ModSecurity Handbook
Second Edition

Christian Folini

Ivan Ristić

Feisty Duck

LONDON

ModSecurity Handbook, Second Edition

by Christian Folini and Ivan Ristić

Copyright © 2017 Feisty Duck Limited. All rights reserved.

ISBN: 978-1-907117-07-7

Published in July 2017 (revision 267). First edition published in March 2010.

Feisty Duck Limited
www.feistyduck.com
contact@feistyduck.com

Address:
6 Acantha Court
Montpelier Road
London W5 2QP
United Kingdom

Production editor: Jelena Girić-Ristić

Copyeditor: Melinda Rankin

Proofreader: Sonia Saruba

Cover design: Peter Jovanović

Cover illustration: Maja Veselinović

Table of Contents

Foreword

As I write this in April 2017, it's been about 14 years since the release of the first-ever version of ModSecurity. The idea for it was in my head probably for a bit longer, but, still—that was a long time ago. The first version wasn't very good, but I persisted and kept steadily improving the project. ModSecurity 2—a complete rewrite based on several years of experience protecting web applications—was much better and very much the tool you know today.

What's really amazing, however, is that the project took on a life of its own. I left ModSecurity in 2009, but it continued to grow and improve. As I write this, there is another rewrite in progress (version 3), this time to natively support multiple web server platforms. The Core Rule Set, an OWASP project, is about to have its third release—a major one. Amazingly, ModSecurity remains the only mainstream open source web application firewall engine. After the license change (thanks, Trustwave!), ModSecurity was incorporated into commercial tools. Its rule-based approach influenced the entire web application firewall industry. Even some vendors that do not use ModSecurity now provide rule-level compatibility.

The first edition of this book was my parting gift to the community; I simply didn't think it would be appropriate to go away without documenting everything I had in my head. Fast-forward several years later, and the book is mildly out of date, but I'm no longer the person who can do anything about it. This is where Christian Folini comes in to save the day.

Christian was one of the early adopters of ModSecurity. His early work on REMO, a whitelisting rule editor, showed the best way to use a web application firewall with a positive security approach, which is superior to blacklisting. Over the years, Christian continued to spend time on Apache and ModSecurity and became part of the Core Rule Set team. Who better to take up the torch and update this book than him? It makes me happy that the ModSecurity community once again will have fully up-to-date documentation at its disposal.

Thank you, Christian, for taking on the important task of making this book new again!

Preface to the Second Edition

I was an early adopter of ModSecurity. I first came across it in about 2005 and was immediately intrigued. Here was a tool that could help me improve my life, indirectly, by improving the security of the systems I manage. I started to use it, although you could say it grew on me slowly over time. You see, I'm a medievalist who landed in web server security when my application for a job at an open air museum was declined. In parallel with the new job, I was also running one of the better known reenactment companies, recreating medieval life for a museum audience. I got married, we started a family, we purchased a historical house (with all the strings attached), and though ModSecurity became more and more important to me over the years, it remained a day job because evenings and weekends were already occupied.

I slowly started to teach Apache and ModSecurity courses, I published blog posts and tutorials on the use of ModSecurity, and, last year, the day job started to expand into evenings and weekends when I became involved with the OWASP ModSecurity Core Rule Set project. I joined a very active team and became invested in the development of the Core Rules Paranoia Mode and Sampling Mode, two core features of the Core Rule Set 3.0 release.

When Ivan asked me to write this new edition of *ModSecurity Handbook*, it felt like a culmination of my work with ModSecurity! This work allowed me to explore features and areas I hadn't used before. It gave me a better view of ModSecurity and—shhh, don't tell anyone—I am probably the person who profited most from it.

I started with an overhaul of the reference section of the book. About one-third of it is brand-new, because many new features were added to ModSecurity in the six years since the first edition of this book was published. Another significant effort was adding more detail throughout and many examples to better explain what each feature did. This is especially visible with the transformations that now come with handy "before" and "after" examples, which provide much-needed clarity about exactly how data is changed. The idea behind this expansion was to describe the usage of the software in a consistent way and to give people who know the online reference substantial value when they buy the book.

The prose part of the book saw fewer updates: some additions to most chapters, small fixes here and there, rewordings, and removing legacy explanations or historical information (e.g., new features in version 2.5.12). All in all, I blew away the dust from that part of the book. This is not true for Chapter 10, *Performance*, which was updated with substantial new data obtained from many different test runs in multiple scenarios. This allowed me to assess performance anew, and I was able to show that the performance of ModSecurity transformations now is not quite how it was when the first edition was written (now it's better!).

You don't write a book on your own, and you don't get into a position to write a technical book on your own, either. Many people contributed in their own way to my work, and I can only name a few of them here. Let their names stand in for many more people like them. First and foremost, my thanks belong to my company of many years, netnea in Berne, Switzerland. Netnea's decision to hire a PhD (me, still hot from the press and hitherto specialized in German mysticism) allowed me to start on this adventure in the first place.

Jelena Girić-Ristić from Feisty Duck, this book's publisher, accompanied me from the moment I accepted this project, and her good spirit kept me working during days when gray clouds covered the sky. Ivan, who wrote the first edition of this book, acted as a technical editor this time around and offered his guiding hand to help achieve clarity when explaining complex topics. Osama Elnaggar, Walter Hop, Marco Pizzoli, and Chaim Sanders reviewed the manuscript and pointed out shortcomings that I had overlooked. Finally, Melinda Rankin came in as copyeditor when they were done and gave the manuscript a most welcome polish.

My marvelous wife Saara is the rare sort of a pastor running a Linux desktop and helping her techie husband configure his mobile phone. She put up with me when I grew grumpy or felt lost with all this book writing, and she cheered me up with her understanding. Our two boys had to put up with me as well, and I feel sorry for all the playing and fun that we missed out on in recent months.

But in the end, what really made this book possible was my experience working with Apache and ModSecurity over the years, in turn possible thanks to my customers, who trusted my growing knowledge and who placed their security projects into my hands. I can't name them all, of course, but I will name Swiss Post, my most important customer. The management at Swiss Post allowed me and the engineering team to invest into a carefully designed reverse proxy platform we are all very proud of. This success was of primordial importance to this book. Other customers bring new challenges with every project, and they all teach me new concepts and new ways to run Apache and ModSecurity. It's a great adventure every day.

Preface to the First Edition

I didn't mean to write this book; I really didn't. In late 2008 I started to work on the second edition of *Apache Security*, deciding to rewrite the ModSecurity chapter first. A funny thing happened: the ModSecurity chapter kept growing and growing. It hit 40 pages; it hit 80 pages; and then I realized that I was nowhere near the end. That was all the excuse I needed to put *Apache Security* aside—for the time being—and focus on a ModSecurity book instead.

I admit that I couldn't be happier, although it was an entirely emotional decision. After spending years working on ModSecurity, I knew it had so much more to offer, yet the documentation wasn't there to show the way—but it is now, I'm thrilled to say. The package is complete. You have an open source tool able to compete with the best commercial products out there, *and* you have the documentation to match.

With this book, I'm also trying something completely new: *continuous writing and publishing*. You see, I published my first book with a major publisher, but I never quite liked the process. It was too slow. You write a book pretty much in isolation, you publish it, and then you never get to update it. I was never happy with that, and that's why I decided to do things differently this time.

Simply said, *ModSecurity Handbook* is a living book. Every time I make a change, a new digital version is made available to you. If I improve the book based on your feedback, you get the improvements as soon as I make them. If you prefer a paper book, you can still get it, of course, through the usual channels. Although I can't do anything about updating the paper version of the book, we can narrow the gap slightly by pushing out book updates even between editions, meaning that even when you get the paper version (as most people seem to prefer to), it's never going to be too much behind the digital version.

Scope and Audience

This book exists to document every single aspect of ModSecurity and to teach you how to use it. It's as simple as that. ModSecurity is a fantastic tool, but it's let down by the poor quality of the documentation. As a result, the adoption is not as good as it could be; application security is difficult on its own, and you don't really want to struggle with poorly documented tools too. I felt a responsibility to write this book and show how ModSecurity can compete with commercial web application firewalls, in spite of being the underdog. Now that the book is finished, I feel I've done a proper job with ModSecurity.

If you are interested in application security, you are my target audience. Even if you're not interested in application security as such, and only want to deal with your particular problems (it's difficult to find a web application these days that's without security problems), you are still my target audience.

You don't need to know anything about ModSecurity to get started. If you just follow the book from the beginning, you'll find that every new chapter advances a notch. Even if you're a long-time ModSecurity user, I believe you'll benefit from a fresh start. I'll let you in on a secret: I have. There's nothing better for completing one's knowledge than having to write about a particular topic. I suspect that long-time ModSecurity users will especially like the second half of the book, which discusses many advanced topics and often covers substantial new ground.

However, there's only so much a book can cover. *ModSecurity Handbook* assumes you already know how to operate the Apache web server. You don't have to be an expert, but you do need to know how to install, configure, and run it. If you don't know how to do that already, you should get my first book, *Apache Security*. I wrote it five years ago, but it's still remarkably fresh. (Ironically, it is only the ModSecurity chapter in *Apache Security* that is completely obsolete—but that's why you have this book.)

On the other end, *ModSecurity Handbook* will teach you how to use ModSecurity and write good rules, but it won't teach you application security. In my earlier book, *Apache Security*, I included a chapter that served as an introduction to application security, but even then I was barely able to mention all that I wanted, and the chapter was still the longest in the book. Since then, the application security field has exploded, and now you have to read several books and dozens of research papers just to begin to understand it.

Contents

Once you move past the first chapter, which is the introduction to the world of ModSecurity, the rest of the book consists of roughly three parts. In the first part, you learn how to install and configure ModSecurity. In the second part, you learn how to write rules. As for the third part, you could say that it contains the advanced stuff—a series of chapters, each dedicated to one important aspect of ModSecurity. At the end of the book is the official reference documentation, reproduced with the permission from Breach Security.

Chapter 1, *Introduction*, is the foundation of the book. It contains a gentle introduction to ModSecurity, and then explains what it can and cannot do. The main usage scenarios are listed to help you identify where you can use ModSecurity in your environment. The middle of the chapter goes under the hood of ModSecurity to give you insight into how it works, and it finishes with an overview of the key areas you'll need to learn in order to deploy it. The end of the chapter lists a series of resources (sites, mailing lists, tools, etc.) that you'll find useful in your day-to-day work.

Chapter 2, *Installation*, teaches you how to install ModSecurity, either compiling from source (using one of the released versions or downloading straight from the development repository) or by using one of the available binary packages, on Unix and Windows alike.

Chapter 3, *Configuration*, explains how each of the available configuration directives should be used. By the end of the chapter, you'll have a complete overview of the configuration options and a solid default configuration for all your ModSecurity installations.

Chapter 4, *Logging*, addresses the logging features of ModSecurity. The two main logging facilities explained are the *debug log*, which is useful in rule writing, and the *audit log*, which is used to log complete transaction data. Special attention is given to remote logging, which you'll need to manage multiple sensors or to use any of the user-friendly tools for alert management. File interception and validation is covered in detail. The chapter ends with an advanced section of logging, which explains how to selectively log traffic and how to use the sanitization feature to prevent sensitive data from being stored in the logs.

Chapter 5, *Rule Language Overview*, is the first of three chapters that address rule writing. This chapter contains an overview of the entire rule language, which will get you started and provide a feature map to which you can return whenever you need to deal with a new problem.

Chapter 6, *Rule Language Tutorial*, teaches how to write rules and how to write them well. It's a fun chapter that adopts a gradual approach, introducing features one by one. By the end of the chapter, you'll know everything about writing individual rules.

Chapter 7, *Rule Configuration*, completes the topic of rule writing. It takes a step back to view the rules as the basic block for policy building. You'll first learn how to put a few rules together and add them to the configuration, then learn how the rules interact with Apache's ability to use different configuration contexts for different sites and different locations within sites. The chapter spends a great deal of time making sure you take advantage of the inheritance feature, which helps make ModSecurity configuration much easier to maintain.

Chapter 8, *Persistent Storage*, is quite possibly the most exciting chapter in the book. It describes the persistent storage mechanism, which enables you to track data and events over time and thus opens up an entire new dimension of ModSecurity. This chapter is also the most practical one in the entire book. It gives you the rules for periodic alerting, brute force attack detection, denial of service attack detection, session and user management, fixing session management weaknesses, and more.

Chapter 9, *Practical Rule Writing*, is, as the name suggests, a tour through many of the practical activities you will perform in your day-to-day work. The chapter starts by covering whitelisting, virtual patching, IP address reputation, and blacklisting. You'll then learn how to integrate with other Apache modules, with practical examples that show how to perform conditional logging and fix insecure session cookies. Special attention is given to the topic of blocking; several approaches, starting from the simple and moving to the very sophisticated, are presented. A section on regular expressions gets you up to speed with the most important ModSecurity operator. The chapter ends with a discussion of rulesets, discussing how to use the rulesets others have written and how to write your own.

Chapter 10, *Performance*, covers several performance-related topics. It opens with an overview of how ModSecurity usually spends its time, a list of common configuration mistakes that should be avoided, and a list of approaches that result in better performance. The second part of the chapter describes how to monitor ModSecurity performance in production. The third part tests the publicly available rulesets in order to give you a taste of what they're like, as well as to document a methodology you can use to test your own rules. The chapter then moves to ruleset benchmarking, which is an essential part of the process of rule writing. The last part of this chapter gives practical advice on how to use regular expressions and parallel matching, comparing several approaches and explaining when to use them.

Chapter 11, *Content Injection*, explains how to reach from ModSecurity, which is a server-side tool, right into a user's browser and continue with the inspection there. This feature makes it possible to detect attacks that were previously thought to be undetectable by a server-side tool—for example, DOM-based cross-site scripting attacks. Content injection also comes in handy if you need to communicate with your users—for example, to tell them that they have been attacked.

Chapter 12, *Writing Rules in Lua*, discusses a gem of a feature: writing rules using the Lua programming language. The rule language of ModSecurity is easy to use and can get a lot done, but for really difficult problems you may need the power of a proper programming language. In addition, you can use Lua to react to events, and it's especially useful when integrating with external systems.

Chapter 13, *Handling XML*, covers the XML capabilities of ModSecurity in detail. You'll learn how to validate XML using either DTDs or XML Schemas and how to combine XPath expressions with the other features ModSecurity offers to perform both whitelist- and blacklist-based validation. The XML features of ModSecurity have traditionally been poorly documented; here, you'll find details never covered before. The chapter ends with an XML validation framework you can easily adapt for your needs.

Chapter 14, *Extending the Rule Language*, discusses how you can extend ModSecurity to implement new functionality. It gives several step-by-step examples, explaining how to implement a transformation function, an operator, and a variable. Of course, with ModSecurity being open source, you can extend it directly at any point, but when you use the official

APIs, you avoid making a custom version of ModSecurity (which is generally time-consuming because it prevents upgrades).

Updates

If you purchased this book directly from Feisty Duck,[1] your purchase includes access to newer digital versions of the book. Updates are made automatically after I update the manuscript, which I keep in DocBook format in a Subversion repository. At the moment, there is a script that runs every hour and rebuilds the book when necessary. Whenever you visit your personal digital download link, you get the most recent version of the book.

In the first two years of its life, I kept *ModSecurity Handbook* up-to-date with every ModSecurity release. There was a full revision in February 2012, which made the book essentially as good and as current as it was on day of the first release back in 2010. Don't take my past performance as a guarantee of what is going to happen in the future, however. At the launch in 2010, I offered a guarantee that the book will be kept up-to-date for at least a year from your purchase. I dropped that promise at the end of 2011, because I could see the possibility that I would stop with the updates at some point. I will keep my promise until the end of 2012, but I don't know what will happen after that.

Feedback

To get in touch with me, please write to *ivanr@webkreator.com*. I would like to hear from you very much, because I believe that a book can fulfill its potential only through the interactions among its author(s) and its readers. Your feedback is particularly important when a book is continuously updated, like this one is. When I change the book as a result of your feedback, all the changes are immediately delivered back to you. There's no more waiting for years to see improvements!

About the Author

Ivan Ristić is a respected security expert and author, known especially for his contribution to the web application firewall field and the development of ModSecurity, the open source web application firewall. He is also the author of *Apache Security*, a comprehensive security guide for the Apache web server. A frequent speaker at computer security conferences, Ivan is an active participant in the application security community, a member of the Open Web Application Security Project (OWASP), and an officer of the Web Application Security Consortium (WASC).

---

[1] Feisty Duck web site (Feisty Duck, retrieved 29 Dec 2016) [fsty.uk/m1]

About the Technical Reviewer

Brian Rectanus is a developer turned manager in the web application security field. He has worked in the past on various security software–related projects, such as the IronBee open source WAF framework, the ModSecurity open source WAF, and the Suricata open source IDS/IPS. Brian is an open source advocate and proud `NIX-loving, Mac-using, non-Windows user who has been writing code on various `NIX platforms with vi since 1993. Today, he still does all his development work in the more modern vim editor—like there is any other—and loves every bit of it. Brian has spent the majority of his career working with web technology from various perspectives, be it manager, developer, administrator, or security assessor. Brian has held many certifications in the past, including GCIA and GCIH certification from the SANS Institute and a BS in computer science from Kansas State University.

Acknowledgments

To begin with, I would like to thank the entire ModSecurity community for their support, and especially all of you who used ModSecurity and sent me your feedback. ModSecurity wouldn't be what it is without you. Developing and supporting ModSecurity was a remarkable experience; I hope you enjoy using it as much as I enjoyed developing it.

I would also like to thank my former colleagues from Breach Security, who gave me a warm welcome, even though I joined them pretty late in the game. I regret that, due to my geographic location, I didn't spend more time working with you. I would especially like to thank—in no particular order—Brian Rectanus, Ryan Barnett, Ofer Shezaf, and Avi Aminov, who worked with me on the ModSecurity team. Brian was also kind to work with me on the book as a technical reviewer, and I owe special thanks to him for ensuring I didn't make too many mistakes.

I mustn't forget my copyeditor, Nancy Kotary, who was a pleasure to work with, despite having to deal with DocBook and Subversion, none of which is in the standard copyediting repertoire.

For some reason unknown to me, my dear wife Jelena continues to tolerate my long working hours—probably because I keep promising to work less, even though that never seems to happen. To her, I can only offer my undying love and gratitude for accepting me for who I am. My daughter Iva, who's four, is too young to understand what she means to me, but that's all right; I have the patience to wait for another 20 years or so. She is the other sunshine in my life.

User Guide

This part, with its 14 chapters, constitutes the main body of the book. The first chapter is the introduction to ModSecurity and your map to the rest of the book. The remaining chapters fall into roughly four groups: installation and configuration, rule writing, practical work, and advanced topics.

1 Introduction

ModSecurity is a tool that will help you secure your web applications—no, scratch that: ModSecurity is a tool that will help you sleep better at night; in this book, we'll explain how. We usually call ModSecurity a *web application firewall* (WAF), the generally accepted term to refer to the class of products designed specifically to secure web applications. Other times, we call it an *HTTP intrusion detection tool*, because we think that name better describes what ModSecurity does. Neither name is entirely adequate, but we don't have a better one. However, it doesn't really matter what we call it. The point is that web applications —yours, ours, everyone's—are terribly insecure on average. We all struggle to keep ahead of security issues and need any help we can get to handle them.

Ivan thought to create ModSecurity while he was responsible for the security of several web-based products. He could see how insecure most web applications were, slapped together with little time spent on design and even less time spent on understanding security issues. Not only were web applications insecure, but people generally had little awareness of whether they were being attacked or exploited. Most web servers kept only standard access and error logs, and they didn't say much.

ModSecurity will help you sleep better at night because, above all, it solves the visibility problem: it lets you see your web traffic. That visibility is key to security; once you can see HTTP traffic, you can analyze it in real time, record it as necessary, and react to the events. The best part of this concept is that you get to do all of that without actually touching web applications. Even better, the concept can be applied to any application—even if you can't access its source code.

Brief History of ModSecurity

Like many other open source projects, ModSecurity started out as a hobby. Back in 2002, producing secure web applications was virtually impossible. (It's the same these days, sadly.) However, that realization led to the idea of a tool that would sit in front of web applications and control the flow of data to and from the system. The first version was released in

November 2002, but a few more months were needed before the tool became useful. Other people started to learn about ModSecurity, and its popularity started to rise.

Initially, most development effort for the tool went into wrestling with Apache to make request body inspection possible. Apache 1.3.x didn't include any interception or filtering APIs, but it was still possible to trick it into submission. Apache 2.x improved the situation by providing APIs that allowed content interception, but no documentation was available.

By 2004, Ivan converted from obsessing about software development to obsessing about web application security. He quit his job and started treating ModSecurity as a business. In the summer of 2006, ModSecurity went head-to-head with other web application firewalls in an evaluation conducted by Forrester Research, and it achieved great results. Later that year, ModSecurity was acquired by Breach Security. A team of one eventually became a team of many: Brian Rectanus came to work on ModSecurity, Ofer Shezaf embarked on the rules, and Ryan C. Barnett handled community management and education. ModSecurity 2.0, a complete rewrite, was released in late 2006. Breach Security also released ModSecurity Community Console, which combined the functionality of a remote logging sensor and a monitoring and reporting GUI.

In 2009, Ivan left Breach Security. He stayed involved with ModSecurity for a while, but mostly worked on the first edition of this book. In his own words, he couldn't leave the project if it wasn't properly documented. Brian Rectanus took the lead. In the meantime, Ryan C. Barnett took charge of the ModSecurity rules and produced significant improvements with Core Rule Set v2. In 2010, Trustwave acquired Breach Security and promised to revitalize ModSecurity. The project was then handed to Ryan C. Barnett and Breno Silva.

Something remarkable happened in March 2011: Trustwave announced that it would change the license of ModSecurity from GPLv2 to Apache Software License (ASLv2). This was a great step toward a wider use of ModSecurity because ASL falls into the category of permissive licenses. Later, the same change was announced for the Core Rule Set project, which is hosted with the Open Web Application Security Project (OWASP). Subsequently, commercial WAF offerings started to incorporate the ModSecurity engine and added the OWASP ModSecurity Core Rules as a default ruleset. With version 2.7.0, ModSecurity was ported to work with Nginx and IIS web servers, but these ports never achieved the stability of the original version. This eventually led to a major rewrite that would be able to support multiple platforms equally well. That will become ModSecurity 3.0, currently in the making.

In 2013, Felipe Costa took over the lead developer position from Breno, and when Ryan left Trustwave in 2015 he handed over the rules to Chaim Sanders, who joined Trustwave in 2014 to support the project with coding and community management.

What Can ModSecurity Do?

ModSecurity is a toolkit for real-time web application monitoring, logging, debugging, and access control. I like to think of it as an enabler. There are no hard rules telling you what to do; instead, it's up to you to choose your own path through the available features. That's why the title of this section asks what ModSecurity *can* do, not what it does.

The freedom to choose what to do is an essential part of ModSecurity's identity and goes well with its open source nature. With full access to the source code, your freedom to choose extends to the ability to customize and extend the tool itself to make it fit your needs. This is a matter not of ideology, but of practicality. I simply don't want my tools to restrict what I can do.

The following is a list of the most important usage scenarios for ModSecurity:

Real-time application security monitoring and access control

At its core, ModSecurity gives you access to the HTTP traffic stream in real time, along with the ability to inspect it. This is enough for real-time security monitoring. There's an added dimension of what's possible through ModSecurity's persistent storage mechanism, which enables you to track system elements over time and perform event correlation. You can block reliably, if you so wish, because ModSecurity uses full request and response buffering.

Virtual patching

Virtual patching is a concept that addresses vulnerability mitigation in a separate layer, in which you get to fix problems in applications without having to touch the applications themselves. Virtual patching is applicable to applications that use any communication protocol, but it's particularly useful with HTTP, because traffic generally can be well understood by an intermediary device. ModSecurity excels at virtual patching because of its reliable blocking capabilities and the flexible rule language that can be adapted to any need. Virtual patching is, by far, the activity ModSecurity offers that requires the least investment, is the easiest to perform, and that most organizations can benefit from straight away.

Full HTTP traffic logging

Web servers traditionally do very little when it comes to logging for security purposes. They log very little by default, and even with a lot of tweaking you can't get all the data that you need. I have yet to encounter a web server that is able to log full transaction data—but ModSecurity gives you the ability to log everything, including raw transaction data, which is essential for forensics. In addition, you get to choose which transactions are logged, which parts of a transaction are logged, and which parts are sanitized. As a bonus, this type of detailed logging is also helpful for application troubleshooting—not just security.

Continuous passive security assessment

Security assessment is seen largely as an active scheduled event, in which an independent team is sourced to try to perform a simulated attack. Continuous passive security assessment is a variation of real-time monitoring in which instead of focusing on the behavior of the external parties, you focus on the behavior of the system itself. It's an early warning system of sorts that can detect traces of many abnormalities and security weaknesses before they are exploited.

Web application hardening

One of my favorite uses for ModSecurity is *attack surface reduction*, in which you selectively narrow down the HTTP features you're willing to accept (e.g., request methods, request headers, content types, etc.). ModSecurity can assist you in enforcing many similar restrictions, either directly or through collaboration with other Apache modules. For example, it's possible to fix many session management issues, as well as cross-site request forgery vulnerabilities.

Something small, yet very important to you

Real life often makes unusual demands of us, and when handling such demands, the flexibility of ModSecurity comes in handy when you need it the most. You may have to address a security need, or maybe you have a completely different issue; for example, some people use ModSecurity as an XML web service router, combining its ability to parse XML and apply XPath expressions with its ability to proxy requests. Who knew?

> **Note**
>
> I'm often asked if ModSecurity can be used to protect Apache itself. The answer is that it can, in some limited circumstances, but that it isn't what it's designed for. You may sometimes be able to catch an attack with ModSecurity before it hits a vulnerable spot in Apache or in a third-party module, but there's a large quantity of code that runs before ModSecurity. If there's a vulnerability in that area, ModSecurity won't be able to do anything about it.

What Are Web Application Firewalls, Anyway?

I said that ModSecurity is a web application firewall, but it's a little known fact that no one really knows what web application firewalls are. It is generally understood that a web application firewall is an intermediary element (implemented either as a software add-on or process, or as a network device) that enhances the security of web applications, but opinions differ once you dig deeper. There are many theories that try to explain the different views, but the best one I could come up with is that, unlike anything we had before, the web application space is so complex that there is no easy way to classify what we do security-wise. Rather than focus on the name, you should focus on what a particular tool does and how it can help.

Guiding Principles

There are three guiding principles on which ModSecurity is based:

Flexibility

ModSecurity was designed and built with a particular user in mind: a security expert who needs to be able to intercept, analyze, and store HTTP traffic. I didn't see much value in hard-coded functionality, because real life is so complex that everyone needs to do things just slightly differently. ModSecurity achieves flexibility by providing a powerful rule language, which allows you to do exactly what you need to, in combination with the ability to apply rules only where you need to: granular control down to the individual byte.

Passiveness

Another key design decision was to make ModSecurity as passive as possible; it will thus never make changes to transaction data unless instructed to do so. The key reason for this was to give users confidence to deploy ModSecurity with entirely passive rulesets that allow them to just observe, safe in knowing that their applications will not be affected. That's why ModSecurity will give you plenty of information, but ultimately leave the decisions to you.

Predictability

There's no such thing as a perfect tool, but a predictable one is the next best thing. Armed with all the facts, you can understand ModSecurity's weak points and work around them.

There are elements in ModSecurity that fall outside the scope of these principles. For example, ModSecurity can change the way Apache identifies itself to the outside world, confine the Apache process within a jail, and even inject security tokens into the traffic. Although these functions are useful, I think that they detract from the main purpose of ModSecurity, which is to be a reliable and predictable tool that enables HTTP traffic inspection.

Deployment Options

ModSecurity supports two deployment options: embedded and reverse proxy deployment. There is no one correct way to use them; choose an option based on what best suits your circumstances. There are advantages and disadvantages of both options:

Embedded

Because ModSecurity is an Apache module, you can add it to any compatible version of Apache. At the moment, that means a reasonably recent Apache version, ideally from the 2.4.x branch. That said, a version from the 2.2.x branch will also work. ModSecurity has been ported to Nginx and to IIS, which introduces wider platform options. The embedded option is a great choice for those who already have their architecture laid out and don't want to change it. Embedded deployment is also the preferred option if you need to protect hundreds of web servers. In such situations, it is impractical to build a separate proxy-based security layer. Embedded ModSecurity not only does not introduce new points of failure, but it scales seamlessly as the underlying web infrastructure scales. The main challenge of embedded deployment is that server resources are shared between the web server and ModSecurity.

Reverse proxy

Reverse proxies are effectively HTTP routers, designed to stand between web servers and their clients. When you install a dedicated Apache reverse proxy and add ModSecurity to it, you get a "proper" network web application firewall, which you can use to protect any number of web servers on the same network. Many security practitioners prefer having a separate security layer, with which you get complete isolation from the systems you are protecting. On the performance front, a standalone ModSecurity installation will have resources dedicated to it, which means that you will be able to do more (i.e., have more complex rules). The main disadvantage of this approach is the new point of failure, which will need to be addressed with a high-availability set-up of two or more reverse proxies.

Getting Started

In this first practical section of the book, I will give you a whirlwind tour of ModSecurity's internals to help you get started.

Hybrid Nature of ModSecurity

ModSecurity is a hybrid WAF engine that relies on the host web server for some of its work. ModSecurity was originally written for the Apache web server but has since been ported to Nginx and to IIS. Although both ports are actively maintained, they suffer from ModSecurity's heritage and tight integration with the Apache source code. The next major version of ModSecurity is being reimplemented to separate it from Apache, allowing it to support all web servers equally well. Until that happens, the best web server to run ModSecurity is Apache 2.x.

Apache does for ModSecurity what it does for all other modules—it handles the following infrastructure tasks:

1. Decrypts SSL

2. Breaks up the inbound connection stream into HTTP requests

3. Partially parses HTTP requests

4. Invokes ModSecurity, choosing the correct configuration context

5. Dechunks request bodies as necessary

There are a few additional tasks Apache performs in a reverse proxy scenario:

1. Forwards requests to backend servers (with or without SSL)

2. Partially parses HTTP responses

3. Dechunks response bodies as necessary

The advantage of a hybrid implementation is that it's efficient; the duplication of work is minimal when it comes to HTTP parsing. A couple of disadvantages of this approach are that you don't always get access to the raw data stream and that web servers sometimes don't process data in the way a security-conscious tool would. In the case of Apache, the hybrid approach works reasonably well, with a few minor issues:

Request line and headers are NUL-terminated

This normally isn't a problem, because what Apache doesn't see can't harm any module or application. In some rare cases, however, the purpose of NUL-byte evasion is to hide something, and this Apache behavior only helps with the hiding.

Request header transformation

Apache will canonicalize request headers, combining multiple headers that use the same name and collapsing those that span two or more lines. The transformation may make it difficult to detect subtle signs of evasion, but in practice this hasn't been a problem yet.

Quick request handling

Apache will handle some requests quickly, leaving ModSecurity unable to do anything but notice them in the logging phase. Invalid HTTP requests, in particular, will be rejected by Apache without ModSecurity having a say.

No access to some response headers

Because of the way Apache works, the Server and Date response headers are invisible to ModSecurity in embedded mode; they can't be inspected or logged.

Main Areas of Functionality

The functionality offered by ModSecurity falls roughly into four areas:

Parsing

ModSecurity tries to make sense of as much data as available. The supported data formats are backed by security-conscious parsers that extract bits of data and store them for use in the rules.

Buffering

In a typical installation, both request and response bodies will be buffered. This means ModSecurity usually sees complete requests before they're passed to the application for processing, and complete responses before they're sent to clients. Buffering is an important feature, because it's the only way to provide reliable blocking. The downside of buffering is that it requires additional RAM to store the request and response body data.

Logging

Full transaction logging (also referred to as *audit logging*) is a big part of what ModSecurity does. This feature allows you to record complete HTTP traffic instead of just rudimentary access log information. Request headers, request body, response header, response body—all those bits will be available to you. It is only with the ability to see what's happening that you will be able to stay in control.

Rule engine

The rule engine builds on the work performed by all other components. By the time the rule engine starts operating, the various bits and pieces of data it requires will all be prepared and ready for inspection. At that point, the rules will take over to assess the transaction and take actions as necessary.

> **Note**
>
> There's one thing ModSecurity purposefully avoids doing: as a matter of design, ModSecurity does not support data sanitization. I don't believe in sanitization, purely because I believe that it is too difficult to get right. If you know for sure that you're being attacked (as you have to before you can decide to sanitize), then you should refuse to process the offending requests altogether. Attempting to sanitize merely opens a new battlefield in which your attackers don't have anything to lose but have everything to win. You, on the other hand, don't have anything to win but everything to lose.

What Rules Look Like

Every part of ModSecurity revolves around two things: configuration and rules. The configuration tells ModSecurity how to process the data it sees; the rules decide what to do with the processed data. Although it's too early to go into how the rules work, I'll include a quick example here just to give you an idea of what they look like. For example:

```
SecRule ARGS "@rx <script>" \
    "id:2000,log,deny,status:404"
```

Even without further assistance, you can probably recognize the part in the rule that specifies what we want to look for in input data (`<script>`). Similarly, you'll easily figure out what will happen if we do find the desired pattern (`log,deny,status:404`). Things will become more clear when you look at the general rule syntax, as follows:

```
SecRule VARIABLES OPERATOR ACTIONS
```

The three parts have the following meanings:

1. The VARIABLES part tells ModSecurity where to look. The ARGS variable, used in the example, indicates all request parameters.

2. The OPERATOR part tells ModSecurity how to look. In the example, we have a regular expression pattern, which will be matched against ARGS.

3. The ACTIONS part is used to add metadata to the rules and to specify what ModSecurity should do when a match occurs. The rule from the previous example assigns ID 2000 to uniquely identify the rule and specifies the following actions on a match: log problem, stop transaction processing, and return HTTP response code 404.

I hope you aren't disappointed with the simplicity of this first rule. I promise you that by combining the various facilities offered by ModSecurity, you will be able to write useful rules that implement complex logic where necessary.

Transaction Lifecycle

In ModSecurity, every transaction goes through five steps, or phases. In each of the phases, ModSecurity will perform some work at the beginning (e.g., parse data that has become available), invoke the rules specified to work in that phase, and perhaps perform a task or two after the phase rules have finished. At first glance, it may seem that five phases are too many, but there's a reason that each phase exists. There is always one task, sometimes several, that can only be performed at a particular moment in the transaction lifecycle.

Request headers (1)
The request headers phase is the first entry point for ModSecurity. The principal purpose of this phase is to allow rule writers to assess a request before the costly request body processing is undertaken. Similarly, there is often a need to influence how ModSecurity will process a request body, and in this phase is the time to do it. For example, ModSecurity will not parse an XML or JSON request body by default, but you can instruct it do so by placing the appropriate rules into phase 1. (If you care about XML processing, it's described in detail in Chapter 13, *Handling XML*.)

Request body (2)
The request body phase is the main request analysis phase and takes place immediately after a complete request body has been received and processed. The rules in this phase have all the available request data at their disposal. Afterward, the web server will either generate the response itself (in embedded mode) or forward the transaction to a backend web server (in reverse proxy mode).

Response headers (3)
The response headers phase takes place after response headers become available but before a response body is read. The rules that need to decide whether to inspect a response body should run in this phase.

Response body (4)

The response body phase is the main response analysis phase. By the time this phase begins, the response body will have been read and all its data made available for the rules to make their decisions.

Logging (5)

The logging phase is special. It's the only phase from which you cannot block. By the time this phase runs, the transaction will have finished, so there's little you can do but record the fact that it happened. Rules in this phase are run to control how logging is performed or to save information in persistent storage.

Lifecycle Example

To give you a better idea of what happens in every transaction, we'll examine a detailed debug log of one POST transaction. The debug log is an additional logging facility provided by ModSecurity that allows you to observe the execution steps of the module in great detail. I've deliberately chosen a transaction type that uses the request body as its principal method to transmit data, because such a transaction will exercise most parts of ModSecurity. To keep things relatively simple, I used a configuration without any rules, removed some of the debug log lines for clarity, and removed the timestamps and some additional metadata from each log line.

> **Note**
>
> Please don't try to understand everything about the logs at this point. The idea is to get a general feel for how ModSecurity works and an introduction to debug logs. Soon after you start to use ModSecurity, you'll discover that debug logs are an indispensable rule-writing and troubleshooting tool.

The transaction I'm using as an example in this section is very straightforward. I made a point of placing request data in two different places—parameter a in the query string and parameter b in the request body—but there's little else of interest in the request:

```
POST /?a=test HTTP/1.0
Content-Type: application/x-www-form-urlencoded
Content-Length: 6

b=test
```

The response is entirely unremarkable:

```
HTTP/1.1 200 OK
Date: Fri, 22 Jul 2016 04:59:13 GMT
Server: Apache
Content-Length: 12
```

```
Connection: close
Content-Type: text/html

Hello World!
```

ModSecurity is first invoked by Apache after request headers become available but before a request body (if any) is read. First comes the initialization message, which contains the unique transaction ID generated by mod_unique_id. With this, you should be able to pair the information in the debug log with the information in your access and audit logs. At this point, ModSecurity will parse the information in the request line and in the request headers. In this example, the query string part contains a single parameter (a), so you'll see a message documenting its discovery. ModSecurity will then create a transaction context and invoke the REQUEST_HEADERS phase:

```
[4] Initialising transaction (txid V5LjWH8AAQEAAFPTr64AAAAA).
[5] Adding request argument (QUERY_STRING): name "a", value "test"
[4] Transaction context created (dcfg 1154668).
[4] Starting phase REQUEST_HEADERS.
```

Assuming that a rule didn't block the transaction, ModSecurity will now return control to Apache, allowing other modules to process the request before control is given back to it.

In the second phase, ModSecurity will first read and process the request body, if it's present. In the following example, you can see three messages from the input filter, which tell you what was read. The fourth message tells you that one parameter was extracted from the request body. The content type used in this request (application/x-www-form-urlencoded) is one of the types ModSecurity recognizes and parses automatically. Once the request body is processed, the REQUEST_BODY rules are processed.

```
[4] Second phase starting (dcfg 1154668).
[4] Input filter: Reading request body.
[9] Input filter: Bucket type HEAP contains 6 bytes.
[9] Input filter: Bucket type EOS contains 0 bytes.
[5] Adding request argument (BODY): name "b", value "test"
[4] Input filter: Completed receiving request body (length 6).
[4] Starting phase REQUEST_BODY.
```

The filters mentioned in the logs are parts of ModSecurity that handle request and response bodies:

```
[4] Hook insert_filter: Adding input forwarding filter (r 7f5fc8002970).
[4] Hook insert_filter: Adding output filter (r 7f5fc8002970).
```

There will be a message in the debug log every time ModSecurity sends a chunk of data to the request handler, and one final message to say that there isn't any more data in the buffers:

```
[4] Input filter: Forwarding input: mode=0, block=0, nbytes=8192 (f 7f5fc800ae90, ↵
r 7f5fc8002970).
[4] Input filter: Forwarded 6 bytes.
[4] Input filter: Sent EOS.
[4] Input filter: Input forwarding complete.
```

The request is now in the hands of Apache's request handler. If the web server is running in embedded mode, the request handler will generate the response itself. If it's running in reverse proxy mode, the server will forward the transaction to a backend server.

Shortly thereafter, the output filter will start receiving data, at which point the RESPONSE_HEADERS rules will be invoked:

```
[9] Output filter: Receiving output (f 7f5fc800aeb8, r 7f5fc8002970).
[4] Starting phase RESPONSE_HEADERS.
```

Once all the rules have run, ModSecurity will continue to store the response body in its buffers, after which it will run the RESPONSE_BODY rules:

```
[9] Content Injection: Not enabled.
[9] Output filter: Bucket type MMAP contains 13 bytes.
[9] Output filter: Bucket type EOS contains 0 bytes.
[4] Output filter: Completed receiving response body (buffered full - 12 bytes).
[4] Starting phase RESPONSE_BODY.
```

Again, assuming that none of the rules blocked, the accumulated response body will be forwarded to the client:

```
[4] Output filter: Output forwarding complete.
```

Finally, the logging phase will commence. The LOGGING rules will be run first to allow them to influence logging, after which the audit logging subsystem will be invoked to log the transaction if necessary. A message from the audit logging subsystem will be the last transaction message in the logs. In this example, ModSecurity tells us that it didn't find anything of interest in the transaction and that it sees no reason to log it:

```
[4] Initialising logging.
[4] Starting phase LOGGING.
[4] Recording persistent data took 0 microseconds.
[4] Audit log: Ignoring a non-relevant request.
```

File Upload Example

Requests that contain files are processed slightly differently. The changes can be best understood by again following the activity in the debug log:

```
[4] Input filter: Reading request body.
[9] Multipart: Boundary: -----------------------ce3de83f6cf79943
```

```
[9] Input filter: Bucket type HEAP contains 140 bytes.
[9] Multipart: Added part header "Content-Disposition" "form-data; name=\"f\"; ↵
filename=\"eicar.com.txt\""
[9] Multipart: Added part header "Content-Type" "text/plain"
[9] Multipart: Content-Disposition name: f
[9] Multipart: Content-Disposition filename: eicar.com.txt
[9] Input filter: Bucket type HEAP contains 116 bytes.
[4] Multipart: Created temporary file 1 (mode 0600): /usr/local/modsecurity/var↵
/tmp/20160723-054018-V5LnIn8AAQEAAFurQfQAAAAA-file-F7zAlU
[9] Multipart: Added file part 7f67b400fd50 to the list: name "f" file name ↵
"eicar.com.txt" (offset 140, length 68)
[9] Input filter: Bucket type EOS contains 0 bytes.
[4] Request body no files length: 96
[4] Input filter: Completed receiving request body (length 256).
```

In addition to seeing the multipart parser in action, you'll see ModSecurity creating a temporary file (into which it will extract the upload) and adjusting its privileges to match the desired configuration.

Then, at the end of the transaction, you'll see the cleanup and the temporary file deleted:

```
[4] Multipart: Cleanup started (remove files 1).
[4] Multipart: Deleted file (part) "/usr/local/modsecurity/var/tmp↵
/20160723-054427-V5LoG38AAQEAAF4SFAoAAAAT-file-bwi2wv"
```

The temporary file won't be deleted if ModSecurity decides to keep an uploaded file. Instead, it will be moved to the storage area:

```
[4] Multipart: Cleanup started (remove files 0).
[4] Input filter: Moved file from "/usr/local/modsecurity/var/tmp↵
/20160723-054018-V5LnIn8AAQEAAFurQfQAAAAA-file-F7zAlU" to "/usr/local/modsecurity↵
/var/upload/20160723-054018-V5LnIn8AAQEAAFurQfQAAAAA-file-F7zAlU".
```

In the example traces, you've observed an upload of a small file that was stored in RAM. When large uploads take place, ModSecurity will attempt to use RAM at first, switching to on-disk storage once it becomes obvious that the file is larger:

```
[9] Input filter: Bucket type HEAP contains 6080 bytes.
[9] Input filter: Bucket type HEAP contains 2112 bytes.
[9] Input filter: Bucket type HEAP contains 5888 bytes.
[9] Input filter: Bucket type HEAP contains 2304 bytes.
[9] Input filter: Bucket type HEAP contains 5696 bytes.
[9] Input filter: Bucket type HEAP contains 2496 bytes.
[9] Input filter: Bucket type HEAP contains 5504 bytes.
[9] Input filter: Bucket type HEAP contains 2688 bytes.
[9] Input filter: Bucket type HEAP contains 5312 bytes.
[9] Input filter: Bucket type HEAP contains 2880 bytes.
[9] Input filter: Bucket type HEAP contains 5120 bytes.
```

```
[9] Input filter: Bucket type HEAP contains 3072 bytes.
[4] Input filter: Request too large to store in memory, switching to disk.
```

A new file will be created to store the entire raw request body:

```
[4] Input filter: Created temporary file to store request body: /usr/local↵
/modsecurity/var/tmp/20160723-054813-V5Lo-X8AAQEAAF4SFAsAAAAQ-request_body-pJs7UV
[4] Input filter: Wrote 128146 bytes from memory to disk.
```

This file is always deleted in the cleanup phase:

```
[4] Multipart: Deleted file (part) "/usr/local/modsecurity/var/tmp↵
/20160723-054813-V5Lo-X8AAQEAAF4SFAsAAAAQ-file-BgWyEd"
[4] Input filter: Removed temporary file: /usr/local/modsecurity/var/tmp↵
/20160723-054813-V5Lo-X8AAQEAAF4SFAsAAAAQ-request_body-pJs7UV
```

Impact on Web Server

The addition of ModSecurity will change how your web server operates. As with all Apache modules, you pay for the additional flexibility and security ModSecurity gives you with increased CPU and RAM consumption on your server. The exact amount will depend on your configuration of ModSecurity—namely, the rules—and the usage of your server. The following is a detailed list of the various activities that increase resource consumption:

- ModSecurity will add to the parsing already performed by Apache, which results in a slight increase in CPU consumption.

- Complex parsers (e.g., XML) are more expensive.

- The handling of file uploads may require I/O operations. In some cases, inbound data will be duplicated on disk.

- The parsing will add to RAM consumption, because every extracted element (e.g., a request parameter) will need to be copied into its own space.

- Request bodies and response bodies are usually buffered in order to support reliable blocking.

- Every rule in your configuration will use some CPU time (for the operator) and RAM (to transform input data before it can be analyzed).

- Some operators used in the rules (e.g., the regular expression operator) are CPU-intensive. Running regular expressions on very large request or response bodies can take a long time—seconds, even.

- Full transaction logging is an expensive I/O operation.

In practice, this list is important because it keeps you informed; what matters is that you have enough resources to support your ModSecurity needs. If you do, then it doesn't matter how expensive ModSecurity is. Also, what's expensive to one person may not be to someone else. If you don't have enough resources to do everything you want with ModSecurity, you'll need to monitor the operation of your system and remove some functionality to reduce the resource consumption; virtually everything that ModSecurity does is configurable, so you should have no problems doing so.

It's generally easier to run ModSecurity in reverse proxy mode, because then you usually have an entire server (with its own CPU and RAM) to play with. In embedded mode, ModSecurity will add to the processing already performed by the web server, so this method is more challenging on a busy server.

For what it's worth, ModSecurity generally uses the minimal necessary resources to perform the desired functions, so this is really a case of exchanging functionality for speed; if you want to do more, you have to pay more.

What's Next?

The purpose of this section is to map your future ModSecurity activities and help you determine where to go from here. Where you'll go depends on what you want to achieve and how much time you have to spend. A complete ModSecurity experience, so to speak, consists of the following elements:

Installation and configuration
> This is the basic step that all users must learn how to perform. The next three chapters will teach you how to make ModSecurity operational, performing installation, general configuration, and logging configuration. Once you're done with those tasks, you need to decide what you want to do with ModSecurity—and that's what the remainder of the book is for.

Rule writing
> Rule writing is an essential skill. You may currently view rules as a tool to detect application security attacks. They are that, but they are also much more. In ModSecurity, you write rules to find out more about HTTP clients (e.g., geolocation and IP address reputation), perform long-term activity tracking (of IP addresses, sessions, and users, for example), implement policy decisions (use available information to make decisions to warn or block), write virtual patches, and even to check on the status of ModSecurity itself.

> It's true that the attack detection rules are in a class of their own, but that's mostly because in order to write them successfully, you need to know a great deal about application security. For that reason, many ModSecurity users generally focus on using third-party rulesets for attack detection. It's a legitimate choice. Not everyone has the time and inclination to become an application security expert. Even if you end up not

using any inspection rules whatsoever, the ability to write virtual patches is reason enough to use ModSecurity.

Rulesets

The use of existing rulesets is the easiest way to get to the proverbial low-hanging fruit: invest small effort and reap big benefits. Traditionally, the main source of Mod-Security rules has been the CRS project, now hosted with OWASP. On the other hand, if you are keen to get your hands dirty, I can tell you that I draw great pleasure from writing my own rules. It's a great way to learn about application security. The only drawback is that it requires a large time investment.

Remote logging and alert management GUI

ModSecurity is perfectly usable without a remote logging solution and without a GUI (the two usually go together). Significant error messages are copied to Apache's error log. Complete transactions are usually logged to the audit log. With a notification system in place, you'll know when something happens and can visit the audit logs to investigate. For example, many installations will divert Apache's error log to a central logging system (via syslog).

The process does become more difficult with more than one sensor to manage. Furthermore, GUIs make the whole experience of monitoring much more pleasant. For that reason you'll probably aim to install one of the available remote centralization tools and use its GUI. The available options are listed in the following Resources section.

Resources

This section contains a list of assorted ModSecurity resources that can assist you in your work.

General Resources

The following resources are the bare essentials:

ModSecurity web site

ModSecurity's web site is probably going to be your main source of information.[1] You should visit the web site from time to time, as well as subscribe to receive the updates from the blog.

---

[1] ModSecurity web site [fsty.uk/m2] (SpiderLabs, retrieved 29 December 2016)

Official documentation

The official ModSecurity documentation is maintained in a wiki, but copies of it are made for inclusion with every release.[2]

Issue tracker

You'll want to visit the ModSecurity issue tracker[3] for one of two reasons: to report a problem with ModSecurity itself (e.g., when you find a bug) or to check the progress on the next (major or minor) version. Before reporting any problems, go through the *support checklist*,[4] which will help you assemble the information required to help resolve your problem. Providing as much information as possible will help the developers understand and replicate the problem and provide a fix (or a workaround) quickly.

Users' mailing list

The users' mailing list (*mod-security-users@lists.sourceforge.net*) is a general-purpose mailing list through which you can discuss ModSecurity.[5] Feel free to ask questions, propose improvements, and discuss ideas. You'll hear about new ModSecurity versions first through this list.

Core Rule Set mailing list

The CRS project[6] is part of OWASP[7] and has a separate mailing list (*owasp-modsecurity-core-rule-set@lists.owasp.org*). Discussions about false positives and the development of new rules also take place in the Core Rules GitHub repository.[8]

Developer Resources

If you're interested in development work, you'll need to access the following resources:

Developers' mailing list

The developers' mailing list is a resource for discussing ModSecurity software development.[9] If you do decide to start playing with the source code, use this list to seek advice and to discuss your work. There is also a ModSecurity developers' guide available with guidelines and examples.[10]

---

[2] ModSecurity documentation [fsty.uk/m3] (SpiderLabs, retrieved 29 December 2016)

[3] ModSecurity issue tracker [fsty.uk/m4] (GitHub, retrieved 29 December 2016)

[4] ModSecurity Support Checklist [fsty.uk/m5] (SpiderLabs, retrieved 29 December 2016)

[5] ModSecurity Users' mailing list [fsty.uk/m6] (SourceForge, retrieved 29 December 2016)

[6] Core Rules Project [fsty.uk/m7] (OWASP, retrieved 29 December 2016)

[7] OWASP [fsty.uk/m8] (OWASP, retrieved 29 December 2016)

[8] CRS GitHub repository [fsty.uk/m9] (GitHub, retrieved 29 December 2016)

[9] ModSecurity developers' mailing list [fsty.uk/m10] (SourceForge, retrieved 29 December 2016)

[10] ModSecurity developers' guide [fsty.uk/m11] (SpiderLabs, retrieved 29 December 2016)

Source code access

The source code of ModSecurity is hosted in a GitHub repository, which allows you to access it directly or through a web-based UI.[11]

AuditConsole

Using ModSecurity entirely from the command line is a lot of fun, but reviewing audit and debug logs is difficult without special scripts or higher-level tools. Your best choice for a log centralization and GUI tool is AuditConsole, built by Christian Bockermann.[12]

AuditConsole is free and provides the following features:

- Event centralization from multiple remote ModSecurity installations
- Event storage and retrieval
- Support for multiple user accounts and support for different views
- Event tagging
- Event triggers, which are executed in the console

Summary

This chapter provided a ModSecurity orientation. I introduced ModSecurity at a high level, discussed what it is and what it isn't, and what it can and can't do. I also gave you a taste of what ModSecurity is like and described its common usage scenarios, as well as covered some of the interesting parts of its operation.

The foundation you now have should be enough to help you set off on a journey of ModSecurity exploration. The next chapter discusses installation.

---

[11] ModSecurity source code [fsty.uk/m12] (GitHub, retrieved 29 December 2016)

[12] AuditConsole [fsty.uk/m13] (Christian Bockermann, retrieved 15 January 2017)

2 Installation

Before you can install ModSecurity, you need to decide if you want to compile it from source or use a binary version—either one included with your operating system or one produced by a third party. Each option comes with advantages and disadvantages, as listed in Table 2.1.

Table 2.1. Installation options

Installation type	Advantages	Disadvantages
Operating system version	• Fully automated installation • Maintenance included	• May not be the latest version
Third-party binary	• Semiautomated installation	• May not be the latest version • Manual download and updates • Must determine if you trust the third party
Source code	• Can always use the latest version • Can use experimental versions • Can make changes, apply patches, and make emergency security fixes	• Manual installation and maintenance required • A lot of work involved with rolling your own version

In some cases, you won't have a choice. For example, if you've installed Apache from source, you will need to install ModSecurity from source too (you will be able to reuse the system packages, of course). The following questions may help you to make the decision:

- Do you intend to use ModSecurity seriously?

- Are you comfortable compiling programs from source?

- Do you have enough time to spend on the compilation and successive maintenance of a custom-installed program?

- Will you need to make changes to ModSecurity or write your own extensions?

Casual users should generally try to use binary packages when they're available (and they are available in most distributions).

Installation from Source

When we build dedicated reverse proxy installations, we tend to build everything from source, because that allows us access to the latest Apache and ModSecurity versions and makes it easier to tweak elements (by changing the source code of either Apache or ModSecurity) when we want to.

Downloading Releases

To download ModSecurity, go to its web site[1] or the GitHub project page.[2] You will need both the main distribution of the source code and its cryptographic signature:

```
$ wget https://www.modsecurity.org/tarball/2.9.1/modsecurity-2.9.1.tar.gz
$ wget https://www.modsecurity.org/tarball/2.9.1/modsecurity-2.9.1.tar.gz.asc
```

Verify the signature before doing anything else, to ensure the package you've just downloaded doesn't contain a Trojan horse planted by a third party and that it hasn't been corrupted during transport:

```
$ gpg --verify modsecurity-2.9.1.tar.gz.asc
gpg: Signature made Wed 09 Mar 2016 19:48:15 CET using DSA key ID E8B11277
gpg: Can't check signature: public key not found
```

Your first attempt may not provide the expected results, but that can be solved easily by importing the referenced key from a key server:

```
$ gpg --keyserver pgp.mit.edu --recv-keys E8B11277
gpg: requesting key E8B11277 from hkp server pgp.mit.edu
gpg: key E8B11277: public key "Felipe Zimmerle da Nobrega Costa ↵
<felipe@zimmerle.org>" imported
gpg: 3 marginal(s) needed, 1 complete(s) needed, classic trust model
gpg: depth: 0  valid:   3  signed:   5  trust: 0-, 0q, 0n, 0m, 0f, 3u
gpg: depth: 1  valid:   5  signed:   5  trust: 2-, 0q, 0n, 2m, 1f, 0u
gpg: depth: 2  valid:   4  signed:   0  trust: 1-, 0q, 0n, 0m, 3f, 0u
gpg: next trustdb check due at 2018-09-26
gpg: Total number processed: 1
gpg:               imported: 1
```

Now you can try again:

---

[1] ModSecurity web site [fsty.uk/m2] (SpiderLabs, retrieved 29 December 2016)

[2] ModSecurity GitHub page [fsty.uk/m12] (GitHub, retrieved 29 December 2016)

```
$ gpg --verify modsecurity-2.9.1.tar.gz.asc
gpg: Signature made Wed 09 Mar 2016 19:48:15 CET using DSA key ID E8B11277
gpg: Good signature from "Felipe Zimmerle da Nobrega Costa ↵
<felipe@zimmerle.org>"
gpg:                    aka "Felipe Zimmerle"
gpg:                    aka "Felipe Costa <fcosta@trustwave.com>"
gpg:                    aka "Felipe Zimmerle (gmail) <zimmerle@gmail.com>"
gpg:                    aka "[jpeg image of size 7280]"
gpg:                    aka "[jpeg image of size 14514]"
gpg: WARNING: This key is not certified with a trusted signature!
gpg:          There is no indication that the signature belongs to the owner.
Primary key fingerprint: 190E FACC A1E9 FA46 6A8E  CD9C E6DF B08C E8B1 1277
```

The warning in the previous snippet might look serious, but it generally isn't a problem; it has to do with the way gpg expects you to verify the identity of an individual. The warning basically tells you that you've downloaded Felipe's key from somewhere, but that you don't *really know* that it belongs to him. The only way to be sure, as far as gpg is concerned, is to meet Felipe in real life, or to meet someone else who knows him personally. If you want to learn more, look up *web of trust* on Wikipedia.

Downloading from Repository

If you want to be on the cutting edge, downloading the latest development version directly from the GitHub repository (the source code control system used by the ModSecurity project) is the way to go. When you do so, you'll get new features days and even months before they make it into an official, stable release. Having said that, however, there is a reason we call some versions "stable." When you use a repository version of ModSecurity, you need to accept that there is no guarantee whatsoever that it will work correctly.

Before you can install a development version of ModSecurity, you need to know where to find it. The repository, which is hosted with GitHub, can be viewed with a browser.[3]

The default view on GitHub is the master source code tree, which shows the most recent development version with the latest accepted changes. Proposed changes are accessible via pull requests or via their own separate branch. These active branches may sometimes contain a feature or a fix that has not been accepted into the master source code. If you want to download a release candidate or a tested release, you can access these archives via a separate submenu.

Once you've determined the location of the version of ModSecurity you want to use, you can get it using the clone command of Git, like this:

```
$ git clone https://github.com/SpiderLabs/ModSecurity.git modsecurity-master
```

---

[3] ModSecurity source code repository [fsty.uk/m12] (GitHub, retrieved 29 Dec 2016)

What you'll get in the modsecurity-master folder is almost the same as what you get when you download a release. Some files need to be generated via a special command first, though. Furthermore, the documentation might not be in sync. The master documentation is kept in a wiki, with copies of the wiki included with releases.

Installation on Unix

Before you can start to compile ModSecurity, you must ensure that you have a complete development toolchain installed. Refer to the documentation of the operating system you're using for instructions. If you'll be adding ModSecurity to an operating system–provided Apache, you're likely to need to install a specific Apache development package too. For example, on Debian and Ubuntu you need to use apache2-dev.

In the next step, ensure that you have resolved all the dependencies before compilation. The dependencies are listed in Table 2.2.

Table 2.2. ModSecurity dependencies

Dependency	In Apache?	Purpose
Apache Portable Runtime (APR)[a]	Yes	Various
APR-Util[b]	Yes	Various
mod_unique_id	Yes, but may not be installed by default	Generate unique transaction ID
libcurl[c]	No	Remote logging (mlogc)
libxml2[d]	No	XML processing
Lua[e]	No	Writing complex rules in Lua (optional)
Perl Compatible Regular Expressions (PCRE)[f]	Yes, but cannot be used by ModSecurity	Regular expression matching
ssdeep[g]	No	Perform fuzzy hash matching
YAJL[h]	No	JSON processing and JSON format logging

[a] Apache Portable Runtime [fsty.uk/m14] (Apache Portable Runtime Project, retrieved 29 December 2016)
[b] APR-Util [fsty.uk/m14] (Apache Portable Runtime Project, retrieved 29 December 2016)
[c] libcurl [fsty.uk/m15] (libcurl, retrieved 29 December 2016)
[d] libxml2 [fsty.uk/m16] (xmlsoft.org, retrieved 29 December 2016)
[e] Lua 5.2 [fsty.uk/m17] (Lua.org, retrieved 29 December 2016)
[f] Perl Compatible Regular Expressions [fsty.uk/m18] (PCRE, retrieved 29 December 2016)
[g] ssdeep [fsty.uk/m19] (SourceForge, retrieved 29 December 2016)
[h] YAJL [fsty.uk/m20] (GitHub, retrieved 29 December 2016)

If you already have Apache installed, you'll only ever need to deal with libcurl, libxml2, Lua, ssdeep, and YAJL. With Apache compiled from source, you'll also need the PCRE library. Apache no longer comes bundled with it. To work around this issue, install PCRE separately and then tell Apache to use the external copy; I explain how to do so later in this section.

If you're installing from source, go to the packages' web sites and download and install the tarballs. If you're using managed packages, you just need to determine what the missing packages are called. On distributions from the Debian family, the following command installs the missing packages:

```
# apt-get install libcurl3-dev liblua5.3-dev libxml2-dev libfuzzy-dev libyajl-dev
```

Refer to the documentation of the package management system used by your platform to determine how to search the package database.

> **Note**
>
> Libcurl, which is used for remote logging, can be compiled to use OpenSSL or GnuTLS. You are advised to use OpenSSL because there have been complaints about remote logging problems when GnuTLS was used. APR-Util is usually compiled without support for cryptographic operations. If you want to use the directive SecRemoteRule with the parameter crypto, you'll need to compile APR-Util yourself.

The process should be straightforward from here on. If you cloned the GitHub repository and did not download a release, then you need to generate the configuration script, which is used to prepare the compilation process:

```
$ ./autogen.sh
```

If you downloaded a release, then you can skip this step and execute the following commands directly in succession:

```
$ ./configure
$ make
```

This set of commands assumes that you don't need any compile-time options. If you do, see the following subsection.

> **Note**
>
> Running additional tests after compilation (make test and make test-regression) is always a good idea and is an especially good idea when using a development version of ModSecurity. If you're going to have any problems, you want to have them before installation, rather than after.

After ModSecurity is built, one more step is required to install it:

```
$ sudo make install
```

This command adds the module to your Apache installation but doesn't activate it; you must do that manually. (While you're doing so, confirm that mod_unique_id is enabled; ModSecu-

---

rity requires it.) The command will also create a folder (/usr/local/modsecurity by default) and store the various runtime files in it. Here's what you get:

```
bin/
    mlogc
    mlogc-batch-load.pl
    rules-updater.pl
lib/
    mod_security2.so
```

Compile-Time Options

The configuration example from the previous section assumed that the dependencies were all installed as system libraries. It also assumed that the configure script will figure everything on its own. It may or may not do so, but chances are good that you'll occasionally need to do something different; this is where the compile-time options listed in Table 2.3 come in handy.

Table 2.3. Main compile-time options

Option	Description
--disable-request-early	Shift the first processing phase of ModSecurity to a later position in the lifecycle of an Apache request. The default is to run the phase early.
--with-apr	Specify the location of the Apache Portable Runtime library.
--with-apu	Specify the location of the APR-Util library.
--with-apxs	Specify the location of Apache through the location of the apxs script.
--with-curl	Specify the location of libcurl.
--with-libxml	Specify the location of libxml2.
--with-pcre	Specify the location of PCRE.
--with-ssdeep	Specify the location of ssdeep.
--with-yajl	Specify the location of YAJL.

Custom-Compiled Apache Installations

Using ModSecurity with a custom-compiled version of Apache is straightforward. With Apache 2.2, there used to be issues with PCRE and the mod_unique_id module not being enabled by default, but these were solved with Apache 2.4.

To configure ModSecurity, use the --with-apxs compile-time option to specify the location of your Apache installation. In the following example, I'm assuming Apache is installed in /usr/local/apache:

```
$ ./configure \
    --with-apxs=/usr/local/apache/bin/apxs
```

From here, install ModSecurity as described in the previous section.

After both Apache and ModSecurity are installed, you should confirm that both products link to the same PCRE library, using ldd:

```
$ ldd /usr/local/apache/bin/httpd | grep pcre
        libpcre.so.3 => /lib64/libpcre.so.3 (0x00007ff2a11fd000)
```

You should get the same result when you compile ModSecurity:

```
$ ldd /usr/local/apache/modules/mod_security2.so | grep pcre
        libpcre.so.3 => /lib64/libpcre.so.3 (0x00007f85995c5000)
```

> **Tip**
>
> Mac OS X does not have ldd, but you can obtain the equivalent functionality by running otool with option -L. If you really get stuck, consider using install_name_tool to change library dependencies after ModSecurity is compiled.

It is quite possible to have a configuration in which Apache uses its bundled PCRE and ModSecurity uses another PCRE version available on the system.

ModSecurity reports the detected library version numbers at startup (in the error log) and compares them to those used at compile time. One or more warnings will be issued if a mismatch is found. This feature is especially handy for troubleshooting various library collisions, which can happen in odd situations.

```
ModSecurity for Apache/2.9.1 (http://www.modsecurity.org/) configured.
ModSecurity: APR compiled version="1.5.2"; loaded version="1.5.2"
ModSecurity: PCRE compiled version="8.39 "; loaded version="8.39 2016-06-14"
ModSecurity: LUA compiled version="Lua 5.2"
ModSecurity: YAJL compiled version="2.0.4"
ModSecurity: LIBXML compiled version="2.9.1"
```

Installation from Binaries

As previously discussed, using a binary version of ModSecurity is often the easiest option, because it just works. Unfortunately, what you gain in ease of installation you lose by sometimes being limited to an older version. Further, packagers often do not include mlogc, which is helpful for remote log centralization. In general, if you're okay with the way the module was compiled, then you'll be fine with binary packages.

Fedora Core, CentOS, and Red Hat Enterprise Linux

If you're a Fedora user, you can install ModSecurity directly from the official distribution, using yum:

```
# yum install mod_security
```

On CentOS and Red Hat Enterprise Linux, you have to use the packages from Extra Packages for Enterprise Linux (EPEL), a volunteer effort that's part of the Fedora community.[4] The installation process is the same as for Fedora.

Debian and Ubuntu

Debian was the first distribution to include ModSecurity. Alberto Gonzalez Iniesta has been a long-time supporter of ModSecurity on Debian, supporting ModSecurity in his own (unofficial) repository and later becoming the official packager.

If you are running a version of the Debian family, the installation is easy:

```
# apt-get install libapache2-mod-security2
```

This single command will download the package and install it, then activate the module in the Apache configuration.

> **Note**
>
> Don't forget that Debian uses a special system of naming configuration files to manage Apache modules and sites. To activate and deactivate modules, use a2enmod and a2dismod, respectively. To manage Apache, use apache2ctl.

Installation on Windows

ModSecurity was ported to Windows early on, in 2003, and has run well on the platform ever since. Windows binary packages of ModSecurity are maintained by Steffen Land, who runs Apache Lounge, a community for those who run Apache on Windows.[5] In addition to ModSecurity, Steffen maintains his version of Apache itself, as well as many third-party modules you might want to run on Windows. The ModSecurity binary packages are consistently up to date, so you'll have little trouble if you want to run the latest version. The download includes ModSecurity and mlogc.

> **Note**
>
> Although it might be possible to run Steffen's ModSecurity binaries with a version of Apache produced elsewhere, you really should use only the packages from a single location that are intended to be used together. Otherwise, you may encounter unusual behavior and web server crashes.

---

[4] Extra Packages for Enterprise Linux [fsty.uk/m21] (Fedora Project, retrieved 29 December 2016)

[5] Apache Lounge web site [fsty.uk/m22] (Apache Lounge, retrieved 29 December 2016)

The installation is quite easy. First, download the package and copy the dynamic libraries into the modules/ folder (of the Apache installation). Then, modify your Apache configuration to activate ModSecurity:

```
LoadModule security2_module modules/mod_security2.so
```

You will also need to activate mod_unique_id. This module may not be already active, but there should already be a commented-out line in your configuration. You just need to find it and uncomment it. If it isn't there, just add the following:

```
LoadModule unique_id_module modules/mod_unique_id.so
```

Summary

It's never been easier to install ModSecurity, now that it's included with so many operating systems and distributions. Although installation from source code gives you guaranteed access to the most recent version, as well as access to the yet-unreleased code, it can be time-consuming if you're not used to it; it's not everyone's cup of tea. There's something to be said for using the provided version and not having to think about upgrading (and saving the time it takes to upgrade).

In the next chapter, I'll explain each of the configuration options, teaching you how to set every single option, step by step, so that everything is just the way you like it.

3 Configuration

Now that you have ModSecurity installed and ready to run, we can proceed to the configuration. This section, with its many subsections, goes through every part of ModSecurity configuration, explicitly configuring every little detail:

- Going through most of the configuration directives will give you a better understanding of how ModSecurity works. Even if there are features that you don't need immediately, you will learn that they exist and you'll be able to take advantage of them when the need arises.

- By explicitly configuring every single feature, you will foolproof your configuration against incompatible changes to default settings that may happen in future versions of ModSecurity.

In accordance with its philosophy, ModSecurity won't do anything implicitly. It won't even run unless you tell it to. There are three reasons for that:

1. By not doing anything implicitly, we ensure that ModSecurity does only what you tell it to. That not only keeps you in control but also makes you think about every feature before you add it to your configuration.

2. It is impossible to design a default configuration that works in all circumstances. We can give you a framework within which you can work (as I'm doing in this section), but you still need to shape your configuration according to your needs.

3. Security is not free. You pay for it by the increased consumption of RAM, CPU, or the possibility that you may block a legitimate request. Incorrect configuration may cause problems, so we need you to think carefully about what you're doing.

The remainder of this section explains the proposed default configuration for ModSecurity. You can get a good overview of the default configuration simply by examining the configuration directives supported by ModSecurity, which are listed in Table 3.1 (with the exception of the logging directives, which are listed in several tables in Chapter 4, *Logging*).

Table 3.1. Main configuration directives

Directive	Description
SecDataDir	Sets the folder for persistent storage
SecRequestBodyAccess	Controls request body buffering
SecRequestBodyInMemoryLimit	Sets the size of the per-request memory buffer
SecRequestBodyLimit	Sets the maximum request body size ModSecurity will accept
SecRequestBodyLimitAction	Controls what happens once the request body limit is reached
SecRequestBodyNoFilesLimit	Sets the maximum request body size, excluding uploaded files
SecResponseBodyAccess	Controls response body buffering
SecResponseBodyLimit	Specifies the response body buffering limit
SecResponseBodyLimitAction	Controls what happens once the response body limit is reached
SecResponseBodyMimeType	Specifies a list of response body MIME types to inspect
SecResponseBodyMimeTypesClear	Clears the list of response body MIME types
SecRuleEngine	Controls the operation of the rule engine
SecTmpDir	Sets the folder for temporary files
SecUploadDir	Sets the folder in which intercepted files will be stored
SecUploadFileLimit	Set the maximum number of file uploads processed in a multipart POST
SecUploadKeepFiles	Controls whether the uploaded files will be kept after the transaction is processed

Folder Locations

Your first configuration task is to decide where on the filesystem to put the various bits and pieces that every ModSecurity installation consists of. Installation layout is often a matter of taste, so it's difficult to give specific advice. Similarly, different choices may be appropriate in different circumstances. For example, if you're adding ModSecurity to a web server and you intend to use it only occasionally, you may not want to use an elaborate folder structure, in which case you'll probably put the ModSecurity folder underneath Apache's. When you're using ModSecurity as part of a dedicated reverse proxy installation, however, a well-thought-out structure is something that will save you a lot of time in the long run.

I always prefer to use an elaborate folder layout, because I like things to be neat and tidy and because the consistency helps me when I am managing multiple ModSecurity installations. I start by creating a dedicated folder for ModSecurity (/usr/local/modsecurity) with multiple subfolders underneath. The subfolders that are written to at runtime are all grouped (in /usr/local/modsecurity/var), which makes it easy to relocate them to a different filesystem using a symbolic link. I end up with the following structure:

Binaries
> /usr/local/modsecurity/bin

Configuration files/rules
/usr/local/modsecurity/etc

Audit logs
/usr/local/modsecurity/var/audit

Persistent data
/usr/local/modsecurity/var/data

Logs
/usr/local/modsecurity/var/log

Temporary files
/usr/local/modsecurity/var/tmp

File uploads
/usr/local/modsecurity/var/upload

Getting the permissions right may involve slightly more effort, depending on your circumstances. Most Apache installations bind to privileged ports (e.g., 80 and 443), which means that the web server must be started as root, and that also means root must be the principal owner of the installation. Because it's not good practice to stay as root at runtime, Apache will switch to a low-privilege account (we'll assume it's apache) as soon as it initializes. You'll find the proposed permissions in Table 3.2.

Table 3.2. Folder permissions

Location	Owner	Group	Permissions
/usr/local/modsecurity	root	apache	rwxr-x---
/usr/local/modsecurity/bin	root	apache	rwxr-x---
/usr/local/modsecurity/etc	root	root	rwx------
/usr/local/modsecurity/var	root	apache	rwxr-x---
/usr/local/modsecurity/var/audit	apache	root	rwx------
/usr/local/modsecurity/var/data	apache	root	rwx------
/usr/local/modsecurity/var/log	root	root	rwx------
/usr/local/modsecurity/var/tmp	apache	apache	rwxr-x---
/usr/local/modsecurity/var/upload	apache	root	rwx------

I've arrived at the desired permission layout through the following requirements:

1. As already discussed, root that owns everything by default, and we assign ownership to apache only when necessary.

2. In two cases (/usr/local/modsecurity and /usr/local/modsecurity/var), we need to allow apache to access a folder so that it can get to a subfolder; we do this by creating a group, also called apache, of which user apache is the only member. We use the same

group for the /usr/local/modsecurity/bin folder, where you might store some binaries Apache will need to execute at runtime.

3. One folder, /usr/local/modsecurity/var/log, stands out; it's the only folder underneath /usr/local/modsecurity/var to which apache is not allowed to write. That folder contains log files that are opened by Apache early on while it's still running as root. On any Unix system, you *must* have only one account with write access to that folder, and it has to be the principal owner. In our case, that must be root. Anything else would create a security hole, whereby the apache user would be able to obtain partial root privileges using symlink trickery. (Essentially, in place of a log file, the apache user creates a symlink to some other root-owned file on the system. When Apache starts, it runs as root and opens for writing the system file that the apache user would otherwise be unable to touch. By submitting requests to Apache, one might be able to control exactly what's written to the log files. That can lead to system compromise.)

4. A careful observer will notice that I've allowed group folder access to /usr/local/modsecurity/var/tmp (which means that any member of the apache group is allowed to read the files in the folder) even though this folder is owned by apache, which already has full access. This is because you'll sometimes want to allow ModSecurity to exchange information with a third user account—for example, if you want to scan uploaded files for viruses (usually via ClamAV). To allow the third user account to access the files created by ModSecurity, make it a member of the apache group and relax the file permissions using the SecUploadFileMode directive.

> **Note**
>
> As an exception to the proposed layout, you may want to reuse Apache's log directory for ModSecurity logs. If you don't, you'll have the error log separate from the debug log (and the audit log if you choose to use the serial logging format). In a reverse proxy installation in particular, it makes great sense to keep everything integrated and easier to find. There may be other good reasons for breaking convention. For example, if you have more than one hard disk installed and you use the audit logging feature a lot, you may want to split the I/O operations across the disks.

Configuration Layout

If you have anything but a trivial setup, spreading configuration across several files is necessary in order to make maintenance easier. The layout depends on what you want to do with ModSecurity. If you plan to run the OWASP ModSecurity Core Rule Set, for example, you'll follow their setup proposal to a certain extent. Other rule layout conventions have more to do with taste than anything else, but in this section I'll describe an approach that's good enough to start with.

Whatever configuration design I use, there is usually one main entry point, typically named modsecurity.conf, which I use as a bridge between Apache and ModSecurity. In my bridge file, I refer to any other ModSecurity files I might have, such as those listed in Table 3.3.

Table 3.3. Configuration files

Filename	Description
main.conf	Main configuration file
rules-first.conf	Rules that need to run first
rules.conf	Principal rule file
rules-last.conf	Rules that need to run last

Your main configuration file (modsecurity.conf) thus may contain only the following lines:

```
Include /usr/local/modsecurity/etc/main.conf
Include /usr/local/modsecurity/etc/rules-first.conf
Include /usr/local/modsecurity/etc/rules.conf
Include /usr/local/modsecurity/etc/rules-last.conf
```

Adding ModSecurity to Apache

As the first step, make Apache aware of ModSecurity, adding the needed components. Depending on how you've chosen to run ModSecurity, this may translate to adding one or more lines to your configuration file. This is what the lines may look like:

```
# Load Lua
LoadFile /usr/lib/x86_64-linux-gnu/liblua5.3.so
# Finally, load ModSecurity
LoadModule security2_module modules/mod_security2.so
```

Now you just need to tell Apache where to find the configuration:

```
<IfModule mod_security2.c>
    Include /usr/local/modsecurity/etc/modsecurity.conf
</IfModule>
```

The <IfModule> tag is there to ensure that the ModSecurity configuration files are used only if ModSecurity is active in the web server. This is common practice when configuring any nonessential Apache modules; it allows you to deactivate a module simply by commenting out the appropriate LoadModule line.

Powering Up

ModSecurity has a master switch—the SecRuleEngine directive—that allows you to quickly turn it on and off. This directive will always come first in every configuration. I generally recommend that you start in detection-only mode, because that way you can be sure nothing will be blocked:

```
# Enable ModSecurity, attaching it to every transaction.
SecRuleEngine DetectionOnly
```

You'll normally want to keep this setting enabled, of course, but there will be cases in which you won't be exactly sure whether ModSecurity is doing something it shouldn't be. Whenever that happens, you'll want to set it to Off, just for a moment or two, until you perform a request without it running.

The SecRuleEngine directive is context-sensitive (i.e., it works with Apache's container tags <VirtualHost>, <Location>, and so on), which means that you can control exactly where ModSecurity runs. You can use this feature to enable ModSecurity only for some sites, parts of a web site, or even for a single script only. I discuss this feature in detail later.

Request Body Handling

Requests consist of two parts: the headers part, which is always present, and the body, which is optional and depends on the HTTP method employed. Use the SecRequestBodyAccess directive to tell ModSecurity to look at request bodies:

```
# Allow ModSecurity to access request bodies. If you don't,
# ModSecurity won't be able to see any POST parameters,
# and that's generally not what you want.
SecRequestBodyAccess On
```

Once this feature is enabled, ModSecurity not only will have access to the content transmitted in request bodies but also will completely buffer them. The buffering is essential for reliable attack prevention. With buffering in place, your rules have the opportunity to inspect requests in their entirety; only after you choose not to block will the requests be allowed through.

The downside of buffering is that, in most cases, it uses RAM for storage, which needs to be taken into account when ModSecurity is running embedded in a web server. There are three directives that control how buffering occurs. The first two, SecRequestBodyLimit and SecRequestBodyNoFilesLimit, establish request limits:

```
# Maximum request body size we will accept for buffering.
# If you support file uploads, then the value given on the
# first line has to be as large as the largest file you
# want to accept. The second value refers to the size of
# data, with files excluded. You want to keep that value
# as low as practical.
SecRequestBodyLimit 1310720
SecRequestBodyNoFilesLimit 131072
```

File uploads generally don't use RAM (and thus don't create an opportunity for a memory-based denial of service attack), which means that it's safe to allow large requests as defined by SecRequestBodyLimit. With all the other requests, the RAM usage has to be considered, and a lower limit is imperative. SecRequestBodyNoFilesLimit is applied in such cases.

Warning

When the SecStreamInBodyInspection directive is enabled, it will attempt to store the entire raw request body in STREAM_INPUT_BODY. In this case, you lose the protection of SecRequestBodyNoFilesLimit; the maximum amount of memory consumed for buffering will be that defined with SecRequestBodyLimit.

Note

In blocking mode, ModSecurity will respond with a 413 (Request Entity Too Large) response status code when a request body limit is reached. This response code was chosen to mimic what Apache does in similar circumstances. See the section called "SecRequestBodyLimitAction" in Chapter 15 for more information.

The third directive that addresses buffering, SecRequestBodyInMemoryLimit, controls how much of a request body will be stored in RAM, but it only works with file upload (multipart/form-data) requests:

```
# Store up to 128 KB of request body data in memory. When
# the multipart parser reaches this limit, it will start
# using your hard disk for storage. That is generally slow,
# but unavoidable.
SecRequestBodyInMemoryLimit 131072
```

The request bodies that fit within the limit configured with SecRequestBodyInMemoryLimit will be stored in RAM. The request bodies that are larger will be streamed to disk. This directive allows you to trade performance (storing request bodies in RAM is fast) for size (the storage capacity of your hard disk is much bigger than that of your RAM).

Response Body Handling

Similarly to requests, responses consist of headers and a body. Unlike requests, however, most responses have bodies. Use the SecResponseBodyAccess directive to tell ModSecurity to observe (and buffer) response bodies:

```
# Allow ModSecurity to access response bodies. We leave
# this disabled because most deployments want to focus on
# the incoming threats, and leaving this off reduces
# memory consumption.
SecResponseBodyAccess Off
```

I prefer to start with this setting disabled, because many deployments don't care to look at what leaves their web servers. Keeping this feature disabled means ModSecurity will use less RAM and less CPU. If you care about output, however, just change the directive setting to On.

There is a complication with response bodies, because you generally only want to look at the bodies of some of the responses. Response bodies make up the bulk of the traffic on most web sites, most of which is just static files that don't have any security relevance in most cases. The response MIME type is used to distinguish interesting responses from those that are not. The SecResponseBodyMimeType directive lists the response MIME types you're interested in:

```
# Which response MIME types do you want to look at? You
# should adjust this configuration to catch documents
# but avoid static files (e.g., images and archives).
SecResponseBodyMimeType text/plain text/html
```

> **Note**
>
> To instruct ModSecurity to inspect response bodies for which the MIME type is unknown (meaning that it was not specified in the response headers), use the special string (null) as a parameter for SecResponseBodyMimeType.

You can control the size of a response body buffer via the SecResponseBodyLimit directive:

```
# Buffer response bodies of up to 512 KB in length.
SecResponseBodyLimit 524288
```

The problem with limiting the size of a response body buffer is that it breaks sites for which pages are longer than the limit. In ModSecurity 2.5, we introduced the SecResponseBodyLimitAction directive, which allows ModSecurity users to choose what happens when the limit is reached:

```
# What happens when we encounter a response body larger
# than the configured limit? By default, we process what
```

```
# we have and let the rest through.
SecResponseBodyLimitAction ProcessPartial
```

If the setting is Reject, the response will be discarded and the transaction interrupted with a 500 (Internal Server Error) response code. If the setting is ProcessPartial, which I recommend, ModSecurity will process what it has in the buffer and allow the rest through.

At first glance, it may seem that allowing the processing of partial response bodies creates a security issue. For the attacker who controls output, it seems easy to create a response that's long enough to bypass observation by ModSecurity—and this is true. However, if you have an attacker with full control of output, it's impossible for any type of monitoring to work reliably. For example, such an attacker could encrypt output, in which case it will be opaque to ModSecurity. Response body monitoring works best to detect information leakage, configuration errors, traces of attacks (successful or not), and data leakage in cases in which an attacker does not have full control of output.

Other than that, response monitoring is most useful when it comes to preventing the data leakage that comes from low-level error messages (e.g., database problems). Because such messages typically appear near the beginning of a page, the ProcessPartial setting will work just as well to catch them.

Dealing with Response Compression

When deploying ModSecurity in reverse proxy mode with backend servers that support compression, make sure to set the SecDisableBackendCompression directive to On. Doing so will hide the fact that the clients support compression from your backend servers, giving ModSecurity access to uncompressed data. If you don't disable backend compression, ModSecurity will see only the compressed response bodies (as served by the backend web servers). To continue to use frontend compression, configure mod_deflate in the proxy itself. The SecDisableBackendCompression directive will not interfere with its operation.

Filesystem Locations

We've made the decisions regarding filesystem locations already, so all we need to do now is translate them into configuration. The following two directives tell ModSecurity where to create temporary files (SecTmpDir) and where to store persistent data (SecDataDir):

```
# The location where ModSecurity will store temporary files
# (e.g., when it needs to handle a multipart request
# body that's larger than the configured limit). If you don't
# specify a location here, your system's default will be used.
# It's recommended that you specify a location that's private.
SecTmpDir /usr/local/modsecurity/var/tmp/
```

```
# The location where ModSecurity will keep its data. This,
# too, needs to be a path that other users can't access.
# IMPORTANT: The path defined by SecDataDir must reside on
# on the same partition as the path defined by SecTmpDir.
SecDataDir /usr/local/modsecurity/var/data/
```

File Uploads

Next, we'll configure the handling of file uploads. We'll configure the folder where ModSecurity will store intercepted files, but keep this functionality disabled for now. File upload interception slows down ModSecurity and can potentially consume a lot of disk space, so you'll want to enable this functionality where you really need it.

```
# The location where ModSecurity will store intercepted
# uploaded files. This location must be private to ModSecurity.
SecUploadDir /usr/local/modsecurity/var/upload/

# By default, do not intercept (nor store) uploaded files.
SecUploadKeepFiles Off
```

For now, we also assume that you will not be using external scripts to inspect uploaded files. That allows us to keep the file permissions more secure, by allowing access only to the apache user:

```
# Uploaded files are by default created with permissions that
# don't allow any other user to access them. You may need to
# relax that if you want to interface ModSecurity with an
# external program (e.g., an anti-virus program).
SecUploadFileMode 0600
```

You should set the maximum number of files that ModSecurity will handle in a request:

```
# Limit the number of files we are willing
# to handle in any one request.
SecUploadFileLimit 32
```

There isn't a limit by default, so setting one in the configuration is very important. The issue here first is that it's easy for an attacker to include many embedded files (hundreds or even thousands) in a single multipart/form-data request, but also you don't want ModSecurity to create that many files on the filesystem (which happens only if the storage or validation of uploaded files is required), because it would create a denial of service situation.

Debug Log

Debug logging is very useful for troubleshooting, but in production you want to keep it at minimum, because too much logging will affect performance. The debug log will duplicate what you'll also see in Apache's error log up to level 3. If the error log is growing fast and has to be rotated quickly, it can be useful to keep the ModSecurity-related messages longer in the debug log. However, if there are a lot of ModSecurity alerts, redundancy will be an issue, and you'll need to make sure you also rotate the debug log regularly. It's perfectly okay to run with a debug log level of 0 and to rely on the Apache error log. Any value above 3 is not recommended in production.

```
# Debug log
SecDebugLog /usr/local/modsecurity/var/log/debug.log
SecDebugLogLevel 3
```

Audit Log

In ModSecurity terminology, *audit logging* refers to the ability to record complete transaction data. For a typical transaction without a request body, this translates to roughly 1 KB. Multiply that by the number of requests you're receiving daily and you'll soon realize that you want to keep this type of logging to an absolute minimum.

Our default configuration will use audit logging only for the transactions that are *relevant*, which means those that have had an error or a warning reported against them. Other possible values for SecAuditEngine are On (log everything) and Off (log nothing).

```
# Log only what's really necessary.
SecAuditEngine RelevantOnly
```

In addition, we'll also log the transactions with response status codes that indicate a server error (500–599). You should never see such transactions on an error-free server. The extra data logged by ModSecurity may help you uncover security issues or problems of some other type.

```
# Also log requests that cause a server error.
SecAuditLogRelevantStatus ^5
```

Alternatively, you can also log client errors in the range of 400–499. This can be useful because affected users often will contact you with support questions. You probably don't want to log status code 404 (Not Found) in this case, so the complete regular expression to keep an audit log of all erroneous requests—with the exception of 404—is as follows:

```
# Also log requests that cause an error.
SecAuditLogRelevantStatus "^(?:5|4(?!04))"
```

The audit log separates its records into multiple parts. Each part is assigned a single letter. You enable the logging of the individual parts by listing them as parameters of the SecAuditLogParts directive. By default, we log all transaction data except response bodies. This assumes that you will seldom log (as it should be), because response bodies can take up a lot of space.

```
# Log everything we know about a transaction.
SecAuditLogParts ABDEFHIJKZ
```

Using the same assumption, we choose to use a single file to store all the recorded information. This is not adequate for installations that will log a lot and it prevents remote logging, but it's good enough to start with:

```
# Use a single file for logging.
SecAuditLogType Serial
SecAuditLog /usr/local/modsecurity/var/log/audit.log
```

As the final step, we'll configure the path that will be used in the more scalable audit logging scheme, called *concurrent logging*, even though you won't need to use it just yet:

```
# Specify the path for concurrent audit logging.
SecAuditLogStorageDir /usr/local/modsecurity/var/audit/
```

Default Rule Match Policy

Now that we're nearing the end of the configuration, you need to decide what you want to happen when a rule matches. We recommend that you start without blocking, because that will allow you to monitor the operation of your installation over a period of time and ensure that legitimate traffic is not being marked as suspicious:

```
SecDefaultAction "phase:1,log,auditlog,pass"
```

This default policy will work for all rules that follow it in the same configuration context. For more information, turn to the section called "Configuration Contexts" in Chapter 7.

> **Note**
>
> It's possible to write rules that ignore the default policies. If you're using third-party rulesets and are not sure how they will behave, consider switching the entire engine to detection only (using SecRuleEngine). No rule will block when you do that, regardless of how it was designed to work.

Handling Processing Errors

As you may recall from our earlier discussion, ModSecurity avoids making decisions for you. It will detect problems as they occur, but it will generally leave it to you to deal with them. In our default configuration, we'll have a couple of rules to deal with the situations that ModSecurity can't deal with on its own: processing errors.

> **Note**
>
> I'm including these rules here because they should be an integral part of every configuration, but you shouldn't worry if you don't understand exactly what it is that they do. The mechanics of the rules will be explained in detail later in the section called "Variable Expansion" in Chapter 6.

There are currently three types of processing errors:

1. Request and response buffering limits encountered

2. Parsing errors

3. PCRE limit errors

Normally, you don't need to be too concerned about encountering buffer limits, because they often occur during normal operation. If you do want to take them into account when making decisions, you can use the INBOUND_DATA_ERROR and OUTBOUND_DATA_ERROR variables for request and response buffering, respectively.

ModSecurity parsers are designed to be as permissive as possible without compromising security. They will raise flags when they fail, but also when they encounter something suspicious. By checking the flags in your rules, you can detect the processing errors.

Currently, the only parsing errors that can happen are request body processor errors. We'll use two rules to handle such errors. The first rule will examine the REQBODY_PROCESSOR_ERROR flag for errors. This flag will be raised whenever a request body parsing error occurs, regardless of which parser was used for parsing:

```
# Verify that we've correctly processed the request body.
# As a rule of thumb, when failing to process a request body
# you should reject the request (when deployed in blocking mode)
# or log a high-severity alert (when deployed in detection-only mode).
SecRule REQBODY_PROCESSOR_ERROR "!@eq 0" \
    "id:2000,phase:2,block,t:none,log,msg:'Failed to parse request body: ↵
%{REQBODY_PROCESSOR_ERROR_MSG}'"
```

The second rule is specific to the multipart/form-data parser, which is used to handle file uploads. If it detects a problem, it produces an error message detailing the flaws:

```
# By default, be strict with what you accept in the multipart/form-data
# request body. If the rule below proves to be too strict for your
# environment, consider changing it to detection-only. You are encouraged
# *not* to remove it altogether.
SecRule MULTIPART_STRICT_ERROR "!@eq 0" \
"id:2001,phase:2,block,t:none,log,msg:'Multipart request body \
```

```
failed strict validation: \
PE %{REQBODY_PROCESSOR_ERROR}, \
BQ %{MULTIPART_BOUNDARY_QUOTED}, \
BW %{MULTIPART_BOUNDARY_WHITESPACE}, \
DB %{MULTIPART_DATA_BEFORE}, \
DA %{MULTIPART_DATA_AFTER}, \
HF %{MULTIPART_HEADER_FOLDING}, \
LF %{MULTIPART_LF_LINE}, \
SM %{MULTIPART_MISSING_SEMICOLON}, \
IQ %{MULTIPART_INVALID_QUOTING}, \
IF %{MULTIPART_INVALID_HEADER_FOLDING}, \
FE %{MULTIPART_FILE_LIMIT_EXCEEDED}'"
```

Errors specific to multipart parsers should never occur unless an attacker genuinely tries to bypass ModSecurity by manipulating the request body payload. Some versions of ModSecurity did have false positives in this area, but the most recent version should be false-positive-free. If you do encounter such a problem, feel free to post it to the ModSecurity users' mailing list, noting that you've encountered an interesting attacker or a ModSecurity bug.

PCRE limits are set to protect the server from denial of service attacks via excessive resource consumption in regular expression calculations. The default limits are very low. Therefore, users can control the setting of the limits via SecPcreMatchLimit and SecPcreMatchLimitRecursion. The debug log will identify rules that have exceeded the limits —for example:

```
[3] Rule 292d670 [id "941140"][file "/usr/local/modsecurity/etc/core-rules↵
/REQUEST-941-APPLICATION-ATTACK-XSS.conf"][line "514"] - Execution error - PCRE ↵
limits exceeded (-8): (null).
```

For now, leave the PCRE limits defaults as they are, but add a rule to warn us when they're exceeded:

```
SecRule TX:MSC_PCRE_LIMITS_EXCEEDED "@eq 1" \
    "id:9000,phase:5,pass,t:none,log,msg:'PCRE limits exceeded'"
```

I've used phase 5 for the rule, but if you're really paranoid and think that exceeding PCRE limits is grounds for blocking, switch to phase 2 (and change pass to something else).

Verifying Installation

After you're done installing and configuring ModSecurity, we recommend undertaking a short exercise to ensure everything is in order:

1. Add a simple blocking rule to detect something in a parameter. For example, the following rule will inspect all parameters for the string MY_UNIQUE_TEST_STRING, responding with a 503 (Service Unavailable) on a match:

```
SecRule ARGS "@contains MY_UNIQUE_TEST_STRING" \
    "id:2000,phase:2,deny,status:503,log"
```

2. Restart Apache, using the graceful restart option if your server is in production and you don't want any downtime.

3. Send a GET request, using your browser, to the ModSecurity-protected server, including the "attack payload" in a parameter (i.e., http://www.example.com/? test=MY_UNIQUE_TEST_STRING). ModSecurity should block the request.

4. Verify that the message has appeared in both the error log and the debug log and that the audit log contains the complete transaction.

5. Submit a POST request that triggers the test rule. With this request, you're testing whether ModSecurity will see the request body and whether it will be able to pass the data in it to your backend after inspection. For this test in particular, it's important that you're testing with the actual application you want to protect. Only doing so will exercise the entire stack of components that make the application. This test is important because of the way Apache modules are written (very little documentation, so module authors generally employ any approach that "works" for them); you can never be 100% certain that a third-party module was implemented correctly. For example, it's possible to write a module that will essentially hijack a request early on and bypass all other modules, including ModSecurity. We're doing this test simply because we don't want to leave anything to chance.

6. If you want to be really pedantic (I have been, on many occasion; you can never be too sure), you may want to consider writing a special test script for your application, which will somehow record the fact that it has been invoked (mine usually writes to a file in /tmp). By sending a request that includes an attack—which will be intercepted by ModSecurity—and verifying that the script has not been invoked, you can be completely sure that blocking works as intended.

7. Remove the test rule and restart Apache again.

8. Finally, and just to be absolutely sure, examine the permissions on all Apache and ModSecurity locations and verify that they're correct.

You're done!

Summary

In this chapter, we looked at the core configuration options of ModSecurity. Strictly speaking, we could have left many of these options set to their defaults and spent about a tenth of this time on configuration, but I've always found it better to explicitly define every setting; with that approach, you end up with the configuration that's tailored to your needs. In addition, you get to know ModSecurity better, which might prove crucial at some point in the future.

Quite a few more optional configuration directives exist. Most of them are highly advanced or only applicable in rare and special situations. They're covered in Chapter 15, *Directives*.

We didn't pay much attention to logging in this chapter, opting to configure both the debug log and the audit log conservatively. However, there's a wealth of logging options in ModSecurity. In the next chapter, I'll discuss logging in detail and conclude with the configuration topics.

4 Logging

This chapter covers the logging capabilities of ModSecurity in detail. Logging is a big part of what ModSecurity does, so it's not surprising that there are extensive logging facilities available for your use.

Debug Log

The debug log is going to be your primary troubleshooting tool, especially initially, while you're learning how ModSecurity works. You're likely to spend a lot of time with the debug log cranked up to level 9, observing why certain things work the way they do. There are two debug log directives, as you can see in Table 4.1.

Table 4.1. Debug log directives

Directive	Description
SecDebugLog	Path to the debug log file
SecDebugLogLevel	Debug log level

In theory, there are 10 debug log levels, but not all are used. You'll find the ones that are in Table 4.2. Messages with levels 1–3 are copied to Apache's error log. The higher-level messages are there mostly for troubleshooting and debugging.

You will want to keep the debug log level in production low (either at 3 if you want a copy of all messages in the debug log or at 0 if you're happy having the messages only in the error log). You can expect in excess of 50 debug log messages (each message is an I/O operation) and at least 7 KB of data for an average transaction; logging all that for every transaction consumes a lot of resources.

This is what a single debug log line looks like:

```
[24/Jul/2016:17:38:25 +0200] [192.168.3.111/sid#15e21f8][rid#7f683c002970]↵
[/index.html][4] Initialising transaction (txid V5Tg8X8AAQEAABXZdiwAAAAA).
```

The line starts with metadata that is often longer than the message itself: the time, client's IP address, internal server ID, internal request ID, request URI, and, finally, the debug log level. The rest of the line is occupied by the message, which is essentially free-form. You will find many examples of debug log messages throughout this guide.

Table 4.2. Debug log levels

Debug log level	Description
0	No logging
1	Errors (e.g., fatal processing errors, blocked transactions)
2	Warnings (e.g., nonblocking rule matches)
3	Notices (e.g., nonfatal processing errors)
4	Handling of transactions and performance
5	Detailed syntax of the rules
6–8	Not used
9	Detailed information about transactions (e.g., variable expansion and setting of variables)

Debugging in Production

There's another reason to avoid extensive debug logging in production, and that's simply that it's very difficult. There's usually so much data that it sometimes takes ages to find the messages that pertain to the transaction you want to investigate. In spite of the difficulties, you may occasionally need to debug in production because you can't reproduce a problem elsewhere.

> **Note**
>
> The audit log can record all the rules that matched during an HTTP transaction. This helpful feature minimizes the need for debugging in production, but it still can't tell you why some rules *didn't* match.

One way to make debugging easier is to keep debug logging disabled by default and enable it only for the part of the site that you want to debug. You can do this by overriding the default configuration, using the <Location> context directive, as shown ahead. While you're doing that, it may be a good idea to specify a different debug log file altogether. That way, you'll keep the main debug log file free of your tests.

```
<Location /myapp/>
    SecDebugLogLevel 9
    SecDebugLog /usr/local/modsecurity/var/log/troubleshooting.log
</Location>
```

This approach, although handy, still doesn't guarantee that the volume of information in the debug log will be manageable. What you really want is to enable debug logging for the requests a specific client sends. ModSecurity provides a solution for this by allowing a debug log level to be changed at runtime, on a per-request basis. This is done by using the special ctl action that allows some of the configuration to be updated at runtime.

All you need to do is somehow uniquely identify yourself. In some circumstances, observing the IP address will be sufficient:

```
SecRule REMOTE_ADDR "@ipMatch 192.168.1.1" \
    id:1000,phase:1,pass,nolog,ctl:debugLogLevel=9
```

Using your IP address won't work in cases in which you're hidden by a network address translation of some sort and share an IP address with a bunch of other users. One straight-forward approach is to modify your browser settings to put a unique identifier in your User-Agent request header. (How exactly that's done depends on the browser you're using.)

```
SecRule REQUEST_HEADERS:User-Agent "@contains YOUR_UNIQUE_ID" \
    id:1000,phase:1,pass,nolog,ctl:debugLogLevel=9
```

This approach, although easy, has a drawback: all your requests will cause an increase in debug logging. You may think of an application in terms of dynamic pages, but extensive debug logging will be enabled for every single embedded object, too. Also, if you're dealing with an application that you're using frequently, you may want to avoid excessive logging.

The most accurate way to dynamically enable detailed debug logging is to manually indicate to ModSecurity the exact requests on which you want it to increase logging. You can do this by modifying your User-Agent string on a request-by-request basis, using one of the tools that support request interception and modification. You can do so via a browser extension or can use an interception proxy. Armed with such a tool, you submit your requests in your browser, modify them in the tool, and then allow them through, modified. It's a bit involved, but a time-saver overall. While you're at it, it's a good idea to make your identifiers similar enough for your rule to always detect them, but different enough to allow you to use a search function to quickly find the exact request in a file with thousands of lines.

Audit Log

It's a little-known fact that the earliest versions of ModSecurity essentially had one feature: the ability to record complete HTTP transaction data. Being able to see exactly what's exchanged between browsers and servers is very important for developers, yet few web servers make it possible. The audit log, which does just that, was one of the first features implemented.

ModSecurity is currently able to log most, but not all, transactions. Transactions involving errors (e.g., 400 and 404 transactions) and some third-party Apache modules like mod_auth_cas use a different execution path, which ModSecurity doesn't support. This means that they shortcut the ModSecurity rule phases 1 to 4, effectively preventing the module from extracting the necessary data out of the request. Audit log directives are shown in Table 4.3.

Table 4.3. Audit log directives

Directive	Description
SecAuditEngine	Controls the audit log engine; possible values are On, Off, or RelevantOnly
SecAuditLog	Path to an audit log file
SecAuditLog2	Path to another audit log file (copy)
SecAuditLogDirMode	Permissions (mode) of the folders created for the concurrent log type
SecAuditLogFileMode	Permissions (mode) of the files created for the concurrent log type
SecAuditLogFormat	Format of the audit log (native or JSON)
SecAuditLogParts	Specifies which part of a transaction will be logged
SecAuditLogRelevantStatus	Specifies which response statuses will be considered relevant
SecAuditLogStorageDir	Path where concurrent audit log files will be stored
SecAuditLogType	Specifies the type of audit log to use: Serial or Concurrent

A typical audit log entry (short, GET request, brief User-Agent, without a body, and no logging of the response body) consumes around 1.5 KB. Requests with bodies will increase the amount of data that needs to be logged, as well as the logging of response bodies.

Logically, each audit log entry is a single file. When serial audit logging is used, all entries will be placed within one file, but with concurrent audit logging, one file per entry is used. There is a native format for the individual entries or an alternative JSON format. Looking at a single audit log entry in the default native format, you'll find that it consists of multiple independent segments (parts):

```
--6b253045-A--
...
--6b253045-B--
...
--6b253045-C--
...
--6b253045-F--
...
--6b253045-E--
...
--6b253045-H--
...
--6b253045-Z--
```

A segment begins with a boundary and ends when the next segment begins. The only exception is the terminating segment (Z), which consists only of the boundary. The idea behind the use of multiple segments is to allow each audit log entry to contain potentially different information. Only parts A and Z are mandatory; the use of the other parts is controlled with the SecAuditLogParts directive. Table 4.4 contains the list of all audit log parts, along with a description of their purpose.

Table 4.4. Audit log parts

Part letter	Description
A	Audit log header (mandatory)
B	Request headers
C	Request body
D	Reserved
E	Response body
F	Response headers
G	Reserved
H	Audit log trailer, which contains additional data
I	Reduced multipart request body, which excludes files (alternative to part C)
J	Information on uploaded files (multipart requests)
K	Contains a list of all rules that matched for the transaction
Z	Final boundary (mandatory)

Native Format Audit Log Entry Example

Every audit log entry begins with part A, which contains the basic information about the transaction: time, unique ID, source IP address, source port, destination IP address, and destination port:

```
--be58b513-A--
[27/Jul/2016:05:46:16 +0200] V5guiH8AAQEAADTeJ2wAAAAK 192.168.3.1 50084 ↵
192.168.3.111 80
```

Part B contains the request headers and nothing else:

```
POST /index.html?a=test HTTP/1.1
Host: example.com
User-Agent: Mozilla/5.0
Accept: text/html,application/xhtml+xml,application/xml;q=0.9,*/*;q=0.8
Accept-Language: en-US,en;q=0.5
Accept-Encoding: gzip, deflate
Referer: http://example.com/index.html
Connection: keep-alive
Content-Type: application/x-www-form-urlencoded
Content-Length: 6
```

Part C contains the raw request body, typically that of a POST request:

```
--be58b513-C--
b=test
```

Part F contains the response headers:

```
--be58b513-F--
HTTP/1.1 200 OK
Last-Modified: Sun, 24 Jul 2016 15:24:49 GMT
ETag: "2d-5386344b7871a"
Accept-Ranges: bytes
Content-Length: 159
Keep-Alive: timeout=5, max=100
Connection: Keep-Alive
Content-Type: text/html
```

Part E contains the response body:

```
--be58b513-E--
<html><body><h1>It works!</h1></body></html>

<form action="index.html?a=test" method="POST">
<textarea name="b">test</textarea>
<input type=submit>
</form>
```

The final part, H, contains additional transaction information:

```
--be58b513-H--
Stopwatch: 1470025005945403 1715 (- - -)
Stopwatch2: 1470025005945403 1715; combined=26, p1=0, p2=0, p3=0, p4=0, p5=26, ↵
sr=0, sw=0, l=0, gc=0
Response-Body-Transformed: Dechunked
Producer: ModSecurity for Apache/2.9.1 (http://www.modsecurity.org/).
Server: Apache
Engine-Mode: "ENABLED"
```

Part K contains a list of rules that matched in a transaction. It isn't unusual for this part to be empty, but if you have a complex ruleset, it may show quite a few rules. Audit logs that record transactions for which there were warnings or those that were blocked will contain at least one rule here. In this example, you'll find a rule that emits a warning on every request:

```
--be58b513-K--
SecAction "phase:2,auditlog,log,pass,msg:'Matching test'"
```

Every audit log file ends with the terminating boundary, which is part Z:

```
--be58b513-Z--
```

JSON Format Audit Log

The JSON audit log format was introduced with ModSecurity 2.9.1. It's enabled via the SecAuditLogFormat directive. It's conceptually similar to the native format, but organizes information in a different way. The native audit log parts can be roughly mapped to the JSON format blocks in the following way:

- Transaction: A
- Request: B and C
- Uploads: J (optional)
- Response: E and F
- Matched_rules: K
- Audit_data: H

More information about this additional audit log format is available in the section called "Parts in JSON Format" in Chapter 20.

Concurrent Audit Log

Initially, ModSecurity supported only the serial audit logging type. Concurrent logging was introduced to address two issues:

- Serial logging is only adequate for moderate use, because only one audit log entry can be written at any one time. Serial logging is fast (logs are written at the end of every transaction, all in one go), but it doesn't scale well. In the extreme, a web server performing full transaction logging practically processes only one request at any one time.
- Real-time audit log centralization requires individual audit log entries to be deleted once they're handled, which is impossible to do when all alerts are stored in a single file.

Concurrent audit logging changes the operation of ModSecurity in two aspects. To observe the changes, switch to concurrent logging without activating mlogc by changing SecAuditLogType to Concurrent (don't forget to restart Apache).

First, as expected, each audit log entry will be stored in a separate file. The files will be created not directly in the folder specified by SecAuditLogStorageDir but in an elaborate structure of subfolders, the names of which will be constructed from the current date and time:

```
20160727
20160727/20160727-0546
20160727/20160727-0546/20160727-054616-V5guiH8AAQEAADTeJ2wAAAAK
20160727/20160727-0546/20160727-054616-V5guBH8AAQEAADTeJ2cAAAAA
```

The purpose of the scheme is to prevent too many files from being created within one directory; many filesystems have limits that can be relatively quickly reached on a busy web server. The first two parts in each filename are based on time (YYYYMMDD and HHMMSS). The third parameter is the unique transaction ID.

In addition to each entry getting its own file, the type of the main audit log file will change when concurrent logging is activated. The file that previously stored the entries themselves will now be used as a record of all generated audit log files:

```
192.168.3.130 192.168.3.1 - - [27/Jul/2016:05:46:16 +0200] "GET / HTTP/1.1" 200 ↵
218 "-" "-" V5guiH8AAQEAADTeJ2wAAAAK "-" /20160727/20160727-0546↵
/20160727-054616-V5guiH8AAQEAADTeJ2wAAAAK 0 1592 md5:48e90bf2a5ab9e7368d8b579f14bf8↵
2b
```

The index file is similar in principle to a web server access log. Each line describes one transaction, duplicating some of the information already available in audit log entries. The purpose of the index file is twofold:

- The first part, which duplicates some of the information available in audit logs, serves as a record of everything that you've recorded so that you can easily search through it.

- The second part tells you where an audit log entry is stored (e.g., /20160727/20160727-0546/20160727-054616-V5guiH8AAQEAADTeJ2wAAAAK), where it begins within that file (always zero, because this feature is not used), how long it is, and its MD5 hash (useful to verify integrity).

When real-time audit log centralization is used, this information isn't written to a file. Instead, it's written to a pipe, which means that it's sent directly to another process, which deals with the information immediately. You'll see how that works in the next section.

Remote Logging

ModSecurity comes with a tool called mlogc (short for ModSecurity Log Collector), which can be used to transport audit logs in real time to a remote logging server. This tool has the following characteristics:

Secure

The communication path between your ModSecurity sensors and the remote logging server is secured with SSL and authenticated using HTTP basic authentication.

Efficient

Remote logging is implemented with multiple threads of execution, which allow for many alerts to be handled in parallel. Existing HTTP connections are reused.

Reliable

An audit log entry will be deleted from the sensor only once its safe receipt is acknowledged by the logging server.

Buffered

The mlogc tool maintains its own audit entry queue, which has two benefits. First, if the logging server is not available, the entries will be preserved and submitted once the server comes back online. Second, mlogc controls the rate at which audit log entries are submitted, meaning that a burst of activity on a sensor will not result in an uncontrolled burst of activity on the remote logging server.

> **Note**
>
> Remote logging uses a simple but effective protocol based on HTTP. You'll find it documented in the section called "Remote Logging Protocol" in Chapter 20.

If you've followed my installation instructions, you'll have mlogc compiled and sitting in your bin/ folder. To proceed, you'll need to configure it, then add it to the ModSecurity configuration.

How Remote Logging Works

Remote logging in ModSecurity is implemented through an elaborate scheme designed to minimize the possibility of data loss. Here's how it's done:

1. ModSecurity processes a transaction and creates an audit log entry file on disk, as explained in the section called "Concurrent Audit Log" earlier in this chapter.

2. ModSecurity then notifies the mlogc tool, which runs in a separate process. The notification contains enough information to locate the audit log entry file on disk.

3. The mlogc tool adds the audit log entry information to the in-memory queue and to its transaction log (the mlogc-transaction.log file by default).

4. One of many worker threads that run within mlogc takes the audit log entry and submits it to a remote logging server. The entry is then removed from the in-memory queue and the transaction log is notified.

5. A periodic checkpoint operation, initiated by mlogc, writes the in-memory queue to the disk (to the mlogc-queue.log file by default) and erases the transaction log.

If mlogc crashes, Apache will restart it automatically. When an unclean shutdown is detected, mlogc will reconstruct the entry queue using the last known good point (the on-disk queue) and the record of all events since the moment the on-disk queue was created, which are stored in the transaction log.

Configuring Remote Logging

The mlogc configuration file is similar to that of Apache, only simpler. We usually place it in /usr/local/modsecurity/etc/mlogc.conf. First, we need to tell mlogc where its "home" is, which is where it will create its log files. The `mlogc` log files are very important, because—as it's Apache that starts `mlogc` and ModSecurity that talks to it—we never interact with `mlogc` directly. We'll need to look in the log files for clues in case of problems:

```
# Specify the folder where the logs will be created
CollectorRoot  /usr/local/modsecurity/var/log

# Define what the log files will be called. You probably
# won't ever change the names, but mlogc requires you
# to define it.
ErrorLog        mlogc-error.log

# The error log level is a number between 0 and 5, with
# level 3 recommended for production (5 for troubleshooting).
ErrorLogLevel  3

# Specify the names of the data files. Similar comment as
# above: you won't want to change these, but they are required.
TransactionLog mlogc-transaction.log
QueuePath       mlogc-queue.log
LockFile        mlogc.lck
```

Then, we tell `mlogc` where to find audit log entries. The value given to `LogStorageDir` should be the same as the one you provided to ModSecurity's `SecAuditLogStorageDir`:

```
# Where are the audit log entries created by ModSecurity?
LogStorageDir /usr/local/modsecurity/var/audit
```

Next, we need to tell `mlogc` where to submit audit log entries. We identify a remote server with a URL and credentials:

```
# Remote logging server details.
ConsoleURI "https://REMOTE_ADDRESS:8888/rpc/auditLogReceiver"
SensorUsername "USERNAME"
SensorPassword "PASSWORD"
```

The remaining configuration directives aren't required, but it's usually a good idea to explicitly configure your programs, rather than let them use their defaults:

```
# How many parallel connections to use to talk to the server,
# and how much to wait (in milliseconds) between submissions.
# These two directives are used to control the rate at which
# audit log entries are submitted.
MaxConnections      10
TransactionDelay    50

# How many entries is a single thread allowed to process
# before it must shut down.
```

```
MaxWorkerRequests    1000

# How long to wait at startup before really starting.
StartupDelay         5000

# Checkpoints are periods when the entries from the transaction
# log (which is written to sequentially) are consolidated with
# the entries in the main queue.
CheckpointInterval  15

# If network communication fails, suspend log
# submission to give the server time to recover.
ServerErrorTimeout  60
```

> **Note**
>
> The `mlogc` tool will take audit log entries created by ModSecurity, submit them to a
> remote logging server, and delete them from disk, but it will leave the empty fold-
> ers (that were used to store the entries) behind. You'll have to remove them your-
> self, either manually or with a script.

Activating Remote Logging

You'll need to make two changes to your default configuration. First, you need to switch to
concurrent audit logging, because that's the only way `mlogc` can work:

```
SecAuditLogType Concurrent
```

Next, you need to activate `mlogc`, which is done using the piped logging feature of Apache:

```
SecAuditLog "|/usr/local/modsecurity/bin/mlogc ↵
/usr/local/modsecurity/etc/mlogc.conf"
```

The pipe character at the beginning of the line tells Apache to treat what follows as a command line. As a result, whenever you start Apache from now on, it will start a copy of `mlogc`
in turn and keep it running in parallel, leaving a one-way communication channel that will
be used by ModSecurity to inform `mlogc` of every new audit log entry it creates.

Your complete configuration should look like this now:

```
SecAuditEngine RelevantOnly
SecAuditLogRelevantStatus ^5
SecAuditLogParts ABDEFHIJKZ
SecAuditLogType Concurrent
SecAuditLog "|/usr/local/modsecurity/bin/mlogc ↵
/usr/local/modsecurity/etc/mlogc.conf"
SecAuditLogStorageDir /usr/local/modsecurity/var/audit/
```

If you restart Apache now, you should see mlogc running:

```
USER      PID  COMMAND
root      11845  /usr/sbin/apache2 -k start
root      11846  /usr/local/modsecurity/bin/mlogc ↵
/usr/local/modsecurity/etc/mlogc.conf
apache    11847  /usr/sbin/apache2 -k start
apache    11848  /usr/sbin/apache2 -k start
apache    11849  /usr/sbin/apache2 -k start
apache    11850  /usr/sbin/apache2 -k start
apache    11851  /usr/sbin/apache2 -k start
```

If you go to the log/ folder, you should see two new log files:

```
-rw-r-----  1 root     root   83K Jul 29 15:12 audit.log
-rw-r-----  1 root     root   68M Jul 29 15:12 debug.log
-rw-r--r--  1 root     root   769 Jul 30 05:31 mlogc-error.log
-rw-r--r--  1 root     root     0 Jul 30 05:31 mlogc-transaction.log
```

If you look at the mlogc-error.log file, there will be signs of minimal activity (the timestamps from the beginning of every line were removed for clarity):

```
[3] [5877/0] Configuring ModSecurity Audit Log Collector 2.9.1.
[3] [5877/0] Delaying execution for 5000ms.
[3] [5897/0] Configuring ModSecurity Audit Log Collector 2.9.1.
[3] [5897/0] Delaying execution for 5000ms.
[3] [5877/0] Queue file not found. New one will be created.
[3] [5877/0] Caught SIGTERM, shutting down.
[3] [5877/0] ModSecurity Audit Log Collector 2.9.1 terminating normally.
[3] [5897/0] Queue file not found. New one will be created.
```

It's normal for two copies of mlogc to have run, because that's how Apache treats all piped logging programs. It starts two (one while it's checking configuration), but leaves only one running. The second token on every line in the example is the combination of process ID and thread ID. Thus, you can see how there are two processes running at the same time (PID 5877 and PID 5897). Because only one program can handle the data files, mlogc is designed to wait for a while before it does anything. Basically, if it still lives after the delay, that means it's the copy that's meant to do something.

What happens if you make an error in the configuration file, preventing mlogc from working properly? As previously discussed, mlogc can't just respond to you on the command line, so it will do the only thing it can—that is, it will report the problem and shut down. (Don't be surprised if Apache continues to attempt to start it. That's what Apache does with piped logging programs.)

If you make a mistake in defining the error log, you may get an error message in response to the attempt to start Apache. The following is the error message you'd get if you left ErrorLog undefined:

```
dev:/usr/local/modsecurity/etc# apache2ctl start
[1] [15997/0] Failed to open the error log (null): Bad address
[3] [15997/0] ModSecurity Audit Log Collector 2.9.1 terminating with error 1
```

If mlogc manages to open its error log, it will do what's expected and write all error messages there. For example:

```
[1] [16402/0] QueuePath not defined in the configuration file.
[3] [16402/0] ModSecurity Audit Log Collector 2.9.1 terminating with error 1
```

At this point, it's a good idea to delete the serial audit log file audit.log, or store it elsewhere. Having switched to concurrent logging, that file won't be updated anymore, and it will only confuse you.

Troubleshooting Remote Logging

Assuming the default logging configuration (level 3), a single audit log entry handled by mlogc will produce one line in the log file:

```
[3] [1748/7f65840009c0] Entry completed (0.109 seconds, 1415 bytes): ↵
V5wORn8AAQEAAAbptJUAAABC
```

That's basically all you need to know—that an entry has been safely transmitted to the intended destination. You'll get more information when something goes wrong, of course. For example, you'll see the following message whenever your logging server goes down:

```
[2] [23743/7ff2840009c0] Flagging server as errored after failure to submit entry ↵
V5wthX8AAQEAAE1D3OYAAAAE (cURL code 7): Failed to connect ↵
to loghost port 8888: Connection refused
```

The message will appear on the first failed delivery, and then once every minute until the server becomes operational. This is because mlogc will shut down its operation for a short period whenever something unusual happens with the server. Only one thread of operation will continue to work to probe the server, with processing returning to full speed once the server recovers. You'll see the following information in the log:

```
[3] [1748/7f65840009c0] Clearing the server error flag after successful entry ↵
submission: V5w1WX8AAQEAAAerQowAAADA
[3] [1748/7f65840009c0] Entry completed (0.887 seconds, 1415 bytes): ↵
V5w1WX8AAQEAAAerQowAAADA
```

Going back to the error message, the first part tells you that there's a problem with the server; the second part tells you what the problem is. In the previous case, the problem was *couldn't connect to host*, which means the server is down. See Table 4.5 for the description of the most common problems.

Table 4.5. Common remote logging problems

Error message	Description
Failed to connect	The server could not be reached. This probably means that the server itself is down, but it could also indicate a network issue. You can investigate the cURL return code to determine the exact cause of the problem.
Possible SSL negotiation error	Most often, this message means that you configured mlogc to submit over plaintext, but the remote server uses SSL. Make sure the ConsoleURI parameter starts with https://.
Unauthorized	The credentials are incorrect. Check the SensorUsername and SensorPassword parameters.
For input string: "0, 0"	A remote server can indicate an internal error, but such errors are treated as transient.

If you still can't resolve the problem, I suggest that you increase the mlogc error log level from 3 (NOTICE) to 5 (DEBUG2), restart Apache (graceful will do), and try to uncover more information that would point to a solution. Actually, I advise you to perform this exercise even before you encounter a problem, because an analysis of the detailed log output will give you a better understanding of how mlogc works.

File Upload Interception

File upload interception is a special form of logging, in which the files being uploaded to your server are intercepted, inspected, and stored—and all that before they are seen by an application. The directives related to this feature are in Table 4.6, but you've already seen them all in the section called "File Uploads" in Chapter 3.

Table 4.6. File upload directives

Directive	Description
SecUploadDir	Specifies the location where intercepted files will be stored
SecUploadFileLimit	Specifies the maximum number of file uploads processed
SecUploadFileMode	Specifies the permissions that will be used for the stored files
SecUploadKeepFiles	Specifies whether to store the uploaded files (On, Off, or RelevantOnly)

Storing Files

Assuming the default configuration suggested in this guide, you only need to change the setting of the SecUploadKeepFiles directive to On to start collecting uploaded files. If, after a few file upload requests, you examine /usr/local/modsecurity/var/upload, you'll find files with names similar to these:

```
20160728-102354-V5nBGn8AAQEAACo1bNgAAAAA-file-b9irlZ
20160728-102354-V5nBGn8AAQEAACo1bNkAAAAC-file-TeZQZF
```

You can probably tell that the first two parts of a filename are based on the time of upload, then the unique transaction ID follows, then the -file- part that is always the same, and finally a random string of characters at the end. ModSecurity uses this algorithm to generate filenames primarily to avoid filename collision and support the storage of a large number of files in a folder. In addition, avoiding the use of a user-supplied filename prevents a potential attacker from placing a file with a known name on a server.

When you store a file like this, it's just a file and doesn't tell you anything about the attacker. Thus, for the files to be useful, you also need to preserve the corresponding audit log entries, which will contain the rest of the information.

> **Note**
>
> Storage of intercepted files can potentially consume a lot of disk space. If you're doing it, you should at least ensure that the filesystem that you're using for storage is not the root filesystem; you don't want an overflow to kill your entire server.

Inspecting Files

For most people, a more reasonable SecUploadKeepFiles setting is RelevantOnly, which enables the storage of only the files that have failed inspection in some way. For this setting to make sense, you need to have at least one external inspection script, along with a rule that invokes it.

There are four separate variables involved with file uploads, and you need to pick the right one for the inspection:

- FILES: Collection of filenames as provided by the client, sometimes including the path to the file on the client's filesystem.

- FILES_NAMES: Collection of names assigned to the files in the upload request—that is, the names of the form fields describing the files.

- FILES_TMP_CONTENT: Collection containing the content of the files.

- FILES_TMPNAMES: Collection of temporary filenames and paths on the ModSecurity server.

The best way to inspect a file is to pass the temporary filename to an inspection script, so we settle on the FILES_TMPNAMES variable. Once this is clear, a file inspection rule is rather simple:

```
SecRule FILES_TMPNAMES "@inspectFile /usr/local/modsecurity/bin/file-inspect.pl" \
    id:2000,phase:2,block,t:none,log
```

This example rule will invoke the /usr/local/modsecurity/bin/file-inspect.pl script for every uploaded file. The script will be given the location of the temporary file as its first and only parameter. It can do whatever it wants with the contents of the file, but it's expected to return a single line of output that consists of a verdict (1 if everything is in order and 0 for a fault), followed by an error message—for example:

```
1 OK
```

Or:

```
0 Error
```

The alert message in the audit log will only display the verdict, but the debug log will display the full error message. The following debug log lines are produced by the inspection file:

```
[4] Recipe: Invoking rule 2735e58; [file "/usr/local/apache/conf/httpd.conf_pod↵
_2016-07-28_10:10"] [line "238"] [id "2000"].
[5] Rule 2735e58: SecRule "FILES_TMPNAMES" "@inspectFile /usr/local/apache/bin↵
/inspect-file.pl" "phase:2,id:2000,block,t:none,log"
[4] Transformation completed in 1 usec.
[4] Executing operator "inspectFile" with param "/usr/local/modsecurity/bin↵
/file-inspect.pl" against FILES_TMPNAMES:f.
[9] Target value: "/tmp//20160728-103559-V5nD738AAQEAAD5bgsAAAAAA-file-yfp59Q"
[4] Executing /usr/local/apache/bin/file-inspect.pl to inspect /usr/local↵
/modsecurity/var/tmp/↵
20160728-103559-V5nD738AAQEAAD5bgsAAAAAA-file-yfp59Q.
[9] Exec: /usr/local/apache/bin/file-inspect.pl
[4] Exec: First line from script output: "1 OK"
[4] Operator completed in 2722317 usec.
[4] Rule returned 0.
```

If an error occurs—for example, if you make a mistake in the name of the script—you'll get an error message that looks similar to this one:

```
[9] Exec: /usr/local/modsecurity/bin/file_inspect.pl
[1] Exec: Execution failed while reading output: /usr/local/modsecurity/bin/file↵
_inspect.pl (End of file found)
```

> **Tip**
>
> If you write your inspection scripts in Lua, ModSecurity will be able to execute them directly using an internal Lua engine. Not only will the internal execution be faster, but from the Lua scripts you'll be able to access the complete transaction context (which isn't available to any external programs).

Integrating with ClamAV

ClamAV is a popular open source anti-virus program. If you have it installed, the following script will allow you to utilize it to scan files from ModSecurity:

```perl
#!/usr/bin/perl

$CLAMSCAN = "/usr/bin/clamscan";

if (@ARGV != 1) {
    print "Usage: modsec-clamscan.pl FILENAME\n";
    exit;
}

my ($FILE) = @ARGV;

$cmd = "$CLAMSCAN --stdout $FILE";
$input = `$cmd`;
$input =~ m/^(.+)/;
$error_message = $1;

$output = "0 Unable to parse clamscan output";

if ($error_message =~ m/: Empty file\.$/) {
    $output = "1 empty file";
}
elsif ($error_message =~ m/: (.+) ERROR$/) {
    $output = "0 clamscan: $1";
}
elsif ($error_message =~ m/: (.+) FOUND$/) {
    $output = "0 clamscan: $1";
}
elsif ($error_message =~ m/: OK$/) {
    $output = "1 clamscan: OK";
}

print "$output\n";
```

> **Note**
>
> If you need a file to test with, you can download one from EICAR's web site.[1] The files at this location contain a test signature that will be picked up by ClamAV.

---

[1] EICAR antimalware test file [fsty.uk/m23] (Retrieved 15 January 2017)

The error message from the integration script will return either the result of the inspection of the file or an error message if the inspection process failed. The following example shows a successful detection of a "virus":

```
[9] Exec: /usr/local/modsecurity/bin/modsec-clamscan.pl
[4] Exec: First line from script output: "0 clamscan: Eicar-Test-Signature"
[4] Operator completed in 2628132 usec.
[2] Warning. File
"/usr/local/modsecurity/var/tmp/20160728-110518-V5nKzn8AAQEAAD5bgsEAAAAC-file-szWj6↵
L" rejected by the approver script "/usr/local/modsecurity/bin/modsec-clamscan.pl":↵
 0 clamscan: Eicar-Test-Signature [file "/usr/local/modsecurity/etc↵
/rules.conf"] [line "238"] [id "2000"]
```

If you look carefully at the example output, you'll see that the inspection took more than two seconds. This isn't unusual (even for my slow virtual server), because we're creating a new instance of the ClamAV engine for every inspection. The scanning alone is fast, but the initialization takes considerable time. A more efficient method would be to use the ClamAV daemon (e.g., the `clamav-daemon` package on Debian) for inspection. In this case, the daemon is running all the time, and the script is only informing it that it needs to inspect a file.

Assuming you've followed the recommendation for the file permissions settings given in the section called "Folder Locations" in Chapter 3, this is what you need to do:

1. Change the name of the ClamAV script from `clamscan` to `clamdscan` (note the added d in the filename).

2. Add the ClamAV user (typically `clamav`) to the `apache` group (don't forget to restart the ClamAV daemon to pick up the new group).

3. Relax the default file permissions used for uploaded files to allow group read by changing `SecUploadFileMode` from `0600` to `0640`.

An examination of the logs after the change in the configuration will tell you that there's been a significant improvement—from seconds to milliseconds:

```
[9] Exec: /usr/local/modsecurity/bin/modsec-clamscan.pl
[4] Exec: First line from script output: "0 clamdscan: Eicar-Test-Signature"
[4] Operator completed in 20581 usec.
[2] Warning. File "/usr/local/modsecurity/var/tmp/20160728-111500-V5nNFH8AAQEAAGO1b↵
38AAAAA-file-vSR2dT" rejected by the approver script "/usr/local/modsecurity/bin↵
/modsec-clamscan.pl": 0 clamscan: Eicar-Test-Signature [file "/usr/local↵
/modsecurity/etc/rules.conf"] [line "239"] [id "2000"]
```

Advanced Logging Configuration

By now, you've seen how you have many facilities you can use to configure logging to work exactly as you need it. The facilities can be grouped into four categories:

Static logging configuration

The various audit logging configuration directives establish the default (or static) audit logging configuration. You should use this type of configuration to establish what you want to happen in most cases. You should then use the remaining configuration mechanisms (listed next) to create exceptions to handle edge cases.

Setting of the relevant flag on rule matches

Every rule match, unless suppressed, increments the transaction's *relevant* flag. This handy feature, designed to work with the RelevantOnly setting of SecAuditEngine, allows you to trigger transaction logging when something unusual happens.

Per-rule logging suggestions

Rule matching and the auditlog and noauditlog actions don't control logging directly. They should be viewed as mere suggestions; it's up to the engine to decide whether to log a transaction. They are also ephemeral, affecting only the rules with which they are associated. They will be forgotten as the processing moves on to the next rule.

Dynamic logging configuration

Rules can make logging decisions that affect entire requests (through the ctl action), but that functionality shouldn't be used lightly. Most rules should be concerned only with event generation. The ability to affect transaction logging should be used by system rules placed in phase 5 and written specifically for the purpose of logging control.

Increasing Logging from a Rule

The SecAuditLogParts directive allows you to configure exactly what parts (how much information) you want logged for every transaction, but one setting won't be adequate in all cases. For example, most configurations won't be logging response bodies, but that information is often required to determine whether certain types of attacks (e.g., XSS) were successful.

The following rule will detect only simple XSS attacks, but when it does, it will cause the transaction's response body to be recorded:

```
SecRule ARGS "@rx <script>" \
    id:2000,phase:2,block,log,ctl:auditLogParts=+E
```

Dynamically Altering Logging Configuration

The feature discussed in the previous section is very useful, but you may not always like the fact that some rules change what you're logging. I know I wouldn't! Luckily, it's a problem that can be resolved with the addition of a phase 5 rule that resets the logged audit log parts:

```
SecAction id:9000,phase:5,pass,nolog,ctl:auditLogParts=ABCDFGH
```

You can then decide on your own whether the logging of part E is justified. If you're using full audit logging in particular, you'll need to manually increase the amount you log per transaction. The HIGHEST_SEVERITY variable, which contains the highest severity of the rules that matched during a transaction, is particularly useful:

```
SecRule HIGHEST_SEVERITY "@le 2" \
    id:9000,phase:5,pass,nolog,ctl:auditLogParts=+E
```

Removing Sensitive Data from Audit Logs

Most web application programmers are taught always to use POST methods for transactions that contain sensitive data. After all, it's well known that request bodies are never logged, meaning that sensitive data will never be logged, either. ModSecurity changes this situation, because it allows for full transaction logging. To deal with sensitive data that may find its way into the logs, ModSecurity uses the sanitiseArg, sanitiseRequestHeader, sanitiseResponseHeader, sanitiseMatched, and sanitiseMatchedBytes sanitization actions. You basically just need to tell ModSecurity which elements of a transaction you want removed, and it will remove them for you, replacing their values in the log with asterisks. The first three actions all require parameters that you will typically know at configuration time, which means that you will invoke them unconditionally with SecAction. Sanitization works when invoked from any phase, but you should always use phase 5, which is designed for this type of activity.

Use sanitiseArg to prevent the logging of the parameters for which you know the names. For example, let's assume that you have an application that uses the password, oldPassword, and newPassword parameters to transmit, well, passwords. This is what you'll do:

```
SecAction "id:9000,phase:5,pass,nolog,\
    sanitiseArg:password,\
    sanitiseArg:oldPassword,\
    sanitiseArg:newPassword"
```

Similarly, use sanitiseRequestHeader and sanitiseResponseHeader to remove the contents of the headers for which you know the names. For example, if you have an application that uses HTTP basic authentication, you'll need the following rule to prevent passwords from being logged:

```
SecAction "id:9000,phase:5,pass,nolog,\
    sanitiseRequestHeader:Authorization"
```

The last action, sanitiseMatched, is used when you need to sanitize a parameter for which you don't know the name in advance. My first example will sanitize the contents of every parameter that has the word *password* in the name:

```
SecRule ARGS_NAMES "@rx password" \
    "id:9000,phase:5,pass,nolog,sanitiseMatched"
```

In the following example, we look for anything that resembles a credit card number and then sanitize it:

```
SecRule ARGS "@verifyCC \d{13,16}" \
    "id:9000,phase:5,pass,nolog,sanitiseMatched"
```

Finally, the sanitiseMatchedBytes action can remove the parts of input that contain sensitive information only, rather than entire parameters. This action works only in conjunction with operators that are based on regular expressions (e.g., @rx, @verifyCC, etc.) and further requires the capture action to be specified:

```
SecRule ARGS "@verifyCC \d{13,16}" \
    "id:9000,phase:5,pass,capture,nolog,sanitiseMatchedBytes"
```

When further parameters are specified, this new operator can even leave parts of the sensitive data in the log. The following example leaves the first four and the last four digits of a credit card number in the log:

```
SecRule ARGS "@verifyCC \d{13,16}" \
    "id:9000,phase:5,pass,capture,nolog,sanitiseMatchedBytes:4/4"
```

> **Warning**
>
> The sanitization actions work only for the data recorded in the audit log. However, sensitive data could end up in the error log if it's involved in a rule match, depending on the logging configuration of the rule. Likewise, sanitization doesn't work with XML and JSON request bodies.

Selective Audit Logging

Although full HTTP transaction logging sounds good in theory, in practice it's very difficult to use, because it slows down your sever and requires large amounts of storage space. There are ways to get some of the same benefits for a fraction of the cost by using partial logging on demand.

The trick is to tie logging into the tracking of IP addresses, users, or sessions. By default, you'll log only what's relevant, but when you spot something suspicious coming from (for example) an IP address, you can change your logging configuration to turn on full logging for the offending IP address only.

To use this functionality, first you need to set up IP address tracking. You do this only once for all your rules, so it should usually be part of your main configuration:

```
SecAction id:1000,phase:1,pass,nolog,initcol:ip=%{REMOTE_ADDR}
```

Now, you need to add a rule that will trigger logging when one of the rules in the ruleset matches. We assume that all the rules in the ruleset assign a severity to their alerts. The default value for HIGHEST_SEVERITY is 255. Any value below 255 thus indicates that an alert has occurred; in practice, you might choose one of the real severity values, matching only on serious events. The following rule will start logging everything coming from an IP address after such a single rule match; to achieve that, we set the flag ip.logflag for up to one hour (3,600 seconds):

```
SecRule HIGHEST_SEVERITY "@lt 4" \
    id:9000,phase:5,pass,nolog,setvar:ip.logflag=1,expirevar:ip.logflag=3600
```

Finally, we add a rule that detects the flag and forces logging for all the requests from the flagged IP address:

```
SecRule IP:logflag "@gt 0" \
    id:9001,phase:5,pass,nolog,ctl:auditEngine=On
```

Summary

This chapter, along with the two before it, covered the configuration of ModSecurity. You learned how to install ModSecurity and how to configure it, with special attention given to the logging facilities. Logging deserved its own chapter, because configuring a tool to perform certain actions is often only half of the entire story, with the other half consisting of tracking exactly what happened and why. Further, remote logging is a gateway to other systems, which may assist you in managing ModSecurity.

The next three chapters discuss a new topic: rule writing. You'll first read an overview of the entire rule language, followed by a tutorial in rule writing, and then a higher-level discussion of how to place ModSecurity configuration within Apache's own directives. Finally, the interesting bits are here!

5 Rule Language Overview

ModSecurity doesn't do anything implicitly, which is why it has the rule language to enable you to implement the inspection logic and policies exactly as you want them. The rule language initially may appear very simple, but it's amazing how powerful and flexible it can be.

This chapter gives an overview of all features of the rule language. In subsequent chapters, you'll see these features in action. They're described in detail in the reference part of this book.

Table 5.1. Rule language directives

Directive	Description
SecAction	Performs an unconditional action. This directive is a rule that always matches.
SecDefaultAction	Specifies the default action list, which will be used in the rules that follow.
SecMarker	Creates a marker that can be used in conjunction with the skipAfter action.
SecRemoteRules	Loads rules from a remote server.
SecRule	Creates a rule.
SecRuleInheritance	Controls whether rules are inherited in a child configuration context.
SecRuleRemoveById	Removes the rules with the given ID or ID range.
SecRuleRemoveByMsg	Removes the rules for which their messages match the given regular expression.
SecRuleRemoveByTag	Removes the rules for which their tags match the given regular expression.
SecRuleScript	Creates a rule implemented using Lua.
SecRuleUpdateActionById	Updates the action list of the rule with the given ID.
SecRuleUpdateTargetById	Updates the target list of the rules with the given ID or ID range.
SecRuleUpdateTargetByMsg	Updates the target list of the rules for which their messages match the given regular expression.
SecRuleUpdateTargetByTag	Updates the target list of the rules for which their tags match the given regular expression.
SecWebAppId	Creates an application namespace that can be matched in rules.

The rule language is implemented using over a dozen directives, which are listed in Table 5.1. The main directive to know is SecRule, which is used to create rules and thus does most of the work. The remainder of this chapter documents the individual elements that make the rules.

Anatomy of a Rule

Every rule defined by SecRule conforms to the same format, as follows:

```
SecRule VARIABLES OPERATOR [TRANSFORMATION_FUNCTIONS] ACTIONS
```

You can see all four building blocks of the rule language on the list. The use of transformation functions is optional. Actions are mostly optional; only the id action is required, to give each rule a unique identifier. So, what do those building blocks do? Here's what:

Variables

Identify the parts of an HTTP transaction that a rule works with. ModSecurity will extract information from every transaction and make it available through variables for rules to use. The important thing to remember about variables is that they contain *raw bytes of data*, meaning that they can contain special characters and bytes of any value. They are not text. Your sites may restrict themselves to using only text in parameters, but that doesn't mean that your adversaries will. In fact, your adversaries will use whatever helps them achieve their goals. A rule must specify one or more variables.

Operators

Specify how a (transformed) variable is to be analyzed. Regular expressions are the most popular choice, but ModSecurity supports many other operators, and you can even write your own. Only one operator is allowed per rule.

Transformation functions

A rule can specify one or more transformation functions. The transformation functions change input in some way before the rule operator is run. They are used commonly to counter evasion, but they can also be used to decode data when necessary.

Actions

Specify what should be done when a rule matches.

> **Note**
>
> Rules don't exist in isolation. In some cases, when a rule doesn't explicitly specify a value for a parameter, the default value is used; you'll learn about these situations in Chapter 6, *Rule Language Tutorial*.

Variables

In ModSecurity, *variables* are used to identify the parts of an HTTP transaction that you want to inspect. One of the main features of ModSecurity is that it preprocesses raw transaction data and makes it easy for rules to focus on the logic of detection. There are over 100 variables in the most recent version of ModSecurity; they're listed and described in this section.

Scalar variables

Contain only one piece of information, which could be data or a number. For example, REMOTE_ADDR always contains the IP address of the client.

Collections

Groups of regular variables. Some collections (e.g., ARGS) allow enumeration, making it possible to use every member in a rule. Some other collections (e.g., ENV) aren't as flexible, but there is always some way to extract individual regular variables out of them.

Read-only collections

Many collections point to some data that can't be modified, in which case the collection itself will be available for reading only.

Read/write collections

When a collection isn't based on immutable data, ModSecurity will allow you to modify it. A good example of a read/write collection is TX, a collection that starts empty and exists only as long as the currently processed transaction exists.

Special collections

Sometimes, a collection is just a handy mechanism to retrieve information from something that isn't organized as a collection but can seem like one. This is the case with the XML collection, which takes an XPath expression as a (mandatory) parameter and allows you to extract values out of an XML file.

Persistent collections

Some collections can be stored in ModSecurity's internal database, where the data can live beyond the life of the current transaction. This feature allows you to adopt a wider view of your systems—for example, tracking access per IP address or per session or per user account.

Request Variables

Request variables (Table 5.2) are those variables extracted from the request part of the transaction being inspected. The variables that describe the request line (request method, URI, and protocol information) and the request headers are available from the very beginning, but the complete information may not be available until phase 2 (request) begins.

Table 5.2. Request variables

Variable	Description
ARGS	Request parameters (read-only collection)
ARGS_COMBINED_SIZE	Total size of all request parameters combined
ARGS_NAMES	Request parameters' names (collection)
ARGS_GET	Query string parameters (read-only collection)
ARGS_GET_NAMES	Query string parameters' names (read-only collection)
ARGS_POST	Request body parameters (read-only collection)
ARGS_POST_NAMES	Request body parameters' names (read-only collection)
FILES	Filenames as provided by client (read-only collection)
FILES_COMBINED_SIZE	Combined size of all uploaded files
FILES_NAMES	File parameter names (read-only collection)
FILES_SIZES	File sizes (read-only collection)
FILES_TMPNAMES	Temporary filenames on server (read-only collection)
FILES_TMP_CONTENT	Content of all uploaded files (read-only collection)
FULL_REQUEST	Full request, including request line, headers, and body
FULL_REQUEST_LENGTH	Total size of full request
MULTIPART_FILENAME	Last filename
MULTIPART_NAME	Last file parameter name
PATH_INFO	Extra path information
QUERY_STRING	Request query string
REMOTE_USER	Remote user
REQUEST_BASENAME	Request URI basename
REQUEST_BODY	Request body
REQUEST_BODY_LENGTH	Total size of the request body
REQUEST_COOKIES	Request cookies (read-only collection)
REQUEST_COOKIES_NAMES	Request cookies' names (read-only collection)
REQUEST_FILENAME	Request URI filename/path
REQUEST_HEADERS	Request headers (read-only collection)
REQUEST_HEADERS_NAMES	Request headers' names (read-only collection)
REQUEST_LINE	Request line
REQUEST_METHOD	Request method
REQUEST_PROTOCOL	Request protocol
REQUEST_URI	Request URI, converted to exclude hostname
REQUEST_URI_RAW	Request URI, as it was presented in the request
STREAM_INPUT_BODY	Raw request body

Server Variables

Server variables (Table 5.3) contain pieces of information that are available to the server but still related to the ongoing transaction.

Table 5.3. Server variables

Variable	Description
AUTH_TYPE	Authentication type
REMOTE_ADDR	Remote address
REMOTE_HOST	Remote host
REMOTE_PORT	Remote port
SCRIPT_BASENAME	Script basename
SCRIPT_FILENAME	Script filename/path
SCRIPT_GID	Script group ID
SCRIPT_GROUPNAME	Script group name
SCRIPT_MODE	Script permissions
SCRIPT_UID	Script user ID
SCRIPT_USERNAME	Script username
SERVER_ADDR	Server address
SERVER_NAME	Server name
SERVER_PORT	Server port
USERAGENT_IP	User agent address

Response Variables

Response variables (Table 5.4) are those variables extracted from the response part of the transaction being inspected. Most response variables will be available in phase 3. The response variable that is arguably the most important, RESPONSE_BODY, is available only in phase 4 (response).

Table 5.4. Response variables

Variable	Description
RESPONSE_BODY	Response body
RESPONSE_CONTENT_LENGTH	Response content length
RESPONSE_CONTENT_TYPE	Response content type
RESPONSE_HEADERS	Response headers (read-only collection)
RESPONSE_HEADERS_NAMES	Response headers' names (read-only collection)
RESPONSE_PROTOCOL	Response protocol

Table 5.4. Response variables (continued)

Variable	Description
RESPONSE_STATUS	Response status code
STREAM_OUTPUT_BODY	Raw response body

Miscellaneous Variables

Miscellaneous variables (Table 5.5) are exactly what they sound like: variables that don't fit into any other category.

Table 5.5. Miscellaneous variables

Variable	Description
HIGHEST_SEVERITY	Highest severity encountered
INBOUND_DATA_ERROR	Flag indicating request body couldn't be buffered
OUTBOUND_DATA_ERROR	Flag indicating response body couldn't be buffered
MATCHED_VAR	Contents of the last variable that matched
MATCHED_VAR_NAME	Name of the last variable that matched
MATCHED_VARS	Contents of all variables that matched in the most recent rule
MATCHED_VARS_NAMES	Names of all variables that matched in the most recent rule
MODSEC_BUILD	ModSecurity build version (e.g., 02090101)
SDBM_DELETE_ERROR	Flag indicating problem with deleting entries in persistent storage
SESSIONID	Session ID associated with current transaction
UNIQUE_ID	Unique transaction ID generated by mod_unique_id
USERID	User ID associated with current transaction
WEBAPPID	Web application ID associated with current transaction
WEBSERVER_ERROR_LOG	Error messages generated by Apache during current transaction

Parsing Flags

Parsing flags are used by ModSecurity to signal important parsing events. The idea behind these flags is to avoid taking implicit action (e.g., blocking in response to an invalid request), instead allowing the rules to decide what to do. See Table 5.6 for details.

Table 5.6. Request body parsing variables

Variable	Description
MULTIPART_BOUNDARY_QUOTED	Multipart parsing error: Quoted boundary encountered
MULTIPART_BOUNDARY_WHITESPACE	Multipart parsing error: Whitespace in boundary

Table 5.6. Request body parsing variables (continued)

Variable	Description
MULTIPART_CRLF_LF_LINES	Multipart parsing error: Mixed line endings used
MULTIPART_DATA_BEFORE	Multipart parsing error: Seen data before first boundary
MULTIPART_DATA_AFTER	Multipart parsing error: Seen data after last boundary
MULTIPART_FILE_LIMIT_EXCEEDED	Multipart parsing error: Too many files
MULTIPART_HEADER_FOLDING	Multipart parsing error: Header folding used
MULTIPART_INVALID_HEADER_FOLDING	Multipart parsing error: Invalid header folding
MULTIPART_INVALID_PART	Multipart parsing error: Invalid part
MULTIPART_INVALID_QUOTING	Multipart parsing error: Invalid quoting
MULTIPART_LF_LINE	Multipart parsing error: LF line ending detected
MULTIPART_MISSING_SEMICOLON	Multipart parsing error: Missing semicolon before boundary
MULTIPART_STRICT_ERROR	At least one multipart error other than unmatched boundary occurred
MULTIPART_UNMATCHED_BOUNDARY	Multipart parsing error: Unmatched boundary detected
REQBODY_ERROR	Request processor error flag
REQBODY_ERROR_MSG	Request processor error message
REQBODY_PROCESSOR	Name of request processor that handled the request body
URLENCODED_ERROR	URL encoding error

Collections

Collections (Table 5.7) are special kinds of variables that can contain other variables. With the exception of persistent storage collections, all collections are essentially one-offs—special variables that give access to the information to which ModSecurity has access.

Table 5.7. Special collections

Variable	Description
ENV	Environment variables (read-only collection)
GEO	Geo lookup information from the last @geoLookup invocation (read-only collection)
GLOBAL	Global information storage, shared by all processes (read/write collection)
IP	IP address data storage (read/write collection)
TX	Transient transaction data (read/write collection)
RESOURCE	Server resource data storage (read/write collection)
RULE	Current rule metadata (read-only collection)
SESSION	Session data storage (read/write collection)
USER	User data storage (read/write collection)
XML	XML DOM tree (read-only collection)

Time and Performance Variables

Time variables (Table 5.8) describe the moment when the current transaction began. The performance variables contain information about internal timings during the transaction. All performance timings are in microseconds.

Table 5.8. Time variables

Variable	Description
DURATION	Duration of transaction since its inception on the server
PERF_ALL	String combining all performance variables
PERF_COMBINED	Sum of all performance variables
PERF_GC	Timing of garbage collection
PERF_LOGGING	Timing of audit logging
PERF_PHASE1	Timing of ModSecurity phase 1
PERF_PHASE2	Timing of ModSecurity phase 2 (request)
PERF_PHASE3	Timing of ModSecurity phase 3
PERF_PHASE4	Timing of ModSecurity phase 4 (response)
PERF_PHASE5	Timing of ModSecurity phase 5 (logging)
PERF_RULES	List of slow rules (read-only collection)
PERF_SREAD	Timing of reading from the persistent storage
PERF_SWRITE	Timing of writing to the persistent storage
TIME	Time (HH:MM:SS)
TIME_DAY	Day of the month (1–31)
TIME_EPOCH	Seconds since January 1, 1970 (e.g., 1473399025)
TIME_HOUR	Hour of the day (0–23)
TIME_MIN	Minute of the hour (0–59)
TIME_MON	Month of the year (1–12)
TIME_SEC	Second of the minute (0–59)
TIME_WDAY	Day of the week (0–6)
TIME_YEAR	Year

Operators

In ModSecurity, operators are invoked to inspect variables. Most rules will use regular expressions for the inspection, but there will be cases in which other operators will be more suitable. Numerical operators, for example, make it possible to compare numerical values, which is difficult to achieve using regular expressions. Similarly, parallel matching, which matches any number of phrases in parallel, achieves much better performance than regular expressions.

There are four operator groups:

- String matching operators
- Numerical operators
- Validation operators
- Miscellaneous operators

We'll discuss these groups in the following subsections.

String Matching Operators

String matching operators (Table 5.9) all take a string on input and attempt to match it to the provided parameter. The @rx and @pm operators are most commonly used, because of their versatility (@rx) and speed (@pm), but the remaining operators are also useful—especially if you need variable expansion, which neither @rx nor @pm support, or in situations in which performance really matters.

Table 5.9. String matching operators

Operator	Description
@beginsWith	Input begins with parameter
@contains	Input contains parameter
@containsWord	Input contains parameter as separate word
@endsWith	Input ends with parameter
@rsub	Manipulation of request and response bodies
@rx	Regular expression pattern match in input
@pm	Parallel pattern matching
@pmFromFile	Parallel pattern matching, with patterns read from a file
@pmf	Alias for pmFromFile
@streq	Input equal to parameter
@strmatch	Alternative to @contains using a different algorithm
@within	Parameter contains input

Numerical Operators

Numerical operators (Table 5.10) make comparing numerical values easy (previously, you had to resort to using complex regular expressions). Numerical operators support variable expansion.

Table 5.10. Numerical operators

Operator	Description
@eq	Equal to
@ge	Greater or equal to
@gt	Greater than
@le	Less than or equal to
@lt	Less than

Validation Operators

Validation operators (Table 5.11) all validate input in some way.

Table 5.11. Validation operators

Operator	Description
@validateByteRange	Validates that parameter consists only of allowed byte values
@validateDTD	Validates XML payload against a DTD
@validateHash	Validates HMAC security tokens
@validateSchema	Validates XML payload against a Schema
@validateUrlEncoding	Validates an URL-encoded string
@validateUtf8Encoding	Validates an UTF-8-encoded string

Miscellaneous Operators

Finally, the miscellaneous category (Table 5.12) offers some useful functionality.

Table 5.12. Miscellaneous operators

Operator	Description
@detectSQLi	Checks for SQL injection attacks using libinjection library
@detectXSS	Checks for cross-site scripting attacks using libinjection library
@fuzzyHash	Checks if a file resembles some other known file in a precompiled database
@geoLookup	Determines the physical location of an IP address
@gsbLookup	Performs a check with Google's Safe Browsing project
@inspectFile	Invokes an external script to inspect a file
@noMatch	Performs a match that will never match (useful for performance testing)
@rbl	Looks up the parameter against a real-time block list (RBL)
@unconditionalMatch	Performs a match that will always match (useful for performance testing and to transform variables)

Table 5.12. Miscellaneous operators (continued)

Operator	Description
@verifyCC	Checks whether the parameter is a valid credit card number
@verifyCPF	Checks whether the parameter is a valid Brazilian social security number
@verifySSN	Checks whether the parameter is a valid US social security number
@ipMatch	Matches input against one or more IP addresses or network segments
@ipMatchFromFile	Functions like @ipMatch, but with IP addresses read from a file
@ipMatchF	Alias for ipMatchFromFile

Actions

Actions make ModSecurity tick. They make it possible to react to events and, more importantly, they're the glue that holds everything else together and makes advanced features possible. They're also the most overloaded element of the rule language. Because of the constraints of the Apache configuration syntax, within the rule language that exists, actions are used to carry everything other than variables and operators.

Actions can be sorted into seven categories:

1. Disruptive actions

2. Flow actions

3. Metadata actions

4. Variable actions

5. Logging actions

6. Special actions

7. Miscellaneous actions

We'll discuss each category in the following subsections.

Disruptive Actions

Disruptive actions (Table 5.13) specify what a rule wants to do on a match. Each rule must be associated with exactly one disruptive action. The pass action is the only exception; it will allow processing to continue when a match occurs. All other actions from this category will block in some specific way.

Table 5.13. Disruptive actions

Action	Description
allow	Stop processing of one or more remaining phases
block	Indicate that a rule wants to block
deny	Block transaction with an error page
drop	Close network connection
pass	Do not block; go to the next rule
pause	Pause for a period of time, then execute allow
proxy	Proxy request to a backend web server
redirect	Redirect request to some other web server

Flow Actions

Flow actions (Table 5.14) alter the way rules are processed within a phase.

Table 5.14. Flow actions

Action	Description
chain	Connect two or more rules into a single logical rule
skip	Skip over one or more rules that follow
skipAfter	Skip after the rule or marker with the provided rule ID or label

Metadata Actions

Metadata actions (Table 5.15) provide additional information about rules. The information is meant to accompany the error messages to make it easier to understand why they occurred.

Table 5.15. Metadata actions

Action	Description
accuracy	Accuracy or quality of the rule
id	Assign unique ID to a rule
maturity	Maturity level
msg	Message string
phase	Phase for a rule to run in
rev	Revision number
severity	Severity
tag	Tag

Table 5.15. Metadata actions (continued)

Action	Description
ver	Version

Variable Actions

Variable actions (Table 5.16) address variables. They allow you to set, change, and remove variables.

Table 5.16. Variable actions

Action	Description
capture	Capture results in one or more variables
deprecatevar	Decrease numerical variable value over time
expirevar	Remove variable after a time period
initcol	Create a new persistent collection
setenv	Set or remove an environment variable
setvar	Set, remove, increment, or decrement a variable
setuid	Associate current transaction with an application user ID (username)
setsid	Associate current transaction with an application session ID

Logging Actions

Logging actions (Table 5.17) influence how logging is performed. The actions that influence logging (auditlog, log, noauditlog, and nolog) only affect the rule in which they reside. To control logging for the transaction as a whole, use the ctl action.

Table 5.17. Logging actions

Action	Description
auditlog	Log current transaction to audit log
log	Log error message; implies auditlog
logdata	Log supplied data as part of error message
noauditlog	Don't log current transaction to audit log
nolog	Don't log error message; implies noauditlog
sanitiseArg	Remove request parameter from audit log
sanitiseMatched	Remove parameter in which a match occurred from audit log
sanitiseMatchedBytes	Remove matched bytes from a regular expression match
sanitiseRequestHeader	Remove request header from audit log

Table 5.17. Logging actions (continued)

Action	Description
sanitiseResponseHeader	Remove response header from audit log

> **Note**
>
> The sanitization functions also exist in American English variants: sanitizeArg, sanitizeMatched, sanitizeMatchedBytes, sanitizeRequestHeader, and sanitizeResponseHeader.

Special Actions

Special actions (Table 5.18) are gateways of a sort; they provide access to another class of functionality. The ctl action has several subactions of its own and allows engine configuration to be changed (but the changes only affect the ongoing transaction). The multiMatch rule activates a special way of matching in which the rule operator is run after every transformation (normally, the operator is run only once after all transformations). The t action is used to specify zero or more transformations that will be applied to variables before an operator is run; together, the transformations create a *transformation pipeline*.

Table 5.18. Special actions

Action	Description
ctl	Change configuration of current transaction
ctl:auditEngine	Control audit logging engine
ctl:auditLogParts	Control which parts are written to the audit log
ctl:debugLogLevel	Set debug log level
ctl:forceRequestBodyVariable	Force creation of REQUEST_BODY for unknown content types
ctl:hashEnforcement	Control the enforcement of the HMAC security token check
ctl:hashEngine	Control the hash engine
ctl:requestBodyAccess	Control request body buffering and processing
ctl:requestBodyLimit	Limit request body size
ctl:requestBodyProcessor	Activate a request body processor (e.g., XML and JSON)
ctl:responseBodyAccess	Control response body buffering and processing
ctl:responseBodyLimit	Limit response body size
ctl:ruleEngine	Control rule engine
ctl:ruleRemoveById	Remove rules by their ID
ctl:ruleRemoveByMsg	Remove rules by their message using a regular expression
ctl:ruleRemoveByTag	Remove rules by their tag using a regular expression

Table 5.18. Special actions (continued)

Action	Description
ctl:ruleRemoveTargetById	Remove a certain target from a rule or multiple rules identified by their ID
ctl:ruleRemoveTargetByMsg	Remove a certain target from a rule or multiple rules identified by their message
ctl:ruleRemoveTargetByTag	Remove a certain target from a rule or multiple rules identified by their tag
multiMatch	Activate multimatching, in which an operator runs after every transformation
t	Specify transformation functions to apply to variables before matching
t:base64Decode	Decode base64-encoded string
t:base64DecodeExt	Decode base64-encoded string, ignoring invalid characters
t:base64Encode	Encode string into base64-encoding
t:cmdLine	Perform several transformations aimed at command execution attacks
t:compressWhitespace	Compress whitespace characters into a single space character
t:cssDecode	Decode CSS-encoded string
t:escapeSeqDecode	Decode ANSI C escape sequences
t:hexDecode	Decode hexadecimal string
t:hexEncode	Encode string into hexadecimal encoding
t:htmlEntityDecode	Decode HTML entity characters
t:jsDecode	Decode JavaScript escape sequences
t:length	Calculate the length of a variable string
t:lowercase	Set lowercase
t:md5	Calculate md5 hash
t:none	Flush transformation pipeline (i.e., remove all configured transformations)
t:normalisePath	Normalize path
t:normalisePathWin	Replace backslash characters with forward slash characters, then normalize path
t:normalizePath	Identical to t:normalisePath
t:normalizePathWin	Identical to t:normalisePathWin
t:parityEven7bit	Calculate even parity of seven-bit data
t:parityOdd7bit	Calculate odd parity of seven-bit data
t:parityZero7bit	Calculate zero parity of seven-bit data
t:removeComments	Remove various forms of comments
t:removeCommentsChar	Remove characters used to create comments
t:removeNulls	Remove NUL bytes
t:removeWhitespace	Remove all whitespace characters
t:replaceComments	Replace C-style comments with a space character
t:replaceNulls	Replace NUL bytes with space characters
t:sha1	Calculate SHA1 hash
t:sqlHexDecode	Decode SQL-style hexadecimal encodings

Table 5.18. Special actions (continued)

Action	Description
t:trim	Trim surrounding whitespace characters
t:trimLeft	Trim whitespace characters from the beginning
t:trimRight	Trim whitespace characters from the end
t:urlDecode	Decode a percent-encoded input string
t:urlDecodeUni	Decode a percent-encoded input string, including support for the %uHHHH form
t:urlEncode	Encode into percent-encoded string
t:utf8toUnicode	Transform UTF-8 characters to Unicode

Miscellaneous Actions

The *miscellaneous actions* (Table 5.19) group contains actions that don't belong in any of the other groups.

Table 5.19. Miscellaneous actions

Action	Description
append	Append content to response body
exec	Execute external script
prepend	Prepend content to response body
status	Specify response status code to use with deny and redirect
xmlns	Specify namespace for use with XPath expressions

Summary

This chapter provided a complete overview of the rule language. I like to think of this chapter as a map of ModSecurity features: as with a real map, whenever you need to do something in ModSecurity, you can return here to discover whether it's possible and how it can be done. For the details, though, visit one of the subsequent chapters or the reference part of the book.

The next chapter focuses on rule writing, and it's going to be the most interesting chapter you've seen so far. I'd like to think that we're setting a trend, with every new chapter being more interesting than the one before it.

6 Rule Language Tutorial

Now that you have a basic understanding of what ModSecurity rules look like, let's walk through some examples that demonstrate the most commonly used functionality.

Introducing Rules

The simplest possible rule will specify only a variable and a regular expression. In the example that follows, we define a rule with ID 2000 and look at the request URI, trying to match the regular expression pattern `<script>` against it:

```
SecRule REQUEST_URI <script> id:2000
```

This simple rule takes advantage of the fact that ModSecurity allows a rule to not specify an operator, in which case it assumes the regular expression operator. This feature is a leftover from ModSecurity 1.x, which supported only regular expressions; there were no operators at all. If you want to, you can always explicitly specify the operator. I usually do. The previous rule is functionally identical to this one:

```
SecRule REQUEST_URI "@rx <script>" id:2000
```

Note how I've had to use double quotes because the second parameter now contains a space.

ModSecurity supports a number of operators. Some often are similar, but have different performance characteristics. For example, the regular expression pattern I used for the example (`<script>`) isn't much of a pattern. It's just a string, because it doesn't contain any special characters. I might just as well have written the same rule using the @contains operator:

```
SecRule REQUEST_URI "@contains <script>" id:2000
```

By now, you've probably realized that the operators are very straightforward: they take a piece of transaction data and analyze it, most commonly by comparing it to some other value that you provided in the same rule.

Working with Variables

You can specify as many variables as you want in a rule, as long as you separate them using the pipe character:

```
SecRule REQUEST_FILENAME|QUERY_STRING "@rx <script>" id:2000
```

Some variables, which we call *collections*, potentially contain more than one piece of information. This is the case with the ARGS variable, for example, which contains all request parameters in a transaction. You use the colon operator to specify only one member of a collection, as in the following rule, which looks only at the parameter named p:

```
SecRule ARGS:p "@rx <script>" id:2000
```

You can use the same collection more than once within the same rule, if you want to do so:

```
SecRule ARGS:p|ARGS:q "@rx <script>" id:2000
```

The colon operator is quite potent and allows you to use a regular expression to specify names, which is helpful when parameter names change at runtime. The following rule will target all parameters with names that begin with the letter p, catching parameters such as password or pea:

```
SecRule ARGS:/^p/ "@rx <script>" id:2000
```

> ## Warning
>
> As always with regular expressions, be sure to use the ^ and $ anchors when you intend to match complete request parameter names. There's also a limitation in this case, because not all characters are allowed; it's not currently possible to use the pipe character, which you might want to use to construct a logical OR (e.g., ARGS:/^(p|q)/ doesn't work).

When you don't restrict a rule to only certain members of a collection, ModSecurity will assume that you want to use all members, which is quite handy when you don't know what parameters a page uses. Not all collections can be used in this way (e.g., ARGS can, but ENV cannot), but when they can, a reference to such a collection will be expanded into individual variables just before a rule is run. You can observe how this works in the debug log. For example, for a request that has the parameters p, q, and z, ARGS expands as follows:

```
[4] Expanded "ARGS" to "ARGS:p|ARGS:q|ARGS:z".
```

Now that you know how expansion works, parameter exclusion will make sense: to remove a parameter from a rule, just put an exclamation point before it. The following rule will look at all request parameters except the one named z:

```
SecRule ARGS|!ARGS:z "@rx <script>" id:2000
```

Combining Rules into Chains

When you specify more than one variable in a rule, you effectively combine the variables using the OR logical operator. The rule will match if any of the variables match. It's also possible to use a logical AND, whereby you combine several rules into one. Let's say that you want to write a rule that matches when something is found in both the parameter p and the parameter q. You write the following:

```
SecRule ARGS:p "@rx <script>" id:2000,chain
    SecRule ARGS:q "@rx <script>"
```

This is called *rule chaining*. The chain action constructs a chain of two or more rules and effectively creates a single rule with more than one evaluation step. The first rule in a chain will always run, but the subsequent rules will run only if all the previous rules (in the same chain) ran. Whenever a rule that belongs to a chain doesn't match, the execution continues with the first rule that isn't part of that chain.

> **Note**
>
> I've made it a habit to indent chained rules for better readability. That way, it's immediately clear that a rule is linked to the previous one, even if a longer list of actions hides the chain keyword.

Rule chains are usually easy to understand and use. However, there's a complication when rules match against more than one parameter (e.g., ARGS). In such a case, the rule will run against all possible values, firing actions on every match, before proceeding to the next rule in the chain. This means that by the time the second rule in the chain is executed, the first match with the captured variables may already be overwritten by additional matches. This usually isn't a problem, but it can be when constructing advanced rules.

Operator Negation

Operator results can be negated by placing an exclamation point right before the operator. For example, if you wanted to write a rule that matches on a username that is neither admin nor root (the opposite of the intent in the previous example), then you'd write the following:

```
SecRule ARGS:username "!@rx ^(admin|root)$" id:2000
```

Operator negation shouldn't be confused with rule negation. The two are the same only when a rule is used against only one variable; the situation changes when there are more. Observe the following rule:

```
SecRule ARGS:p|ARGS:q "!@eq 5" id:2000
```

This rule will match if any one parameter doesn't equal 5. If you want to write a rule that matches when both parameters do not equal 5, you'll have to use rule chaining, as follows:

```
SecRule ARGS:p "!@eq 5" id:2000,chain
    SecRule ARGS:q "!@eq 5"
```

Variable Counting

Here's a question: how do you detect something that isn't there? Take, for example, the common rule that addresses all parameters in a request:

```
SecRule ARGS "@rx <script>" id:2000
```

In a request without any parameters, ARGS will expand to zero variables. Without any variables to work with, any operator will fail and the rule (or a chain) will not match. You might argue that this is fine, but let's assume that you want to make a parameter mandatory; writing a rule that checks for an empty value won't exactly work as desired.

The solution is to use ModSecurity's ability to count how many variables there are in a collection. With the help of the ampersand modifier, we can look into ARGS and detect a case in which there are no parameters:

```
SecRule &ARGS "@eq 0" id:2000
```

The ampersand operator can be applied to any collection, including a partial one. The following rule will match whenever it sees a request with more than one parameter named username:

```
SecRule &ARGS:username "@gt 1" id:2000
```

Using Actions

So far, most of the examples in this tutorial have used only the mandatory id action. I chose to focus initially only on the mechanics of detection, without worrying about anything else. However, it's practically impossible to write a rule without specifying any additional actions.

Actions are placed in the third parameter of SecRule and the first parameter of SecAction. Because the id action is mandatory, a rule can have one or more actions. If there's more than one action, the actions are separated with commas and any number of whitespace characters in between. The following rule specifies three actions:

```
SecRule ARGS "@rx K1" id:2000,deny,log
```

Some actions have parameters, in which case you must place a colon after the action name and follow with the parameter. To deny with status 404, you could use the following:

```
SecRule ARGS "@rx K1" id:2000,deny,log,status:404
```

Finally, if you want to supply a parameter that uses whitespace or contains a comma, enclose the value in single quotes. This method of parameter handling is needed often with messages:

```
SecRule ARGS "@rx K1" "id:2000,deny,log,msg:'Acme attack detected'"
```

In addition to using single quotes around the parameter for the msg action, I enclosed the entire third directive parameter in double quotes. This is needed for Apache to correctly parse the directive line whenever there's whitespace in the directive parameters. Later, you'll see that some actions take complex parameters (e.g., ctl and setvar), but the syntax discussed here applies to them as well.

Understanding Action Defaults

You now know how to specify rule actions—but what would happen if you didn't? ModSecurity has a *default action list*. Whenever a new rule is added to the configuration, the action list of the rule is merged with the default action list. The default action list is currently phase:2,pass,log,auditlog, but you can override that at any time using the SecDefaultAction directive.

In the simplest case, when the rule being added has no action outside of id, the default action list is used instead. Take the following rule (and assume there are no other rules or defaults in the configuration):

```
SecRule ARGS "@rx K1" id:2000
```

After the default action list is taken into consideration, the previous rule looks like this:

```
SecRule ARGS "@rx K1" id:2000,phase:2,pass,log,auditlog
```

In general, when a rule has one or more actions, merging means one of two things:

The rule action replaces an action in the default action list
This will typically happen with disruptive actions, of which there can only be one per rule. If there's a disruptive action specified in both the default actions list and the rule, the one in the rule will prevail.

The rule action is appended to the ones in the default action list
Some actions can appear more than once in an action list. This is the case with many nondisruptive actions, such as t, setvar, ctl, and so on. In some cases, it's possible for the rule actions to completely remove the default actions, but how that's done de-

pends on the action in question. With the transformation action, for example, using t:none clears the list of transformations and starts over.

The idea with SecDefaultAction was to make the job of rule writing easier by allowing you to specify the commonly used actions only once. For example, you could write something like this:

```
SecDefaultAction phase:2,log,deny,status:404
SecRule ARGS "@rx K1" id:2000
SecRule ARGS "@rx K2" id:2001
...
SecRule ARGS "@rx K99" id:2098
```

This approach works well when you're in complete control of your configuration, but it complicates things, because the rules are no longer self-contained. The rules are perhaps easier to write initially, but at the price of being more difficult to understand when you come back to them in a couple of months. Furthermore, there's always a danger that there will be unforeseen interaction between the defaults and the rule. For example, suppose that you write a rule that relies on certain default values, but then you later change the defaults without realizing how you're affecting the rules.

This is particularly true if you place any transformation functions in the default list:

```
SecDefaultAction phase:2,log,pass,t:lowercase
...
SecRule ARGS "@rx K1" t:urlDecode id:2000
```

For this reason, it's never a good idea to use transformation functions in SecDefaultAction. In fact, such usage is officially deprecated.

> **Note**
>
> You should always write rules to specify the complete list of transformation functions that they depend on. To achieve this, always specify t:none as the first transformation function, which will reset the transformation pipeline.

Another peculiarity with the SecDefaultAction directive is that it can be used more than once. Every time you use it, the default action list is changed—for example:

```
# First we have some rules that only warn
SecDefaultAction phase:2,log,pass
SecRule ARGS "@rx W1" id:2000
SecRule ARGS "@rx W2" id:2001
...
SecRule ARGS "@rx W19" id:2018

# Now we have some rules that block
```

```
SecDefaultAction phase:2,log,deny,status:500
SecRule ARGS "@rx B1" id:2100
...
SecRule ARGS "@rx B89" id:2188
```

The bottom line is that even though SecDefaultAction is powerful and allows you to specify any action, you should use it only to specify the default blocking method. Anything other than that is asking for trouble! Because of this, and because of some other issues that occur whenever SecDefaultAction is used in configuration with multiple contexts (which will be explained in the section called "SecDefaultAction Inheritance Anomaly" in Chapter 7), there's a good probability that SecDefaultAction will be deprecated and replaced with a safer mechanism in the future.

Before we leave SecDefaultAction, I'd like to highlight another use case it supports. If you combine multiple applications on a single server or you centralize the log files of multiple services, then it helps to tell the alerts apart if you add a default tag to individual services containing the application name. A security operations center (SOC) can get alerts from hundreds of ModSecurity sensors, and providing a link to the documentation of the individual services together with the alert can be very helpful:

```
# Add default tags to all alerts for service "Production dashboard"
SecDefaultAction "phase:2,pass,log,auditlog,\
                tag:'Production dashboard',\
                tag:'https://docs.example.org/services/dashboard'"
```

Actions in Chained Rules

Special rules apply to the placement of actions in chained rules. Because several chained rules form a single complex rule, there can only be one disruptive action for the entire chain. Similarly, there can only be one set of metadata rules. By convention, the disruptive action and the metadata actions are placed with the first rule in a chain:

```
SecRule ARGS "@rx K1" id:2000,deny,log,chain
    SecRule ARGS "@rx K2"
```

That example looks innocent enough, but trouble begins once you start to write complex chained rules (as most are), when you will have to mix nondisruptive actions with the disruptive ones—for example:

```
SecRule ARGS "@rx K1" id:2000,deny,log,setvar:TX.score=+1,chain
    SecRule ARGS "@rx K2" setvar:TX.score=+1
```

Although disruptive actions require special treatment when used in rule chains, most other actions don't. This means that a nondisruptive action associated with a rule executes as soon as the rule matches, even when the rule is a part of a chain. Disruptive actions, on the other hand, execute at the end, when the last rule in the chain matches. The flow control actions (e.g., skipAfter) and msg share this trait.

In hindsight, the last rule in a chain is a much better location for the disruptive and metadata rules, but it's too late to change at this point.

Unconditional Rules

The actions that you specify in SecRule execute when a match occurs, but you can use the SecAction directive to do something unconditionally. This directive accepts only one parameter, which is identical to the third parameter of SecRule, and it's a list of actions that you want to be executed:

```
SecAction id:2000,pass,nolog,setvar:TX.counter=10
```

The SecAction directive is useful in the following cases:

- To initialize one or more variables before the rules that use them are processed

- To initialize a persistent collection, most often using a client's IP address

- In combination with skip, to implement an *if-then-else* construct (described later in this chapter)

Using Transformation Functions

You already know that rules typically work by taking some data determined by a variable name and applying an operator to it. However, direct matching like that happens only in the simplest case. In general, the data processed by a rule will be transformed by one or more transformation functions before it's fed to an operator. The transformation functions are often referred to as a *transformation pipeline*.

Take the following rule, for example, which transforms input by converting all characters into lowercase, then compressing multiple consecutive whitespace characters:

```
SecRule ARGS "@contains delete from" \
    id:2000,phase:2,block,t:lowercase,t:compressWhitespace
```

As a result, the rule will match all the following forms of input:

```
delete from
DELETE FROM
deLeTe    fRoM
Delete From
```

There are several reasons you might want to apply operators to something other than the original variable values:

- Your input isn't available in a form that's useful to you. For example, it might be base64-encoded, in which case you won't be able to do anything useful with it. By applying the transformation function that decodes base64 data (`t:base64Decode`), you open up the data for inspection.

- Similarly, you may need a piece of data in some other form. If you have some binary data that you need to record in a user-friendly manner, you'll probably encode it as hex characters using `t:hexEncode`.

- Sometimes rules are difficult or impossible to write in order to deal with input in its original form. Take, for example, case sensitivity. Most ModSecurity operators are case-sensitive, but there are many occasions when case doesn't matter. If you attempt to match a nontrivial string using a case-sensitive matching function, you'll soon discover that you need to write either a number of rules (each with a different combination of lowercase and uppercase letters) or a rule with a very ugly and difficult to decipher regular expression. You can address this particular problem by transforming input into lowercase characters before matching.

- In the majority of cases, you'll use transformation functions to counter evasion. *Evasion* is a technique often used by attackers to bypass existing detection and protection mechanisms. Attackers will take advantage of the specific context in which attack payload data is processed to modify it in such a way that it can evade detection but remain effective.

runs before the first transformation function and then again after every transformation that's carried out in the same rule.

Blocking

Regardless of whether you use actions, every ModSecurity rule is always associated with one (and only one) disruptive action. Disruptive actions are those that interrupt rule processing within a phase. A disruptive action can do one of three things:

Continue with the next rule

This is a special case of a disruptive action that doesn't disrupt. Use the `pass` action whenever you want to only warn about a potential issue or when you want to have a rule that changes something else in the transaction or persistent state (e.g., increments a counter).

Stop processing phase but continue with transaction

The `allow` action is used for whitelisting. It allows transactions to proceed without further inspection. Depending on how you use `allow`, you may choose to skip just the current phase, the request inspection phases (phases 1 and 2), or all remaining inspection phases (the logging phase always runs). Skipping rules is used so often that the section called "Whitelisting" in Chapter 9 is dedicated to the topic.

Stop processing phase and block transaction

Blocking is a last-resort measure you can undertake to protect your web applications and to turn away undesirable clients (e.g., worms, bots, and the like). The best way for a rule to block is by using the `block` action, which indicates blocking but doesn't state how it's to be done. Another advantage of `block` is that it can be overridden by the rule administrator. If you use any other blocking actions (`deny`, `drop`, `redirect`, or `proxy`), you're essentially hard-coding policy in rules. That may be all right if you're writing one-off rules for yourself, but be warned that for others to use your rules, they'll probably have to change them to suit their circumstances.

If you'd like to read more about blocking, head to the section called "Advanced Blocking" in Chapter 9, which covers the topic in detail.

Changing Rule Flow

The assumption with ModSecurity rules is that they'll be processed one by one, starting with the first rule in a phase and ending with the last. If a match occurs somewhere in the phase and blocking takes place, phase processing will stop, but the execution of the rules is still linear. However, there is only so much you can achieve by executing rules in that fashion. Sometimes you'll want to form rule groups and create if-then-else constructs, and for that you'll need actions that change the way rules flow.

The best way to design a desired flow is to use a combination of the SecMarker directive and the skipAfteraction. In the following example, we inspect the p and q parameters only if the admin parameter is also part of the request:

```
SecRule &ARGS:admin "@eq 0"  "id:2000,pass,nolog,skipAfter:END_ADMIN"
SecRule ARGS:p      "@rx K1" "id:2001,block,log"
SecRule ARGS:q      "@rx K2" "id:2002,block,log"
SecMarker END_ADMIN
```

When you use skipAfter and the rule matches, ModSecurity will examine all the subsequent rules to find the one with the specified marker. Once found, rule execution will continue with the rule immediately after.

Historically, the first skipping action supported by ModSecurity was skip, which takes one parameter and skips over as many rules as you specify. The following example demonstrates skip:

```
SecRule ARGS "@rx K1" id:2000,pass,nolog,skip:2
SecRule ARGS "@rx K2" id:2001,pass,nolog
SecRule ARGS "@rx K3" id:2002,block,log
```

In this example, when rule 1 matches, ModSecurity will skip the next two rules.

Keep the following points in mind:

- When you form a chain of two or more individual rules, the entire chain counts as one rule for the sake of skipping with the skip action.
- You can use skip in a chain, but the same rules as for the disruptive actions apply: only one skip is allowed and it has to be placed within the chain starter rule.
- The skip action works only within the same phase as the rule that initiated it. As far as ModSecurity is concerned, the rules in other phases simply do not exist.

Skipping is often used as an optimization technique. Sometimes, executing a group of rules makes sense only under a specific condition; executing them otherwise is a waste of CPU power. In such cases, you'll typically precede the group with a single rule that tests for the condition and jumps over the entire group of rules if the condition is not true. This is the use case for the previous skipAfter example.

If-Then-Else

You can implement an *if-then-else* construct with the skipAfter action we just introduced:

```
SecMarker IF
SecRule &ARGS:admin "@gt 0"  "id:2000,pass,nolog,skipAfter:ELSE"
SecMarker THEN
SecRule ARGS:p      "@rx K1" "id:2001,block,log"
```

```
SecRule ARGS:q        "@rx K2" "id:2002,block,log"
SecAction                      "id:2003,pass,nolog,skipAfter:END"
SecMarker ELSE
SecRule ARGS:p        "@rx K3" "id:2003,block,log"
SecRule ARGS:q        "@rx K4" "id:2004,block,log"
SecMarker END
```

Technically, you don't need the first two `SecMarker` directives in this example, but they make for a more readable ruleset.

Controlling Logging

There are several logging actions that a rule can use, and they fall into two groups. (As a reminder, you can find the list of all logging rules in Table 5.17.) The first group consists of the actions that influence only what happens during the processing of the current rule; such actions are used in virtually every rule, and I cover them in this section. The actions in the second group influence how logging is performed on a transaction level, and they're normally only used in configuration rules. I won't cover the second group here, because the common use cases are already covered in the section called "Advanced Logging Configuration" in Chapter 4.

Going back to the first group, the most common usage is as follows:

```
SecRule ARGS "@rx K1" id:2000,block,log,auditlog
```

If the rule matches, the `log` and `auditlog` actions tell the engine to emit an alert and log the transaction to the audit log, respectively. I'll let you in on a secret: the `log` action implies `auditlog`, so it's always safe to use only the first. (The same is true for the actions that ask for no logging: `nolog`, the opposite of `log`, implies `noauditlog`, which is the opposite of `auditlog`.) There are two points to consider:

1. An alert is a record of a rule match that will appear in the debug log, in Apache's error log, and in the H section of an audit log entry. Because there are two pairs of actions (`log` and `nolog`, and `auditlog` and `noauditlog`), you can decide exactly what happens, logging-wise, when a rule matches. Most rules will want both logs, but you can log a match to the error log only and not have an audit log entry at all (which you achieve with `log,noauditlog`).

2. When a rule specifies `auditlog`, that doesn't mean an audit log will be created. You should think about audit log as *asking* for a transaction to be recorded, but a detection rule won't normally have full control over what will actually happen. ModSecurity classifies transactions as relevant or not relevant. When a rule matches and it specifies `auditlog` (either explicitly, or implicitly through `log` without `noauditlog`), then ModSecurity will set the relevancy flag. This will normally cause the transaction to be

recorded, but, as you saw in the section called "Advanced Logging Configuration" earlier, a subsequent rule can override that decision. This separation of concerns is intentional. Rules should only indicate what they want to achieve; the administrator should have the final say.

Capturing Data

The TX collection has 10 variables with names that are just digits from 0 to 9. Those variables are reserved for *substring data capture*, which is primarily a feature of the @rx operator. To make use of this feature, you have to do two things:

1. Use capturing parentheses within regular expression patterns to specify where capture should take place

2. Add the capture action to the rule in which you want data capture to take place

As an example, suppose you're dealing with a web application that places session identifiers in the request line. In order to support session state, you want to extract the session information and initialize a parallel session in ModSecurity. The URI used in the application and containing a session identifier could look like this:

```
https://www.example.com/69d032331009e7b0/index.html
```

Your rule to extract the session identifier will use a regular expression data capture:

```
# Initialize session state from the session identifier in URI
# Example REQUEST_URI value: /69d032331009e7b0/index.html
SecRule REQUEST_URI "@rx ^/([0-9a-fA-F]{16})/" \
    "id:1000,phase:1,pass,capture,nolog,setsid:%{TX.1}"
```

> **Note**
>
> Although the previous example neatly demonstrates the data capture mechanism, that one rule alone isn't enough for a robust implementation of session management. For complete coverage, refer to the section called "Session Management" in Chapter 8.

Here's what happens on a successful match:

```
[4] Recipe: Invoking rule ecbc90; [file "/usr/local/modsecurity/etc↵
/rules.conf"] [line "132"] [id "1000"].
[5] Rule ecbc90: SecRule "REQUEST_URI" "@rx ^/([0-9a-fA-f]{16})/" ↵
"phase:1,id:1000,pass,capture,nolog,setsid:%{TX.1}"
[4] Transformation completed in 1 usec.
[4] Executing operator "rx" with param "^/([0-9a-fA-f]{16})/" against REQUEST_URI.
[9] Target value: "/69d032331009e7b0/index.html"
[9] Added regex subexpression to TX.0: /69d032331009e7b0/
```

```
[9] Added regex subexpression to TX.1: 69d032331009e7b0
[4] Operator completed in 75 usec.
```

The TX.0 variable will always contain the entire part of the input that was matched (/69d032331009e7b0/ in the example; note the forward slashes at the beginning and the end of the value). If your regular expression uses the ^ and $ anchors, TX.0 will contain the entire input. In the example, I used only one of the anchors, so TX.0 contains the data from the beginning of input, but only until the end of the matching part (the second forward slash). The TX.1 variable will contain just the part that was enclosed in the first parentheses set that appeared in the pattern. The TX.2 variable will draw its contents from the second set of parentheses, and so on. Up to nine captures will be created.

> **Note**
>
> If there is no match, the data capture variables won't be changed. However, if there is a match, the unused data capture variables will be unset.

The @pm and @pmFromFile operators have limited support for data capture: if the capture action is specified, the TX.0 variable will be populated with the input data matched. There's no need to use parentheses in the patterns anywhere.

Variable Manipulation

Although most of the data you'll be dealing with will be read-only, generated by Apache and ModSecurity as they parse transaction data, there are certain variables and collections that you're allowed to change. The TX collection is a private, per-transaction space that rules can use to collaborate. The variables placed in TX can be retrieved using the same approach as for other collections. The setvar action, however, allows the values to be changed.

To create a new variable, simply set its value to something:

```
SecAction id:2000,pass,nolog,setvar:TX.score=1
```

To delete a variable, place an exclamation point before the name:

```
SecAction id:2000,pass,nolog,setvar:!TX.score
```

Numerical values can be incremented or decremented. The following example first increments a variable by 2 then decrements it by 1:

```
SecAction id:2000,pass,nolog,setvar:TX.score=+2
SecAction id:2001,pass,nolog,setvar:TX.score=-1
```

Although collaboration within the same transaction is interesting and useful, variable manipulation becomes more exciting when combined with the persistent storage functionality and the expirevar and deprecatevar actions (covered in Chapter 8, *Persistent Storage*).

Variable Expansion

In many text contexts, ModSecurity supports a feature known as *variable expansion*. The reference manual refers to it as *macro expansion*, but I think that's rather ambitious, at least at this time. Variable expansion enables you to output data into text, which can be useful. You may recall that I used variable expansion in the system rules in the section called "Handling Processing Errors" in Chapter 3:

```
SecRule REQBODY_PROCESSOR_ERROR "!@eq 0" \
    "id:2000,phase:2,block,log,t:none,msg:'Failed to parse request body: ↵
%{REQBODY_PROCESSOR_ERROR_MSG}'"
```

The idea is that when a fault occurs during request body parsing, you can see what the actual error was. Variable expansion takes place whenever ModSecurity encounters a variable name enclosed in %{...}, which is a syntax that ModSecurity adopted from mod_rewrite. The variable name can be anything, and you can access collections using the familiar %{COLNAME.VARNAME} syntax.

> **Note**
>
> The difference between COLNAME:VARNAME and COLNAME.VARNAME is that the former potentially returns more than one result, whereas the latter will always return only one result (or no result at all).

Most parts of the rule language support variable expansion; many features actually require it. For example, session or IP address tracking would be impossible without the ability to somehow handle a piece of data received from a client. Having said that, don't be surprised if you encounter a part of the rule language that doesn't support this feature. If that happens, you're advised to report the problem to the issue tracker. Initially, the support for this feature was added only where it was needed. By popular demand, the support expanded over time, but there may still be areas in which variable expansion does not work.

Here's an interesting example that uses variable expansion, in which one piece of a request is compared to another one from the same request:

```
# If an absolute URI (containing hostname) was given on the request
# line, check that the same hostname is used in the Host header
SecRule REQUEST_URI_RAW "@beginsWith https" "id:2000,phase:2,block,\
    msg:'Hostname mismatch',chain"
    SecRule REQUEST_URI_RAW "!@beginsWith https://%{REQUEST_HEADERS.Host}"
```

There's a performance penalty when using variable expansion with regular expression and parallel matching operators. Both @rx and @pm split their work into two steps. They do as much work as possible up front, compiling patterns into more efficient internal representations. Then, in the second step, they perform matching. Compilation of patterns usually is performed only once, at configure-time, thus profiting from static patterns. However, if variable expansion is being used, the regular expression pattern will be compiled every time the rule is executed, which can be costly.

Recording Data in Alerts

The one remaining log action we've yet to discuss is logdata, the purpose of which is to take a piece of data you specify and include it along with other alert information.

Consider the following rule, which looks for JavaScript event handlers in input:

```
SecRule ARGS "@rx \bon(abort|blur|change|click|dblclick|dragdrop|end|error|\
focus|keydown|keypress|keyup|load|mousedown|mousemove|mouseout|mouseover|\
mouseup|move|readystatechange|reset|resize|select|submit|unload)\
\b\W*?=" \
    id:2000,phase:2,deny,capture,t:none,t:lowercase,log,logdata:%{TX.0}
```

This rule may seem a bit intimidating at first glance, although it's conceptually simple. If you read the regular expression pattern carefully, you'll see that all the patterns we're looking for share the beginning, have a part in the middle that's different, and share the end—so it's not that difficult after all. However, consider the following points:

- Alert messages don't display input data by default. Thus, looking at an alert message alone, you won't be able to tell which part of the pattern matched; you'll have to seek access to the entire audit log. Even when it's possible to understand it, it will still be time-consuming.

- Even with access to the audit log, tracking down the part of the input that matched may not be simple. When this sort of rule matches, it typically happens with request parameters that are quite long. Thus, you need to first understand what the rule does and then effectively perform manual pattern matching by reading through every parameter.

- Matching takes place against potentially transformed input, so often the raw input won't contain the data in the form used for matching.

These problems are resolved when you use the logdata action. Examine the following alert (focusing on the emphasized part):

```
ModSecurity: Access denied with code 403 (phase 2). Pattern match ↵
"\\\\bon(abort|blur|change|click|dblclick|dragdrop|end|error|focus|keydown|keypress↵
|keyup|load|mousedown|mousemove|mouseoutmouseover|mouseup|move|readystatechange|res↵
```

```
et|resize|select|submit|unload)\\\\\b\\\\\W*?=" at ARGS:a. [file "/usr/local↵
/modsecurity/etc/rules.conf"] [line "135"] [id "2000"] [data "onblur=alert('attack'↵
)"] [hostname "localhost"] [uri "/"] [unique_id "V6lfaX8AAQEAAGFLGmEAAAAE"]
```

The capture action from the rule told the regular expression operator (@rx) to place the entire matching area into the TX.0 variable. The logdata:%{TX.0} part of the rule told the engine to include the value of the TX.0 variable in the alert. The end result is that you now know, at a glance, exactly what matched.

> ### Note
>
> At this point, you may ask why we have logdata when it's perfectly possible to use variable expansion in the msg action. There's only one reason: when you set a piece of data as part of a message, a program parsing it won't know where the data starts. To a computer, the entire message is just some text. However, if you include the same data in an alert with logdata, the same parser will know that it's something that originated in input, and it can do something useful with it. It could, for example, highlight the piece of data on the alert page.

Adding Metadata

Although some rules are simple and don't require much thought to understand, many aren't. Also, even when the rule itself is simple, that doesn't mean that it will be easy to understand what it does and why it does it. ModSecurity generally tries to add as much metadata to alerts as possible. Consider the following rule, which gets the job done:

```
SecRule REQUEST_METHOD "!@rx ^(GET|HEAD)$" \
    id:1000,phase:1,block,t:none,log
```

This rule restricts request methods to either GET or HEAD, which is suitable only for a static web site. The rule will, on a match, produce the following alert:

```
[2016-08-09 06:53:06.787899] [-:error] 127.0.0.1:49751 V6lhsn8AAQEAAGtNO1kAAAAC ↵
[client 127.0.0.1] ModSecurity: Warning. Match of "rx ^(GET|HEAD)$" against ↵
"REQUEST_METHOD" required. [file "/usr/local/modsecurity/etc/rules.conf"] [line ↵
"133"] [id "1000"] [hostname "localhost"] [uri "/"] [unique_id "V6lhsn8AAQEAAGtNO1k↵
AAAAC"]
```

Alert messages contain quite a lot of information by default, but they don't provide enough. For example, the default message generated by ModSecurity gives you some idea about what the rule looks like, but it doesn't tell you what the rule writer wanted to accomplish. This is where metadata actions come into play. These actions are primarily used to document rules and make them easier to handle. Here's the same rule as earlier, but with additional metadata:

```
SecRule REQUEST_METHOD "!@rx ^(GET|HEAD)$" \
    "id:1000,phase:1,block,t:none,log,rev:2,\
    severity:WARNING,msg:'Request method is not allowed'"
```

Technically, `id` is a metadata action. There are also several additional metadata actions:

- The `rev` action (short for *revision*) is essentially a change counter, or a serial number: it starts at 1 and increments by one every time a rule changes. The idea is to make it possible to determine at a glance whether a rule changed and, even better, to make it possible for a program (that wouldn't be able to understand the differences between two rule versions anyway) to do the same.

- The `severity` action tells you how serious a detected problem is. ModSecurity adopted the *syslog* system of severities, which are listed in Table 19.1. The least serious severity is DEBUG (7) and the most serious one is EMERGENCY (1). At any given moment, the `HIGHEST_SEVERITY` variable will hold the numerical value of the rule match with the highest severity (with 1 being higher than 7, as far as severity is concerned).

- The `msg` action adds another message to the rule, which should explain the goal of a rule, or its result.

The information in metadata actions is always used in alerts. The improved rule listed earlier produces the following alert:

```
[2016-08-09 07:05:40.074810] [-:error] 127.0.0.1:49755 V6lkpH8AAQEAAHcirqoAAAAA ↵
[client 127.0.0.1] ModSecurity: Warning. Match of "rx ^(GET|HEAD)$" against ↵
"REQUEST_METHOD" required. [file "/usr/local/modsecurity/etc/rules.conf"] [line ↵
"135"] [id "1000"] [rev "2"] [msg "Request method is not allowed"] [severity ↵
"WARNING"] [hostname "localhost"] [uri "/"] [unique_id "V6lkpH8AAQEAAHcirqoAAAAA"]
```

That's much better, but the alert still doesn't explain why any request method other than GET or HEAD is restricted. Let's try again:

```
# Do not allow request methods other than GET or HEAD. The
# site does not currently use any other methods; restricting
# the methods allowed reduces the attack surface.
SecRule REQUEST_METHOD "!@rx ^(GET|HEAD)$" \
    "id:1000,phase:1,block,t:none,log,rev:2,\
    severity:WARNING,msg:'Request method is not allowed because \
it is not used by the application',tag:HARDENING"
```

This latest batch of improvements added a long description of the rule functionality and also improved the alert message. In addition, it also uses the tag action to categorize the rule. *Tags* are pieces of text that can be attached to rules, and it's possible to attach one or more tags. By convention, the first tag defines a rule's primary category, and all other tags define secondary categories. Knowing the category for a rule helps you understand what the rule does. Categories also enable monitoring systems that collect alerts to construct pretty alert pie charts with little effort (e.g., displaying how many alerts of each category occurred in a time period). There are no clear guidelines for how to use tags; the Core Rule Set does use them to categorize rules, but it doesn't document the categories (and doesn't guarantee that the categories won't change).

Rule ID Namespace

As you're already aware, every ModSecurity rule must have a unique identifier. For your local rules, you'll be using the local range of identifiers (from 1 to 99,999), giving you ample space from which to select your IDs. However, even though you're technically free to use IDs as you wish, in practice it's better to design a strategy before you start writing your rules. You'll find that some planning early on saves a lot of time later.

Consider the following possibilities:

- Different ModSecurity phases could each use their own ranges.

- Rules shared between different services (servers) could use a range of their own so as not to clash with one another.

- Whitelisting rulesets used to lock down a specific service (via a positive security model) typically need a lot of rules. I've found that assigning a separate rule range helps with the organization.

- If you work with the OWASP ModSecurity Core Rule Set and possibly other rulesets, it's likely that you'll need to write rules to handle false positives at runtime. Use a separate range for this purpose.

- If there are multiple applications running on the same server, perhaps you'll want to assign different rule ranges to different applications.

Considering the previous points, I've developed the following approach for this book:

- 1,000–1,999: Phase 1

- 2,000–2,999: Phase 2

- 3,000–3,999: Whitelisting rules (phase 1 and phase 2)

- 4,000–4,999: Ruleset tuning (phase 1 and phase 2)

- 6,000–6,999: Phase 3

- 7,000–7,999: Phase 4

- 9,000–9,999: Phase 5

- 10,000 onwards: Shared rules

Table 6.1. Variables sensitive to operating mode

Variable	Availability in reverse proxy mode
AUTH_TYPE	Reverse proxy authentication
ENV	Reverse proxy environment
PATH_INFO	Not available
SCRIPT_BASENAME	Can't be trusted on reverse proxy
SCRIPT_FILENAME	URL with prefix proxy:// on reverse proxy
SCRIPT_GID	Not available
SCRIPT_GROUPNAME	Not available
SCRIPT_MODE	Not available
SCRIPT_UID	Not available
SCRIPT_USERNAME	Not available
SERVER_ADDR	Reverse proxy address
SERVER_NAME	Reverse proxy name
SERVER_PORT	Reverse proxy port
WEBSERVER_ERROR_LOG	Reverse proxy error log

Embedded Versus Reverse Proxy Mode

ModSecurity doesn't care whether it's deployed in embedded or reverse proxy mode. In reverse proxy mode, Apache takes care of the transfer of data to the backend server and back, so there's very little for ModSecurity to worry about. There are only few small differences, which I'm listing here for reference:

1. In an embedded scenario, there will typically be a resource (a script or a file) used to fulfill each request. ModSecurity rules can inspect the properties of such files (the SCRIPT_* family of variables allows access). In reverse proxy mode, virtually all requests will be fulfilled by backend servers, which means that local resources won't be used and that the use of the variables that reference them makes little sense.

2. When embedded, ModSecurity gives access to the web server environment and error log. When used in reverse proxy mode, you still get access to both the environment and the error log, but to those of the reverse proxy. The backend servers will have their own environments and error logs, which ModSecurity can't access.

3. Apache's Directory, DirectoryMatch, Files, and FileMatch configuration contexts never match when used in a reverse proxy.

4. There are potential evasion issues when a reverse proxy is used in front of a backend system that interprets URIs differently (e.g., if you have a Unix box in front of a Windows box). In such cases, you have to be very careful if you're using the <Location> or <Proxy> configuration context. They are case-sensitive and recognize only forward

slashes, whereas other platforms may have filesystems that are case-insensitive or web servers that support the backslash as the URI path separator. Some variables are sensitive to the operating mode (see Table 6.1).

Summary

Now that you've completed the rule tutorial, you should have a good understanding of rule writing. I thoroughly enjoyed working on this chapter, because it reminded me of every single rule feature—even the ones I don't use very often.

In the next chapter, we turn our attention to ModSecurity's existence within Apache. You'll learn the minimum necessary about how Apache handles its configuration files, which will help you organize your rules effectively. You'll also learn about configuration contexts and inheritance, concepts that will allow you to both simplify your configuration and use different configurations for different sites and applications in the same server.

7 Rule Configuration

This chapter is the last of those that cover the core language. Whereas the previous chapter focused on how to write individual rules, this chapter focuses on higher-level concepts, such as the following:

- Apache configuration syntax
- How ModSecurity fits into Apache configuration files
- Configuration contexts and inheritance
- Rule manipulation

Apache Configuration Syntax

First, you should view Apache configuration as a single file that consists of many lines of text. In reality, any configuration can be split among many files, but that's only for our convenience. To Apache, it's just line after line after line.

If you look at a typical configuration file, you'll find that every line falls into one of three groups:

Empty lines
Empty lines (either those that are genuinely empty, or those that contain only whitespace characters) have no function as far as Apache is concerned, but they help make configuration files easier to read.

Comment lines
Comment lines have the # character as the first nonwhitespace character; any text can follow. Comment lines are often used to make configuration files user-friendly by providing documentation. They're also used to deactivate parts of configuration without deleting them, which is handy if you ever want to put the deactivated parts into use again.

Data lines

If a line is neither empty nor a comment line, then it's a *data line*, and Apache will use it in configuration building.

With all this in mind, let's look at an example configuration fragment:

```
# It's always useful to begin configuration with a comment.
# Perhaps you have something important to say—for
# example, what's this configuration for?

# The one empty line above helps separate one comment from another.

# The following line is a single data line.
SecRuleEngine On
```

Breaking Lines

In practice, configuration lines can be as long as you need them to be. Apache's configuration files do have their limits—16 MB for normal configuration files on Apache 2.4 and 8,190 bytes for .htaccess files—but I've never encountered them, and you probably won't either. You'll want your lines to be on the short side anyway. Most configuration tweaking and maintenance takes place remotely, so for best results your lines need to fit within your shell window. Otherwise, you'll either have to do a lot of scrolling or use the automated word-wrapping facility, if your editor supports it.

To split a long line into two, use a single backslash character followed by a newline:

```
SecRule ARGS "@rx <script>" \
    id:2000,phase:2,block,t:none
```

Apache will interpret the previous two-line configuration snippet as a single line. You can use this trick as many times as you want to create single logical lines that consist of multiple actual lines.

You can place a break at any location, but some places are better than others. I prefer to indent continued lines, but although my eye doesn't see the indentation, the whitespace actually ends up in the line. Unless you break the line somewhere that whitespace doesn't matter, you'll end up with a gap. The best place for a continuation is between directive parameters, as in the previous example. With rules, the first two parameters are generally short, so in most cases you'll place the continuation after the second parameter—again, as in the example. Action lists are often too long to fit even on a broken line; I often find myself breaking the parameter across lines. When you do that, the best place for a break is just after a comma (that's where whitespace doesn't matter).

Directives and Parameters

Every data line begins with a directive name, followed by zero or more parameters. Apache supports the following directive parameter styles:

- No parameters.

- A single boolean parameter, which allows for only On or Off values (e.g., SecRuleInheritance).

- One, two, or three free-form parameters, where each parameter has a separate meaning; parameters other than the first can be optional (e.g., SecRule and SecRuleScript).

- Any number of free-form parameters, but all must have the same meaning (e.g., SecResponseBodyMimeType).

Directive parameter values are separated from one another using whitespace:

```
SecRule ARGS "@rx <script>" "id:2000,phase:2"
```

If you have a value that contains one or more whitespace characters, you'll have to enclose the entire value in quotation marks, a signal that will enable Apache to understand that there's only one parameter inside:

```
SecRule RESPONSE_BODY "@rx Error has occurred" "id:7000,phase:4"
```

When there are no whitespace characters inside parameter values, you don't have to use quotes (even when the value contains a lot of unusual characters), but you can. Whatever you do, just be consistent and always use the same approach.

Spreading Configuration Across Files

As your configuration grows, you'll find it more difficult to find your way around. That's especially true with ModSecurity, because not only will you have the configuration, but there will be many rules, some of which you may be writing yourself and some of which you may be downloading from an external source.

Apache configuration always begins with a single file, but you are allowed to include other configuration files using the Include directive. The following, for example, could be a skeleton for your ModSecurity configuration:

```
Include conf/modsecurity/main.conf
Include conf/modsecurity/preamble.conf
Include conf/modsecurity/rules1.conf
Include conf/modsecurity/rules2.conf
Include conf/modsecurity/rules3.conf
Include conf/modsecurity/epilogue.conf
```

The paths I used in this example are all relative; Apache will resolve them using its main installation path (e.g., /usr/local/apache) as a starting point. Of course, you can use absolute paths if you like, but that usually means more typing.

The Include directive can also include several files in one go when you use the following Unix shell-style wildcard characters:

- ?: Any one character

- *: Zero or more characters

- \: Escapes the character that follows

- []: Exactly one character from the range (e.g., [0-9] for a digit)

The most common way to use this feature is to include all files that end with a particular suffix:

```
Include conf/modsecurity/*.conf
```

If an Include line resolves to multiple files, they'll be included in alphabetical order in Apache. That's quite logical, but doesn't always work as desired, because we tend to choose names based on the purpose the files serve. A common strategy is to use numbers in file-names to control the order in which they're included. The example Include line used with the previously discussed hypothetical ModSecurity configuration wouldn't include the files in the correct order, but the inclusion will be in the correct order if we rename the files as follows:

```
00-main.conf
10-preamble.conf
20-rules1.conf
30-rules2.conf
40-rules3.conf
90-epilogue.conf
```

I've intentionally selected a larger range than needed (0–99) and left gaps between numbers, because that will allow me to insert new files in between the existing ones.

> **Warning**
>
> Explicitly listing each file you want to include is probably the safest approach. If you point Include to a directory, it will include all files in it and all the files in all its subdirectories. This particular feature isn't very useful, because you'll virtually never have a directory that will contain just configuration files; there will always be something else, and that something will break your configuration. Also note that when using ModSecurity with Nginx and IIS, the Include directive doesn't sort files by name when including folders.

Container Directives

Apache supports two directive types. The standard variant, which you've already seen, is defined by a single configuration line (which may be split across several physical lines). The other variant, container directives, uses a syntax similar to XML. Container directives have the following characteristics:

- They always come in pairs, which we call tags.
- The starting tag begins with < and ends with >.
- For parameters, the starting tag uses the same format as all other directives.
- The ending tag begins with </ and ends with >.
- The ending tag can't have parameters.
- The directives enclosed in the pair of tags (possibly including other container directives) are nested in a new configuration context.

Look at the following example:

```
# This is the main configuration context

<VirtualHost demo1.example.com>
    # This is the configuration context
    # used by demo1.example.com

    <Location /special/>
        # This is the configuration context
        # used by demo1.example.com/special
    </Location>
</VirtualHost>

<VirtualHost demo2.example.com>
    # This is the configuration context
    # used by demo2.example.com
</VirtualHost>
```

The main configuration context exists in every configuration. There are two further <VirtualHost> contexts, nested in the main configuration context, and one <Location> context, nested in one of the virtual hosts.

ModSecurity doesn't define any container directives itself (modules are allowed to create such directives, too), but it integrates with all the container directives used by Apache.

Configuration Contexts

Apache allows for several types of configuration contexts using container directives. *Configuration contexts* are mechanisms that allow you to apply configuration to only parts of the server. The example in the previous section demonstrated the three most commonly used configuration contexts—the main configuration context, `<VirtualHost>`, and `<Location>`—but there are others. The following is the complete list:

Main

> The main (implicit) configuration context is used by default. Unless a configuration uses explicit configuration contexts, the entire server will use a single configuration context.

`<VirtualHost>`

> The `<VirtualHost>` configuration context is used to create a new virtual host, possibly using a configuration unique to it. Apache will automatically choose the correct virtual host to use for a request, based on the host information supplied in every request.

`<Location>` and `<LocationMatch>`

> The `<Location>` and `<LocationMatch>` directives both create location-specific configuration contexts. Apache will automatically choose the correct location-specific configuration context to use based on the active virtual host and the information provided in every request's URI.

`<Directory>` and `<DirectoryMatch>`

> The `<Directory>` and `<DirectoryMatch>` directives both create directory-specific configuration contexts. This type of context makes sense only when there's no proxying, because proxies typically don't interact with local filesystems. Directory-specific contexts will be used, but Apache determines which file on the local filesystem will be used to serve a request.

`<Files>` and `<FilesMatch>`

> The `<Files>` and `<FilesMatch>` directives both create file-specific configuration contexts. Apache automatically chooses the correct file-specific configuration context to serve a request, but only after it determines which file will be used.

`<Proxy>` and `<ProxyMatch>`

> The `<Proxy>` and `<ProxyMatch>` directives both create proxy-specific configuration contexts. Apache will automatically choose the correct proxy-specific configuration to use based on the `<ProxyPass>` directive or the rewrite rule used to initiate a proxy connection.

> **Note**
>
> There are subtle differences between the `<Location>`, `<Directory>`, `<Files>`, and `<Proxy>` directives and their respective `<LocationMatch>`, `<DirectoryMatch>`, `<FilesMatch>`, and `<ProxyMatch>` counterparts. Each provides a different way to achieve the same effect. You should invest some time in studying the Apache documentation to understand how and why these directives are different.

Configuration Merging

When configuration is simple, a request will use only one configuration context, but when configuration is complex, configuration contexts may overlap. For example, you may define some rules for a specific virtual host and some further rules for a specific location. Those two configuration contexts have to be merged into a single configuration context before a request that triggers both can be handled. Merging always takes place between two contexts at one time. Multiple merging operations will be performed when there are three or more configuration contexts to merge.

There are two aspects to understand about merging:

- The parent-child relationship is significant, as is the order in which contexts are merged. For example, if you define a setting in both contexts, one of the two values may be overwritten by the other. If there are three contexts to be merged, with a different value for the same setting in each context, you need to understand the order in which merging operations will happen.

- Apache initiates the process, but every individual module handles the merging of its configuration. Thus, to understand merging, you need to study the documentation of each module you're using. Some simpler modules may not support merging at all, whereas complex modules (e.g., ModSecurity) will use different merging strategies for different configuration directives.

The order in which contexts are merged can be quite complex to understand if you want to use every possible combination, but my advice is to simplify, as follows:

- Outside of the main configuration context, use only the <VirtualHost> and <Location> container directives.

- Remember that multiple <Location> containers (in the same virtual host) are processed in the order in which they appear in the configuration file.

If you follow this advice, your configuration will start with rules in the main configuration context, which will then be overwritten by the per-virtual-host configuration, which will then be overwritten by the per-location configuration. In this way, the behavior is easily predictable. However, if you chose to mix multiple container directives, you'll need to test the exact behavior of the server.

Configuration and Rule Inheritance

ModSecurity uses two inheritance (configuration merging) strategies. The first strategy is used for nonrule directives (e.g., SecRuleEngine); the second applies to rules.

Configuration Inheritance

For configuration settings, ModSecurity implements a straightforward merging strategy:

- The child context inherits all settings from the parent configuration context.
- The settings explicitly defined in the child context will overwrite those defined in the parent context.

Consider the following example:

```
SecRuleEngine On
SecAuditEngine RelevantOnly

<VirtualHost www.example.com>
    SecRuleEngine DetectionOnly
</VirtualHost>
```

The effective configuration of the main context is exactly as it appears in the configuration file:

```
SecRuleEngine On
SecAuditEngine RelevantOnly
```

As for the configuration of the one virtual host, you can work it out using the two previously mentioned rules. First, start with the configuration of the parent configuration context, then use the value of SecRuleEngine with DetectionOnly instead of the inherited On.

> **Warning**
>
> The only exception to the preceding rules is SecDefaultAction, the values of which aren't inherited across configuration contexts. The default action list will always revert to default in every new configuration context.

Rule Inheritance

Because rules can't overwrite one another in the way predefined settings can, different merging rules apply:

1. The child context inherits the rules from the parent context.
2. The rules defined in a child context are added after the rules defined in the parent context.

This, too, should be intuitive—for example:

```
SecRule ARGS "@rx K1" id:2000,phase:2

<VirtualHost www.example.com>
```

```
        SecRule ARGS "@rx K2" id:2001,phase:2
    </VirtualHost>
```

In this example, there will be one rule defined in the main configuration context (the rule 2000), but two in the virtual host (2000 first, then 2001).

The positioning of a child context within the parent context doesn't influence the configuration of either context. The following segment, which uses a different layout, arrives at the same configuration as the previous example:

```
<VirtualHost www.example.com>
    SecRule ARGS "@rx K2" id:2000,phase:2
</VirtualHost>

SecRule ARGS "@rx K1" id:2001,phase:2
```

This is because configuration processing is a two-step process in Apache: all configuration contexts are created in the first step, with merging following in the second. From that point of view, the two previous configuration snippets are practically identical.

Rule inheritance is a desired feature in most circumstances, because you'll specify your general configuration in the main configuration context or in the virtual host container and then use more specific per-location contexts for tweaking. In such circumstances, it makes sense to begin with the rules specified in the parent configuration context. If you ever need to completely redefine the rules that run in a specific location, ModSecurity allows you to disable rule inheritance using the SecRuleInheritance directive, as follows:

```
SecRule ARGS "@rx K1" id:2000,phase:2

<VirtualHost www.example.com>
    SecRuleInheritance Off
    SecRule ARGS "@rx K2" id:2001,phase:2
</VirtualHost>
```

In this example, in the virtual host context the configuration will contain only the rule 2001, because rule inheritance was disabled.

Location-Specific Configuration Restrictions

There is a significant problem related to how inheritance (of both configuration and rules) is implemented in ModSecurity: phase 1 takes place before anything specified in a <Location> configuration container is evaluated. This is an implementation detail, but one with significant consequences:

- Phase 1 rules must be placed in the main configuration context or within <VirtualHost> contexts.

- Any phase 1 rules placed in `<Location>` will be ignored silently.

- Any configuration changes made in `<Location>` will take effect, but only for whatever happens in phase 2 and later.

The execution phases were implemented in this way to enable ModSecurity to act as early as possible in the transaction lifecycle, the reasoning being that acting early might help protect against flaws within Apache and third-party modules.

> **Note**
>
> If you need to place phase 1 rules within `<Location>` containers, there's a compile time configuration option called `--disable-request-early` that allows you to shift the execution of phase 1 later into the lifecycle of the request. Phase 1 will now happen after the `<Location>` container has been evaluated, and phase 1 rules within `<Location>` are now active.

SecDefaultAction Inheritance Anomaly

There is one exception to the configuration merging rules outlined in the previous sections: the SecDefaultAction setting isn't inherited. This exception is more of a bug than anything else, and it can lead to some very subtle problems and unexpected behavior—for example:

```
SecDefaultAction phase:2,deny,log,auditlog
SecRule ARGS "@rx K1" id:2000,phase:2


<VirtualHost www.example.com>
    SecRule ARGS "@rx K2" id:2001,phase:2
</VirtualHost>
```

In this example, the first line of the configuration will change the built-in default action list to activate blocking. The change will be picked up by rule 2000, which follows in the same configuration context; rule 2000 thus will block. In the nested configuration context for the www.example.com virtual host, because there's no inheritance of SecDefaultAction, the default action list will revert to the built-in value (phase:2,pass,log,auditlog). Rule 2001 thus will only warn, although it would be more intuitive if it blocked.

Rule Manipulation and Exclusion

When you write your own rules, it makes sense to change them directly whenever you want to make a change. The same approach doesn't work with third-party rules; it effectively creates a fork and makes upgrades difficult. ModSecurity has a mechanism or two that you can use to exclude or change rules without actually changing them at their original location. Instead, you're manipulating the rules either after they're loaded at configure-time or as transactions are evaluated at runtime.

Whenever possible, you should choose configure-time manipulation, because this approach results in the best performance and better readability. On the other hand, configure-time manipulation is quite limited, because it's unconditional; it results in a permanent modification of a rule within a context. Runtime manipulation is slower but flexible: with it, you can use the rule language to evaluate a transaction in any way you choose and then make your modifications.

> ### Note
>
> There is a subtle difference in how the two approaches to rule manipulation are implemented. Configure-time manipulation has to be performed after the rules being changed are defined. In contrast, runtime manipulation needs to happen before the rule you want changed is evaluated.

Removing Rules at Configure-Time

ModSecurity supports a configure-time mechanism that allows the removal of a rule for which you know the ID, after the rule has been defined. Alternatively, you can also remove rules for which you know the messages or a group of rules that share a tag. Such removals are achieved using SecRuleRemoveById, SecRuleRemoveByMsg, and SecRuleRemoveByTag, respectively. The following example demonstrates all three directives:

```
# Example of removing a rule by its ID
SecRule ARGS "@rx K1" id:2000,phase:2,deny,log
SecRuleRemoveById 2000

# Example of removing a rule by its message
SecRule ARGS "@rx K2" "id:2001,phase:2,deny,log,msg:'Strange error occurred'"
SecRuleRemoveByMsg "Strange error occurred"

# Example of removing rules using tag matching
SecRule ARGS "@rx K3" "id:2002,phase:2,deny,log,tag:'Strict pattern match/K3'"
SecRule ARGS "@rx K4" "id:2003,phase:2,deny,log,tag:'Strict pattern match/K4'"
SecRuleRemoveByTag "Strict pattern match"
```

SecRuleRemoveById is quite flexible, because it allows you to list any number of rule IDs and rule ranges (e.g., 2000–2099), and it will remove all the rules that match. The SecRuleRemoveByMsg and SecRuleRemoveByTag directives are similar in flexibility: their one parameter is a regular expression that also supports removing multiple rules at once.

Removing rules at configuration time as presented in the examples thus far doesn't make any sense, of course—but it will once I change the example slightly. Imagine that you have a third-party ruleset you want to use:

```
Include /usr/local/modsecurity/core-rules/rules/*.conf
```

When you deploy the ruleset, you discover that there's one rule that produces a high volume of false positives. You're now faced with a dilemma: do you remove the offending rule, or do you live with it? If you choose the former, you'll be forced to assume the maintenance of the ruleset and you won't be able to update it automatically. If you choose the latter, you'll have to tolerate the false positives.

However, armed with SecRuleRemoveById, its friends, and the IDs (or messages or tags) extracted from the false positives, you can now remove the offending rule without actually modifying the third-party ruleset:

```
Include /usr/local/modsecurity/core-rules/rules/*.conf

# Excluding rule 920320: Request Missing a User Agent Header
SecRuleRemoveById 920320
```

Thus, we've established that removing rules at configuration time can be very useful if you're unable for some reason to modify the original rulesets. You'll find another application for this technique if you ever need to customize your rulesets for parts of application, which is done by creating a more specific configuration context in Apache, as follows:

```
<VirtualHost www.example.com>
    # Your ModSecurity configuration directives and rules here
    # ...

    # A more-specific configuration context in which
    # you don't want to run the rule 2000
    <Location /moreSpecific/>
        SecRuleRemoveById 2000
    </Location>
</VirtualHost>
```

Updating Rule Actions at Configure-Time

Speaking of changing rules at runtime, sometimes you'll encounter a rule that isn't a false positive, but just does something you don't want it to. For example, there may be a rule that was hard-coded to block in a particular way, but you want it to warn or to block in another way. You can change what the rule does on a match at runtime, using the SecRuleUpdateActionById directive:

```
SecRule ARGS "@rx K1" id:2000,phase:2,deny,log

# ...

SecRuleUpdateActionById 2000 pass
```

For simplicity, this example shows two rules in the same configuration context, but—as discussed in the previous section—changing rule actions like that is only useful when you can't change the rules themselves—or when you don't want to.

The ability to change rule actions was designed primarily to allow you to change disruptive actions, which is why this ability supports changing action lists only for standalone rules or for the first rule in a chain. However, you can change action lists in rule chains by specifying a rule offset after a rule ID and separating the two with a colon. The following example updates the second rule in the chain and lets you call a script in case of a match:

```
SecRule ARGS "@rx K1" id:2000,phase:2,deny,log,chain
    SecRule ARGS "@rx K2"

# ...

# Fork execution of external script
SecRuleUpdateActionById 2000:1 exec:/path/to/my.script
```

Updating Rule Targets at Configure-Time

You can change a rule's target list at configure-time. For example, you may find that a group of rules is matching on a parameter that you know isn't vulnerable, and you want to stop the rules from looking at it. Instead of removing the rules completely like we did in previous sections, we can exclude the rules for a certain parameter only:

```
Include /usr/local/modsecurity/core-rules/rules/*.conf

# ...

SecRuleUpdateTargetByTag attack-xss "!ARGS:content"
```

The second rule will find the offending rules by tag (attack-xss) and then append the second parameter to the list of inspection variables. At runtime, the list of target variables will be generated, with your appended instructions removing the parameter content from inspection.

Removing Rules at Runtime

As explained previously, you can exclude rules at runtime. This has a small performance impact, but allows for greater flexibility. Armed with one or more rule IDs (or messages or tags), a rule that runs first can prevent other rules from running, as in the following example:

```
SecRule REMOTE_USER "@rx admin" \
    "id:1000,phase:1,pass,nolog,ctl:ruleRemoveByTag=attacks-sqli
```

```
Include /opt/modsecurity/core-rules/rules/*.conf
```

If the first rule matches, the associated `ctl` action runs. Because the `ctl` action specifies the `ruleRemoveByTag` action, the engine will make a note that it shouldn't run rules that have the `attacks-sqli` tag. Later in the phase, if the engine reaches a rule matching the tag, it will skip over it and exclude the rule from running.

> **Note**
>
> The order of the directives is very important, because the `ctl` action must run before the rules that you wish to remove or manipulate. There will be no effect if the rules have run already.

Updating Rule Targets at Runtime

You can change a rule's target list at runtime—provided, of course, that you do so before the rule you want to change runs. Consider the following example, in which I've written three rules to manipulate several rules from the Core Rule Set at runtime:

```
SecRule REQUEST_URI "@beginsWith /submit" \
    "id:2000,phase:1,pass,nolog,ctl:ruleRemoveTargetById=930120;ARGS:mailbody"
SecRule REQUEST_URI "@beginsWith /submit" \
    "id:2001,phase:1,pass,nolog,\
    ctl:ruleRemoveTargetByMsg=Restricted.*Character\sAnomaly\sDetection;↵
ARGS:mailbody"
SecRule REQUEST_URI "@beginsWith /submit" \
    "id:2002,phase:1,pass,nolog,ctl:ruleRemoveTargetByTag=attack-sqli;ARGS:mailbody"

Include /opt/modsecurity/core-rules/rules/*.conf
```

All three rules activate on transactions the URIs of which begin with /submit; they're designed to reduce what's being inspected, from the default `ARGS` to `ARGS:mailbody`. The idea is to reduce the rate of false positives. The first rule changes only one rule, that with ID 930120. The second changes all rules for which their messages match the regular expression defined with `ctl:ruleRemoveTargetByMsg`. Finally, the third rule affects all rules that have the `attack-sqli` tag.

Configuration Tips

As described in this chapter, ModSecurity provides great flexibility in organizing your rules. There isn't one best method, so you should use the approach that makes maintenance easy for you. The following tips may help you choose a method:

- The simplest approach is to define all your rules in the main server body. Then, if there's a need to do something differently in a particular site, you can take one of the following actions:

  - Append new rules by placing them into the correct `<VirtualHost>` tag.

  - Override the rules from the main server body using the techniques described earlier in this chapter.

  - Turn off rule inheritance completely, then implement a new policy from scratch.

- There is also a middle way in which you keep all your rules in the main server body but write them in such a way that they behave differently, depending on the host. For example, you could have a rule that determines which host is running it, then takes different paths in the ruleset. Alternatively (and somewhat more safely), your `<VirtualHost>` contexts could make use of the `SecWebAppId` directive to define all your applications; in your rules, you could use the `WEBAPPID` variable to change processing at runtime.

- The same advice applies equally to those cases in which you need to use different policies within one site, the only difference being that you'll be using the `<Location>` tags instead of `<VirtualHost>`.

- A different approach to rule organization is to leave the main server configuration empty, configuring only the individual sites. That's fine too, so long as you understand that there may be some requests that won't fall within any of the sites (e.g., bad requests), which ModSecurity won't be able to see. In most cases it won't matter, but your view of your web server activity may no longer be complete.

- If your sites require significantly different policies, define each policy in a separate file (or several files, if the policy is highly complex) and use the `Include` directive to activate it. By doing so, you maximize reuse and minimize maintenance.

- Third-party rulesets are best left in their own files, allowing you to easily replace them with newer versions. If they're well-written, you'll be able to use the exclusion techniques described in the section called "Rule Manipulation and Exclusion" earlier in this chapter.

Summary

This chapter is the last in the series of chapters that discuss rule writing, a three-part journey that started with an overview, proceeded through a step-by-step explanation of every rule feature, and concluded with the high-level "glue" to tie everything together.

Rule writing was the second main topic of this book, after configuration. The next seven chapters provide an in-depth look at the most important features of ModSecurity, with each chapter generally focusing on only one aspect. The only exception is Chapter 9, *Practical Rule Writing*, which contains a collection of topics that, although important, aren't big enough to be in chapters of their own.

The next chapter discusses persistent storage, quite possibly the single most important facility in ModSecurity. You'll soon see why.

8 Persistent Storage

This chapter is about the *persistent storage* mechanism, which adds long-term memory to ModSecurity. Without persistent storage, you're condemned to look at only one transaction at a time without knowledge of what came before it or whether what came before it is important. With persistent storage, you can construct data models that mirror the main elements of the models used in applications. Some of the elements you'll want to track are IP addresses, application sessions, and application users.

The persistent storage mechanism in ModSecurity can be described as a free-form database. Every collection is a separate table. Within each table, you can have any number of records, and the records will hold any number of variables. There's no need for the records to be uniform. You don't need to know in advance what you'll store, and you can even store different data in different records. The storage mechanism was designed with ultimately transient data in mind, so each record has an expiry mechanism built in, which enables the database to essentially keep itself in shape, automatically removing expired records over time.

That's all fine, I hear you say, but what's the persistent storage for? Here are a couple of things that you can do (I'll show you how in the remainder of this chapter):

- Track IP address activity, attack, and anomaly scores

- Track session activity, attack, and anomaly scores

- Track user behavior over a long period of time

- Monitor for session hijacking

- Enforce session inactivity timeouts and absolute life span

- Implement periodic alerting

- Detect denial of service and brute force attacks

I'm sure that you'll find plenty of additional scenarios to use persistent storage in your own environment. As a bonus, this chapter includes several examples to give you an idea of what you can do with the Lua scripting language in ModSecurity. I could have written the examples using ModSecurity rules, but for complex tasks Lua is a much better choice.

Manipulating Collection Records

In this section, I'll cover the basics of collection manipulation. We'll discuss creating records first. In most cases, creation is all you need to do, and ModSecurity will take care of everything else. The rest of the section will provide the details you need to know when you want full control of the persistent storage mechanism.

Creating Records

Creating a record is a matter of deciding on a key and invoking the initcol action. The IP collection, for example, is almost always initialized unconditionally using the remote IP address. Because the REMOTE_ADDR variable is always available, it's a good idea to initialize the IP collection early, in phase 1, as follows:

```
# Track IP addresses
SecAction id:1000,phase:1,pass,nolog,initcol:IP=%{REMOTE_ADDR}
```

A collection can be initialized with a record only once per transaction. If there are multiple invocations of the initcol action for the same collection (IP in the example), the first invocation will be processed and all the subsequent invocations will be ignored.

> **Note**
>
> The case of the collection names used in initcol doesn't matter (i.e., IP is equivalent to ip, Ip, or iP). That said, it's customary to write collection names in uppercase.

Although most collections use single variables for their keys, it's perfectly possible to create a key out of two or more variables. For example, sometimes you may have a large number of users behind the same IP address but still may want to attempt to track them individually. Although there's not a way to do that reliably, a more granular method is to generate record keys using a combination of the IP address and a hash of the User-Agent field:

```
# Generate a readable hash out of the User-Agent
# request header and store it in TX.uahash
SecRule REQUEST_HEADERS:User-Agent "@unconditionalMatch" \
    id:1000,phase:1,pass,t:none,t:sha1,t:hexEncode,setvar:TX.uahash=%{MATCHED_VAR}

# Initialize the IP collection using a
# combination of IP address and User-Agent hash
SecAction id:1001,phase:1,pass,nolog,initcol:IP=%{REMOTE_ADDR}_%{TX.uahash}
```

Currently, it's only possible to use the predefined collection names listed in Table 8.1. A future version of ModSecurity might allow you to use any name (so long as the name doesn't clash with the built-in variables).

Table 8.1. Predefined collections

Collection	Create with	Description
GLOBAL	initcol	Global (per-server) data store
IP	initcol	Per-IP-address data store
RESOURCE	initcol	Per-resource (typically URL) data store
SESSION	setsid	Per-session data store
USER	setuid	Per-user data store

The collection names were chosen to give clues about their intended usages, and I trust you won't have any difficulty figuring out what those usages are. However, the rest of this section will show you how to use each collection.

You'll notice that not all collections can be created using the initcol action. The SESSION and USER collections each have a special initialization action to support application namespaces (described in the section called "Application Namespaces" in this chapter).

> **Note**
>
> There's no practical difference between creating a record and retrieving an existing record. The initcol action will automatically create a new record if one doesn't already exist.

Application Namespaces

A single server running ModSecurity can serve many different sites with their own separate session IDs and user accounts. Although the session IDs will overlap only very rarely (assuming that the ID generation algorithm is solid), there's a good chance that username collisions will be quite frequent if you run multiple applications on the same server. For example, I imagine that every other application uses admin as the username for the main administration account.

ModSecurity uses *application namespaces* to deal with this problem, allowing you to manually specify application boundaries. Each application then receives a private space for its SESSION and USER collections, preventing overlaps. Applications are defined using the SecWebAppId directive. Your goal should be to use one unique application ID per application —for example:

```
<VirtualHost www.ssllabs.com>
    SecWebAppId ssllabs
```

```
    </VirtualHost>

    <VirtualHost www.feistyduck.com>
        SecWebAppId feistyduck
    </VirtualHost>
```

The method by which application namespaces are implemented is very simple. For normal collections, the collection name is used to name the file in which its data will be stored. For namespace-aware collections, the namespace is part of the name. Assuming the configuration in the previous example, the data persistence directory may contain the following files:

```
default_SESSION.dir
default_SESSION.pag
feistyduck_SESSION.dir
feistyduck_SESSION.pag
IP.dir
IP.pag
ssllabs_SESSION.dir
ssllabs_SESSION.pag
```

You can see that there's one global database for the IP collection, but three databases for sessions: one each for ssllabs and feistyduck applications, and one (default) for all other applications together. Each database uses two files: the .dir files contains indexes, and the .pag files contain data.

Initializing Records

After a collection is initialized, the record is entirely empty, but for complex rules you'll most likely need to populate it with some initial values. The special record variable IS_NEW can be used to determine whether a record is new; you can test whether this variable is set, and perform the initialization of the record if it is. In the following example, we'll set an initial reputation in the IP.reputation variable, which will be saved automatically as a part of the persistent IP address record:

```
# Enable IP address tracking
SecAction id:1000,phase:1,pass,nolog,initcol:IP=%{REMOTE_ADDR}

# Set the default reputation value for new IP records
SecRule IP:IS_NEW "@eq 1" \
    id:1001,phase:1,pass,nolog,setvar:IP.reputation=100
```

Controlling Record Longevity

The number of records in a collection can grow very quickly, especially in cases in which you use one or more records per IP address and you have many users. To preserve space and improve performance, you want your records to be deleted as soon as you no longer need them, but no sooner.

The principal way to control the removal of records is through the *inactivity timeout mechanism* built into the persistence subsystem. This mechanism ensures the removal of records that are no longer updated. Its operation is straightforward:

1. An inactivity timeout value is associated with every record.

2. Records are scheduled for deletion as soon as they're created.

3. If a record is written to, the expiry time is recalculated using the current timeout value. This means that every activity prolongs the lifetime of a record.

4. The default inactivity timeout value is 3,600 seconds, but it can be changed by assigning a different value to the TIMEOUT collection variable (e.g., setvar:IP.TIMEOUT=300). A different default value also can be selected using the SecCollectionTimeout directive.

It's a best practice to configure the desired inactivity timeout value only once, in a separate rule that checks IS_NEW before making any changes (as demonstrated in the previous section).

Choose the correct value depending on what your collection does. Use the following list as guidance:

- IP tracking: hours

- Session tracking: days

- User tracking: months

However, there are also security concerns to take into consideration: if your application has a session inactivity timeout of 30 minutes, then you shouldn't let your ModSecurity session last much longer than that. Therefore, you need to look at each individual case and make reasonable decisions.

Deleting Records

In most cases, you won't need to delete collection records explicitly; it's much better to configure the correct timeout period and let the garbage collection process deal with inactive records after they expire. There are currently two ways in which records are deleted:

- A special garbage collection process runs periodically to examine all records in all known collections (i.e., the collections that have been activated during the transaction using initcol, setsid, or setuid). This process will remove all expired records.

- When an attempt to retrieve an expired record is made, the expired record is deleted and replaced with a new one.

If you know that you no longer need a record, it's most efficient to delete it immediately. That's possible to do, in a roundabout sort of way; you can force its deletion by unsetting the special KEY collection variable as follows:

```
# Delete record
SecAction id:1000,phase:1,pass,nolog,setvar:!IP.KEY
```

Detecting Very Old Records

Because the expiry time of a record potentially can be reset indefinitely, it isn't impossible to have a record survive for a very long time. Although ModSecurity won't complain about a record that's too old, it does record the creation time, making it possible to write a custom rule to inspect it. My first attempt at detecting very old records used the following Lua rule (because I thought the calculations would be impossible to do in ModSecurity's rule language):

```
function main()
    -- Retrieve CREATE_TIME of the current IP record
    local createTime = m.getvar("IP.CREATE_TIME");

    -- If the variable is available and if the record is older
    -- than 24 hours, report the problem back
    if ((createTime ~= nil) and (os.time() - createTime > 86400)) then
        -- Retrieve the record key, which will
        -- make the error message more useful
        local key = m.getvar("IP.KEY");
        -- Match
        return "IP record older than 24 hours (" ..
            (os.time() - createTime) .. "s): " .. key;
    end

    -- No match
    return nil;
end
```

To use the rule, place it in a file called check_ip_create_time.lua, and call it as follows:

```
# Check the CREATE_TIME of the IP collection
SecRuleScript check_ip_create_time.lua \
    id:9000,phase:5,pass,log
```

If you want to delete such old records (using the technique described in the previous section), use the following rule instead:

```
# Delete very old IP collection records
SecRuleScript check_ip_create_time.lua \
    id:9000,phase:5,pass,nolog,setvar:!IP.KEY
```

To learn more about writing rules in Lua, see Chapter 12, *Writing Rules in Lua*.

After seeing my Lua rule, Brian Rectanus came up with the following rule language equivalent:

```
# Detect very old IP records
SecAction "id:9000,phase:5,pass,log,\
    msg:'IP record older than 24 hours',\
    setvar:TX.exp=%{TIME_EPOCH},\
    setvar:TX.exp=-%{IP.CREATE_TIME},\
    chain"
SecRule TX:exp "@gt 86400" "setvar:!IP.KEY"
```

Although the rule language doesn't support arithmetic operations in operators, it does support addition and subtraction in the `setvar` action. The preceding example starts with an unconditional rule that uses two `setvar` actions to calculate the age of an IP record. The second rule then checks the result, which has been saved in the transient variable `TX.exp`.

Collection Variables

What makes collections beautiful is that they allow you to store any variable, and on a whim. Once you initialize a collection (and thus obtain a record), you can use the `setvar` action to create, modify, and delete collection variables. This section covers three additional features that persistent collections do support, but ordinary collections don't:

- Built-in variables, which give you insight into how a record is used
- Variable expiry, which allows you to remove (expire) a variable at some point in the future
- Variable value depreciation, which allows you to reduce the value of a variable over time

Built-In Variables

Every persistent collection contains certain built-in variables, as described in Table 8.2. The use of these variables is explained throughout this section, but generally they're populated using the information provided by the underlying persistence mechanism, allowing you to understand how individual records are used.

Table 8.2. Built-in collection variables

Name	Access	Description
CREATE_TIME	Read-only	Record creation time, in seconds, since January 1, 1970 (*epoch time*).
IS_NEW	Read-only	This flag is set on a record that has been created during this transaction.
KEY	Read/delete	Record key. Can be unset, in which case the record will be deleted.
LAST_UPDATE_TIME	Read-only	The last record update time, in seconds (prior to this transaction).
TIMEOUT	Read/write	The current timeout value, which will be used to extend the life of the record on the next write. The timeout is initially set to the value of SecCollectionTimeout, which is 3,600 seconds by default.
UPDATE_COUNTER	Read-only	Update counter, which is incremented every time the record is persisted.
UPDATE_RATE	Read-only	Update rate in updates per minute. Measured over the entire lifetime of the record.

Variable Expiry

The *variable expiry* mechanism enables you to schedule a variable to be expired (unset) at some point in the future. You can use this feature whenever you want to execute an action that will remain active for a period of time (long after the HTTP transaction that initiated it is gone).

A good example of how to use this feature can be seen with IP address blocking. Assuming you have the IP collection initialized, IP address blocking requires two rules:

1. One rule will decide when to block an IP address and set the appropriate flag in the IP collection (let's use IP.blocked for this example).

2. The second rule will block transactions originating from the flagged IP addresses.

For example:

```
# Detect attack and install a persistent IP address block
SecRule ARGS "@rx attack" \
    "id:2000,phase:2,block,log,msg:'Blocking IP address for 60s',\
    setvar:IP.blocked,\
    expirevar:IP.blocked=60"

# Enforce a persistent IP address block
SecRule IP:blocked "@eq 1" \
    "id:2001,phase:2,block,msg:'Enforcing earlier IP address block'"
```

> **Note**
>
> If you want blocking to remain active for a very long period of time, make sure that the IP collection timeout value is longer than the blocking period. If an IP collection record expires, the block will expire with it.

Variable Value Depreciation

Variable expiry works well for things that are black or white, right or wrong—but when you have shades of gray, you'll need to use variable value depreciation (with the deprecatevar action), which is designed to work with variables that contain numerical values. When you employ depreciation, the numerical value of your choice is gradually reduced over time until it reaches zero. This mechanism is typically used to work with anomaly or attack scores.

> **Note**
>
> The deprecatevar action is implemented differently than expirevar. Whereas expirevar uses a "fire-and-forget approach" and needs to run only once, the deprecatevar action needs to be invoked continuously—in most cases, on every request—for as long as you need the depreciation to remain active. The recommended approach for expirevar is to use it in the same rule that creates (or updates) a variable. The recommended approach for deprecatevar is to use it unconditionally (with SecAction) in phase 5.

The deprecatevar action takes two positive integer parameters, separated by a forward slash. The first number defines by how much the variable value will be reduced in a single change. The second number defines the duration between changes. Together, the parameters define the speed of depreciation. In the following example, the value of the IP.score variable will be reduced by 1 every 5 seconds:

```
SecAction id:9000,phase:5,pass,nolog,deprecatevar:IP.score=1/5
```

The way in which you choose the numbers matters, because the reduction in value is made at the discrete intervals defined by the duration parameter. That means that although both 1/5 and 60/300 will result in the same variable value after 300 seconds, in the first case there would be 60 decrements of 1 at 5-second intervals, whereas in the second case you will get just one decrement of 60 after 300 seconds. On every request, ModSecurity will check the interval since the last update of the variable. As soon as the interval is greater than or equal to the duration parameter, the depreciation will be executed in a single step. If there are no transactions, then there will be no depreciation. However, if a new request is served after a longer idle period, then multiple depreciation steps will be executed all at once.

For a complete example using depreciation, consider the following implementation of IP address attack scoring:

```
# Increment IP address attack score with every attack
SecRule ARGS "@rx attack" \
    id:2000,phase:2,pass,log,setvar:IP.score=+1

# Block IP addresses whose attack score is greater than 10
SecRule IP:score "@gt 10" \
```

```
    "id:2001,phase:2,block,log,msg:'IP address anomaly score over 10 ↵
(%{IP.score})'"

# Decrement attack score by 1 every 5 seconds
SecAction id:9000,phase:5,pass,nolog,deprecatevar:IP.score=1/5
```

If you look at the debug log, you may find the following two lines for each variable being depreciated:

```
[9] Deprecating variable: IP.score=1/5
[4] Deprecated variable "IP.score" from 17 to 15 (10 seconds since last update).
```

As you would expect, depreciation doesn't occur when there's no change in value. In such a case, you'll see the following message in the debug log:

```
[9] Not deprecating variable "IP.score" because the new value (15) is the same as ↵
the old one (15) (4 seconds since last update).
```

> **Note**
>
> Because the reduction in value happens only in the logging phase, a request arriving after a longer idle period will be blocked before the reduction is executed. Only subsequent requests will pass rule 2001 in the earlier example.

Implementation Details

Persistent storage in ModSecurity is implemented using the SDBM library, which is part of Apache Portable Runtime (APR). SDBM was selected because it was already available (ModSecurity depends on APR anyway) and because it allows for control of concurrent access. The latter reason is very important, because in ModSecurity we potentially deal with many concurrent transactions.

Retrieving Records

Collection records are retrieved when the `initcol` action is encountered. Assuming that the collection wasn't previously initialized, ModSecurity will look for the appropriate SDBM database and fetch the record with the corresponding key. You can examine the process when you increase the debug log level to 9:

```
[9] Resolved macro %{remote_addr} to: 192.168.3.1
[9] collection_retrieve_ex: collection_retrieve_ex: Retrieving collection ↵
(name "ip", filename "/opt/modsecurity/var/data/ip")
[9] collection_unpack: Read variable: name "__expire_KEY", value "1471235160".
[9] collection_unpack: Read variable: name "KEY", value "192.168.3.1".
[9] collection_unpack: Read variable: name "TIMEOUT", value "3600".
```

```
[9] collection_unpack: Read variable: name "__key", value "192.168.3.1".
[9] collection_unpack: Read variable: name "__name", value "ip".
[9] collection_unpack: Read variable: name "CREATE_TIME", value "1471231223".
[9] collection_unpack: Read variable: name "UPDATE_COUNTER", value "30".
[9] collection_unpack: Read variable: name "LAST_UPDATE_TIME", value "1471231560".
[9] collection_unpack: Read variable: name "blocked", value "1".
[9] collection_unpack: Read variable: name "__expire_blocked", value "1471231570".
[9] collection_retrieve_ex: Removing key "blocked" from collection.
[9] collection_retrieve_ex: Removing key "__expire_blocked" from collection.
[4] collection_retrieve_ex: Removed expired variable "blocked".
[4] collection_retrieve_ex: Retrieved collection (name "ip", key "192.168.3.1").
[9] Recorded original collection variable: ip.UPDATE_COUNTER = "30"
[4] Added collection "ip" to the list.
```

The first line gives a clue about what key was used. Following that, there will be one line for every variable retrieved from the database. You'll notice that some variable names begin with two underscore characters (__). Those variables are internal to ModSecurity; you can probably guess from their names what they do. The variables with names that begin with the __expire_ prefix are created by the expirevar action to keep track of when individual variables need to be expired.

Storing a Collection

All the records initialized during a transaction will be persisted after the transaction completes. Usually, persistence will require a straightforward write to the database:

```
[9] collection_store: Wrote variable: name "__expire_KEY", value "1471237309".
[9] collection_store: Wrote variable: name "KEY", value "192.168.3.1".
[9] collection_store: Wrote variable: name "TIMEOUT", value "3600".
[9] collection_store: Wrote variable: name "__key", value "192.168.3.1".
[9] collection_store: Wrote variable: name "__name", value "ip".
[9] collection_store: Wrote variable: name "CREATE_TIME", value "1471231223".
[9] collection_store: Wrote variable: name "UPDATE_COUNTER", value "36".
[9] collection_store: Wrote variable: name "reputation", value "100".
[9] collection_store: Wrote variable: name "LAST_UPDATE_TIME", value "1471233709".
[9] collection_store: Wrote variable: name "blocked", value "1".
[9] collection_store: Wrote variable: name "__expire_blocked", value "1471233719".
[4] collection_store: Persisted collection (name "ip", key "192.168.3.1").
[4] Recording persistent data took 0 microseconds.
```

> **Note**
>
> If, while looking at your debug logs, you discover that an initialized collection isn't being persisted, that's because nothing was changed in it. When there are no changes in the record, the copy in storage will be identical to that in memory, so there's no need to perform the expensive write operation.

Because the writing is delayed until the end of a transaction and because there's no record locking (there can't be any, because it would create a terrible bottleneck), there's always a race condition, due to the time gap between the moment a rule retrieves a record and the moment it writes the record back to storage. By the time a record is persisted, some other request may have changed the stored record values.

ModSecurity uses a double-retrieval mechanism with write-locking to deal with the concurrent access problem. It performs the following operations:

1. Locks the database

2. Retrieves the record again to obtain up-to-date values

3. For every numerical value that was changed, calculates the difference between what it originally saw and what it has

4. Updates the numerical values in the record retrieved in step 2 by making relative changes using the calculation from the previous step

5. Writes the record to disk

6. Unlocks the database

The debug log will show something similar to the following (note the delta calculations in between the read and write operations):

```
[4] collection_retrieve_ex: Retrieved collection (name "ip", key "192.168.3.1").
[9] collection_store: Delta applied for ip.UPDATE_COUNTER 35->36 (1): 35 + (1) = ↵
36 [36,2]
[9] collection_store: Delta applied for ip.counter 35->36 (1): 35 + (1) = 36 [36,2]
[9] collection_store: Wrote variable: name "__expire_KEY", value "1471237309".
```

The locking and the delta calculations are necessary in order to ensure the integrity of the persisted numerical values. Without them, multiple concurrent transactions would overwrite one another's values and the numerical values would be incorrect. By remembering the changes rather than absolute values, ModSecurity ensures that numerical values are always correctly persisted. Unfortunately, there's no way to ensure the integrity of nonnumerical values in the concurrent access scenario (not without severe performance degradation, that is). On the positive side, nonnumerical values are not frequently used in persistent storage, and, when they are, they're used in situations in which there is little concurrent access.

Record Limits

The SDBM library imposes an arbitrary limit of 1,008 bytes on the combined size of key length and record length. If you break this limit, the persistence operation will fail and you'll see the following message in your logs:

```
Failed to write to DBM file "/usr/local/modsecurity/var/data/ip": Invalid argument
```

ModSecurity uses about 200 bytes for its needs (mostly the built-in collection variables), which means that you have about 800 bytes left in a practical sense. Although 800 bytes doesn't sound like much, it's enough in most situations, because rules usually only save numerical values in persistent storage.

> **Note**
>
> If you're running out of space, avoid using very long keys. Keys are stored in three copies: two copies are used by ModSecurity, and one copy is used by SDBM itself. If everything else fails, you can always resort to "brute force" and recompile APR and APR-util to increase the size limit to a much higher value. Look for `PAIRMAX 1008` in the SDBM source code in APR-util.

As a rule of thumb, you should avoid storing anything user-controlled in persistent storage. For example, you might want to store the value of the `User-Agent` request header in a `SESSION` collection to check for possible session hijacking attacks, but that value can be as much as 8,190 bytes long (that's Apache's default request header limit). In such situations, it's better to store a value derived from the `User-Agent` value than to store the value itself.

Practically speaking, you can use the `sha1` or `md5` transformation function to "compress" input of any size to a fixed-length value. Because the output of those two transformation functions is binary, it's a good idea to follow them with a `hexEncode` transformation, making the final value printable. The following is the rule from an earlier example, which takes the value of the `User-Agent` request header and transforms it into a value (stored in `TX.uahash`) that can be used with persistent storage:

```
SecRule REQUEST_HEADERS:User-Agent @unconditionalMatch \
    id:1000,phase:1,t:none,t:sha1,t:hexEncode,setvar:TX.uahash=%{MATCHED_VAR}
```

Applied Persistence

In this section, I will apply the previously discussed persistence techniques to several real-life problems:

- Periodic alerting
- Denial of service attack detection
- Brute force attack detection

The combination of the persistence facilities and the rule language makes the examples that follow particularly interesting. The techniques you'll learn in the remainder of this chapter will help you take your own rules to the next level!

Periodic Alerting

Periodic alerting is a useful technique when you only need to see one alert about a particular situation and when further events would only create clutter. You can implement periodic alerting to work once per IP address, session, URL, or even an entire application. First, you choose the collection you want to work with, and then you create a special flag the presence of which will tell you that an alert needs to be suppressed.

The best case for periodic alerting can be made when you're dealing with problems that aren't caused by an external factor, which typically happens with rules that perform *passive vulnerability scanning*. Such rules detect traces of vulnerabilities in output and alert you to them. They are quite handy because they can alert you of problems before they're exploited. If passive scanning rules are stateless, they may cause far too many alerts, because they'll report a problem whenever they see it, which may happen very frequently on busy sites. If you're faced with such a problem, you'll have probably seen the first couple of alerts, and even if you aren't doing anything to address the discovered issue, you don't really want to be reminded about it. That annoyance can be solved by updating passive vulnerability scanning rules to alert only once, as I'll demonstrate.

To start, here's a simple rule that detects application version leakage in the X-Powered-By response header:

```
SecRule RESPONSE_HEADERS:X-Powered-By @unconditionalMatch \
    "id:6000,phase:3,pass,log,msg:'X-Powered-By information leakage'"
```

PHP version leakage is a minor issue that's good to know about, but not with an alert on every web server hit. The leakage is caused by a site-wide problem in the configuration of the PHP engine, which means that we can use the GLOBAL collection to track it. We'll create a special record (in the GLOBAL collection) for this one problem and use it to keep track of the previous activity.

The following rule will detect X-Powered-By information leakage, but will warn about the problem only once every 60 seconds:

```
SecRule RESPONSE_HEADERS:X-Powered-By @unconditionalMatch \
    "id:9000,phase:5,pass,log,\
    msg:'X-Powered-By information leakage (%{TX.temp} hits since last alert)',\
    initcol:GLOBAL=1,\
    setvar:GLOBAL.id9000_counter=+1,\
    chain"
    SecRule &GLOBAL:id9000_flag "@eq 0" \
        "setvar:GLOBAL.id9000_flag,\
        expirevar:GLOBAL.id9000_flag=60,\
        setvar:TX.temp=%{GLOBAL.id9000_counter},\
        setvar:GLOBAL.id9000_counter=0"
```

Let's walk through what this rule does:

1. The first rule checks whether the problem exists by looking for a nonempty X-Powered-By response header.

2. Upon successful detection, two actions are carried out:

   a. A record in the GLOBAL collection is initialized, using the constant key 1. By performing the initialization only after a match, we enhance performance of requests without the leakage problem.

   b. The counter value is increased by 1. Even if we don't alert on the problem, we keep track of how many violations there were.

3. The second rule—which, being part of the same chain, is tested only after the first rule matches—tests the GLOBAL.id9000_flag variable, which will tell us if we've alerted in the previous period of time. The presence of the variable is a sign that we shouldn't alert (you'll see why in the next step). If the variable isn't present, the rule will match, and the following actions will be carried out:

   a. The GLOBAL.id9000_flag variable will be created.

   b. The GLOBAL.id9000_flag will be set to expire 60 seconds in the future.

   c. The value of the GLOBAL.id9000_counter variable is preserved in the temporary variable TX.temp.

   d. The counter (GLOBAL.id9000_counter) is then reset to zero.

   e. The match of the second rule will cause the entire chain to match and create an alert. Note how the chain message makes use of the temporary variable TX.temp, which stored the earlier value of the counter (which we've since reset).

> **Note**
>
> If you don't need to track how many alerts were suppressed, omit the incrementation of the GLOBAL.id9000_counter, which will save you a write to disk for every suppressed alert (which could be a write for every request to your site, depending on the nature of the problem being detected).

Even with this elaborate scheme to implement periodic alerting, it's possible to get more than one alert for a problem that occurs often (e.g., on every request). This is because processing a request takes time, so it's entirely possible for two requests to execute so close to each other that they don't realize the alert has already taken place. We're minimizing the chances of that happening by choosing phase 5 for the rule and using late initialization. Collections are persisted right after the rules in phase 5 complete, which means that the window of opportunity for the collision is minimized.

If you need suppression to work per application script, use the RESOURCE collection. The following rule is identical to the previous example, except that the collection initialization is slightly different:

```
SecRule RESPONSE_HEADERS:X-Powered-By @unconditionalMatch \
    "id:9000,phase:5,pass,log,\
    msg:'X-Powered-By information leakage (%{TX.temp} hits since last alert)',\
    initcol:RESOURCE=%{SCRIPT_FILENAME},\
    setvar:RESOURCE.id9000_counter=+1,\
    chain"
    SecRule &RESOURCE:id9000_flag "@eq 0" \
        "setvar:RESOURCE.id9000_flag,\
        expirevar:RESOURCE.id9000_flag=60,\
        setvar:TX.temp=%{RESOURCE.id9000_counter},\
        setvar:RESOURCE.id9000_counter=0"
```

The RESOURCE collection can give you access to a record that's unique for the script that will process the request. When ModSecurity is embedded in a web server, initialize the RESOURCE collection in phase 2 using SCRIPT_FILENAME (which will map to the actual script on disk, no matter what the request URI looks like). In a proxy situation, bear in mind that a single script can be used for an unlimited number of request URIs. A proxy doesn't understand the path info portion of an URI, so when a transaction requests /index.php/1001 and then /index.php/1002, it sees them as two different request URIs. A web server would see them as only one script (when you use SCRIPT_FILENAME). Furthermore, it's possible to have two locations (e.g., /index.php in two different virtual hosts). To avoid the chance of a collision, you should use the current hostname as part of the key.

Denial of Service Attack Detection

In general, reacting to denial of service attacks from within a web server is less than ideal. When the target of an attack is the web server itself (e.g., the attacker is trying to overwhelm it by sending a large number of requests or keeping a large number of connections open), by the time a request reaches the web server, it will have already caused damage. Denial of service attacks based on brute force should be handled by the network layer, where you can minimize the attack impact. This doesn't rule out deploying a detection mechanism on the web server, but you need to implement the active defense at the network layer.

When it comes to attacks against applications, that's another story, and you may actually find ModSecurity very useful. Application attacks rely on being able to send cheap requests (in terms of resources needed to send them) to applications that will use disproportionately more resources (CPU, I/O, and RAM) to process them. Any application function that performs intensive work is a good attack choice. For example, most simple database-backed sites exercise no control over how many database connections they open and are easy prey.

Send more than a handful of requests to such a site and it will suddenly start to malfunction.

The simplest approach to detecting DoS attacks is to check the value in the UPDATE_RATE variable of a collection. However, because collections are persisted only when there's a change to record, you need to ensure that the collection you're using is written to on every request that matters. A simple way to do that is to increment a counter on every request, as in the following example using the IP collection:

```
SecAction id:1000,phase:1,pass,nolog,setvar:IP.counter=+1
SecRule IP:UPDATE_RATE "@gt 10" \
    "id:1001,phase:1,block,msg:'Request rate (%{IP.UPDATE_RATE}) too high for IP ↵
address %{REMOTE_ADDR}'"
```

I have one concern about this approach, though: I don't like the fact that the IP collection is written to on every request. Unless you're already doing something with the IP collection, constantly updating the collection will add to your overall resource consumption. That doesn't mean that it's not going to work well, but it does mean that you need to watch it.

It's possible to improve performance by focusing only on those requests that really matter. If you examine your access logs, chances are good you'll find that only a fraction of all requests are forwarded to the application, with the rest being requests for static resources, such as images, JavaScript, and CSS files. Static files are delivered efficiently by the web server, and you can probably avoid tracking them in ModSecurity. By amending the first rule in the previous example to increment only on a nonstatic request (using an unreliable method of checking the file extension, which will be sufficiently good in this case), we can increase the efficiency of our application DoS detection—for example:

```
# Only increment the counter if the
# request is for a dynamic resource
SecRule REQUEST_FILENAME "!@rx \.(jpg|png|gif|js|css|ico)$" \
    id:1000,phase:1,pass,nolog,setvar:IP.counter=+1
```

> **Note**
>
> The UPDATE_RATE value is calculated over the lifetime of a record. If you keep the records alive for a long period of time, a spike of activity (which may or may not be a DoS) won't affect the overall rate significantly.

You can use the DURATION variable to discover how long a transaction has been running. This information is useful to keep track of how much time the web server is spending per IP address, session, or user.

The following example keeps track of the resources spent on every IP address:

```
# Initialize IP collection and immediately
# deprecate existing load data
```

```
SecAction "id:1000,phase:1,pass,nolog,\
    initcol:IP=%{REMOTE_ADDR},\
    deprecatevar:IP.load=250/1"

# Block the IP addresses that use too
# much of the web server's time
SecRule IP:load "@gt 10000" \
    "id:1000,phase:1,block,t:none,\
    msg:'IP address load too high: %{IP.load}'"

# Keep track of how much web server
# time is consumed by each IP address
SecAction "id:9000,phase:5,pass,nolog,\
    setvar:IP.load=+%{DURATION}"
```

You mustn't forget to use the deprecatevar action to ensure that the load value goes down during periods of inactivity; otherwise, the load will keep increasing and the block will never drop. Please note that the values I used in the example are completely arbitrary and aren't likely to work on your sites. Use the trial and error approach until you arrive at values that work for you. Similarly, keep in mind that a client's communication speed may affect the time he or she spends with a transaction. Excessively large pages may have skewed DURATION values. If you're buffering response bodies, I suggest that you move the tracking rule from phase 5 (which occurs after a transaction is complete) to phase 4 (which occurs just before a response body is sent).

Finally, if you get tired of looking at the debug log as you test your persistent rules, consider displaying the update rate (or load) as a part of the access log of the server, together with the duration of the full request and possibly other performance indicators, like the time spent in every ModSecurity phase.

Brute Force Attack Detection

Brute force attack detection is conceptually similar to the approach used to detect denial of service attacks. You keep track of the authentication failures and you react when you feel an attack is taking place. Performance-wise, brute force detection uses less resources, because the rules only have to work when authentication takes place.

To start, you need to understand how authentication failure manifests, because the condition will be different for every application. You learn that by using the application, recording all traffic to the logging script, and performing both successful and unsuccessful authentication. Your goal is to write a rule that will trigger on a failure, but not on success.

Let's assume that we're dealing with an application that uses the URL /login.php for all authentication requests. On success, the application redirects the user to /index.php. On failure, the application redirects back to /login.php, asking the user to try again. Our brute force attack detection rule could thus begin as follows:

```
<Location /login.php>
    # Check for authentication failure
    SecRule RESPONSE_HEADERS:Location "@endsWith login.php" \
        "id:9000,phase:5,pass,t:none,log,msg:'Failed authentication'"
</Location>
```

Once we verify that this works as expected, we can move on to managing the counters. Let's start with the IP collection first. The following rule will keep a per-IP-address counter and alert only after seeing 25 authentication attempts, at which point it will clear the counter and start over:

```
<Location /login.php>
    # Check for authentication failure, maintaining
    # a counter that keeps track of how many failures were
    SecRule RESPONSE_HEADERS:Location "@endsWith login.php" \
        "id:9000,phase:5,pass,t:none,log,\
        msg:'Multiple authentication failures from IP address',\
        setvar:IP.bf_counter=+1,\
        chain"
        SecRule IP:bf_counter "@ge 25" t:none,setvar:!IP.bf_counter
</Location>
```

What we really want to do is block access for a period of time when too many authentication attempts are seen. We can do that with an additional flag and a rule that checks for it, as follows:

```
<Location /login.php>
    # Enforce an existing IP address block
    SecRule IP:bf_block "@eq 1" "id:2000,phase:2,block,\
        msg:'IP address blocked because of suspected brute force attack'"

    # Check for authentication failure
    SecRule RESPONSE_HEADERS:Location "@endsWith login.php" \
        "id:9000,phase:5,pass,t:none,log, \
        msg:'Multiple authentication failures from IP address',\
        setvar:IP.bf_counter=+1,\
        chain"
        SecRule IP:bf_counter "@ge 25" "t:none,\
            setvar:IP.bf_block=1,\
            setvar:!IP.bf_counter,\
            expirevar:IP.bf_block=3600"
</Location>
```

And there we have our brute force detection rules, which will block anyone who misbehaves for one hour. Now, let's implement another layer of brute force attack defense, keeping track of the per-username authentication failures. This is possible, but with some restrictions, as you'll soon see.

For the second layer of defense, we need a place to store the second counter, of which we need to keep track no matter which IP address is used for access. It's only natural to use the USER collection, which was designed for that sort of thing—that is, for keeping track of information on a per-user basis:

```
<Location /login.php>
    # Enforce an existing IP address block
    SecRule IP:bf_block "@eq 1" \
        "id:2000,phase:2,deny,\
        msg:'IP address blocked because of suspected brute force attack'"

    # Retrieve the per-username record
    SecAction id:2001,phase:2,pass,nolog,setuid:%{ARGS.username}

    # Enforce an existing username block
    SecRule USER:bf_block "@eq 1" \
        "id:2002,phase:2,deny,\
        msg:'Username %{USER.key} blocked because of suspected brute force attack'"

    # Check for authentication failure and increment counters
    SecRule RESPONSE_HEADERS:Location "@endsWith /login.php" \
        "id:9000,phase:5,pass,t:none,nolog,\
        setvar:IP.bf_counter=+1,\
        setvar:USER.bf_counter=+1"

    # Check for too many failures from a single IP address
    SecRule IP:bf_counter "@ge 25" \
        "id:9001,phase:5,pass,t:none,\
        setvar:IP.bf_block=1,\
        setvar:!IP.bf_counter,\
        expirevar:IP.bf_block=1800"

    # Check for too many failures for a single username
    SecRule USER:bf_counter "@ge 25" \
        "id:9002,phase:5,pass,t:none,\
        setvar:USER.bf_block=1,\
        setvar:!USER.bf_counter,\
        expirevar:USER.bf_block=1800"
</Location>
```

This example uses a user-supplied value (whatever's in the username parameter) as a collection key. In such situations, you should always check that the user-supplied data is safe. You'll find more information about the dangers of using user-supplied data in the rest of this chapter.

Session Management

Session management is one of the more fun aspects of ModSecurity, and it's an area in which ModSecurity truly can be useful. The reason is simple: unlike with other methods, sessions allow you to understand and monitor in practice what one single user does. The usefulness of session tracking will vary depending on what you're protecting, but it's best used with applications that use sessions to enable users to establish a "relationship" with the application. Because sessions are required to use an application in a meaningful way, adversaries are compelled to use them, too, and that makes monitoring easier.

Initializing Sessions

Before you start to think about session initialization, think about how many applications you have on the same server. If you have more than one, you must create a separate application namespace using the SecWebAppId directive. Even if you have only one application, it doesn't hurt to use SecWebAppId, because it causes the application ID to be recorded in audit logs. Over time, you may add more applications, in which case it would be useful to know which audit log entries belong to which application.

To initialize a session, you need to do two things:

Extract session token from request

Most applications use cookies to transmit session tokens. Session cookies' names vary, but they should be easy to identify, because they usually contain a large, random-looking string (e.g., 64c24d4e35dc753cd085ca574def4131). A small number of applications embed session tokens in their URLs, and those are even easier to identify, because the large string can be seen in your browser's URL bar.

Configure sufficient session lifetime

ModSecurity collections have a default lifetime value of 3,600 seconds, but that's too short for sessions, which may remain active for hours under normal circumstances. Some faulty applications might even not impose a limit on session duration. To be able to monitor sessions throughout their lives, you need to choose a timeout value that is at least as long as the duration of the longest possible application session. In most cases, however, you should aim for the SESSION collection to remain alive for several times the maximum duration of the application session, because that will allow you to perform reliable session blocking. The examples in this section will use 48 hours (172,800 seconds) as the SESSION collection timeout value.

To initialize a session from a cookie, you first need to identify the correct cookie. Look at the following request that contains session information:

```
GET /index.php HTTP/1.1
Host: example.com
```

```
User-Agent: Mozilla/5.0 (X11; Ubuntu; Linux x86_64; rv:47.0) Gecko/20100101 ↵
Firefox/47.0
Accept: text/html,application/xhtml+xml,application/xml;q=0.9,*/*;q=0.8
Accept-Language: en-US,en;q=0.5
Accept-Encoding: gzip, deflate
Connection: keep-alive
```
Cookie: PHPSESSID=64c24d4e35dc753cd085ca574def4131

I've emphasized the session cookie, and you can see that it's easy to identify the session token. In your effort to extract the session token, you won't have to deal with the request header directly. Because ModSecurity parses inbound cookies, you'll be able to retrieve it by name using the REQUEST_COOKIES variable. Session initialization is thus as simple as the following:

```
# Initialize SESSION from PHP session token
SecRule REQUEST_COOKIES:PHPSESSID "!@rx ^$" \
    "id:1000,phase:1,pass,nolog,\
    setsid:%{REQUEST_COOKIES.PHPSESSID},\
    setvar:SESSION.TIMEOUT=172800"
```

It is advisable, however, to verify session tokens before you use them as collection keys. Anything user-supplied should be validated first, because you never know what you'll get. For all you know, an attacker may try to bypass your session defenses by submitting multiple session cookies. Also, if the token is invalid, then it probably won't be recognized by the application, in which case you probably don't have any reason to use it either.

In the following example, we first perform the necessary checks (and block if something suspicious is discovered), then use the value of the session token to initialize the SESSION collection:

```
# Check that we have at most one session token
SecRule &REQUEST_COOKIES:PHPSESSID "@gt 1" \
    "id:1000,phase:1,block,log,msg:'More than one session token'"

# Catch invalid PHP session tokens
SecRule REQUEST_COOKIES:PHPSESSID "!@rx ^[0-9a-z]{32}$" \
    "id:1001,phase:1,block,log,msg:'Invalid session token'"

# Initialize SESSION from PHP session token
SecRule REQUEST_COOKIES:PHPSESSID "@rx ^[0-9a-z]{32}$" \
    "id:1002,phase:1,pass,nolog,\
    setsid:%{REQUEST_COOKIES.PHPSESSID}"

# Set the default timeout value for new records
SecRule SESSION:IS_NEW "@eq 1" \
    "id:1003,phase:1,pass,nolog,\
    setvar:SESSION.TIMEOUT=172800"
```

If your application uses URI-based session tokens, head to the section called "Capturing Data" in Chapter 6, where I give a complete example showing how to use the data capture facility to extract session tokens from URIs.

Blocking Sessions

After the SESSION collection is initialized, blocking a session is a matter of setting a flag (with the correct expiry time) and checking for it on all requests. You have seen this technique earlier in this chapter. I describe the flag method, as well as several variations and other blocking methods, in the section called "Advanced Blocking" in Chapter 9.

In addition to blocking sessions with ModSecurity rules, you should consider communicating with the application so that it too blocks the session or signs the user out. Signing out the user can be as simple as proxying the current request to the sign-out page:

```
SecAction "id:2000,phase:2,proxy:/sign-out.php,log,msg:'Logging out current user'"
```

An alternative to using the proxy action is to write a Lua script that can then communicate with an external system to achieve a similar effect. Some information on this approach is available in the section called "External Blocking" in Chapter 9.

If you couple the signing out with a block on the user account (described in the section called "Restricting Session Lifetime"), a potentially rogue user can be banned from the application until an investigation can be carried out.

Forcing Session Regeneration

Blocking sessions might work well for security, but it isn't very user-friendly. If you use session blocking alone, you may leave your users confused, because they won't be able to continue to use the application and won't know how to obtain a new session (i.e., close all browser windows and restart the application). The solution to that problem is to generate a new session for the user. There are two ways to achieve session regeneration, and I'll demonstrate both here.

Both approaches use header manipulation, which means that you'll need to use ModSecurity in tandem with mod_headers. (At this point, you should probably go read the section called "Integration with Other Apache Modules" in Chapter 9 before proceeding; there, I explain how to get ModSecurity to collaborate with other Apache modules.)

The following code contains two mod_headers rules, each activated by setting an environment variable:

```
# Neutralize the cookies containing disabled session IDs
RequestHeader edit Cookie "(?i)^(PHPSESSID)=(.+)$" "DISABLED_$1=$2" \
    env=DISABLE_INBOUND_SESSION
```

```
# Instruct browser to delete session cookie
Header always set Set-Cookie "PHPSESSID=;expires=Fri, 31-Dec-1999 00:00:00 GMT" \
    env=DISABLE_OUTBOUND_SESSION
```

The first rule is activated by the DISABLE_INBOUND_SESSION environment variable, after which it renames inbound session cookies. When a session cookie is renamed, it's no longer a session cookie, but some cookie the value of which will be ignored. As a result, the application will likely generate a brand-new session cookie.

The second rule is activated by the DISABLE_OUTBOUND_SESSION environment variable and sends a command to the user's browser to delete the session cookie (by using the same name as the session cookie, with an expiry time in the past).

To maximize both security and usability, use both mechanisms in your rules: delete the session cookie of a session you're deciding to block (by executing setenv:DISABLE_OUTBOUND_SESSION in any phase except phase 5), and suppress inbound session cookies of the sessions that have previously been blocked (by executing setenv:DISABLE_INBOUND_SESSION in phase 1 or in phase 2).

Restricting Session Lifetime

Because sessions in today's web applications function as temporary passwords, it's important to cancel them as soon as they're not needed. Two mechanisms are typically used to do so:

Inactivity timeout

> When a session isn't used for a period of time, it's reasonable to assume that it has been abandoned. Allowing such sessions to remain active only increases the danger of them being reused by someone other than the original user.

Session duration timeout

> You should also put an absolute limit on session duration. A very long session life span is unusual and may be an indication of automated activity or of a bad guy trying to extract as much information as possible from a hijacked session.

Here's what we need to do to implement the two limits:

1. Record the last time a session was used. As you may recall from earlier sections, whenever a collection record is persisted, its LAST_UPDATE_TIME variable is updated. We need that value. Therefore, to force session records to be persisted, we'll use the same approach as we used with the IP collection: increment an arbitrary variable on every request.

2. Now that we have access to LAST_UPDATE_TIME, we can check it on every request to ensure that it hasn't been too long since the previous request.

3. All collections have the `CREATE_TIME` variable, which we'll use to enforce maximum session duration.

We'll use the following Lua rule (placed in the `check_session.lua` file) to check those two conditions:

```lua
function main()
    -- Retrieve session key
    local key = m.getvar("SESSION.KEY");

    -- If there's no key there's no session,
    -- so return without a match.
    if (key == nil) then
        return nil;
    end


    -- Retrieve CREATE_TIME
    local createTime = m.getvar("SESSION.CREATE_TIME");

    -- If the session was created more than 8
    -- hours ago, trigger a match
    if (os.time() - createTime > 28800) then
        -- Match
        return "Session older than 8 hours: " .. key;
    end


    -- Retrieve LAST_UPDATE_TIME
    local lastUpdateTime = m.getvar("SESSION.LAST_UPDATE_TIME");

    -- Check for lastUpdateTime (new sessions do not have this value)
    if (not lastUpdateTime) then
        return nil;
    end
    -- Check for a period of inactivity
    if (os.time() - lastUpdateTime > 600) then
        -- Match
        return "Session inactive for more than 10 minutes ("
            .. (os.time() - lastUpdateTime) .. "s):" .. key;
    end


    -- No match
    return nil;
end
```

Because this particular feature is more complex than your average rule, I'm going to put all the required rules together in the following self-contained example, which combines everything we've discussed about session initialization, collection timeouts, session inactivity detection (the Lua rule), session blocking, and header manipulation:

```
# Check that we have at most one session token
SecRule &REQUEST_COOKIES:PHPSESSID "@gt 1" \
    "id:1000,phase:1,block,log,msg:'More than one session token'"

# Catch invalid PHP session tokens
SecRule REQUEST_COOKIES:PHPSESSID "!@rx ^[0-9a-z]{32}$" \
    "id:1001,phase:1,block,log,msg:'Invalid session token'"

# Initialize SESSION from PHP session token
SecRule REQUEST_COOKIES:PHPSESSID "@rx ^[0-9a-z]{32}$" \
    "id:1002,phase:1,pass,nolog,\
    setsid:%{REQUEST_COOKIES.PHPSESSID}"

# Set the default timeout value for new SESSION records
SecRule SESSION:IS_NEW "@eq 1" \
    "id:1003,phase:1,pass,nolog,\
    setvar:SESSION.TIMEOUT=172800"

# Check for expired session
SecRule SESSION:expired "@eq 1" \
    "id:1004,phase:1,redirect:/session-timeout.html,log,\
    setenv:DISABLE_INBOUND_SESSION,\
    setenv:DISABLE_OUTBOUND_SESSION"

# Check session inactivity and duration
SecRuleScript check_session.lua \
    "id:1005,phase:1,redirect:/session-timeout.html,log,\
    setenv:DISABLE_INBOUND_SESSION,\
    setenv:DISABLE_OUTBOUND_SESSION,\
    setvar:SESSION.expired"

# Increment the session counter
SecRule REQUEST_FILENAME "!@rx \.(jpg|png|gif|js|css|ico)$" \
    id:1006,phase:1,pass,nolog,setvar:SESSION.counter=+1

# Neutralize cookies containing disabled session IDs
RequestHeader edit Cookie "(?i)^(PHPSESSID)=(.+)$" "DISABLED_$1=$2" \
    env=DISABLE_INBOUND_SESSION

# Instruct browser to delete the session cookie
Header always set Set-Cookie "PHPSESSID=;expires=Fri, 31-Dec-1999 00:00:00 GMT" \
    env=DISABLE_OUTBOUND_SESSION
```

Detecting Session Hijacking

Session hijacking is a potentially devastating attack, often executed as the next step after a successful XSS attack. Once the attacker obtains a session token, he or she can assume the identity of the original user. Although it isn't possible to detect and prevent session hijacking 100 percent reliably, a few defenses can prove to be highly effective. Before you resort to stateful session monitoring as a measure against session hijacking, however, you should verify that you've done everything you can to secure the session cookies; if you make them safe from compromise, then session hijacking isn't possible. (I'll discuss the necessary session cookie rewriting in the section called "Integration with Other Apache Modules" in Chapter 9.)

Our session hijacking detection measures are going to focus on two pieces of information:

Session IP address

Sessions aren't attached to IP addresses; anyone with knowledge of the session token is allowed to participate in a session. That said, the IP address to which the session was initially assigned (on the first request) will in many situations remain the same throughout a session. For example, a user accessing an application from his or her workstation attached to the internal network isn't likely to change his or her IP address. That's probably the best-case scenario.

When it comes to Internet users and roaming users, a change of IP address is possible, and you can never be quite sure whether a hijacking is taking place. People using their smartphones seamlessly switch from their mobile connections to Wi-Fi networks, and with every switch there's an IP address change. However, it's rare to roam from one country into another, so the IP address may change, but the GeoIP Country usually remains the same.

Also note that it's possible for the attacker and the victim to have the same IP address as far as you're concerned. That could happen, for example, if they're behind the same proxy or a network address translation (NAT) system.

Ultimately, the value of this detection mechanism will depend on your user base. My advice is to try the mechanism out as a warning system initially and see if it produces false positives.

Session user-agent

Although it's possible as noted that the session IP address will change, it's far less likely that the user agent identification will. If you start a session in one browser, it's unlikely that you'll finish it in another—unless you hijack someone's session, that is. Research carried out by the Electronic Frontier Foundation (EFF) indicated that one in about 1,500 users have the same User-Agent request field.[1] Checking that the user

---

[1] Tracking by user agent [fsty.uk/m24] (EFF, retrieved 30 December 2016)

agent identification remains the same across all session requests is thus a decent detection mechanism. It's also a mechanism that can be easily defeated by a determined attacker who knows that it exists and who can somehow uncover the victim's own identification string (with a bit of social engineering, for example).

Putting that lengthy discussion aside, here's how to store the original IP address, geographic information, and User-Agent values into a previously established session collection and check them on subsequent requests:

```
# Initialize GeoIP database and look up IP address
SecGeoLookupDB /usr/local/modsecurity/var/GeoIP.dat
SecRule REMOTE_ADDR "@geoLookup" "id:1000,phase:1,nolog,pass"

# Generate a readable hash out of the User-Agent
# request header and store it in TX.uahash
SecRule REQUEST_HEADERS:User-Agent "@unconditionalMatch" \
    "id:1001,phase:1,pass,t:none,t:sha1,t:hexEncode,nolog,\
    setvar:TX.uahash=%{MATCHED_VAR}"

# Initialize SESSION, storing a hash of the User-Agent
# value, as well as the originating IP address.
SecRule SESSION:IS_NEW "@eq 1" \
    "id:1002,phase:1,pass,nolog,\
    setvar:SESSION.uahash=%{TX.uahash},\
    setvar:SESSION.ip=%{REMOTE_ADDR},\
    setvar:SESSION.country=%{GEO.COUNTRY_CODE},\
    skipAfter:END_SESSION_CHECK"

SecRule SESSION:country "!@streq %{GEO.COUNTRY_CODE}" \
    "id:1003,phase:1,pass,\
    msg:'Possible session hijacking: Expected country code \
%{SESSION.country} but got %{GEO.COUNTRY_CODE}'"

SecRule SESSION:ip "!@streq %{REMOTE_ADDR}" \
    "id:1004,phase:1,pass,\
    msg:'Possible session hijacking: Expected session IP address \
%{SESSION.ip} but got %{REMOTE_ADDR}'"

SecRule SESSION:uahash "!@streq %{TX.uahash}" \
    "id:1005,phase:1,pass,\
    msg:'Possible session hijacking: Expected session User-Agent hash \
%{SESSION.uahash} but got %{TX.uahash}'"

SecMarker END_SESSION_CHECK
```

There's nothing in these rules that you haven't already seen; they use a combination of the techniques already covered in this chapter.

User Management

When it comes to persistent state, user management is the final piece of the puzzle. By following individual users, you come as close as possible to using the same data model applications do. We've already used the USER collection in this chapter to keep track of authentication attempts. Now, we're going to see if it's possible to detect users as they sign in and out. (Of course it is!) If we manage to detect those two events, we might be able to associate each session with a user account and use that information to initialize the USER collection.

Keep in mind that tracking users in ModSecurity isn't going to be an exact science. You have to work with the information you have available, which means that you're going to have to rely on many assumptions—some of which may not be true. That will be just fine, so long as you use the user management facilities with that unreliability in mind.

Detecting User Sign-In

The work we'll need to perform to detect a sign-in event is just the opposite of what we did to detect brute force attacks against authentication. I'll base the examples in this section on the assumption that we're dealing with an application for which the sign-in form is located at /login.php and that the application redirects back to the home page (/index.php) when authentication is successful. If you recall, in the case of failed authentication, the redirection was back to the same /login.php page.

```
# Initialize session based on the session ID in the request. We
# skip this step when authentication is taking place because then
# it's possible to have two sessions on a single HTTP transaction,
# and ModSecurity doesn't support that.
SecRule REQUEST_FILENAME "!@streq /login.php" \
    "id:1000,phase:1,pass,nolog,chain"
    SecRule REQUEST_COOKIES:PHPSESSID "@rx ^([0-9a-z]{32})$" \
        "setsid:%{REQUEST_COOKIES.PHPSESSID}"


<Location /login.php>
    # First try to find a new session cookie in the response headers. We
    # do this because some applications set a new session ID after
    # authentication (a best practice).
    SecRule RESPONSE_HEADERS:Set-Cookie "@rx PHPSESSID=([^;]+)" \
        "id:9001,phase:5,pass,nolog,capture,setvar:TX.SESSIONID=%{TX.1}"


    # If that fails, accept the session cookie from the request.
    SecRule &TX:SESSIONID "@eq 0" \
        id:9002,phase:5,pass,nolog,chain
        SecRule REQUEST_COOKIES:PHPSESSID "@rx ^([0-9a-z]{32})$" \
            capture,setvar:TX.SESSIONID=%{TX.1}
```

```
                # In case of successful authentication, create a new session
                # and associate the authenticated username with it.
                SecRule REQUEST_METHOD "@streq POST" \
                    "id:9000,phase:5,pass,log,\
                    msg:'Initializing a new session after successful login',\
                    logdata:%{TX.SESSIONID},chain"
                    SecRule RESPONSE_HEADERS:Location "@endsWith /index.php" chain
                        SecRule &TX:SESSIONID "!@eq 0" \
                            "setsid:%{TX.SESSIONID},\
                            setvar:SESSION.user=%{ARGS.username},\
                            setvar:SESSION.TIMEOUT=2592000"
        </Location>
```

The main rule in the example is rule 9000, which runs in the last processing phase to monitor for successful authentication. That's relatively straightforward: we watch for POST requests (for the sign-in URL only, via the `<Location>` tags) and trigger on the redirection that happens only when authentication is successful. When everything is aligned, we initialize a new session and associate the just-authenticated username with it.

Rules 9001 and 9002 are necessary to handle the change of session ID after authentication, which is a best practice designed to counter session fixation.[2] In rule 9001, we look for a new session ID; if there isn't one, then in rule 9002 we fall back to the session ID supplied in the request.

Finally, rule 1000 is necessary to work around ModSecurity's inability to reinitialize collections. Normally, we always initialize a session as early as possible with the session ID from the request. However, if we do that here and the application sends a new session ID after authentication, we won't be able to do what we need to. Thus, for the authentication URL only, we suspend session creation until we're sure we have the correct session ID.

> ### Warning
>
> Look at the previous example carefully and try to answer what will happen if the sign-in function receives two (different) username parameters. Do you think it's possible for the application to choose one of those parameters while the rules choose the other? If that happens, the rules may end up associating the session with the wrong user account. A best practice is to use a positive security model to verify every aspect of the entire sign-in operation, as discussed in the section called "Virtual Patching" in Chapter 9.

---

[2] *Session fixation attacks* occur when attackers first create a new application session then trick victims (usually via social engineering) to reuse the session ID. After authentication, attackers can hijack user sessions because they already know their session IDs.

Detecting User Sign-Out

Detecting the sign-out function is much easier, because the action is rarely conditional. In the following example, assume an application in which it's sufficient to visit the /signout.php page in order to sign out of the application:

```
<Location /signout.php>
    # Disassociate user from session
    SecAction id:9000,phase:5,pass,nolog,setvar:!SESSION.KEY
</Location>
```

When we're on the sign-out page, we simply remove the session from our collection and trust the application to remove the corresponding session cookie.

Summary

Now that you've worked through this persistence chapter, I hope that you understand why I was so excited about this aspect of ModSecurity. The persistent storage facility is the feature that quite literally adds a completely new dimension to ModSecurity: that of time. With the ability to track external parties over time and correlate events, you gain a far more useful tool in ModSecurity.

In the next chapter, aptly named *Practical Rule Writing*, we'll tie together everything you've learned so far by discussing a number of practical issues that you'll encounter in your every-day life with ModSecurity.

9 Practical Rule Writing

This chapter is dedicated to the many practical aspects and requirements of rule writing. We go beyond looking at features in isolation to discuss what we can achieve when multiple features are used together. This is the chapter in which, finally, everything comes together.

Whitelisting

Rulesets are usually written to single out unusual requests, but it turns out that most deployments actually require some "unusual" requests to operate properly. The more complex the deployment, the more likely it is that you'll need to use whitelisting. In most cases, there will be at least one crude monitoring script that's practically indistinguishable from some other Perl script that will be attacking you. In others, you might have outsourced security testing to a third party, and you won't want your rules to interfere with their work. Finally, even if none of that applies, you won't be able to avoid the unexpected: Apache sending requests to itself.

In all those cases, you need a mechanism that allows certain requests to bypass your ruleset completely. We call this *whitelisting*. In a general sense, we use this term when we talk about rules that actively promote (allow) types of requests we want. For example, later in this chapter, we'll use the term *whitelisting* to refer to the practice of writing rules that allow only known to be good parameters for certain scripts. Anything not conforming to what's good will be forbidden.

Whitelisting Theory

You have to be very careful when writing whitelisting rules, because each addition to your ruleset creates a bond of trust. If you make a mistake, you can end up with a hole in your ruleset that can be used by your adversaries. You should ask yourself three questions:

How do I know the request is from the person or device I want to whitelist?
In the ideal case, the remote client will authenticate itself in some way. For example, allowing requests that arrive from known, good IP addresses is an easy and secure

solution. This is something you can easily do with ModSecurity, and even with Apache itself. Other possibilities include using client certificates and basic authentication credentials.

Is there anything specific about the requests I want to whitelist?

You may have established that requests are coming from a source you can reasonably trust, but it's still a good idea to narrow down the attack vector as much as possible. You should think about your rules as walls that defend you from attackers; when you write rule exclusions, you create holes in these walls. Therefore, it's a best practice to keep the hole as small as possible. Observe, over time, the requests you want to whitelist. Is there a recurring pattern? For example, most monitoring requests are identical. In other cases, the requests will be restricted to a part of your web site and will have predictable parameters.

What changes do I want to make to the default configuration?

This last question pertains to the action you want to take after you decide definitely that you want to go through with whitelisting. The easiest thing to do is simply use the `allow` action to let the remote party continue unconditionally, but are you really comfortable with giving that party unrestricted access? A better solution might to be to switch the rule engine to detection mode. You won't regret it, so long as you get false positives only occasionally.

In the next section, I'll discuss the placement of whitelisting rules, followed by several simple examples, then finish with the rule that you'll need to silence the Apache web server itself.

Whitelisting Mechanics

Whitelisting rules need to be executed before all your other detection rules, which means that they should always follow your configuration and system rules. It's a good idea to have a special file for this category of rules alone to make them easy to find with a simple glance at the list of your configuration files.

Most whitelisting rules look at the remote address first, so let's do that now. Let's assume that there are two trusted employees to whom you want to give unrestricted access to your web site. The IP addresses of their workstations are 192.168.1.1 and 192.168.15.7. The corresponding whitelisting rule will be as follows:

```
SecRule REMOTE_ADDR "@ipMatch 192.168.1.1,192.168.15.7" \
    id:1000,phase:1,allow,t:none,nolog
```

As previously discussed, you generally should avoid using the `allow` action; a better idea instead is to switch the rule engine to detection-only mode:

```
SecRule REMOTE_ADDR "@ipMatch 192.168.1.1,192.168.15.7" \
    id:1000,phase:1,pass,t:none,nolog,ctl:ruleEngine=DetectionOnly
```

In this rule, I replaced allow with pass, and added an invocation of the ctl action with an instruction to change the operating mode of the rule engine.

> **Note**
>
> If you need to list many different IP addresses, the alternative operator @ipMatchFromFile allows you to list IP addresses in a separate file. Both operators, @ipMatch and @ipMatchFromFile, support CIDR notation.

Granular Whitelisting

Although every invocation of the allow action interrupts the phase in which it runs, you can choose whether and how other phases in the same transaction are affected. The allow action has an optional parameter, and the following rules apply:

Interrupt current phase and skip all other inspection phases

If you invoke allow without a parameter, then regardless of the current phase, all inspection phases will be skipped.

Interrupt current phase only

When allow is invoked with phase as a parameter (allow:phase), it restricts the effect of this action to the current phase.

Interrupt current phase and any remaining request phase

When allow is invoked in phase 1 with request as a parameter (allow:request), the processing of phase 1 will be interrupted and phase 2 will be skipped completely. The processing will continue with the first response phase (phase 3).

Full Whitelisting Example

Earlier, I mentioned how Apache talks to itself. Because it's a situation that every ModSecurity administrator will have to deal with, I'll use it as an example to demonstrate how to implement whitelisting.

First, let's look at the complete request we need to ignore:

```
::1 - - [26/Oct/2009:16:01:06 +0000] "OPTIONS * HTTP/1.0" 200 - ↵
"-" "Apache (internal dummy connection)"
```

What can we deduce from the example log line? Note the following points:

1. The first thing that you will notice about this request is that it always arrives from the server itself. In the example, the remote address is ::1 (IPv6 localhost). In other cases,

you'll see 127.0.0.1 there. We can use this information to restrict the source of requests that our rule will take into account.

2. The request is always the same and involves the OPTIONS request method. This is even more helpful, because it allows us to write a rule that only matches that specific usage.

3. The user agent identification is the same for all requests.

Using the obtained information, we can write a robust and reasonably safe rule:

```
SecRule REQUEST_LINE "@streq OPTIONS * HTTP/1.0" \
    "id:1000,phase:1,allow,t:none,log,\
    msg:'Allowing wake-up request from Apache itself',\
    chain"
    SecRule REMOTE_ADDR "@ipMatch ::1,127.0.0.1" t:none
```

I used only the first two facts for my rule, because I felt that they allow me to uniquely identify a request and that no more narrowing is needed. Besides, the User-Agent request header is trivial to subvert.

Virtual Patching

In the ideal world, when you identify a flaw in an application, you get the developers to fix the problem. You then get the developers to examine the entire code base for similar problems, fixing other flaws that they discover. In the real world, however, there are many obstacles to fixing problems in this way:

No access to source code

When you're running third-party applications or using third-party libraries, you don't have a choice. You're at the mercy of the vendors to deal with the issues. Many vendors won't have the same sense of urgency; in some cases, months and even years may pass before an issue is fixed.

No legal right to change source code

When you outsource your development, you may have access to the source code, but you may not be able to do anything with it until the contract with the developer expires. At best, you can identify the location of the problem and assist the developer.

Changing source code prohibitively expensive

Let's say there are no legal issues in fixing the problem in an application for which you have the source code. If you're currently using the stock version (e.g., the one that comes with the operating system), to fix a flaw requires an additional packaging and distribution of the new package, and you also need to continue to produce new application versions until the original flaw is fixed upstream.

Lack of expertise to fix flaw

All the source code in the world won't mean a thing if you lack the expertise needed to devise a fix. Employing a random developer won't cut it; you need access to a senior developer with security expertise who already understands the application. Otherwise, you risk the danger of breaking the application and creating a bigger problem. Lack of expertise especially can be a problem especially when the flaw is in a legacy application that's long been forgotten. How on earth are you going to find someone to not only fix the problem but also build a complete development, staging, and deployment environment from scratch?

In the best-case scenario for fixing problems in the source code, the flaw will be in a critical internal application developed by an agile experienced team with security expertise. However, even in that case, there may be issues with timing and with costs:

- Should you disrupt a development cycle halfway?
- How will that affect the quality of the release?
- Will subsequent releases (and features) be affected?
- How will the changes have an impact on the business?
- Can you roll out an update to the application?
- Is the production version a freeze during the critical time of the year?
- Is the key developer out sick or away on a vacation?
- Do you dare make changes without him or her?
- Are there any bigger fires to deal with?

Virtual patching presents a way to deal with a known problem in a web application—almost any application—without actually touching the application itself. Because most web application traffic uses standard data transport protocols, it's relatively easy to reroute information flow and install a policy capable of preventing the exploitation. This technique is also sometimes referred to as *just-in-time patching*, or *dynamic patching*.

The principal advantage of virtual patching is that it's very effective and quick to deploy. Assuming you've laid the foundation for virtual patching in advance, it can take literally minutes to mitigate a problem. Compare that to the days, weeks, and months that it might take to fix the same problem in the source code. In addition, if you neutralize a problem in this way, you relieve pressure on your developers, giving them enough time to fix the problem properly and roll out the fix in the next scheduled software update.

Some application security practitioners are concerned that the use of virtual patching, as effective as it can be, contributes to the culture of not caring about security flaws and leaving them to linger in the source code. That's a legitimate concern, but the culture in an organization ultimately will be exactly what the people in charge want it to be. The truth is that virtual patching is an operational tool, which shouldn't affect how problems are treated on the development level.

Vulnerability Versus Exploit Patching

There are two ways in which virtual patches can be written: vulnerability-oriented and exploit-oriented. *Vulnerability-oriented* virtual patches are designed to address the core issue; you work to understand the problem and write a policy that essentially does the work that the vulnerable application should have done—typically, adding the required input validation. This approach is also known as the *positive security model* or *whitelisting*. You make no attempts to determine whether something is unsafe. Instead, you just figure out what *is* safe (which is much easier), and you then write the policy to implement just that.

Exploit-oriented patches focus on the known exploits instead. No attempts are made to understand the root cause; the focus is on trying to catch the attacks instead. This approach is also known as the *negative security model* or *blacklisting*. Exploit-oriented patches are not as effective as vulnerability-oriented patches, because they will fail if someone reworks an existing exploit to be different yet remain effective. Similarly, such defense measures will fail if someone discovers another way to exploit the underlying problem.

I prefer to use the term *virtual patching* only for policies that employ the whitelisting approach.

Failings of Exploit Detection

Let's assume we're dealing with a web application that's vulnerable to SQL injection. We'll say that the vulnerable page has a parameter called `articleid`, which is supposed to be just an integer, but that no checks are made on what the supplied value actually contains. Normally, you'd use the page with a URL such as this one:

```
http://www.example.com/showArticle.jsp?articleid=4
```

However, there's nothing preventing you from adding a bit of SQL to the parameter and getting it to execute in the site's database:

```
http://www.example.com/showArticle.jsp?articleid=4;↵
drop%20table%20articles
```

If you were to circulate this "exploit," someone might write a rule that focuses on detecting the SQL keywords used in it:

```
SecRule ARGS:articleid "@rx (drop|table)" \
    id:2000,phase:2,block,t:none,t:lowercase,t:compressWhitespace,log
```

This rule creates an imperfect net that catches some attacks, but not necessarily all of them. Someone with enough time on his hands could perform many tests and work methodically to reverse-engineer your rule by sending varying requests. In the end, he might find a way to bypass the rule. To illustrate this possibility, consider the following rule, which uses evasion and which many databases will accept:

```
http://www.example.com/showArticle.jsp?articleid=4;0x44524F50%200x7461626c65%20arti↵
cles
```

If you want to be safe, write positive security patches, allowing only what you know to be safe. Let's try to do that:

```
# Allow only requests whose "articleid" parameters match the expected format
SecRule ARGS:articleid "!@rx ^[0-9]{1,10}$" \
    "id:2000,phase:2,block,t:none,log"
```

This rule, being vulnerability-based, is a great improvement over the previous attempts. The key difference is that now the attacker can try to use every SQL injection technique available, but she'll fail unless she can make the exploit payload be an integer. The attacker won't be able to do that, and you'll be safe. Or will you?

Impedance Mismatch

When you use the whitelisting approach to virtual patch creation, the attacker should no longer be able to successfully attack the application. What he or she can do, however, is attack the web application firewall—or, in our case, ModSecurity. If you look at the previous rule carefully, you may realize that it depends entirely on the ability to correctly inspect the articleid parameter.

A common attack technique is to use multiple parameters with the same name, with some using a correct value and some containing exploit payloads, and hope that the inspection device will allow the request after seeing one of the correct values. This technique doesn't work against ModSecurity, because when you use the named parameter syntax (e.g., ARGS:articleid), it inspects all parameters with that name.

What if the attacker changes the name of the parameter in some way to make ModSecurity see it as a different name, while the target application sees it as the original name? Strictly speaking, that shouldn't be possible. After all, we have standards that define how parameter names are specified. In reality, however, it's quite easy with some application servers, because they will handle input in nonstandard ways.

PHP, for example, is quite liberal as to how it handles parameter names. It's trying to be helpful, correcting things it thinks are wrong, but it ultimately causes problems from a security perspective. One thing it will do is ignore whitespace at the beginning of parameter names. Take the following request, for example:

```
http://www.example.com/showArticle.jsp?%20articleid=4;drop%20table%20articles
```

You might be surprised to learn that the application would process the request as if you used the parameter articleid without the space as the first character. Meanwhile, ModSecurity will process the parameter exactly as supplied, causing the virtual patch to fail. Back to the drawing board!

Using the negative security mentality, you might want to detect parameters that have spaces in them:

```
SecRule ARGS_NAMES "@rx \s+" \
    "id:2000,phase:2,block,log,msg:'Whitespace in parameter name'"
```

You don't want to only look for the whitespace at the beginning of parameter names, because PHP will also convert whitespace inside parameter names, replacing it with underscores. Anyway, the approach in the previous rule would probably be good enough, assuming you're not running any applications that actually have whitespace in the parameter names. However, you shouldn't rely on that approach, because you don't know all the weird ways in which PHP will change parameter names. A positive security approach would be to define what you consider to be normal—like the following rule, for example, which allows only the characters you would normally expect in a parameter name:

```
SecRule ARGS_NAMES "!@rx ^[-0-9a-zA-Z_.]+$" \
    "id:2000,phase:2,block,log,msg:'Invalid parameter name'"
```

That's an improvement: now, if we accept a parameter name, we'll know exactly what it can be.

Preferred Virtual Patching Approach

The preferred virtual patching approach is to cast a wider net and lock down the entire script that exhibits the vulnerability you're patching. With the previously described vulnerability in mind, consider the following group of rules:

```
<Location /index.php>
    SecDefaultAction phase:2,t:none,log,deny

    # Validate parameter names
    SecRule ARGS_NAMES "!@rx ^(articleid)$" \
        "id:2000,phase:2,msg:'Unknown parameter name: %{MATCHED_VAR_NAME}'"

    # Validate each parameter's cardinality
    SecRule &ARGS:articleid "!@eq 1" \
        "id:2001,phase:2,msg:'Multiple parameters: articleid'"

    # Validate parameter 'articleid'
    SecRule ARGS:articleid "!@rx ^[0-9]{1,10}$" \
```

```
        "id:2002,phase:2,msg:'Invalid parameter: articleid'"
</Location>
```

The preferred virtual patching approach is to use the following methodology:

1. Use the `<Location>` or `<Directory>` (preferred, but only works in embedded mode) configuration containers, or any other sort of URI condition to focus on only a single script or page.

2. Allow only known parameter names.

3. Check that each parameter appears only once (or as many times as needed).

4. Check that the value provided in each parameter matches what is desired.

Although my example demonstrates the concept on a script with only one parameter, the same approach can be used with any number of parameters.

> **Note**
>
> After writing the first edition of this book, Ivan wrote a research paper to highlight in more detail all the possible ways in which web application firewalls can be evaded. This paper is useful not only for its coverage of generic evasion techniques but also because it includes a section geared specifically to ModSecurity users.[1]

Whitelisting Rulesets

Building on the previous virtual patching example, we can take things one step further and evolve the rules into a tight whitelisting ruleset. In this section, we're no longer limiting ourselves to a single URI, and we'll also defend against advanced evasion methods that work against reverse proxies.

It's generally well understood that whitelisting is a very strong defense method. However, though network firewalls do use whitelisting, people don't write their web application firewall rules this way. The main reasons are the perceived amount of work it takes to do it properly and the dynamic nature of applications, which forces you to update the ruleset in sync with application releases. It's hard to get around the latter problem, but the amount of work is usually overestimated.

In fact, you don't need to develop a holistic whitelisting ruleset; a partial whitelist often is a reasonable compromise. Imagine an application exposed on the Internet. Users access it and are immediately taken to a login page. After successful login, they have access to the complex and dynamic application. It would be hard to develop a whitelisting ruleset for the full application, but you can focus your efforts on protecting the most exposed part of the application. Protecting the login page provides a real improvement in terms of security without

---

[1] Protocol-level evasion of web application firewalls [fsty.uk/m25] (Ivan Ristić, 25 July 2012)

too much work, and it's simple compared to the effort it would take to protect the entire application.

Let's write a whitelisting ruleset for such an imaginary login page. It isn't overly complicated, but there are a few things to consider. I'll present the individual parts of the ruleset, which you can then put together and adopt for your server.

Because we're writing a partial whitelist, we have to make sure an attacker can't evade our whitelist rules by manipulating the path somehow. As part of normal processing, the web server (e.g., Apache) always will normalize the request URI. Because we want to be extra sensitive here, we'll take the normalized REQUEST_URI from the web server, transform it with our own normalization routine, and then compare it to the original request URI stored in REQUEST_URI_RAW. If there's a difference between the original submission and the normalized URI, then we might face an evasion attempt, and therefore we'll deny access:

```
# START whitelisting block for URI /login (rule IDs 3000-3499)
SecRule REQUEST_URI "!@streq %{REQUEST_URI_RAW}" \
    "id:3000,phase:2,deny,t:lowercase,t:normalizePathWin,log,msg:'Path evasion ↵
attempt.'"
```

Next, we'll examine the request path. For this example, assume everything related to the login page is stored in the /login path. Also apply the lowercase transformation to the URI; some backends are case-insensitive, and we want to make sure requests attempting to exploit this behavior have to pass our whitelisting ruleset as well. If the request doesn't match the /login path prefix, we skip to the END_WHITELIST_login marker. The following parts of the complete recipe have to be put inside the block created between the skipAfter action and this marker:

```
SecRule REQUEST_URI "!@beginsWith /login" \
    "id:3001,phase:2,pass,t:lowercase,nolog,skipAfter:END_WHITELIST_login"

# ...

SecMarker END_WHITELIST_login
```

The first property of the transactions we're validating is the HTTP method. We'll accept the standard GET, HEAD, and POST methods, as well as the OPTIONS method. OPTIONS requests are issued by various clients automatically to check out the functionality of the server. If you don't allow them, you'll get quite a few unnecessary alarms:

```
# Validate HTTP method
SecRule REQUEST_METHOD "!@pm GET HEAD POST OPTIONS" \
    "id:3010,phase:2,deny,log,msg:'Method %{MATCHED_VAR} not allowed'"
```

Next, we'll inspect the request path in more detail:

```
# Validate request path
SecRule REQUEST_FILENAME "@beginsWith /login/static/css" \
    "id:3100,phase:2,pass,nolog,skipAfter:END_URIBLOCK_WHITELIST_login"
SecRule REQUEST_FILENAME "@beginsWith /login/static/img" \
    "id:3101,phase:2,pass,nolog,skipAfter:END_URIBLOCK_WHITELIST_login"
SecRule REQUEST_FILENAME "@beginsWith /login/static/js" \
    "id:3102,phase:2,pass,nolog,skipAfter:END_URIBLOCK_WHITELIST_login"
SecRule REQUEST_FILENAME \
    "@rx ^/login/(displayLogin|login|logout|)\.do$" \
    "id:3103,phase:2,pass,nolog,skipAfter:END_URIBLOCK_WHITELIST_login"

# If we land here, we are facing an unknown URI,
# which is why we will respond using the 404 status code
SecAction "id:3199,phase:2,deny,status:404,log,\
    msg:'Unknown URI %{REQUEST_URI}'"

SecMarker END_URIBLOCK_WHITELIST_login
```

Our login page supports a series of URIs, and we want to make sure clients can request only these predefined URIs. The whole block is constructed with the help of a series of skipAfter actions. I primarily rely on the @beginsWith operator but employ the standard regular expression check as well. The rules aren't overly strict when it comes to static files; anything within three different folders is permissible. That way, we won't have to update the ruleset if a new image is deployed.

The situation is different with the dynamic URIs. Here, we want to make sure that we're allowing only a predefined list of actions. Note the use of the double anchor in the regular expression and the REQUEST_FILENAME variable. This variable contains the URI without the query string and thus is preferred in this situation, because the query string will be covered in the next rule block. Rule 3199 marks the end of the URI validation block. The previous rules all issued skips across 3199 down to the END_URIBLOCK_WHITELIST_login marker. This means that every request arriving at 3199 has to be a request to an unknown URI, and we can thus deny access in this rule.

Now, it's time to look at the parameters, following the layout of the rules in the example from the previous section—name, cardinality, and value:

```
# Validate parameter names
SecRule ARGS_NAMES "!@rx ^(username|password|sectoken)$" \
    "id:3200,phase:2,deny,log,msg:'Unknown parameter: %{MATCHED_VAR_NAME}'"

# Validate each parameter's cardinality
SecRule &ARGS:username "@gt 1" \
    "id:3300,phase:2,deny,log,msg:'Parameter username submitted multiple times'"
SecRule &ARGS:password "@gt 1" \
    "id:3301,phase:2,deny,log,msg:'Parameter password submitted multiple times'"
```

```
SecRule &ARGS:sectoken "@gt 1" \
    "id:3302,phase:2,deny,log,msg:'Parameter sectoken submitted multiple times'"

# Check individual parameter values
SecRule ARGS:username "!@rx ^[a-zA-Z0-9.@-]{1,32}$" \
    "id:3400,phase:2,deny,log,\
    msg:'Invalid parameter format: %{MATCHED_VAR_NAME} (%{MATCHED_VAR})'"
SecRule ARGS:password "@gt 128" \
    "id:3403,phase:2,deny,log,t:length,\
    msg:'Invalid parameter format: %{MATCHED_VAR_NAME} too long (%{MATCHED_VAR} ↵
bytes)'"
SecRule ARGS:sectoken "!@rx ^[a-zA-Z0-9]{32}$" \
    "id:3401,phase:2,deny,log,\
    msg:'Invalid parameter format: %{MATCHED_VAR_NAME} (%{MATCHED_VAR})'"
```

> **Note**
>
> For simplicity, we're using the ARGS collection to retrieve parameters, which ignores parameter origin. If you prefer to treat GET and POST parameters separately, you can use ARGS_GET and ARGS_POST instead. When dealing with POST parameters, make sure you put the rules in phase 2.

This whitelisting example is fairly elaborate, but it doesn't cover every detail. However, I think it represents a good balance between effort and an increase in security overall.

JSON Requests

JSON support is a fairly recent addition to ModSecurity that arrived with the 2.8.0 release. When the JSON parser is enabled, individual variables embedded in a JSON request body will be converted into ModSecurity variables. To enable the parser, you need to detect JSON payloads in phase 1, just before request body processing begins, which is what the following rule does:

```
SecRule REQUEST_HEADERS:Content-Type "@beginsWith application/json" \
    "id:1000,phase:1,pass,t:lowercase,nolog,ctl:requestBodyProcessor=JSON"
```

Now, as soon as the request body is received, it will be handed over to the JSON processor. The parsing will happen in between phases 1 and 2. At the beginning of phase 2 (request) we can check if the JSON payload was well-formed or if there have been any processing errors. Add the following general rule, if you don't yet have it in your ruleset:

```
SecRule REQBODY_ERROR "!@eq 0" \
    "id:2000,phase:2,deny,log,msg:'%{REQBODY_ERROR_MSG}'"
```

Assuming the payload was well-formed, we can then access the individual parameters. To illustrate how that works, let's consider the following example of a JSON request body taken from JSON RFC 4627:[2]

```
{
    "Image": {
        "Width":  800,
        "Height": 600,
        "Title":  "View from 15th Floor",
        "Thumbnail": {
            "Url":     "http://www.example.com/image/481989943",
            "Height": 125,
            "Width":  "100"
        },
        "IDs": [116, 943, 234, 38793]
    }
}
```

The JSON processor will make this data available within the standard ARGS collection using the keys used in the data. We can access this the same way we would access standard arguments, as shown in the following example:

```
SecRule ARGS:Image.Width            "!@rx ^([0-9]+)$"  "id:2001,phase:2,deny"
SecRule ARGS:Image.Height           "!@rx ^([0-9]+)$"  "id:2002,phase:2,deny"
SecRule ARGS:Image.Thumbnail.Height "!@rx ^([0-9]+)$"  "id:2003,phase:2,deny"
SecRule ARGS:Image.IDs              "!@rx ^([0-9]+)$"  "id:2004,phase:2,deny"
SecRule &ARGS:Image.Height          "@gt 1"            "id:2005,phase:2,deny"
SecRule &ARGS:Image.IDs             "@gt 4"            "id:2006,phase:2,deny"
```

As you can see, accessing the JSON data is straightforward. Writing rules thus is easy, and it's also possible to incorporate this factor into the whitelisting ruleset in the previous section.

> **Note**
>
> Unfortunately, it isn't possible to access the individual items of an array like the IDs array in the example payload. A rule like the one with ID 2004 in the example will always evaluate all items of the array in parallel. It thus will be executed four times for the example payload.

IP Address Reputation and Blacklisting

Only two things are guaranteed for every HTTP request you get: you will have an IP address and a port to work with. Even when everything else is wrong or broken, these two pieces of

---

[2] The application/json Media Type for JSON [fsty.uk/m26] (IETF, retrieved 30 December 2016)

information can be retrieved from the TCP network level. At first, you might think that an IP address isn't worth much, but it's surprising how much you can do with it:

- Using geolocation, you can determine a client's geographic location.

- You can ban an IP address from your site forever.

- You can keep long-term information on an IP address in a local database and use it to influence your policies.

- You can ask a remote fraud-detection service whether it believes the IP address is "bad."

IP Address Blocking

Conceptually, blacklisting is performed in the same way as whitelisting. You keep a list of IP addresses you don't want to do business with, and you refuse requests that arrive from them. There's often a difference in the number of IP addresses that are used. Blacklists often contain hundreds and even thousands of IP addresses, which means that you need to work harder to maintain good performance.

Individual IP addresses and networks are easiest to blacklist with the help of the `@ipMatch` operator. When you need to cover more addresses, you should assemble them into an external file and integrate with the help of the `@ipMatchFromFile` operator or its shortcut alias, `@ipMatchF`:

```
SecRule REMOTE_ADDR "@ipMatchF blacklist.dat" \
    "id:1000,phase:1,block,log,msg:'IP address on blacklist'"
```

The file `blacklist.dat` contains one IP address or network per line. You can use CIDR notation and you can enter comment lines as well, as follows:

```
# Known Zeus botnet command servers
91.121.240.111
195.20.44.0/24
```

If you're concerned about performance, there's a parallel matching alternative for IPv4 addresses. This is faster than the `@ipMatch` family of operators, but because `@pm` wasn't designed for matching IP addresses, you'll need to do some extra work to implement it correctly. The problem is that the `@pm` operator doesn't understand pattern boundaries. If you ask it to match "192.168.1.1", it will match it no matter where in the string pattern it sits, which means that it will match "192.168.1.10" and "192.168.1.100" as well, to list just a couple of the possible false positives.

The extra work I mentioned is needed to create artificial boundaries where they're needed. First, you need to create a new variable to keep the remote IP address, adding something in front of the IP address and something at the end. I'll use a forward slash character:

```
SecAction "id:1000,phase:1,pass,nolog,\
    setvar:TX.REMOTE_ADDR=/%{REMOTE_ADDR}/"
```

The actual blacklisting is just a normal use of the `@pmFromFile` operator, but you use `TX:REMOTE_ADDR` instead of `REMOTE_ADDR`:

```
SecRule TX:REMOTE_ADDR "@pmFromFile blacklist.dat" \
    "id:1000,phase:1,block,log,msg:'IP address on blacklist'"
```

The file `blacklist.dat` contains one IP address per line, with a forward slash character at the beginning and end of every line:

```
/192.168.1.1/
/192.168.1.2/
/192.168.1.3/
```

Because we have the forward slash characters in both places (in the rule and in the file), the matching will work as it should, without the previously described false positives. As a matter of fact, now you can take advantage of the side effect, making the blacklisting of entire segments easier. For example, if you want to match an entire class C address space (256 IP addresses), you could have the following line in the file:

```
/192.168.1.
```

Geolocation

Geolocation is the identification of the geographic location of an HTTP client by means of an IP address. The identification is done by performing a lookup against a database that "knows" where every IP address belongs. The process is not 100 percent accurate and may not work at all for some addresses.

ModSecurity supports geolocation through integration with the free GeoLite Country or GeoLite City databases.[3] To start using this feature, first download the database and put it somewhere on the local filesystem where ModSecurity can get to it. To obtain the geographic location of someone whose IP address you have, you'll need one configuration directive and one rule:

```
# Initialize GeoIP database
SecGeoLookupDb /usr/local/modsecurity/var/GeoIP.dat

# Perform geolocation
SecRule REMOTE_ADDR "@geoLookup" \
    "id:1000,phase:1,pass,t:none,nolog"
```

---

[3] GeoLite legacy downloadable databases [fsty.uk/m27] (MaxMind, retrieved 30 December 2016)

You can afford to perform a lookup on every request, because the database is available locally. It's unlikely that performance will be an issue, even though the lookup is not cached. From this point on, you can use geographic information in your rules. For example, to detect access from outside Great Britain, write the following rule:

```
# Forbid all foreign access
SecRule GEO:COUNTRY_CODE3 "!@streq GBR" \
    "id:1000,phase:1,block,log,msg:'Access from outside Great Britain'"
```

In practice, you'll want to add the geographic information to the list of variables that influence your rules and your policies. Here are a couple of ideas for how to use this information:

Assign a risk score to each country
> When deciding whether a request is an attack or whether to block, you can use the risk score to sway your decision one way or another.

Know where your users are
> Keep track of where your users are. If a user session changes country or if a user "travels" a great distance in a short period of time, that may be an indication that his or her account was compromised.

Implement defense conditions
> The majority of your users may be in one or a few countries, but you normally don't want to restrict access, because some users travel often. However, in extraordinary circumstances (e.g., when you're under attack), you may want to lock down your systems and allow access only from a small number of countries.

Real-Time Block Lists

A *real-time block list* (RBL) is an IP address reputation tool that can tell you whether an IP address or domain name is bad. RBLs are most commonly used to fight email spam, but they can be quite useful for web applications. After all, if you know that there's a spammer behind an IP address, do you really want that spammer in your application? In recent years, we've seen the rise of RBLs designed to work with application security in mind.

Unlike geolocation, RBLs are usually accessed over the network. The upside is that there's usually zero maintenance. The downside is that there can be a significant performance hit, depending on where the servers that power the RBL are located (relative to your own servers). When I recently experimented with an RBL, I discovered that I had introduced additional latency of about 400 ms. Because RBL lookups are performed over the DNS infrastructure, there's limited caching support, which means that not all requests will take the latency hit. If you're planning on using RBLs in production, a best practice is to install a local caching DNS server (e.g., rbldnsd).[4] Because some lists are available for download, with a local DNS server you solve the latency problem.

In ModSecurity, a lookup of an address against an RBL is performed with the @rbl operator:

```
# Only allow the IP addresses cleared by multi.surbl.org
SecRule REMOTE_ADDR "@rbl multi.surbl.org" \
    "id:1000,phase:1,block,log,msg:'IP address denied by multi.surbl.org'"
```

If you get a match, that means that the IP address is listed in the RBL. You don't have to block immediately, but if you don't, you should store the information in a TX variable so that you can refer to it later. I've found the following RBLs to be widely used:

- Spamhaus[5]

- SURBL[6]

- URIBL[7]

- Project Honey Pot[8]

Local Reputation Management

Every time you create a whitelist or a blacklist, you practice local reputation management. Similarly, the various persistent storage techniques used to track IP addresses and application sessions are part of the same concept, including the following:

Static network access control
> Keep track of IP addresses that require special treatment, be it whitelisting or blacklisting. Using @ipMatchFromFile is the standard method, but you may want to look into @pmFromFile for performance reasons, as discussed in the section called "IP Address Blocking" earlier in this chapter. The disadvantage of the static approach is that every change to the list requires a restart of Apache (even when the IP addresses are kept in an external file and used with @ipMatchFromFile or @pmFromFile).

Local (internal) geographic and organizational information
> For sites for which users are strongly clustered (e.g., internal applications used by different departments and company groups), consider creating a local database for geographic and organization lookups. Again, you can write the rules in any way, but use parallel matching if there are too many IP addresses on the list.

---

[4] rbldnsd: Small Daemon for DNSBLs [fsty.uk/m28] (Michael Tokarev, retrieved 30 December 2016)

[5] The Spamhaus Project [fsty.uk/m29] (Spamhaus, retrieved 30 December 2016)

[6] SURBL URI reputation data [fsty.uk/m30] (SURBL, retrieved 30 December 2016)

[7] URIBL - Real-time URI Blacklist [fsty.uk/m31] (URIBL, retrieved 30 December 2016)

[8] Project Honey Pot [fsty.uk/m32] (Unspam Technologies, Inc., retrieved 18 January 2017)

Dynamic network, session, and user access control

Write rules to keep track of the behavior of the individual system elements (IP addresses, sessions, users, and so on, as discussed in Chapter 8, *Persistent Storage*), denying access to those elements that cross thresholds. The rules from this category should ideally require little or no maintenance and use only temporary bans that don't require manual intervention. For example, if you keep an anomaly score per IP address, you want to ensure the score will go up and down as needed.

Integration with Other Apache Modules

One of the biggest advantages of Apache is its modular nature. With modularity and popularity combined, it sometimes seems that there's already a module to fulfill whatever need you can think of it. In most cases, modules are used on their own, but multiple modules can sometimes communicate with one another. ModSecurity generally tries to avoid reimplementing features available in other modules, even for functionality that could come under the security label. Thus, there will be times when you'll need to send or receive instructions to and from other modules.

There are two mechanisms in Apache that allow for communication among modules:

Environment variables

Intermodule communication using environment variables is a common approach to allow modules to exchange information and influence one another. Whenever two modules need to communicate, the receiving module will be configured to watch for the presence (and possibly the value) of a particular environment variable and act on it. Many modules are built with environment variables in mind, so whenever you discover that a particular module supports these variables, you can use them to talk to the module from ModSecurity using the `setenv` action. Because you can use the `ENV` collection in ModSecurity to retrieve the value of a named variable, you can write rules that use the information prepared by other modules.

Optional functions

Optional functions make it possible for a module to export one or more named functions for other modules to consume. This mechanism is intended for module developers to use; chances are that you won't use it very often. ModSecurity builds its extension APIs on top of optional functions. The extension APIs are described in Chapter 14, *Extending the Rule Language*.

The modules you may find yourself integrating with are as follows:

- `mod_deflate`
- `mod_headers`

- mod_log_config
- mod_proxy
- mod_rewrite
- mod_sed
- mod_setenvif

You should be aware that it may not be possible to get any two modules to communicate successfully. If you want to send information from ModSecurity to another module, you must verify that ModSecurity runs first. If you want to consume information in ModSecurity, you need to verify that the other module runs first. In some cases, the order of execution is obvious. For example, if you do something in a request phase in ModSecurity, you'll always be able to consume it in the response phase in mod_headers, and vice versa.

The process becomes tricky when both modules operates on the request or both modules operate on the response. Apache has many extension points, but modules don't document which ones they use. Experimentation is one way to determine whether something is possible; another way is to get your hands dirty, read the source code, and even sometimes change the order in which things happen.

Conditional Logging

Normally, an access log will record every transaction processed by Apache, but sometimes you'll want to record only some transactions. This is called *conditional logging*, and Apache's logging facilities support it, enabling the use of environment variables to decide what to log as follows:

- Log by default, but do not log if an environment variable is set
- Do not log by default, but log if an environment variable is set

The following example creates a custom access log that logs only transactions from a specific IP address:

```
# Detect the condition that requires logging
SecRule REMOTE_ADDR "@ipMatch 192.168.1.1" \
    id:1000,phase:1,pass,nolog,setenv:SPECIAL_ACCESS_LOG

# Create a special access log file, which reacts to
# the SPECIAL_ACCESS_LOG environment variable.
CustomLog logs/special_access.log combined env=SPECIAL_ACCESS_LOG
```

Header Manipulation

In Apache, the mod_headers module is used for header manipulation. Its Header and RequestHeader directives know how to look up an environment variable, as described in the previous section, which means that you can use them to conditionally change request and response headers. As before, the aim is to check for a condition using ModSecurity and set an environment variable if the condition is met.

The following example uses ModSecurity to instruct mod_headers to delete the session cookie from the client:

```
# Simulate a condition that would want us
# to force the user to use another session
SecRule ARGS "@rx attackPattern" \
    "id:2000,phase:2,pass,t:none,log,setenv:DISABLE_OUTBOUND_SESSION"

# Expire session cookies when instructed
Header set Set-Cookie "PHPSESSID=;expires=Fri, 31-Dec-1999 00:00:00 GMT" \
    env=DISABLE_OUTBOUND_SESSION
```

Securing Session Cookies

In web applications that support user authentication, session cookies function as temporary passwords. Users provide their credentials only once and then, assuming they're correct, their sessions are marked as authenticated. From that point on, whoever knows a session's ID can exercise full control over it. Great care needs to be taken when constructing session cookies to ensure that they're secure. In many applications, the security of session cookies can be improved by changing two aspects of how they're constructed:

Use of the HttpOnly flag

> The HttpOnly flag is an Internet Explorer innovation that aims to prevent access to session cookies from JavaScript (which is the most common way to steal a session ID after a successful XSS attack). The idea is that session cookies are needed only by the server-side code and that we lose nothing by forbidding access from JavaScript. With the HttpOnly flag in place, session hijacking becomes significantly more difficult.

Use of the Secure flag

> When a site uses SSL, there is no way for an attacker to gain access to the data being exchanged between the site and the users. When using SSL, marking session cookies as secure is frequently omitted. This omission can lead to a compromise of users' session cookies, giving an attacker complete access to the corresponding sessions.

If you're using Apache, you can fix these problems quickly by using just two mod_headers instructions. The following example improves the security of the session cookies used by PHP:

```
# Add missing HttpOnly flag
Header edit Set-Cookie "(?i)^(PHPSESSID=(?:(?!httponly).)+)$" "$1; HttpOnly"
```

Chapter 9: Practical Rule Writing

```
# Add missing Secure flag
Header edit Set-Cookie "(?i)^(PHPSESSID=(?:(?!secure).)+)$" "$1; Secure"
```

Here, we look at the Set-Cookie header, which is used to create new cookies, and look for session cookies that don't have the desired flags set. If such incorrectly set cookies are found, we modify the headers to append the missing flags. The example uses several rarely used but highly useful features:

- The regular expression patterns both begin with (?i), which ensures that matching is case-insensitive.

- In the second part, there is a *negative lookahead assertion*, causing the entire pattern to match only if the bits in the assertion don't appear anywhere in the header.

- The fourth parameter, which contains the value that will replace an existing Set-Cookie value, makes use of backreferences ($1), which are replaced by the existing header value. Finally, after a semicolon, we append the appropriate missing flag (HttpOnly or Secure).

It's interesting to see how much information can be contained in a single line of text, isn't it?

Advanced Blocking

Chapter 8, *Persistent Storage*, introduced many advanced blocking techniques, but that was only half of the story. This section is the second half, discussing a few practical details and introducing the concept that blocking doesn't need to be a purely black and white affair. In fact, as you'll soon see, the wealth of facilities provided in ModSecurity allows you to do what you want when and how you want.

Immediate Blocking

When we talk about blocking, we tend to have in mind the straightforward approach, in which you detect a problem and block immediately, as follows:

```
SecRule ARGS "@rx attack" \
    "id:2000,phase:2,deny,status:403,log,msg:'Attack detected'"
```

When you use the deny action, which is the primary blocking mechanism, ModSecurity will instruct Apache to cut short transaction processing and respond with an HTTP status code of your choice. By default, the status code 403 (Forbidden) is used, but you can specify any other status code using the status action. Responding with the 403 status code is probably the best choice if you don't have a desire to hide your actions from a potential attacker.

Having said that, there's a case to be made for laying low and keeping the attacker guessing. I often use the 500 status code (Internal Server Error), because that's how a malfunctioning site would respond. On the other hand, if you have a false positive with a 500, you create an impression in your user base that your web site is crashing.

> **Note**
>
> When working with whitelisting rulesets, I sometimes respond with the 404 status code to requests for forbidden URIs. That's technically not correct, but it leaves an attacker in the dark about the existence of a resource I want to protect.

To some errors, you can respond with a meaningful status code, such as 405 (Method Not Allowed) and 501 (Not Implemented). Responding with an inappropriate status code (e.g., blocking with 504 or 501) is not recommended, because it may confuse many HTTP clients and also makes it easy for others to fingerprint your rules.

Not all phases are created equal when it comes to blocking. You can block reliably from some but not from others. The full details are presented in Table 9.1.

Table 9.1. Phase blocking suitability

Phase	Blocking notes
REQUEST_HEADERS (1)	Request and response always possible.
REQUEST_BODY (2)	Request and response always possible.
RESPONSE_HEADERS (3)	Response blocking always possible. Request already processed.
RESPONSE_BODY (4)	Response blocking possible, but only when response buffering is enabled. Request already processed. Response headers might have been sent.
LOGGING (5)	Never possible. Request already processed. Response already sent.

Keeping Detection and Blocking Separate

Although ModSecurity rules have the ability to be very specific about blocking, specifying whether to block and how to block, I take the view that those decisions are none of the rules' business. The rules should focus on detecting issues and raising flags and generally leave it to the system administrator to decide what to do. There's a facility in ModSecurity that enables the rule writers to ensure just that—the block action.

When a rule uses the block action, it essentially gives the system a hint that it believes blocking should take place, but the administrator is free to specify what really happens. In the following example, the rules rely on the blocking policy specified at the beginning of the block:

```
# Define how blocking takes place
SecDefaultAction phase:2,log,deny,status:403

# Detect attacks
```

```
SecRule ARGS "@rx attack1" id:2000,phase:2,block
SecRule ARGS "@rx attack2" id:2001,phase:2,block
```

The advantage of this approach is that there is now only one location in which you change the blocking policy. You don't have to make extensive changes in the rules. More important-ly, the blocking policy defined in this way will work with third-party rulesets (but only as-suming they were correctly implemented, avoiding the use of any specific blocking instruc-tions):

```
# Define how blocking takes place
SecDefaultAction log,deny,status:403

# Include Acme Rule Set
Include conf/acme/*.conf
```

It's even possible to avoid blocking, if the default action list uses pass:

```
# No blocking by default
SecDefaultAction id:2000,phase:2,pass,log
```

User-Friendly Blocking

Whenever you use blocking, you need to be aware that your rules will probably produce false positives. These false alerts will likely catch a few innocent users over time. The securi-ty of your system may be your primary concern (otherwise, you wouldn't be blocking, right?), but the innocent users that get caught as collateral damage won't be very happy. In fact, the experience is likely to frustrate them and lose you money.

To lessen users' frustration, you need to set up a user-friendly response page where you ex-plain to users why they were blocked. Depending on the nature of the block, you may even be able to give them some practical advice (e.g., "try again in a few minutes").

A simple blocking response page can be set up by using redirection as a blocking method:

```
# Respond to attacks with a user-friendly response
SecRule ARGS "@rx attack" \
    id:2000,phase:2,redirect:https://%{REQUEST_HEADERS.Host}/security-error.shtml
```

A disadvantage of this approach is that the action of redirection makes users move away from the original transaction that may have caused a problem. If they contact support, you'll only have their account name to work with and not much else. In real life, you'll want to have a way to connect your support tickets to the actual problems you can find in the logs. We can use the UNIQUE_ID variable for this purpose. In the following example, we prop-agate the unique transaction ID to the response page:

```
SecRule ARGS "@rx attack" \
    "id:2000,phase:2,\
```

```
    redirect:https://%{REQUEST_HEADERS.Host}/security-error.shtml?↵
uniqueid=%{UNIQUE_ID}"
```

The client will then follow the redirect to the security error page and provide the unique ID of the request behind the redirect as a query string parameter. Depending on your environment, there are various options to display a query string parameter back to the client. The following example is particularly lean; it uses Apache's mod_include, which can be installed on a reverse proxy without much overhead. Here's the Apache configuration to make this work:

```
LoadModule include_module modules/mod_include.so
# ...

AddType text/html .shtml
AddOutputFilter INCLUDES .shtml
# ...

<Location />
    Options IncludesNoExec
    # ...
</Location>
# ...

SecRule ARGS:uniqueid "!@rx ^[a-zA-Z0-9@-]{24}$" "id:1000,phase:1,deny"
SecRule ARGS:uniqueid "@unconditionalMatch" \
    "id:1001,phase:1,pass,nolog,setenv:UNIQUEID=%{MATCHED_VAR}"
```

The mod_include module requires a few options to configure correctly. First, we assign the filename suffix .shtml to the module, then we enable the module using the IncludesNoExec option. We follow up with a ModSecurity whitelisting rule that validates the uniqueid parameter. Because we intend to display the contents of this variable back to the user, we have to be certain that it doesn't contain a XSS attack. Our rule guarantees this by allowing only a set of known, safe characters that Apache normally uses. Then, we put the query string variable into an environment variable named UNIQUEID, which will subsequently be displayed by the Include module.

Here's the security error page we're displaying:

```
<html>
<head>
<title>Security Error</title>
<meta http-equiv="Content-Type" content="text/html;charset=utf-8" />
</head>

<body>
<h1>Security Error</h1>
```

```
<pre>
Your request has been blocked for security reasons. Please try again
in a few minutes. Should the problem persist and you need to call
support, please write down the following problem information:

    <!--#echo var="UNIQUEID" -->

We apologize for any inconvenience.
</pre>

<!--
This comment is here to increase the page size and prevent Internet
Explorer from masking the message. More information is available at
the following address:

    http://support.microsoft.com/default.aspx?scid=kb;en-us;Q294807
-->

</body>
</html>
```

External Blocking

In some cases, such as when you're under a denial of service attack, friendly blocking won't be a priority—but efficient blocking will. While discussing the defense against DoS attacks in Chapter 8, *Persistent Storage*, I mentioned that defending against this type of attack on the web server level isn't the most efficient approach. If you move your blocking (of some attack types) to the network level, you can simply block all traffic from the offending IP address, taking the load off your web server.

ModSecurity can't perform network-level blocking, but there are several ways in which you can pass the required information to an external system that can, including the following:

External scripts

> By using the exec action on a rule match, you can invoke a system program that can initiate external blocking. The external script will have access to the offending IP address through the REMOTE_ADDR environment variable.

Lua scripts

> Using Lua along with the Curl bindings (the lua-curl package on my Debian server), you can perform an HTTP request, passing on the offending IP address to some remote system. From Lua, you have full access to transaction data, so you can send anything you need.

Honeypot Diversion

If you have a lot of extra time on your hands, an interesting option is to block without the attacker being aware of it happening. You can implement this type of blocking by using the proxy action to redirect an attacker's requests to a separate system. Such a system is usually called a *honeypot*. The idea behind honeypots is that you want to be able to observe attackers' actions for as long as possible, because each additional request may tell you more about the problems you have in your system. Honeypots have the potential to unearth information your rules never could.

Honeypot diversion isn't practical implemented on a per-transaction level. Your honeypot system may see only some transactions, and the transactions that happen after an attack will again go to the main production system, which defies the purpose of the honeypot. However, activating your honeypot in a persistent manner can work reasonably well. Working on a per-session or per-user basis is a good choice; a per-IP-address honeypot could catch many innocent users.

Delayed Blocking

Immediate blocking is the easiest approach to use, but it prevents the remaining phase rules from running. You've blocked the transaction, but the messages associated with it may not tell you the whole story. For example, your block could have been for a generic problem, but a specific attack could be hiding in the request data somewhere. In my experience, rulesets tend to order their rules from generic to more specific, and that adds to the problem of information loss.

Delayed blocking, in which you wait until the end of each phase to decide whether to block, solves the information loss problem. With it, all rules in a phase run, which means that you get all the messages you can in the audit log.

To implement delayed blocking, use one transaction variable (e.g., TX.block) as an indicator of whether blocking is needed. In your rules, you no longer block, but set the indicator instead. Then, you add a rule to check the indicator at the end of each phase. The following example demonstrates the concept:

```
# Detect attack X
SecRule ARGS "@rx attackX" \
    "id:2000,phase:2,pass,msg:'Detected attack X',\
    setvar:TX.block"

# Detect attack Y
SecRule ARGS "@rx attackY" \
    "id:2001,phase:2,pass,msg:'Detected attack Y',\
    setvar:TX.block"
```

```
# Delayed blocking
SecRule TX:block "@eq 1" \
    "id:2002,phase:2,deny,log,msg:'Phase block due to an earlier match'\
    setvar:!TX.block"
```

In addition to blocking, the last rule unsets the blocking indicator, which prevents it from "leaking" into subsequent phases when the engine is running in detection-only mode.

Score-Based Blocking

Score-based blocking is a variation on the delayed-blocking approach. Instead of using an indicator, you use a score and decide whether to block depending on the resulting phase score—for example:

```
# Detect attack X
SecRule ARGS "@rx attackX" \
    "id:2000,phase:2,pass,msg:'Detected attack X',\
    setvar:TX.score=+1"

# Detect attack Y
SecRule ARGS "@rx attackY" \
    "id:2001,phase:2,pass,msg:'Detected attack Y',\
    setvar:TX.score=+5"

# Delayed blocking
SecRule TX:score "@gt 5" \
    "id:2002,phase:2,deny,log,msg:'Phase block due to high score'\
    setvar:!TX.score"
```

The interesting thing about scoring is that you aren't restricted to using only one score; you can have a score for any transaction characteristic you choose. Consider the following approaches:

Phase scores

Keep a separate score for every phase. This enables you to implement delayed per-phase blocking, but if blocking doesn't take place, the scores remain available for use in subsequent phases.

Attack class score

Each attack class could have a score of its own, which would allow for a fine-grained approach to detection. The OWASP ModSecurity Core Rule Set uses this approach (as well as a few others).

Transaction score

Keep a combined transaction score, possibly combining the individual phase scores.

Request and response scores

>Keep one score for the first two phases and another for the second two phases. This approach allows for a correlation between attack detection and attack results detection. For example, suppose the request score reflects your suspicion that an SQL injection attack is taking place. If the response score indicates a trace of the attack (e.g., a database error message), you can decide to block.

Persistent scores

>Once persistent collections are initialized, the concept of scoring can be applied to higher-level elements such as IP addresses, sessions, and users. The only difference is that transactions always start fresh with a score of zero, whereas persistent elements keep their scores until they expire. A persistent score thus needs to involve a depreciating element so that it effectively maintains itself. I discussed persistent scoring at length in Chapter 8, *Persistent Storage*.

Score-based blocking is neat, but it can be difficult to implement. The burden is on the rule writer to come up with a meaningful way to combine rule scores into combined values, which is necessary for that final threshold check to work. For example, it can be an issue to have several rules match for the same underlying problem, because that will artificially push the score over the threshold.

Making the Most of Regular Expressions

Although ModSecurity supports many operators, regular expressions are so powerful and versatile that they remain the most often seen choice in rules. ModSecurity uses the Perl Compatible Regular Expressions library, better known as PCRE.[9] This is a well-known and widely used regular expression library, and it's also used by Apache. Because they are so powerful, regular expressions will often surprise you, and you'll realize that they're more capable than you thought. This section will highlight the most important aspects of PCRE and the way this library is used in ModSecurity, but it only covers the tip of the iceberg. I highly recommend that you familiarize yourself with the PCRE documentation, which contains everything you need to know.

How ModSecurity Compiles Patterns

Regular expression patterns are *compiled* (converted into an efficient internal representation) before they're used. The compilation step helps the library improve performance, doing as much work as possible only once, at configure-time. The compilation flags affect how patterns are used, and you need to be aware of them. In the most important operator in

---

[9] Perl Compatible Regular Expressions library [fsty.uk/m18] (PCRE, retrieved 30 December 2016)

which regular expressions are used, the @rx operator, ModSecurity uses two compilation flags:

PCRE_DOLLAR_ENDONLY

By default, a dollar metacharacter will match a newline at the end of a string. Users often don't expect this, and it messes with rules that want to have complete control over what's allowed in certain places. By using PCRE_DOLLAR_ENDONLY to compile patterns, the dollar character is made to match only at the end of the input.

PCRE_DOTALL

Also by default, a dot metacharacter in a pattern matches all characters except those indicating newlines. In a security context, that opens a potential weakness, by which an attacker is able to use a newline to break up the attack payload and prevent a pattern from matching. With PCRE_DOTALL set, a dot metacharacter will genuinely match any character.

Table 9.2. Pattern compilation flags

Usage	Compilation flags used
@gsbLookup	PCRE_DOTALL, PCRE_MULTILINE
@rx	PCRE_DOLLAR_ENDONLY, PCRE_DOTALL
@validateHash	PCRE_DOLLAR_ENDONLY, PCRE_DOTALL
@verifyCC	PCRE_DOTALL, PCRE_MULTILINE
@verifyCPF	PCRE_DOTALL, PCRE_MULTILINE
@verifySSN	PCRE_DOTALL, PCRE_MULTILINE
SecAuditLogRelevantStatus	PCRE_DOTALL
SecHashMethodRx	No flags used
SecRuleRemoveByMsg	No flags used
SecRuleRemoveByTag	No flags used
SecRuleUpdateTargetByMsg	No flags used
SecRuleUpdateTargetByTag	No flags used
Variable selection (e.g., ARGS)	PCRE_CASELESS, PCRE_DOLLAR_ENDONLY, PCRE_DOTALL

Now you know which compilation flags are used, but it's important also to learn about two that are *not* used:

PCRE_CASELESS

Enables case-insensitive matching. Because this flag is absent when the @rx patterns are compiled, all patterns are case-sensitive. (Use the t:lowercase transformation function to achieve case-insensitive matching, or read the next section, which shows another way.)

PCRE_MULTILINE

This flag changes the behavior of the ^ and $ metacharacters to force them to match at the beginning of a line and at the end of a line, respectively. Without it, PCRE will treat the entire input string as a single line. The PCRE default is used for the @rx operator, which means that a ^ metacharacter will *always* match at the beginning of the string, and $ will *always* match at the end.

There are several other points at which regular expressions are used, and although they are not as security-sensitive as the @rx operator, you should still be aware of how they're compiled. Table 9.2 gives a complete picture.

Changing How Patterns Are Compiled

If you aren't happy with how ModSecurity compiles patterns, you'll be glad to hear that PCRE allows you to override the compile flags from within the pattern itself. For example, the following rule—which doesn't use any transformation functions—will match the word attack no matter what case is used:

```
SecRule ARGS "@rx (?i)attack" \
    id:2000,phase:2,deny,t:none
```

The (?i) part, placed at the beginning of the pattern, activates the PCRE_CASELESS flag for the entire pattern. It's also possible to change a setting for only a part of a pattern by placing the modifier within:

```
SecRule ARGS "@rx attack (?i)keyword" \
    id:2000,phase:2,deny,t:none
```

The previous expression will match attack keyword and attack KeYWORD, but not ATTACK keyword. If you place the modifier in a subpattern, then only the remainder of the subpattern will be modified:

```
SecRule ARGS "@rx (key(?i)word) attack" \
    id:2000,phase:2,deny,t:none
```

The previous expression will match keyWORD attack, but not keyWORD ATTACK, nor KeyWORD attack.

To remove a flag, use a hyphen in front of the letter. The following pattern unsets the PCRE_DOTALL flag that's used by ModSecurity by default:

```
SecRule ARGS "@rx (?-s)keyword" \
    id:2000,phase:2,deny,t:none
```

The complete list of the modifiers you can use in this way is in Table 9.3. For complete meanings, look up the modifiers in the PCRE documentation.

Table 9.3. Pattern modifiers

Modifier	Meaning
i	PCRE_CASELESS
J	PCRE_DUPNAMES
m	PCRE_MULTILINE
s	PCRE_DOTALL
U	PCRE_UNGREEDY
x	PCRE_EXTENDED
X	PCRE_EXTRA

Common Pattern Problems

Mistakes in regular expression patterns are common, but two are seen more often than others:

Forgetting to escape the metacharacters

The most frequently unescaped metacharacter is the dot. It most commonly happens when you're writing patterns to match IP addresses, which have many dots in them. An unescaped dot will match any character, matching against unintended characters if it wasn't meant to be used as a metacharacter. Other metacharacters that have to be escaped are ?, *, +, {, }, (,), [,], \, ^, $, and |.

Not using the ^ and $ anchors when matching entire input

The use of the ^ and $ anchors is required when you want your patterns to match complete input strings. If you omit one or the other, you allow an attacker to send anything before your pattern (when you don't have the ^ at the beginning) and anything after your pattern (when you don't have the $ at the end). Without these anchors, a pattern may match a substring in the middle, ignoring anything else.

Regular Expression Denial of Service

Regular expression denial of service (ReDoS) is a relatively obscure problem that affects every regular expression writer. Some regular expression constructs are known to suffer from bad performance when certain edge cases are encountered; in the worst case, the reduction in performance is exponential with input length. If you aren't careful, you can write a pattern that can be manipulated from the outside by an attacker to consume most or all of your server's resources.

Here are some examples of vulnerable patterns (borrowed from Roichman and Weidman 2009):

- `^(a+)+$`

- `^(a|aa)+$`

- `^(a|a?)+$`

- `^(.*a){x}$`, for x >= 2; depending on your PCRE limits

Triggering these types of regular expressions with a parameter value like aaaaaaaaaaaaaaaaaaaX can cause a denial of service on your server's CPU.

In ModSecurity, regular expressions are configured with conservative limits by default, allowing only up to 1,500 matches and up to 1,500 internal recursions. This means that an attacker exploiting one of your weak regular expressions will be stopped before problems escalate too much.

On the other hand, when this self-defense mechanism kicks in, the rules don't complete and may miss the attack they were designed to catch. An attacker could "spice" their exploits with ReDoS, evade your defenses, and hit the application.

You have several options to defend against this weakness. First and best, you can construct your regular expressions in a way that makes them safe from ReDoS. This approach requires advanced knowledge and is outside the scope of this book, but we recommend the following resources:

- Alex Roichman and Adar Weidman: "Regular Expression Denial of Service" (OWASP presentation slides, 2009)[10]

- Michael Hidalgo: "Regular Expression Denial of Service," blog post (2015)[11]

- OWASP: ReDoS[12]

- Wikipedia: ReDoS[13]

You can also raise the PCRE matching limits using the `SecPcreMatchLimit` and `SecPcreMatchLimitRecursion` directives. The default of 1,500 matches each is conservative; I've successfully used values of up to one million in production setups. For example, with this limit, the attack pattern presented previously took around 12 milliseconds to evaluate (and abort) on my mediocre server. That isn't yet a proper DoS attack, but if executed by a large group of requests in parallel, it could very well become one. Therefore, you need to weigh the risk of a DoS attacks against the possibility of a rule bypass. My answer to this question is to raise the limit and to monitor for DoS, then react if necessary.

Finally, as a safety net, you can refuse to serve requests that breach PCRE limits. This can be achieved with a rule that monitors the `WEBSERVER_ERROR_LOG` variable. If you place such a

---

[10] Regular Expression Denial of Service [fsty.uk/m33] (Alex Roichman and Adar Weidman, retrieved 22 March 2017)

[11] Regular Expression Denial of Service [fsty.uk/m34] (Michael Hidalgo, retrieved 22 March 2017)

[12] Regular expression denial of service—ReDoS [fsty.uk/m35] (OWASP, retrieved 30 December 2016)

[13] ReDoS [fsty.uk/m36] (Wikipedia, retrieved 30 December 2016)

rule at the end of phase 2 and block offending requests, you can be sure that ReDoS can't be used for rule bypass:

```
SecRule WEBSERVER_ERROR_LOG "@rx PCRE\ limits\ exceeded" \
    "id:2999,phase:2,deny,log,msg:'PCRE limit error (Possible ReDoS)'"
```

Be aware that false positives are likely in this situation. In fact, PCRE limit errors are frequent when running the OWASP ModSecurity Core Rules. You need to balance PCRE limits and the security of your site against typical user input. A combination of the three defense options therefore will provide the best results, especially because it isn't always possible to construct every rule in such a way as to be safe from denial of service.

Resources

Don't be surprised if you sometimes become overwhelmed working with regular expressions. That's entirely normal and will vanish in time. You don't have to buy a book to become proficient in regular expressions, but it will certainly help if you do. My only issue with available books is that they all cover many regular expression flavors, and I'm interested only in PCRE. However, there are at least two classic books you should consider:

- *Mastering Regular Expressions*, by Jeffrey Friedl (O'Reilly, 2006), is widely considered to be a classic work on regular expressions.
- *Regular Expressions Cookbook*, by Jan Goyvaerts and Steven Levithan (O'Reilly, 2012), is a decent addition to the regular expression work and adopts a more practical style of learning.

You should also consider one of the following tools, which will enable you to interactively design and analyze regular expressions:

- Regex101,[14] often mentioned as the best online tool.
- RegExr[15] provides somewhat simpler explanations.
- RegexBuddy,[16] a commercial tool written by *Regular Expressions Cookbook* co-author Jan Goyvaerts, is often recommended as the ultimate regular expression assistant.
- Expresso[17] is a free tool from Ultrapico.

Working with Rulesets

Rulesets are packaged collections of rules designed to address a particular problem. In this section, I'll discuss rulesets first from a user's point of view and then from a ruleset writer's

---

[14] Regex101 web site [fsty.uk/m37] (Regex101, retrieved 30 December 2016)

[15] RegExr web site [fsty.uk/m38] (RegExr, retrieved 30 December 2016)

[16] RegexBuddy web site [fsty.uk/m39] (RegexBuddy, retrieved 30 December 2016)

[17] Expresso web site [fsty.uk/m40] (Ultrapico, retrieved 30 December 2016)

point of view. You should read both sections no matter which group you belong to, because they're just different aspects of the same story.

Deploying Rulesets

If a ruleset is well-written, deploying it is a matter of deciding how to react to its alerts and adding the ruleset to your configuration. In other words:

```
# Configure default blocking policy
SecDefaultAction "phase:1,pass,log,auditlog"

# Activate Ultimate rules
Include conf/ultimate-rules-9.99/*.conf
```

You shouldn't use blocking when you deploy a ruleset for the first time, because you don't know if it will produce many false positives. Warnings will be sufficient for the first couple of days or weeks. Once you gain confidence that the ruleset won't ruin you financially, you can switch to blocking if you want.

There are only two maintenance activities you should ever do when it comes to rulesets: dealing with false positives and updating to new releases.

Dealing with False Positives: Exclusion Rules

Big rulesets tend to have false positives. If an application has free-form text fields, sooner or later a legitimate user will enter some text that will trigger a rule and cause a false positive.

Occasional false alarms can be ignored, but just where should you draw the line? In my experience, it depends on the application and the users involved. As a rule of thumb, anything more than one false alarm in 10,000 requests is certainly too much. However, there are services that need this rate to be as low as one false positive in every one million requests.

ModSecurity offers many options to deal with false positives, providing tools to exclude certain rules in certain situations. In effect, you're writing rules to manipulate (typically exclude) some other rules. I thus call them *exclusion rules*.

This chapter started with several sections dedicated to the concept of whitelisting. The concept of exclusion rules is close to that idea, but instead of bypassing ModSecurity, we're now excluding a particular request or parameter from a group of rules—often from a single rule. Therefore, the artificial hole you pierce into your ruleset is much smaller with this approach, making it the preferred method to deal with false positives.

Exclusion rules fall into two categories: 1) manipulations at configuration time during the startup of the server and 2) manipulations at runtime as requests come in. We'll start with the former category; Table 9.4 lists the necessary directives.

Table 9.4. Directives for rule manipulation at startup

Directive	Meaning
SecRuleRemoveById	Deactivate rules, matching by ID
SecRuleRemoveByMsg	Deactivate rules, matching by message pattern
SecRuleRemoveByTag	Deactivate rules, matching by tag pattern
SecRuleUpdateActionById	Change rules' action lists of rules, matching by ID
SecRuleUpdateTargetById	Change rules' targets, matching by ID
SecRuleUpdateTargetByMsg	Change rules' targets, matching by message pattern
SecRuleUpdateTargetByTag	Change rules' targets, matching by tag pattern

All these directives are used by placing them after the rules they intend to manipulate. Because larger rulesets are usually loaded via Include statements, exclusion rules are best placed immediately after.

This approach to rule exclusion provides the best performance because everything occurs at startup time. Longer lists of these directives are also easy to read and understand, which helps with maintenance. Unfortunately, they can be a bit coarse (i.e., the hole they drill is too wide); if you need more granular control, you can try the second approach, which is to manipulate rules at runtime as requests are being processed. Table 9.5 lists the control actions that perform this manipulation.

Table 9.5. Control actions for rule manipulation at runtime

Directive	Meaning
ctl:ruleRemoveById	Deactivate rules, matching by ID
ctl:ruleRemoveByMsg	Deactivate rules, matching by message pattern
ctl:ruleRemoveByTag	Deactivate rules, matching by tag pattern
ctl:ruleRemoveTargetById	Remove parameters from rules, matching by ID
ctl:ruleRemoveTargetByMsg	Remove parameters from rules, matching by message pattern
ctl:ruleRemoveTargetByTag	Remove parameters from rules, matching tag pattern

To manipulate rules at runtime, the control actions must be placed *before* the rules they target. In the case of rulesets loaded via an Include statement, place the control actions immediately before. Consider the following example, which allows a health monitor to submit a request without a host header, which is forbidden in the OWASP ModSecurity Core Rules:

```
# RULE EXCLUSIONS (Runtime) : Rule IDs 4000-4999

# Rule exclusions for health monitoring from 192.168.5.45
# 920280 : Request Missing a Host Header
SecRule REMOTE_ADDR "@ipMatch 192.168.5.45" \
```

```
"id:4000,phase:1,pass,nolog,ctl:ruleRemoveById=920280,chain"
SecRule REQUEST_FILENAME "@beginsWith /healthcheck.do"
```

Although this approach is more flexible, it comes with a performance penalty, because all the work is done during request processing, over and over again. However, the ultimate benefit is that with this approach, you can choose to react based on the content of each requests, which means that the effective rule configuration can be slightly different for different requests.

Upgrading to New Releases

Updating to a new version should involve downloading the new files, going through the documentation to understand the changes, and possibly using `diff` to see exactly what changed. Some people prefer to switch back to detection-only for a while, just to make sure there won't be any nasty surprises. Others, who have adequate budgets, will first try the new rules in a staging environment. It's advisable to keep the previous version of the rules around, just in case you don't find the new version satisfactory.

If you've copied and modified any of the rules, then when upgrading to a new release don't forget to check if the rule has been improved in the meantime.

Writing Rules for Distribution

When you're writing rules for yourself, you're often able to make design shortcuts, because you do things in certain ways and there's little sense in allowing for different behavior. When writing for others, however, about the only certainty is that they will want things done differently. When people download a ruleset, they basically expect to be able to plug it into their web site and use it with little fuss. What they don't expect is to have their site overtaken by the newly installed rules. Thus, the key to writing rules for distribution is to give your users options and let them decide what to do, as follows:

Avoid mixing rules with configuration

Your users will have spent significant time deciding exactly how they want to run ModSecurity; you don't want to surprise them by overriding their configuration with something else. Besides, your configuration choices may not be adequate for their circumstances.

Detect problems, but don't react to them

Your job as a ruleset writer is to detect problems, not react to them. Leave the reacting to your users. If you're writing straightforward blocking rules, you only need to remember to use `block` as your disruptive action. If you're writing advanced rules that produce attack scores, don't take any action, but document what the outcome of your rules is going to be and leave it to your users to do the rest.

Split rules into modules

Splitting complex rulesets into modules is always a good idea, especially if you can make the modules differ in terms of precision and performance. The split into modules is a recipe for user satisfaction when coupled with good documentation that explains the characteristics of each module.

Document your rules

Everything is game, provided you tell your users in advance what to expect. Include such items as installation instructions, performance, the update mechanism, and so on. The more you tell them, the happier they'll be. On the rule level, make sure that every rule contains every little bit of metadata you can think of.

For practical advice, consider the following:

- Always specify id, rev (unless 1), msg, and severity.
- IDs must be allocated from the pool assigned to the publisher.
- Once allocated, the rule IDs must not be reused for other rules.
- The rule revision number must be incremented with every change to the rule.
- List all desired transformation functions, starting with t:none.
- Use only pass and block as disruptive actions.
- Never use nolog in combination with block.
- Use logdata:%{TX.0} with complex rules, which will help your users understand exactly what matched.

Use only the following directives:

- SecAction
- SecComponentSignature
- SecMarker
- SecRule
- SecRuleScript

Never use the following actions:

- allow
- append
- ctl
- drop
- exec
- initcol

- pause
- prepend
- proxy
- redirect
- setuid
- setsid
- status

Summary

This chapter touched on a number of practical tasks, most of which are needed by every single ModSecurity user. Whitelisting, blacklisting, and virtual patching constitute the core of what ModSecurity was designed to do. The section on regular expressions provided a good introduction to the topic, but you should consider buying another book or two and learning everything there is to know about it. Regular expressions are the single most powerful tool for inspection, and to this day I'm sometimes amazed with what they can do.

The next step is to discuss everyone's favorite topic—performance. I'll give you the information you need to understand performance, which is important for your ability to write efficient rules, and to measure performance, which is important so that you can know how your ModSecurity installations perform.

10 Performance

In this chapter, I present a detailed analysis of the performance of ModSecurity. Performance is everybody's favorite topic, but judging by the evidence (i.e., few users are complaining), ModSecurity runs fast enough. That said, there's no reason for it to run slower than it could, and this chapter will both teach you how to measure performance and explain how to make ModSecurity run efficiently.

Understanding Performance

Our first task is to understand where ModSecurity spends its time. Different sites have different usage profiles, and when you consider that the rules will be different too, you realize that a performance aspect that isn't important to you may be very important to someone else.

With three key resources in mind (CPU, RAM, and I/O), the following list details the performance hot spots in ModSecurity:

Parsing

ModSecurity reuses the work performed by Apache—but because it goes deeper, it needs to do more parsing of its own. It's not much work, however. On a simple GET request, only the parameters in the query string will be parsed. On POST requests, the parameters placed in a request body will be parsed. Unless you're parsing XML or JSON (both of which are disabled by default), the overhead from parsing won't be a cause of concern.

Buffering

I guess you could say that ModSecurity uses a lot of RAM, which is necessary to allow for reliable blocking. Even without the buffering requirement, the additional data processed by ModSecurity has to be stored somewhere. The difficult thing about RAM is that the added consumption is difficult to measure; it can be measured only indirectly, by observing differences in behavior with and without ModSecurity.

File upload interception

Handling file uploads can slow things down, for two reasons. First, to avoid using too much RAM, request bodies typically will be stored on disk, which adds to I/O requirements. There will be two passes: one to store a request body and another to read it (so that it can be forwarded for processing). The I/O overhead is further increased if you choose to use file upload interception, because ModSecurity will also need to extract individual files from the stream of request body data to store them separately.

Rule processing

The rule processing CPU requirements constitute the bulk of the ModSecurity overhead. The good news is that you're in full control: the fewer rules you have in your configuration, the better the performance. If you read this book and follow my advice, I don't expect you'll have any performance trouble. Be careful with third-party rulesets, though. Don't assume that they'll perform well, and always test them before using them in production.

Persistent storage operations

By definition, a persistent storage mechanism is going to cost more than just storing data in RAM, because you need to ensure that the data you put in survives application restarts. ModSecurity's persistent storage is disk-based, which means that it isn't as fast as it could be (if it used shared memory, for example). Modern operating systems are very good at buffering filesystem operations, so the performance should be decent. This isn't something to be concerned about, but it should be monitored.

External operations

External operations aren't going to cost you anything unless you use them, which means that this entry is here to remind you of the potential cost. Features such as the @rbl operator (which performs a DNS request) and the exec action (which executes an external binary) are outside the control of ModSecurity and should be watched for.

Logging

Assuming you don't make any configuration mistakes (e.g., enabling debug logging in production), logging won't cost you much. Most of the cost will go toward performing audit logging, which, after all, should take place only once in a while. If you're keen to use full audit logging, you should consider using a separate disk array for that purpose alone.

Top 10 Performance Rules

If there's one thing that people love more than talking about performance, it's top 10 lists—so what better way to discuss performance than with a top 10 list of its own! If you have just 10 minutes to spend thinking about this problem, try the following list—in no particular order:

Avoid debug logging in production

The debug log is verbose, especially at higher levels. At best, the `SecDebugLogLevel` directive should be kept at 3 in production, in which case it will contain only the essential messages. A copy of the essential messages will be recorded in the error log, so it's even possible to completely turn debug logging off. If your web server installation uses an error log per virtual host, however, you may benefit from keeping the debug log level at 3, because you'll then have a record of all ModSecurity actions on the server for all virtual hosts.

Understand performance

The previous section gave an overview of where performance issues may appear. With that information, and now that you also know what affects the performance of the rules, you're halfway to achieving desired performance levels.

Enforce limits

The role of runtime limits is to put a cap on the unknown. You can never control external factors, but you can (and should) refuse to process a request that would endanger your system. For more information on what to configure and how, refer to the detailed configuration instructions in Chapter 3, *Configuration*.

Minimize false positives

Eliminating false positives will not only make it easier to spot real problems but also eliminate the unnecessary I/O operation required to perform audit logging.

Be reasonable in what you expect

Extensive content inspection can be costly. That usually isn't a problem on a dedicated reverse proxy (especially one designed to work as a web application firewall), but if you're dealing with a web server that's already running at the limit of its capacity, you can't expect to add ModSecurity and get away with it.

Use adequate matching techniques

If you're writing your own rules, the best way to make them run efficiently is to use the pattern matching techniques that have performance characteristics which are a good match for the job. You'll find a good overview of the available approaches later in this chapter, in the section called "Optimizing Pattern Matching" later in this chapter.

Know your sites and your rules

Knowing what your sites do and what your rules do (even if you didn't design either yourself) will give you a rough idea of what to expect. The more you know about the system, the better.

Keep track of performance

Always keep a performance log. It will give you peace of mind when you're doing fine and help you spot performance issues early when you aren't. Having a performance log is also essential to address (usually unsubstantiated) "your site is slow" accusations.

Test response content types before buffering

Another configuration mistake that's easy to make is to use response body buffering on all requests, which increases RAM consumption and wastes the time used on the response inspection.

Test your limits

You should know what your system is capable of before you post your link to Slashdot. Finding out later usually isn't good. It's also a good idea to have a plan for what you'll do when your system becomes overloaded.

Performance Tracking

If performance is a concern, your first step should always be to measure it. ModSecurity has excellent features to accurately track its performance with detailed data down to the individual execution of a rule.

Performance Metrics

The implementation of performance tracking in ModSecurity always keeps track of a number of performance metrics. Partial access to that data is available in real time, using any of the variables from the PERF_ family. You can, for example, retrieve the duration of a previously completed phase, but you can't get any information for the phase currently being processed.

All the basic metrics, apart from the duration of the audit logging phase, are recorded in the audit log entry of a transaction, for which the Stopwatch2 header is used:

```
Stopwatch2: 1264256494438648 5131; combined=3917, p1=11, p2=3653, p3=3, p4=29, ↵
p5=221, sr=0, sw=0, l=0, gc=0
```

The first two values are the same as in the original Stopwatch header (request start time and duration). The performance metrics follow after the semicolon:

- combined: Combined processing time
- p1–p5: Time spent in each of the rule phases
- sr and sw: Time spent reading from and writing to persistent storage, respectively
- l: Time spent on audit logging
- gc: Time spent on garbage collection

All the values are given in microseconds.

Performance Logging

Performance logging must be performed when all work ModSecurity does on a transaction is complete. That means that you'll have to use Apache's logging facilities (mod_log_config). You can choose to add the additional information to your existing access log or create a separate log file. By using a feature that was added as part of the performance tracking improvements, it's possible to log any ModSecurity variable from within mod_log_config using the special %{VARNAME}M format string (only the uppercase M works; the case is not important in variable names). That improvement, along with moving phase 5 to happen prior to Apache performing its logging, makes the final performance logging possible.

Use Apache's CustomLog directive as follows to create a special log to track ModSecurity performance:

```
CustomLog logs/modsec_performance.log "%V %h %l %u %t \"%r\" %>s %b | \
%{UNIQUE_ID}e %D | %{PERF_ALL}M"
```

The variables on the first line all come standard with mod_log_config; if you're not sure about their meaning, look them up in the Apache documentation. On the second line, we're taking advantage of the special PERF_ALL variable, which was designed to include all the combined performance metrics in the same format as in the Stopwatch2 header. What other information you include is up to you, but I suggest that you always record the UNIQUE_ID value, which will enable you to cross-reference an entry in this log to other information you might have (a complete audit log entry, for example).

If you don't want to keep a separate performance log, you should at least add %{PERF_COMBINED}M to your existing access log.

Real-Time Performance Monitoring

Because you can access performance counters from within ModSecurity itself, you can write a rule to track the performance in real time. Assuming that you want to be warned about the requests on which ModSecurity spends more than 2.5 milliseconds working, write the following:

```
SecRule PERF_COMBINED "@gt 2500" \
    "id:9000,phase:5,pass,log,msg:'Slow ModSecurity rules detected'"
```

The PERF_COMBINED variable contains the time, in microseconds, spent in ModSecurity during the current transaction.

Load Testing

The only way to truly measure the performance of a ruleset is in production or with a staging platform on which production traffic can be faithfully replicated. Web performance testing is difficult on its own, even when ModSecurity isn't involved. Because rulesets do many things, using anything but real traffic will mean that you're testing only one aspect of the ruleset, which may or may not be important for you.

> **Note**
>
> The rulesets tested here were current when the second edition of this book was written, but they're continually being superseded by newer, improved releases. However, the purpose of this section is not to benchmark the rulesets but to show how the benchmarking is done. Ruleset performance can change from version to version, and—given time—you should always run a quick test to verify that there was no significant degradation compared to the version you are using.

Still, having some idea about what the performance will be like is advisable. In this section, I'll test the performance of several ModSecurity rulesets:

- The whitelisting ruleset introduced in the previous chapter

- OWASP ModSecurity Core Rule Set 2.2.9 (the latest point release of the former major release)

- Core Rule Set 3.0.0 with default settings (paranoia level [PL] 1)

- Core Rule Set 3.0.0 with PL 4

The whitelisting ruleset was adapted to the specific request used for testing. The CRS 2.2.9 test used all the rules from the base_rules folder. CRS 3.0.0 is a new major release with a consolidated ruleset; it gives you the option to enable additional, more aggressive rules via the so-called paranoia level setting. The CRS 3.0.0 PL 4 installation had to be tuned for the test request to pass without a false positive.

In addition to the ruleset tests, I made two baseline tests: one without ModSecurity, and the other with ModSecurity but without any rules.

In preparing for the test, I opted for a simple approach that will test the rulesets with a non-trivial request. It's not the best-case scenario, but not the worst-case scenario, either:

1. I wrote a PHP script that simulates an application doing some work. I tweaked the script until I got it to spend about 30 ms "working." In the real world, the application will become slower under load. However, I built it in such a way that the 30 ms time would remain stable, because I wasn't interested in load-testing PHP, but only the ruleset. In practice, this corresponds with a reverse proxy in front of a potent farm of application servers that aren't affected by the load.

2. I performed some initial tests without ModSecurity to determine the limits of the installation. The hardware used was a dedicated AWS EC2 cloud instance of the m4.large type—that is, an octo-core 2.4 GHz Xeon processor with 8 GB RAM. Based on the results, I settled on testing using between 100 and 1,200 requests per second. I

also made sure that neither the Apache configuration nor network bandwidth was going to create a performance bottleneck. For performance tests, you want the CPU to be the bottleneck, so the load was coming from a second machine of the same type.

3. For the test, I picked up a GET request with 12 parameters, with the size just under 300 bytes.

For the testing, I used the autobench tool, with the following command line:

```
$ autobench --single_host --host1 IPADDRESS --uri1 /index.php\?firstname=John\
\&lastname=Smith\&username=john.smith\&password=12345678\&password_repeat=\
12345678\&addressline1=First%20line%20of%20address\&addressline2=Second%20\
line%20of%20address\&postcode=WXXXX\&city=London\&country=United%20Kingdom\
\&phone=+447766XXXXXX\&param=john.smith@example.com --low_rate 1 \
--high_rate 15 --rate_step 1 --num_call 10 --num_conn 100 \
--timeout 5 --file results-baseline.tsv
```

I extracted two sets of data from the test results: response rate and response time. I then used gnuplot to create the graphs:

```
set terminal postscript eps mono dashed
set output "response_rate.ps"
set key inside left
set key box

set style data linespointsset ylabel "Response rate [req/s]"
set xlabel "Request rate [req/s]"
set grid
set xrange [100:1200]
set yrange [0:800]

plot "data/results-baseline.tsv" using 1:5 title "Baseline", \
     "data/results-no_rules.tsv" using 1:5 title "No Rules", \
     "data/results-whitelisting.tsv" using 1:5 title "Whitelisting", \
     "data/results-2.2.9.tsv" using 1:5 title "CRS 2.2.9", \
     "data/results-3.0.0-pl1.tsv" using 1:5 title "CRS 3.0.0 PL1", \
     "data/results-3.0.0-pl4.tsv" using 1:5 title "CRS 3.0.0 PL4"
```

The resulting graphs are shown in Figure 10.1 and Figure 10.2.

Figure 10.1. Response time test

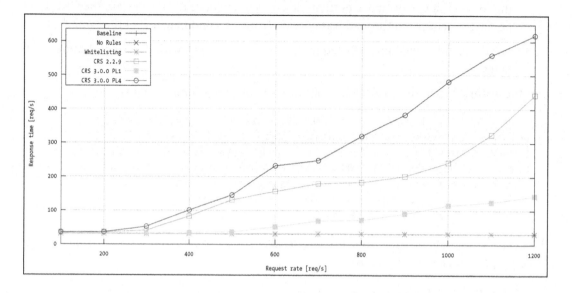

The response time graph is the more informative one:

1. The performance of the application without ModSecurity is the same for the entire duration of the test. Even at the high end, Apache is able to serve 1,200 responses per second without a drop in performance. It would start to deteriorate at around 2,000 requests (outside the chart).

2. There's virtually no difference in performance when ModSecurity is added without any rules or with the whitelisting rule set. The naked ModSecurity overhead and small individual rules like the partial whitelist are basically free, as far as performance is concerned.

3. The three Core Rule Set versions vary greatly in performance:

   - CRS 2.2.9 starts to make a significant impact at around 400 requests per second. This gets increasingly worse as the load rises.

   - The default CRS 3.0.0 option supports much higher loads than CRS 2.2.9.

   - Enabling more rules by raising the paranoia level to its highest setting has a bad effect on performance. Clearly, there's a price to pay in return for the additional security benefit.

4. Each ruleset has a different point at which the performance is significantly degraded. With CRS 2.2.9, you'll notice a lag starting at about 400 requests per second. CRS 3.0.0 can sustain 900 requests per second, whereas CRS 3.0.0 with PL 4 slows down at roughly the same rate as CRS 2.2.9.

Figure 10.2. Response rate test

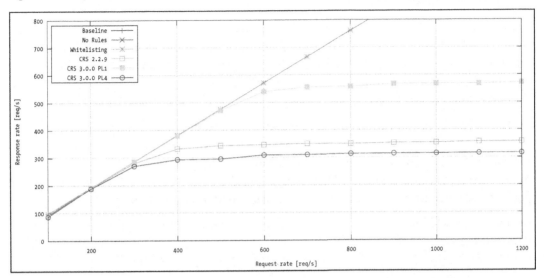

Now, let's look at the response rate. The graphs show a typical plateau effect. With the naked Apache or the simple whitelisting ruleset, we're still far from the plateau. Meanwhile, CRS 2.2.9 and CRS 3 PL 4 are able to deliver about 300 responses per second, whereas the default CRS 3 comes in at 550 responses.

During the tests, I used `vmstat` to keep my eye on the overall state of the test system. I noticed a rough correlation between the speed of a ruleset and its RAM consumption, but none of the rulesets made a significant dent in free RAM on the 8 GB server.

> **Note**
>
> Keeping a historical record of the vital system information of production systems is important in case you ever need to troubleshoot a problem after the fact. On systems from the Debian family, install the `sysstat` package; for others, consult vendor documentation.

The test results show us that not all rulesets are created equal: some are focused on performance more than others. Whenever possible, you should test the ruleset you're evaluating under circumstances that are as close as possible to the ones it will encounter in production. Also, rulesets consist of many parts, and you don't necessarily have to run all of them. If you invest some time into understanding what a ruleset does, you'll probably be able to remove some parts you don't need and achieve better performance.

Rule Benchmarking

Accurately measuring the performance of individual rules isn't possible using the same version of ModSecurity that you use in production. Because the rules run for only a short period of time, not only would any attempts to measure the individual performance be inaccurate, but, because the measurements themselves take time too, the overall execution speed would be noticeably reduced.

To allow for fine-grained performance measurement, ModSecurity has a compile-time option called --enable-performance-measurement, which activates the normally inactive performance measurement code. The version of ModSecurity you produce this way isn't usable in production, because it will be 5,000 times slower than a normal one. That's because in the performance measurement mode, each rule is run 5,000 times in a loop!

In this section, I'll guide you through the steps to accurately measure the performance of your rules.

Preparation

For your rule performance tests, you'll need to prepare a specially compiled version of ModSecurity as follows:

1. Choose a computer that isn't used for anything else, which will enable you to get consistent performance numbers. This computer will be used as a test server. You won't need a client computer, because the nature of the tests is such that virtually no resources are consumed on the client side.

2. Install Apache on the test server.

3. Run ModSecurity configure with --enable-performance-measurement and any other configure-time option that you need.

4. Compile, install, and configure ModSecurity.

5. Make sure to disable audit logging and set the debug log level to 0. This is important to prevent logging from interfering with the tests.

At this point, you may want to perform a request or two to see how performance measurement works. Add a couple of rules to your configuration, and send one request to the web server. In your error log, you'll see output similar to the following (I've removed a bunch of nonessential stuff to make it easier to read):

```
ModSecurity: Phase 1
ModSecurity: Phase 2
ModSecurity: Rule f54d90 [id "2000"][file "/usr/local/modsecurity/etc/rules.conf"]↵
[line "107"]: 1 usec
ModSecurity: Phase 3
```

```
ModSecurity: Phase 4
ModSecurity: Phase 5
```

In performance measurement mode, ModSecurity will run all the rules it has in the configuration quietly (looping 5,000 times around each rule) and print the results at the end of transaction processing. The results will contain an average measurement taken for every rule (i.e., the total time of the rule execution divided by 5,000). In my example, I had only one rule in my configuration. This particular rule ran quite fast, because it wanted to look at request parameters, but my request didn't have any. To experiment for a while before moving on to more complex tests, add the following rule to your configuration:

```
SecRule ARGS "@rx test" \
    id:2000,phase:2,pass,t:none,nolog
```

After you restart Apache, start sending requests with a varying number of parameters and observe the differences in rule performance.

How you write your rules—every little difference—will affect the performance, just as it would in real life. For consistent results, you need to watch for two things:

Your rules shouldn't block

If a rule blocks, the rules that follow won't get a chance to run. You can easily fix this problem by using the detection-only mode of deployment.

Your rules shouldn't log

If you can't avoid matching, use the nolog action to suppress logging.

Test Data Selection

Not all transactions are equal when it comes to rule testing. For example, most rules focus on request parameters, which means that a request that has no parameters will complete very quickly (as our first performance test showed). For your tests, you should select several transactions that are representative of the workload on the target system. You can construct test data based on what you know about the production system, or you can simply guess. If you have the time, the best approach is to record key characteristics and build tests based on that data.

The key characteristics are the following:

- Timestamp
- Duration
- Request method
- Query string length
- Request content type

- Request body length

- Combined size of all parameters, with file data excluded

- Number of parameters

- Response status

- Response content type

- Response body size

To record these characteristics, you'll need a few ModSecurity rules and one `CustomLog` directive. The rules are used to collect the required information and transform it into a form that can be logged by Apache:

```
# How many parameters are there? We have to do this because
# variable expansion does not currently support counting
SecRule &ARGS @unconditionalMatch \
    "id:9000,phase:5,pass,capture,t:none,nolog,\
    setvar:TX.ARGS_COUNT=%{MATCHED_VAR}"

# Find out the length of the query string
SecRule QUERY_STRING @unconditionalMatch \
    "id:9001,phase:5,pass,capture,t:none,t:length,nolog,\
    setvar:TX.QUERY_STRING_LENGTH=%{MATCHED_VAR}"

# Record per-transaction statistics
CustomLog logs/stats.log "%V %h %t %D \"%r\" | %{TX.QUERY_STRING_LENGTH}M \
\"%{REQUEST_CONTENT_TYPE}M\" %{REQUEST_BODY_LENGTH}M %{ARGS_COMBINED_SIZE}M \
%{TX.ARGS_COUNT}M %>s \"%{RESPONSE_CONTENT_TYPE}M\" %B"
```

If you collect a representative sample of your site's traffic over a period of time, you should be able to build an accurate profile for testing.

> **Note**
>
> Most of the variables you'll be logging depend on ModSecurity having access to request body data, which means that the `SecRequestBodyAccess` directive must be enabled for the statistics to be accurate.

Now that I've described this thorough approach to performance testing, I'll admit that I often use a much simpler approach. I have four requests that I use:

1. A simple `GET` request, representative of the requests used to retrieve static resources, with no parameters.

2. A short `POST` request that simulates a registration form or a feedback form. It has 12 parameters with about 300 bytes of data. This request is designed to show how performance changes as the number of parameters grows.

3. A long POST request with a single long parameter (about 15 KB), aimed at determining how rules handle large amounts of data.

4. A very long POST request with a single very long parameter (about 150 KB), which sheds light on the handling of very large amounts of data.

I'll use these four requests for testing in the remainder of this section.

Performance Baseline

Without further ado, I use the following rules to establish the baseline performance of the ModSecurity rule engine. Each test is designed to exercise one aspect of rule engine performance while minimizing all others. Examine the comments that precede the rules to understand what each rule does.

```
# A rule that uses a nonexistent variable.
SecRule XML @noMatch id:1000,phase:1,pass,nolog

# A rule that always has one target variable,
# but which never matches (and there's no operator cost).
SecRule REMOTE_ADDR @noMatch id:1001,phase:1,pass,nolog

# A rule that always matches, designed to assess the cost
# of the tasks performed on a match. (Also no operator cost.)
SecRule REMOTE_ADDR @unconditionalMatch id:1002,phase:1,pass,nolog

# Unconditional action that doesn't do anything.
SecAction id:1003,phase:1,pass,nolog

# Unconditional action that sets a variable.
SecAction id:1004,phase:1,pass,nolog,setvar:TX.x=1

# A rule that applies a no-cost operator to every parameter,
# which was designed to see how the cost rises with the
# number of parameters present.
SecRule ARGS @noMatch id:2000,phase:2,pass,nolog

# A rule designed to determine the cost of a single-parameter
# match with no operator cost and no transformation functions.
SecRule ARGS:param @noMatch id:2001,phase:2,pass,t:none,nolog

# A rule designed to determine the cost
# of the lowercase transformation function.
SecRule ARGS:param @noMatch id:2002,phase:2,pass,t:lowercase,nolog

# A rule designed to determine the cost
# of the base64Encode transformation function.
```

```
SecRule ARGS:param @noMatch id:2003,phase:2,pass,t:base64Encode,nolog

# A rule designed to determine the cost
# of the compressWhitespace transformation function.
SecRule ARGS:param @noMatch id:2004,phase:2,pass,t:compressWhitespace,nolog

# One complete, reasonably complex rule, with
# no transformation functions.
SecRule ARGS "@rx \bon(abort|blur|change|click|dblclick|dragdrop|end|error|\
focus|keydown|keypress|keyup|load|mousedown|mousemove|mouseout|\
mouseover|mouseup|move|readystatechange|reset|resize|select|submit|\
unload)\b\W*?=" \
    id:2005,phase:2,pass,t:none,nolog
```

The baseline performance testing results (of ModSecurity 2.9.1) are shown in Table 10.1. The results are given in microseconds.

Table 10.1. Baseline performance results

Rule	GET	POST	Long POST	Very long POST
No variable cost	0	0	0	0
One variable, no match, no operator cost	0	0	0	0
One variable, match, no operator cost	1	1	1	1
Unconditional match, but no actions	1	1	1	1
Unconditional match, set variable	2	2	2	2
All arguments, no match, no operator cost	0	7	0	0
One argument, no match	0	0	18	175
One argument with t:lowercase, no match	0	0	18	175
One argument with t:base64Encode, no match	0	0	18	199
One argument with t:compressWhitespace, no match	0	0	25	248
Nontrivial regular expression	0	9	23	230

We draw the following conclusions:

- There seems to be a very small per-variable handling cost (engine overhead) of about a half microsecond. This becomes visible when you look at the line with all 12 arguments. They took seven microseconds to execute. Divide this by 12 and you realize why the table reports 0 microseconds for a single variable. The engine overhead may seem small, but it is in fact significant, because that's what most rules will do: iterate through all available parameters.

- There's a per-match cost of about one microsecond. Because matches are relatively rare, it's not something we need to be concerned about.

- Rules without any parameters are processed quickly.

- The larger the arguments, the longer the transactions take. The growth is almost linear.

- With transformations, performance depends on the type, but they all cost less than regular expressions.

Optimizing Pattern Matching

Using the performance measurement mode of ModSecurity, we established that there's an inherent cost to every rule. Now, we'll explore several optimization techniques that increase the overall performance of pattern matching, especially when dealing with a large number of patterns.

The basis for our tests will be 236 SQL function names, which I've retrieved from Core Rule Set 3.0.0. Here are a few, just to give you an idea of what they look like:

```
abs
acos
adddate
addtime
aes_decrypt
aes_encrypt
ascii
asciistr
asin
atan
atan2
avg
benchmark
bin
bin_to_num
bit_and
... 220 more keywords
```

As you can see, some of these functions are likely to result in many false positives (`bin`, `avg`, `benchmark`, etc.); however, the goal of those keywords is not necessarily to detect an SQL injection but rather to give an indication, based on which you could decide to perform further tests.

Rule per Keyword Approach

We'll start with the naïve approach to implementing keyword detection, using one rule per keyword and arriving at exactly 236 rules. The performance of this approach will be the baseline against which we'll compare all other tests:

```
SecRule ARGS "@rx abs" "id:2001,phase:2,deny"
SecRule ARGS "@rx acos" "id:2002,phase:2,deny"
SecRule ARGS "@rx adddate" "id:2003,phase:2,deny"
... 233 more rules
```

Although this approach isn't likely to result in great performance, it's straightforward and allows us to handle each keyword individually. For example, if you determine that a keyword is causing too many false positives in a particular location, you can use SecRuleRemoveById to remove the entire rule. The ability to deal with false positives in this way is especially important for third-party rules, for which the ability to update easily from one release to another is important. You want to be able to tweak third-party rules without modifying the actual files.

Combined Regular Expression Pattern

To eliminate the per-rule overhead, we can combine all the keywords in a single regular expression pattern using alternation:

```
SecRule ARGS "@rx (?i)(abs|acos|adddate|addtime|aes_decrypt|aes_encrypt|ascii|↵
asciistr|asin|atan|atan2|avg|benchmark|bin|bin_to_num|bit_and|bit_count|↵
bit_length|bit_or|bit_xor|cast|ciel|cieling|char_length|char|character_length|↵

... 35 lines of text omitted from the middle

year|yearweek|xmltype)" "id:2000,phase:2,deny"
```

The single-rule approach is likely to provide a significant speed boost, but we've lost the ability to suppress individual keywords. On the plus side, it's fairly easy to locate a keyword in the entire regular express pattern and remove it manually.

Optimized Regular Expression Pattern

Regular expression patterns are compiled into state machines. Our crude attempt at combining keywords is easy to understand and do, but it doesn't produce very efficient results. The more keywords you have, the more likely it is that they have a lot in common. If you can figure out what they have in common, you can write an efficient regular expression pattern. I did just that, and this is the resulting regular expression:

```
SecRule ARGS "@rx (?:c(?:o(?:n(?:v(?:ert(?:_tz)?)?)?|cat(?:_ws)?|nection_id)|↵
(?:mpres)?s|ercibility|(?:un)?t|llation|alesce)|ur(?:rent_(?:time(?:stamp)?|↵
date|user)|(?:dat|tim)e)|h(?:ar(?:(?:acter)?_length|set)?|r)|iel(?:ing)?|↵

... 30 lines of text omitted from the middle

qu(?:arter|ote)|year(?:week)?|xmltype)) "id:2000,phase:2,deny"
```

The result is most certainly an incomprehensible mess. You can probably make out the original keywords in the text, but they've all been "melted" together. You'll notice that alternation is still used, but with deep nesting, combining the shared keyword bits. In addition, data capture is disabled.

Increased pattern matching performance comes at a further maintenance cost. In addition to not being able to work with individual keywords directly (the same problem as with our earlier attempt at optimization), now it isn't even possible to modify the one resulting regular expression by hand.

> **Note**
>
> Although the combined regular expressions can't be maintained by hand, nothing says that manual maintenance is the only option. You easily can put together a script or two to generate optimized regular expressions from a simple list of individual ones. That way, you get the best of both worlds!

Of course, I didn't manually construct the heavily optimized regular expression. I used a clever Perl module called `Regexp::Assemble`[1] and followed the instructions written by Ofer Shezaf in a blog post on the ModSecurity blog.[2] Ofer pioneered the use of heavily optimized regular expressions in the first generation of the Core Rule Set.

I used `apt-get install libregexp-assemble-perl` to install `Regexp::Assemble` on my Debian box. In the blog post, Ofer provides instructions for installation on Windows, and there's even a Windows binary available for download.

A trivial script is needed to operate `Regexp::Assemble`:

```perl
#!/usr/bin/perl

use strict;
use Regexp::Assemble;

my $ra = Regexp::Assemble->new;

while (<>) {
  $ra->add($_);
}

print $ra->as_string . "\n";
```

You feed the script a list of keywords (one per line), and it spits back the optimized regular expression:

---

[1] Regexp::Assemble [fsty.uk/m41] (David Landgren, retrieved 5 January 2017)

[2] ModSecurity blog [fsty.uk/m42] (Ofer Shezaf, retrieved 5 January 2017)

```
$ ./optimize-regex.pl < sql-function-names.data
(?^:(?:c(?:o(?:n(?:v(?:ert(?:_tz)?)?)?|cat(?:_ws)?|nection_id)
```

...and so on

Parallel Pattern Matching

An alternative optimization technique is to use the parallel matching facilities of ModSecurity, which use the Aho-Corasick algorithm to match all supplied keywords at once. I'll use the @pmFromFile operator, which allows me to refer to the file in which the keywords are stored (which is nice, because it keeps the configuration file neat and tidy):

```
SecRule ARGS "@pmFromFile sql-function-names.data" \
    id:2000,phase:2,deny
```

When using @pm and @pmFromFile, you need to be aware that the underlying algorithm doesn't distinguish between uppercase and lowercase letters. If you want to use it in a whitelisting scenario, you need to combine it with the t:lowercase transformation to make sure there is no ambiguity in paths and parameters that could be used to evade your rules.

Test Results

The testing results of the four pattern-matching techniques are shown in Table 10.2. The results are given in microseconds. We got pretty much the results we'd expected and can draw the following conclusions:

- The multirule approach carries a measurable cost, even with requests with no parameters. It may take less than one microsecond to process a rule, but those microseconds add up.

- Parallel matching is very fast. You should therefore aim to use it whenever you can, which in practice means whenever you have a large number of keywords and the expressiveness of regular expressions isn't required.

- If you must use regular expressions, using optimized combinations may increase the speed several-fold.

- Using a large number of regular expressions against large amounts of data (e.g., response bodies) isn't recommended. Doing so will consume significant amounts of CPU power.

Table 10.2. Performance comparison of pattern-matching approaches

Approach	GET	POST	Long POST	Very long POST
Rule (@rx) per keyword (all rules summed up)	41	2,074	4,631	54,903
Combined regular expression (@rx)	0	293	373	479
Optimized regular expression (@rx)	0	64	56	161
Parallel matching (@pm)	0	12	18	122

Summary

In the course of writing this chapter, I learned more about ModSecurity than ever before. You see, I too was happy with the performance of ModSecurity and rarely felt the need to look deeper into the topic—but I always wondered how ModSecurity was performing in various usage scenarios. Having tested multiple setups, I am pleased to confirm that the performance is really good when you pay attention to the correct use of the directives, operators, and transformations.

The next chapter discusses content injection, an interesting feature that enables you to extend your inspection capabilities from the server side into your users' browsers.

11 Content Injection

Content injection is a security technique that allows you to inject arbitrary content into HTTP response bodies. The technique was designed to address attacks that take place in the browser itself, which is outside the reach of most server-side defenses.

With content injection, a server can reach out to inject dynamic content and code (JavaScript) into responses, gaining in-browser inspection capabilities. First, you perform your normal server-side inspection, after which you inject JavaScript into the HTTP response to continue the inspection with full access to the browser's internal state. This chapter will give you a good overview of several useful and easy-to-use techniques based on content injection.

> **Note**
>
> Nothing says that content injection has to be used only for defense. There's a school of thought that says offense is the best defense. If you subscribe to that view, you could use content injection to attack the attackers, injecting malware directly into their browsers. Just make sure that you understand your legal position before you do anything that might be crossing the line.

Writing Content Injection Rules

Content injection allows you to inject content, possibly on a per-response basis, either at the beginning of a response or at the end. Injecting at the beginning is useful if you want to attempt to prevent attacks. Injecting at the end is useful if you want to inspect the content of the page and the internal browser state after all other JavaScript code has already been run.

> **Warning**
>
> The injected code will be placed outside the body of the HTML document, producing a page with markup that's technically invalid. Most browsers will render (and execute) the injected code just fine, but that behavior might change in the future.

To start, enable the injection feature using the `SecContentInjection` directive:

```
# Enable content injection
SecContentInjection On
```

> **Note**
>
> Content injection doesn't require that you have SecResponseBodyAccess enabled.

In the next step, determine whether injection would make sense. Web servers process many types of requests, and only some responses can be injected. You wouldn't, for example, want to inject anything into an image; it would end up being corrupted. To find out whether a response is injectable, check its content type, which you'll find in the RESPONSE_CONTENT_TYPE variable, in phase 3. (You shouldn't try to use RESPONSE_HEADERS:Content-Type, which may not always contain the necessary information.)

I suggest the following framework for all of your content injection rules:

```
SecContentInjection On

# First check if we should inject anything
SecRule RESPONSE_CONTENT_TYPE "!@rx ^text/html" \
    id:6000,phase:3,pass,nolog,skipAfter:END_CONTENT_INJECTION

# ... your content injection rules here

SecMarker END_CONTENT_INJECTION
```

First, check for the correct content type, skipping over all your content injection rules if an incorrect type is used in a response. If you're going to inject into more than one type of document (e.g., text/plain and text/html), then you're probably going to need different rules, with different content for each type. In that case, just repeat the previous example fragment, making sure to choose the content type correctly and to use a unique SecMarker value in each group.

Finally, to inject content, use the append and prepend actions. The following example injects a header and a footer into an HTML response:

```
SecAction id:6001,phase:3,pass,nolog,prepend:'Header<hr>'
SecAction id:6002,phase:3,pass,nolog,append:'<hr>Footer'
```

> **Note**
>
> The content injection facilities won't perform any output encoding, which means that you must manually encode everything you want injected. The prepend and append actions do support variable expansion and make it possible to inject dynamically generated content, but you *must* take care to *never* inject any user-con-

---

Chapter 11: Content Injection

trolled content. Doing so would create a XSS vulnerability, right there in your web application firewall! Inject only what you have 100 percent control over.

For testing purposes, you can also try the following simple JavaScript code, which will write the URL of the current page on the screen:

```
SecAction "id:6001,phase:3,pass,nolog,\
    prepend:'<script>document.write(document.location)</script>'"
```

Now, we've established that you can have your JavaScript code inside the browser—but what can you do with this ability? Here are some ideas:

- Inspect request parameters, including the fragment identifier, which normally isn't sent to servers.

- Inspect the browser state. For example, a popular technique used to assist in XSS attacks is to store the payload in window names (property window.name). That field is out of bounds to a server, but not to the injected JavaScript code.

- Inspect the browser configuration; for example, look for vulnerable plug-ins.

- Inspect the page state and structure (DOM) at the end of page execution.

- Redefine the built-in JavaScript functions to detect unusual activity patterns.

JavaScript is a fascinating language that's endlessly tweakable. Describing advanced JavaScript attacks is out of the scope of this book, but if you want to learn more, simply pick up the most advanced JavaScript book you can find and use it as a starting point.

Communicating Back to the Server

When you detect a problem using JavaScript, you need to somehow communicate that fact back to the server. The best way to do so is to get the browser to send a special request. The simplest way to do that is by writing some HTML into the response:

```
document.write("<script src=/security-error.js><" + "/script>");
```

> **Note**
>
> The injected payload must never contain the string </script> anywhere except at the very end. If it does, then that's where browsers will terminate the entire payload and probably even cause a JavaScript error. String concatenation, as illustrated in the previous example, is often used to deactivate the closing tag.

To the special request, add a rule that detects it and raises an alert in ModSecurity. While you're there, you might want to consider doing other things, such as canceling the victim's application session. You might want to consider including an error code in the request (e.g., as a parameter), which will help you establish exactly where the problem was. You should also be aware that this communication mechanism can be discovered and subverted by the attacker. Therefore, don't use any information obtained from such requests for anything other than logging.

Interrupting Page Rendering

Perhaps you'll decide that detection isn't enough and that you want to prevent in-browser attacks. JavaScript doesn't offer a way to stop page rendering, but you can do the next best thing: redirect the user someplace else using `location.replace()`. In my tests, the invocation has the effect of effectively stopping rendering and moving the browser elsewhere. For example:

```
location.replace("http://www.example.com/security-error.html");
```

Stopping page rendering when `location.replace()` is invoked is a side effect; in general, you shouldn't expect it to work across all browsers or to continue to work in the browsers it works in today. For example, some browsers may continue to process JavaScript while another page is being loaded. You should assume that some attacks may get through.

If you choose to implement prevention in this way, don't forget to add a user-friendly explanation for the sudden redirection to another page. Your users will appreciate it. The advantage of using prevention like this is that it also notifies you of the problem: whenever someone accesses that special page, you'll know that user has been attacked.

Using External JavaScript Code

In the current implementation of content injection, you're limited to the content you can put in a parameter of the append and prepend actions. In particular, you won't be able to inject any nonprintable characters. You can escape a single quote with a backslash, but that's the only escape option ModSecurity supports at present. If you do run into trouble, you can always store the JavaScript code in a separate file and inject a link to it.

If you can place a file onto the root of the web site being protected, use this:

```
SecAction "id:6000,phase:3,pass,nolog,prepend:'<script src=/ids.js></script>'"
```

If you have several web sites and you'd like to use one file for all of them, use a fully qualified address:

```
SecAction "id:6000,phase:3,pass,nolog,\
    prepend:'<script src=https://www.example.com/ids.js></script>'"
```

Finally, if you need to construct the address dynamically, you can do that by injecting JavaScript that will generate the HTML code needed to include the external JavaScript:

```
SecAction "id:6003,phase:3,pass,nolog,\
    prepend:'<script>document.write(unescape(\"<script src=\'\" \
    + document.location.protocol + \"//localhost/ids.js\'>%3c↵
/script>\"));</script>'"
```

Several aspects of this rule need explaining:

1. Use `document.write()` to output HTML to the document body.

2. Make sure to escape all single and double quotes in the code.

3. The preceding example used URL encoding (converting the opening angle bracket to `%3c`) in combination with `unescape()` to deactivate the closing script tag. This approach also can be used if you need special characters in JavaScript (and you can't write them directly because of ModSecurity's poor escape syntax).

4. The code uses the `document.location.protocol` property, which will be `http:` for plaintext connections and `https:` for encrypted connections.

Communicating with Users

Another interesting application of content injection is "talking" to application users. Ages ago, I wrote some code, practically as a party trick, that would detect access using vulnerability scanners (e.g., Arachni) and send a message back that we don't like being probed.

Such a rule can be as simple as this example:

```
SecRule REQUEST_HEADERS:User-Agent "@rx Arachni" \
    "id:6000,phase:3,pass,\
    prepend:'<script>alert(\"Use of Arachni is strictly forbidden\");</script>'"
```

If your site uses sessions and you've configured ModSecurity to track them, you can send per-session messages that expire after a period of time. I will show you how to do that, using an example that detects the word attack anywhere in request parameters (let's pretend we're detecting an SQL injection attack), then sets a message that will be displayed to the same session for 60 seconds (even in requests that don't contain the attack). The example consists of only two rules.

The first rule is used to trigger the message:

```
# The following rule triggers a message. Session must have been
# established (using setsid) beforehand; otherwise the execution
# of this rule will cause an error.
SecRule ARGS "@rx attack" \
    "id:2000,phase:2,pass,log,msg:'Detected SQL Injection',\
    setvar:SESSION.message_flag=1,\
    expirevar:SESSION.message_flag=60,\
    setvar:'SESSION.message=SQL Injection is lame'"
```

The detection itself is trivial, but the rest needs an explanation:

1. The first setvar action (setvar:SESSION.message_flag=1) creates a per-session flag used to indicate that a message exists.

2. The expirevar action (expirevar:SESSION.message_flag=60) is used to delete the SESSION.message_flag variable after 60 seconds.

3. The second setvar action (setvar:'SESSION.message=SQL Injection is lame') defines the message.

A second rule is used to detect the presence of SESSION.message_flag and display the message stored in SESSION.message:

```
# The following rule displays the message for 60 seconds. As before, the prepend
# action must be executed only if the response content type is right.
SecRule SESSION:message_flag "@eq 1" \
    "id:6000,phase:3,pass,nolog,\
    prepend:'<script>alert(\"%{SESSION.message}\");</script>'"
```

When, after 60 seconds, the expirevar statement from the first rule kicks in, the SESSION.message_flag variable will be deleted and the message will go away.

Summary

To me, content injection is a fascinating ability of ModSecurity, because you get to move into the ever-complex world of JavaScript. You can extend your virtual hand into every single user's browser and take a look at what they know. It's all right to look, by the way, because you'll have access only to the pages that come from your own sites; everything else will be off-limits.

We've only scratched the surface with this brief chapter. Other ideas can be found in an inspirational presentation by Denis Kolegov and Arseny Reutov about client-side WAF capabilities using JavaScript.[1] Another interesting topic to discuss is injecting code into responses in order to run a browser fingerprint regularly and detect session hijacking when the fingerprint of the browser changes. The ClientJS project is a good start in this direction.[2]

In the next chapter, we'll discuss a topic that's possibly even more interesting than the one covered here: the ability to write rules in Lua, a proper programming language.

---

[1] How to Protect Web Applications using JavaScript [fsty.uk/m43] (SlideShare, Denis Kolegov and Arseny Reutov, 24 May 2016)

[2] ClientJS project [fsty.uk/m44] (Jack Spirou, retrieved 11 April 2017)

12 Writing Rules in Lua

The ModSecurity Rule Language is relatively easy to use, but it's fairly limited. After all, the directives have to obey the Apache configuration syntax, so there's only so much we can do within those boundaries. I like to think that you can use the rule language to get 80 percent of your tasks done, and quickly too: common things are simple to do; complex things are possible. At some point, however, the rule language stops being an appropriate tool for the task, and you need to look elsewhere. Starting with ModSecurity 2.5, you can write rules in Lua, a fast and memory-efficient scripting language.[1] These attributes make Lua very popular with game programmers, who are always trying to get that extra ounce of performance.

The advantage of Lua is that it's a proper programming language, which means that you're limited only by your programming skills. The disadvantage, as you might expect, is a performance penalty. Some of that penalty comes from the fact that Lua scripts need to be interpreted at runtime, and some comes about because the current implementation in ModSecurity isn't as efficient as it could be. That said, performance is adequate in most cases.

There are two ways in which Lua can be used to enhance your rulesets. First, you can write detection rules in it. Second, you can write scripts that are executed on a rule match. The remainder of this chapter explains both of these features.

Rule Language Integration

Although the chapter introduction made it sound like Lua rules are separate from the rule language, that's not true. In ModSecurity, Lua is implemented as a rule language extension, via the SecRuleScript directive. For example, this is how you run a Lua script:

```
SecRuleScript /path/to/script.lua \
    id:2000,phase:2,deny,log
```

If you compare that to the SecRule directive, you'll see the variables and the operators are gone. They're replaced with a single parameter, which is the location of the Lua script you

---

[1] Lua web site [fsty.uk/m45] (Lua.org, retrieved 5 January 2017)

wish to run. That means the script will choose which variables it wants to inspect and in what order. The action list is still there, though. You can see that the rule in the previous example runs in phase 2 and that it logs and blocks on a match.

Lua Rules Skeleton

Every Lua rule needs to have an entry point that ModSecurity can find: the main function. This is what the simplest Lua rule looks like:

```
function main()
    -- Never match
    return nil;
end
```

As you may suspect, the previous rule doesn't do much. It only returns nil, which means that there's no match. For a Lua rule to match, it needs to return a message:

```
function main()
    -- Always match
    return "Error message";
end
```

The beauty of the way Lua is integrated with ModSecurity is that once you return an error message, the rule language takes over and processes the action list. Thus, with Lua rules, you still get to use what you already know. For example, you provide all the metadata information for Lua rules in the exact same way as you do for normal rules:

```
SecRuleScript /path/to/script.lua \
    id:2000,phase:2,deny,log,rev:1,severity:3
```

Whatever you can do with a SecRule directive, you can do with SecRuleScript.

Accessing Variables

Once inside a Lua rule, the first thing you'll need to do is access some variables. The following example retrieves two variables from ModSecurity:

```
function main()
    -- Retrieve remote IP address
    local remote_addr = m.getvar("REMOTE_ADDR");

    -- Retrieve username
    local username = m.getvar("ARGS.username", {"lowercase"});

    -- Admin access outside 192.168.1.1 not allowed
```

```
    if ((username == "admin") and (remote_addr ~= "192.168.1.1")) then
        return "Admin sign-in not allowed from IP address: " .. remote_addr;
    end


    -- No match
    return nil;
end
```

A call to the m.getvar() function will retrieve the variable named in the first parameter. In the example, the value of REMOTE_ADDR is retrieved and placed into the Lua variable remote_addr.

The function has an optional second parameter. If used, it must contain a list of transformation functions that will be applied to the variable before it's returned to Lua. In the example, the value of ARGS.username is retrieved from ModSecurity, passed through the lowercase transformation function, and placed into the Lua variable username.

It's also possible to retrieve more than one variable at once, but for that you use the m.getvars() function (note the additional s in the name). The following example retrieves all request parameters, then examines them one at a time:

```
function main()
    -- Retrieve all parameters
    local vars = m.getvars("ARGS", {"lowercase", "htmlEntityDecode"});

    -- Examine all variables
    for i = 1, #vars do
        -- Examine one value
        if (string.find(vars[i].value, "<script")) then
            return ("Suspected XSS in variable: " .. vars[i].name .. ".");
        end
    end

    -- Nothing wrong found
    return nil;
end
```

The m.getvars() function works differently. It doesn't return just the value of the requested variable; instead, it returns an object with two members: name, which contains the name of the variable, and value, which contains the corresponding value. The preceding example demonstrates how both are used.

Setting Variables

You can modify or add transaction variables from within a Lua script using the m.setvar() function. The following example will take an existing variable and increment it by 1:

```
function main()
    -- Retrieve parameter
    local var = m.getvar("TX.test");

    var = var + 1;

    m.setvar("TX.test", var);

    -- No match
    return nil;
end
```

With this addition, you can set variables from Lua in two ways. One way is to use a setvar action triggered by a Lua script returning with a match. The second way enables you to set variables directly from the script, even if there's no match.

Logging

Sometimes, a Lua rule won't work as you expect, but you won't have any clue as to why. You can troubleshoot your scripts by emitting debug log messages, using the m.log() function:

```
function main()
    -- Log something
    m.log(3, "Hello World from Lua!");

    -- Never match
    return nil;
end
```

The m.log() function takes two parameters, the first of which is the desired log level (1–9); the second is the desired message. Messages with log level 1–3 will be written to the error log and to the debug log.

Lua Actions

With the addition of Lua, the exec action was extended to support Lua natively. Normally, you supply the exec action with a path to an external script, and ModSecurity executes that script in a separate process. If the script path ends with .lua, however, ModSecurity will process the script using the embedded Lua interpreter. This approach not only achieves better performance (no need to start a new process), but also gives the Lua script access to the current transaction context:

```
SecRule ARGS "@rx test" \
    id:2000,phase:2,pass,log,exec:/path/to/script.lua
```

A Lua script called from exec must define the same entry point as all other Lua scripts. There's no need to return anything from the main() function:

```
function main()
    -- Log something
    m.log(3, "Lua executed in exec!");
end
```

Now, the preceding example looks deceptively simple—so much so that you may wonder what use Lua could possibly have. The answer is that you can do pretty much anything you want from Lua. You not only get the programming language and the standard Lua libraries, but you also get access to a number of extensions that take care of filesystem access, sockets, database access, and so on. In addition, because Lua scripts executed in this way have access to the transaction context and the persistent storage, the result is a seamless scripting extension of ModSecurity.

Summary

This chapter is short, but the topic is important enough to warrant its own chapter. When implementing a particular functionality using just the rule language fails or when the resulting rules are too difficult to maintain, you'll turn to Lua. Support for Lua has been around for many years, but while everybody agrees it has big potential, it hasn't seen the wide deployment it deserves. I suspect the standard ModSecurity rule language is good enough to perform all day-to-day tasks, and the few people with more advanced recipes hardly publish their code. Maybe this will change in the future. It would certainly be welcome to see more ModSecurity Lua scripts being published.

In the next chapter, we'll focus on XML processing. The XML features of ModSecurity aren't used by all installations, but those that do use them find the capabilities crucial.

13 Handling XML

ModSecurity has very good XML support, which is made possible through tight integration with libxml2.[1] Libxml2 is one of the fastest XML libraries available, making it suitable for the performance-sensitive work of ModSecurity. The integration is seamless, effectively making XML payloads just another source of data to which you can apply your usual rule-writing techniques. The following functionality is supported:

- XML parsing

- DTD validation

- XML Schema validation

- XPath expressions

> **Note**
>
> You don't want to use ModSecurity as an XML testing tool, because the entire cycle (write rules, then send payload, then analyze the debug log) is very slow. You should instead use an XML validation tool. Probably the best option is xmllint, because it's based on the same library used by ModSecurity.

The examples used in this chapter were adapted from the sample written by Steve Traut for the former XMLBeans project.[2]

XML Parsing

Although ModSecurity is capable of parsing XML, it won't attempt any parsing by default. XML parsing is resource-intensive, and many installations don't need it. Even when they do, recognizing that XML parsing is needed isn't something that can be done in a way that works for everyone. Other request body processors (URLENCODED and MULTIPART) rely on us-

---

[1] libxml2 web site [fsty.uk/m16] (xmlsoft, retrieved 5 January 2017)

[2] XMLBeans project [fsty.uk/m46] (Apache.org, retrieved 5 January 2017)

ing a standardized content type for detection when they're needed, but there's no such option for XML.

To enable XML parsing, you'll have to go through the manual request body processor activation. There are two steps you'll need to take:

1. Analyze the request to determine whether XML parsing is needed. Most requests won't need XML parsing enabled. Figuring out which ones do will depend on the exact content type used by your application. In many cases, the Content-Type header will contain text/xml, and that's what I'll assume in my examples.

2. Instruct ModSecurity to use the XML request body processor for the requests that do need it.

For example:

```
# Detect XML payloads and activate XML parsing
SecRule REQUEST_HEADERS:Content-Type "@rx ^text/xml$" \
    id:1000,phase:1,pass,t:none,t:lowercase,nolog,ctl:requestBodyProcessor=XML
```

This example uses the @rx operator, but a straightforward @streq would have worked as well. Notice how I used t:lowercase to ensure that the comparison is case-insensitive (which is always appropriate when working with Content-Type).

It's important always to use phase 1 (REQUEST_HEADERS) when determining request body processors. Request body parsing is performed directly after phase 1 completes, and the processor choice must be made before then.

When you're writing ModSecurity rules, you usually have to test a lot, and when you're working with XML, you'll have to test even more. For my testing, I use the command line utility curl. With this tool in hand, you can construct and send raw HTTP requests to your web server to test your rules. For example, I used the following file (which I named xml.t) to test XML parsing:

```
<employees>
    <employee>
        <name>Fred Jones</name>
        <address location="home">
            <street>999 Aurora Ave.</street>
            <city>Seattle</city>
            <state>WA</state>
            <zip>98115</zip>
        </address>
        <address location="work">
            <street>2022 152nd Avenue NE</street>
            <city>Redmond</city>
            <state>WA</state>
            <zip>98052</zip>
```

```
        </address>
        <phone location="work">(425)555-0100</phone>
        <phone location="home">(206)555-0101</phone>
        <phone location="mobile">(206)555-0102</phone>
    </employee>
</employees>
```

To send a file to a web server, you specify the server information (in the following example, both the IP address and the port) and the file you want to send. I also often use the verbose switch (-v), which makes the tool output all traffic to standard output:

```
curl -v --data "@xml.t" --header "Content-Type: text/xml" http://127.0.0.1:8080
```

Let's see how ModSecurity processed this test request. First, the rule ran in phase 1 to check the value of the Content-Type request header. It matched, causing the ctl action to set the request body processor to XML. The following is the debug log output at level 8 (which is shorter than the level 9 output, but equally meaningful in this case):

```
[4] Recipe: Invoking rule 20fa670; [file "/usr/local/modsecurity/etc↵
/rules.conf"] [line "139"] [id "1000"].
[5] Rule 20fa670: SecRule "REQUEST_HEADERS:Content-Type" "@rx ^text/xml$" ↵
"phase:1,id:1000,pass,t:none,t:lowercase,nolog,ctl:requestBodyProcessor=XML"
[4] Transformation completed in 3 usec.
[4] Executing operator "rx" with param "^text/xml$" against REQUEST↵
_HEADERS:Content-Type.
[4] Operator completed in 10 usec.
[4] Ctl: Set requestBodyProcessor to XML.
[2] Warning. Pattern match "^text/xml$" at REQUEST_HEADERS:Content-Type. [file "↵
/usr/local/modsecurity/etc/rules.conf"] [line "139"] [id "1000"]
[4] Rule returned 1.
```

Then, we see the second phase starting and ModSecurity reading the request body and forwarding it to the XML parser:

```
[4] Second phase starting (dcfg 20b7878).
[4] Input filter: Reading request body.
[4] XML: Initialising parser.
[4] XML: Parsing complete (well_formed 1).
```

The last line indicates the completion of XML parsing. It also indicates that the XML was well-formed. If it wasn't, the message would display a 0 instead of a 1. This message makes a good point, in fact: you need to not only enable XML parsing, but also verify that it was successful.

To verify how well XML parsing went in a rule, use the REQBODY_PROCESSOR_ERROR variable, as you do with all request body processors. I covered this topic in detail in the section called "Handling Processing Errors" in Chapter 3. If you follow my advice from that section and

---

XML Parsing   227

use the rule to check for request body processor errors (also reproduced here), you'll be covered for XML parsing errors, too:

```
# Verify that we've correctly processed the request body.
# As a rule of thumb, when failing to process a request body
# you should reject the request (when deployed in blocking mode)
# or log a high-severity alert (when deployed in detection-only mode).
SecRule REQBODY_PROCESSOR_ERROR "!@eq 0" \
    "id:2000,phase:2,block,t:none,log,\
    msg:'Failed to parse request body: %{REQBODY_PROCESSOR_ERROR_MSG}'"
```

We can check easily whether that's correct. Make a copy of xml.t, calling the new file xml-invalid.t, then replace one of the angle brackets with a space. When you send such a modified file to the server, the debug log will report the problem:

```
[4] Second phase starting (dcfg e9a878).
[4] Input filter: Reading request body.
[4] XML: Initialising parser.
[2] XML parsing error: XML: Failed parsing document.
```

Then, a few lines down in the log file, you'll see the second rule be triggered:

```
[4] Recipe: Invoking rule 16490c0; [file "/usr/local/modsecurity/etc↵
/rules.conf"] [line "144"] [id "2000"].
[5] Rule 16490c0: SecRule "REQBODY_PROCESSOR_ERROR" "!@eq 0" "phase:2,id:2000,block↵
,t:none,log,msg:'Failed to parse request body: %{REQBODY_PROCESSOR_ERROR_MSG}'"
[4] Transformation completed in 2 usec.
[4] Executing operator "!eq" with param "0" against REQBODY_PROCESSOR_ERROR.
[4] Operator completed in 6 usec.
[4] Rule returned 1.
[1] Access denied with code 403 (phase 2). Match of "eq 0" against "REQBODY↵
_PROCESSOR_ERROR" required. [file "/usr/local/modsecurity/etc/rules.conf"] [line ↵
"144"] [id "2000"] [msg "Failed to parse request body: XML parsing error: XML: ↵
Failed parsing document."]
```

> **Note**
>
> Just because an XML payload isn't well-formed doesn't mean that your subsequent rules aren't going to run. They will run, but they'll have access only to a partial XML tree, created until the parsing error was encountered. What this tree will contain depends on the nature of the error. If you choose not to block on a request body processor failure, then you need to at least ensure that you don't rely on the results of your subsequent XML rules. For example, you could evaluate REQBODY_PROCESSOR_ERROR again and skip over them. If you don't mind working with a partial XML payload, or even if that's desired, then you don't need to do anything.

DTD Validation

Sometimes, you'll be happy to work with a partial (invalid) XML payload, but other times you'll want to perform further validation. The validation requires one further rule, in which you specify the type of validation and the file that contains the rules. ModSecurity supports two types of XML validation: DTD (short for *Document Type Definition*) and Schema validation. First, let's look at DTD validation:

```
SecRule XML "@validateDTD /path/to/apache2/conf/xml.dtd" \
    "id:2000,phase:2,block,log,msg:'Failed to validate XML payload against DTD'"
```

The `xml.dtd` file, which contains a DTD for the XML payload used earlier in this section, contains the following lines:

```
<!ELEMENT phone (#PCDATA)>
<!ATTLIST phone location CDATA #REQUIRED>
<!ELEMENT street (#PCDATA)>
<!ELEMENT city (#PCDATA)>
<!ELEMENT state (#PCDATA)>
<!ELEMENT zip (#PCDATA)>
<!ELEMENT address (street, city, state, zip)>
<!ATTLIST address location CDATA #REQUIRED>
<!ELEMENT name (#PCDATA)>
<!ELEMENT employee (name, address+, phone+)>
<!ELEMENT employees (employee)>
```

When you submit the same XML payload as before, you get the following result:

```
[4] Recipe: Invoking rule 13bfa70; [file "/usr/local/modsecurity/etc↵
/rules.conf"] [line "148"] [id "2000"].
[5] Rule 13bfa70: SecRule "XML" "@validateDTD /usr/local/apache/conf/xml.dtd" ↵
"phase:2,log,id:2000,block,msg:'Failed to validate XML payload against DTD'"
[4] Transformation completed in 0 usec.
[4] Executing operator "validateDTD" with param "/usr/local/apache/conf/xml.dtd" ↵
against XML.
[4] XML: Successfully validated payload against DTD: /usr/local/apache/conf/xml.dtd
[4] Operator completed in 544 usec.
[4] Rule returned 0.
```

> **Note**
>
> The `@validateDTD` operator returns a match if it fails to validate and no match if everything is all right.

When validation fails, the error messages from libxml2 will be recorded as notices (level 3), which means that they'll appear in the debug log, the audit log, and the Apache error log.

For example, when I changed the payload to transmit the employee name with the first name and the last name separately, as follows:

```
<firstname>Fred</firstname>
<lastname>Jones</lastname>
```

I received three libxml2 errors in return:

```
[3] Element employee content does not follow the DTD, expecting (name , address+ , ↵
phone+), got (firstname lastname address address phone phone phone )
[3] No declaration for element firstname
[3] No declaration for element lastname
```

There was also one fatal error from the validation rule itself:

```
[1] Access denied with code 403 (phase 2). XML: DTD validation failed. [file "/usr↵
/local/modsecurity/etc/rules.conf"] [line "148"] [id "2000"] [msg "Failed to ↵
validate XML payload against DTD"]
```

XML Schema Validation

The XML Schema validation rule is functionally identical to that used for DTD validation:

```
SecRule XML "@validateSchema /path/to/apache2/conf/xml.xsd" \
    "id:2000,phase:2,block,log,msg:'Failed to validate XML payload against schema'"
```

XML Schemas allow for much stricter validation, but the rule files are much more complicated. The following is the XML Schema equivalent of the DTD used in the previous section:

```
<?xml version="1.0" encoding="UTF-8"?>
<xs:schema xmlns:xs="http://www.w3.org/2001/XMLSchema">
  <xs:element name="employees">
    <xs:complexType>
      <xs:sequence>
        <xs:element name="employee" type="employeeType" maxOccurs="unbounded"/>
      </xs:sequence>
    </xs:complexType>
  </xs:element>
  <xs:complexType name="employeeType">
    <xs:sequence>
      <xs:element name="name" type="xs:string"/>
      <xs:element name="address" type="addressType" maxOccurs="unbounded"/>
      <xs:element name="phone" type="phoneType" maxOccurs="unbounded"/>
    </xs:sequence>
  </xs:complexType>
  <xs:complexType name="addressType">
```

```
    <xs:sequence>
      <xs:element name="street" type="xs:string"/>
      <xs:element name="city" type="xs:NCName"/>
      <xs:element name="state" type="xs:NCName"/>
      <xs:element name="zip" type="xs:integer"/>
    </xs:sequence>
    <xs:attribute name="location" type="xs:NCName" use="required"/>
  </xs:complexType>
  <xs:complexType name="phoneType">
    <xs:simpleContent>
      <xs:extension base="xs:string">
        <xs:attribute name="location" type="xs:NCName" use="required"/>
      </xs:extension>
    </xs:simpleContent>
  </xs:complexType>
</xs:schema>
```

Libxml2, the underlying XML library used by ModSecurity, is known to not fully implement the XML Schema standards. You may encounter validation problems that aren't a result of a problem in a request, but are the result of the incomplete XML Schema implementation in libxml2. In that case, your best bet is to try to upgrade the library to a newer version (ModSecurity will use the same library version as used by your operating system). If that doesn't help, try seeking help from the libxml2 users mailing list.

XML Namespaces

Initially, XML was simple and easy to understand, like the one example I've used many times in this chapter. As it gained in popularity, however, people decided that they wanted to combine XML documents of different types and needed a way to distinguish which elements belong to which types. Thus, XML namespaces were born.

To demonstrate how namespaces work, I've reworked the original example to split it into two namespaces—one for the employees element and the other for the address element:

```
<employees xmlns="http://www.example.org/employees">
    <employee>
        <name>Fred Jones</name>
        <a:address location="home" xmlns:a="http://www.example.org/address">
            <a:street>999 Aurora Ave.</a:street>
            <a:city>Seattle</a:city>
            <a:state>WA</a:state>
            <a:zip>98115</a:zip>
        </a:address>
        <a:address location="work" xmlns:a="http://www.example.org/address">
            <a:street>2022 152nd Avenue NE</a:street>
            <a:city>Redmond</a:city>
```

```
            <a:state>WA</a:state>
            <a:zip>98052</a:zip>
        </a:address>
        <phone location="work">(425)555-0100</phone>
        <phone location="home">(206)555-0101</phone>
        <phone location="mobile">(206)555-0102</phone>
    </employee>
  </employees>
```

To use a namespace, choose a prefix (it can be anything) and associate it with a namespace URI. In the preceding example, the prefix is a (nice and short) and the URI is http://www.example.org/address (it's not necessary for the URI to work; its role is just to serve as a unique identifier). Once a namespace has been introduced, you need to rewrite all the tags that belong to it to use the prefix.

Of course, the original XML Schema we used for validation won't work any more. The assumption, with the new XML payload, is that two Schemas are needed. The address Schema (xml-address.xsd) defines the rules only for addresses:

```
<?xml version="1.0" encoding="UTF-8"?>
<xs:schema xmlns:xs="http://www.w3.org/2001/XMLSchema"
  elementFormDefault="qualified"
  targetNamespace="http://www.example.org/address"
  xmlns="http://www.example.org/address">

  <xs:element name="address" type="addressType"/>

  <xs:complexType name="addressType">
    <xs:sequence>
      <xs:element name="street" type="xs:string"/>
      <xs:element name="city" type="xs:NCName"/>
      <xs:element name="state" type="xs:NCName"/>
      <xs:element name="zip" type="xs:integer"/>
    </xs:sequence>
    <xs:attribute name="location" type="xs:NCName" use="required"/>
  </xs:complexType>

  <xs:complexType name="phoneType">
    <xs:simpleContent>
      <xs:extension base="xs:string">
        <xs:attribute name="location" type="xs:NCName" use="required"/>
      </xs:extension>
    </xs:simpleContent>
  </xs:complexType>

</xs:schema>
```

The employees Schema (xml-employees.xsd) defines the rules for everything else:

```xml
<?xml version="1.0" encoding="UTF-8"?>
<xs:schema xmlns:xs="http://www.w3.org/2001/XMLSchema"
  elementFormDefault="qualified"
  targetNamespace="http://www.example.org/employees"
  xmlns="http://www.example.org/employees"
  xmlns:a="http://www.example.org/address">

  <xs:import namespace="http://www.example.org/address"
  schemaLocation="xml-address.xsd"/>

  <xs:element name="employees">
    <xs:complexType>
      <xs:sequence>
        <xs:element name="employee" type="employeeType" maxOccurs="unbounded"/>
      </xs:sequence>
    </xs:complexType>
  </xs:element>
  <xs:complexType name="employeeType">
    <xs:sequence>
      <xs:element name="name" type="xs:string"/>
      <xs:element ref="a:address" maxOccurs="unbounded"/>
      <xs:element name="phone" type="phoneType" maxOccurs="unbounded"/>
    </xs:sequence>
  </xs:complexType>
  <xs:complexType name="phoneType">
    <xs:simpleContent>
      <xs:extension base="xs:string">
        <xs:attribute name="location" type="xs:NCName" use="required"/>
      </xs:extension>
    </xs:simpleContent>
  </xs:complexType>
</xs:schema>
```

Notice how this second Schema uses the XML Schema import facility to refer to xml-address.xsd and then uses the address element by reference.

When you need to validate a document that uses multiple Schemas, as in the preceding example, the parameter that you supply to @validateSchema must be the path to the main Schema. You should also place all dependent Schemas in the same directory as the main one, which will enable libxml2 to find them. The validation rule is the same as before:

```
SecRule XML "@validateSchema /path/to/apache2/conf/xml-employees.xsd" \
    "id:2000,phase:2,block,log,msg:'Failed to validate XML payload against schema'"
```

If the validation fails, you'll see the following information in your debug log:

```
[4] Executing operator "validateSchema" with param "/usr/lib/modsecurity/etc↵
/xml-employees.xsd" against XML.
[9] Target value: "[XML document tree]"
[3] Element '{http://www.example.org/employees}name': Element content is not ↵
allowed, because the type definition is simple.
[4] Operator completed in 1297 usec.
[4] Rule returned 1.
```

XPath Expressions

XML Path Language (XPath) is a language for addressing parts of an XML document. The addressing is done by writing XPath expressions, which are powerful and easy to use. I've compiled several examples in Table 13.1, but if you've never worked with XPath expressions before, I recommend that you go through the very nice tutorial available at zvon.org.[3]

Table 13.1. XPath expression examples

XPath expression	Description
/	Root element
/employees/employee	All employees
//address	An address, under any parent element
//*	All elements in payload
/employees/employee/address[2]	The second employee address
//phone[@location='work']	All work phone numbers

XPath expressions can be used only against the XML collection, and only in phase 2 (request) and later—for example:

```
SecRule XML:/employees/employee/name/text() "!@rx ^[a-zA-Z ]{3,33}$" \
    "id:2000,phase:2,deny,msg:'Invalid employee name'"
```

Unless you've worked with XPath expressions before, the results may not always be what you expect. Some XPath expressions will give tidy results; for example, the one used in the preceding example will return Fred Jones. However, that happens only when you select a simple element (one that doesn't have any children). If the element you select has children, you get back everything the children contain too, excluding the markup.

Try this, for example:

```
# Get the complete second employee address
SecRule XML:/employees/employee/address[2] "@rx TEST" \
    "id:2000,phase:2,deny"
```

---

[3] XPath tutorial [fsty.uk/m47] (zvon.org, retrieved 5 January 2017)

Chapter 13: Handling XML

The address fragment in the XML payload contains the following text (notice the whitespace, which I left the same as it is in the original payload):

```
<address location="work">
    <street>2022 152nd Avenue NE</street>
    <city>Redmond</city>
    <state>WA</state>
    <zip>98052</zip>
</address>
```

The debug log reveals what was used for matching (now in log level 9):

```
[4] Recipe: Invoking rule 1a173c0; [file "/usr/local/modsecurity/etc↵
/rules.conf"] [line "159"] [id "2000"].
[5] Rule 1a173c0: SecRule "XML:/employees/employee/address[2]" "@rx TEST" ↵
"phase:2,log,id:2000,deny"
[4] Transformation completed in 0 usec.
[4] Executing operator "rx" with param "TEST" against XML:/employees/employee↵
/address[2].
[9] Target value: "              2011 152nd Avenue NE          Redmond          ↵
WA            98052          "
```

You can see that the whitespace is all there, including the newline characters.

As a rule of thumb, when working with XML you should restrict yourself to the analysis of specific fields. Bulk analysis (e.g., using //*, which returns all elements in an XML payload) just isn't going to be very effective, because even smaller payloads will be broken into dozens, and larger ones into possibly hundreds and thousands of small pieces. The performance of bulk XML matching is likely to be very bad. When the //* expression is used with our short XML example, it creates 16 variables.

XPath and Namespaces

Once you move away from simple XML documents to those using namespaces, your XPath expressions might stop working. For example, we could have used the following "clean" XPath expression to validate ZIP codes in the first XML example:

```
SecRule XML://address/zip "!@rx ^\d+$" \
    "id:2000,phase:2,deny,msg:'Invalid ZIP code'"
```

To get the rule working with an XML document that uses prefixes, like the second XML example, you could try to modify the XPath expression to include the prefixes, but that will just cause XPath evaluation to fail, because libxml2 will try to match the prefix to a namespace but won't know how. You'll see XML: Unable to evaluate xpath expression in the debug log. Even if libxml2 didn't complain, this approach wouldn't work, because the choice of prefix is in the hands of the request sender. You don't get to control it on the server.

The solution is to use prefixes in XPath expressions, but also tell libxml2 about the namespace, using the xmlns action:

```
SecRule XML://a:address/a:zip "!@rx ^\d+$" \
    "id:2000,phase:2,deny,msg:'Invalid ZIP code',xmlns:a=http://www.example.org↵
/address"
```

This example will work as it would in the original example, returning two ZIP codes. It will even work if the sender chooses an entirely different prefix.

XML Inspection Framework

The validation examples so far all assumed one validation per request, but an average application will have many entry points, with a different set of rules needed for each. In this section, I sketch a framework that you can use whenever you need to deal with XML in ModSecurity.

```
# Establish the baseline for all XML entry points
<Location /api/>
    # Is the Content-Type correct?
    SecRule REQUEST_HEADERS:Content-Type "!@rx ^text/xml$" \
        "id:1000,phase:1,deny,t:lowercase,msg:'Invalid Content-Type for XML API'"

    # Activate XML parsing
    SecAction id:1001,phase:1,pass,t:lowercase,nolog,ctl:requestBodyProcessor=XML

    # Was the payload successfully parsed?
    SecRule REQBODY_PROCESSOR_ERROR "!@eq 0" \
        "id:2000,phase:2,deny,t:none,log,\
        msg:'Failed to parse request body: %{REQBODY_PROCESSOR_ERROR_MSG}'"

    # By default, we assume that XML validation did not take place
    SecAction id:2001,phase:2,pass,nolog,setvar:TX.xml_validated=0
</Location>

# Entry point One
<Location /api/entryPointOne.php>
    # Validate payload first
    SecRule XML "@validateDTD /path/to/conf/entryPointOne.dtd" \
        "id:2002,phase:2,deny,msg:'Failed to validate XML against ↵
entryPointOne.dtd'"

    # Restrict employee name to known good characters only
    SecRule XML:/employees/employee/name/text() "!@rx ^[a-zA-Z ]{3,33}$" \
        "id:2003,phase:2,deny,msg:'Invalid employee name'"
```

```
    # Validation was successful
    SecAction id:2004,phase:2,pass,nolog,setvar:TX.xml_validated
</Location>

# Entry point Two
<Location /api/entryPointTwo.php>
    # Validate payload first
    SecRule XML "@validateDTD /path/to/conf/entryPointTwo.dtd" \
        "id:2005,phase:2,deny,msg:'Failed to validate XML against ↵
entryPointTwo.dtd'"

    # Implement additional restrictions
    # ...

    # Validation was successful
    SecAction id:2006,phase:2,pass,nolog,setvar:TX.xml_validated
</Location>

# Finally, verify that the entry point was valid
<Location /api/>
    # The xml_validated flag will only be set after a
    # successful validation
    SecRule TX:xml_validated "!@eq 1" \
        "id:2007,phase:2,deny,msg:'Invalid API entry point'"
</Location>
```

With this example framework, we achieve the following:

1. First, there is one <Location> section in which we establish the baseline for all XML entry points. It's here that we activate XML parsing but also reject all requests that aren't XML. The assumption is that the /api/ folder contains only XML entry points. This assumption is usually valid, because API calls don't need any accompanying files (e.g., embedded images, stylesheet files, etc.).

2. With an additional one <Location> section per entry point, we ensure that we apply the correct validation rules to each entry point, followed by the per-entry point rules.

3. We finalize the XML rules by adding another global <Location> section, in which we use one rule that checks whether validation was successfully completed. This final check is needed in case a request specifies an unlisted entry point, in which case the xml_validated flag will be 0 (set in the first global section).

> **Note**
>
> Remember that configuration merging for the <Location> directive works in the same order in which the sections appear in the configuration file. Thus, the rules will be processed as they appear in the configuration too. If you aren't familiar with

> Apache's configuration merging, there's a refresher available in the section called "Apache Configuration Syntax" in Chapter 7.

With XML rules, as with all other rules, the best approach is to use whitelisting, or positive security. Through this approach, you look at every single bit of data you accept and check that it's correct. You don't try to discover "bad" characters (that would be negative security, or blacklisting). DTD validation generally isn't powerful enough, but you may be able to use XML Schemas as a good validation mechanism. Then, if there are parts that you can't cover with Schemas, you should use custom XPath expressions as the last line of validation.

Summary

Being able to properly process XML is always important, especially if you're dealing with XML-based APIs. In ModSecurity, generally you'll find everything you need to parse, validate, and inspect XML in a meaningful way. If you find certain parts of the XML support difficult to work with, that's probably not because of ModSecurity, but because the XML world continues to increase in complexity. No effort on the part of ModSecurity developers can make that go away, and you may have to resort to advanced validation techniques using external logic developed in Lua or some other language.

There's only one chapter left in this User Guide, and it will teach you how to extend ModSecurity by writing native code, which is something that you may need to do when you reach the edges of ModSecurity's capabilities. Don't worry; it's easy to do. I promise!

14 Extending the Rule Language

The ModSecurity rule language is pretty good at meeting users' requirements, but sometimes you'll need it to do something that it can't. We looked at Lua previously, but if you want to stay in ModSecurity and you can program in C, then there's an easy way to extend the rule language. There are four extension points, enabling you to add custom variables, operators, transformation functions, and request body processors.

Because ModSecurity is part of Apache, it doesn't have to implement its own extension infrastructure: you extend ModSecurity by writing Apache modules. This is a great time-saver if you have previous Apache programming experience. However, even if you don't, finding people who do generally will be easy. After all, Apache is one of the most popular programs ever.

For years, the common way to learn how to write Apache modules was to study existing modules, especially the ones bundled with Apache itself. (My favorite has always been mod_rewrite.) If you prefer a book, then Nick Kew's *The Apache Modules Book* (Prentice Hall, 2007) is the standard reference on the topic. Nick's book is now 10 years old, but it's still invaluable. For simple efforts, what's in this section should be sufficient.

With or without the book, you should familiarize yourself with the Apache Portable Runtime (APR) and Apache Portable Runtime Utility (APR-Util) libraries, which form the infrastructure on top of which Apache is built.[1] Whenever you program an Apache module, you have full access to the APR and APR-Util libraries—which is quite handy, because they contain tons of useful functionality.

The remainder of this chapter will introduce a template module, which you can use as a starting point for your ModSecurity extensions, and then implement four modules, one for each extension point. For the examples, I'll use the sample code included with ModSecurity and stored in the ext subfolder.

---

[1] Apache Portable Runtime Project [fsty.uk/m14] (Apache.org, retrieved 5 January 2017)

Extension Template

First, I'll show you how to create a template module that establishes the infrastructure on top of which we'll build later.

> **Note**
>
> Before you begin, ensure that you have the ability to compile custom Apache modules. This is the same process as that for custom-compiling ModSecurity itself. In addition, you'll need the source code for the exact version of ModSecurity you're writing extensions for.

The template module is a complete Apache module, which you should be able to compile and install. You can practice with it to ensure that your environment has all the right components for custom Apache module development. The following is the complete module source code:

```c
#include "httpd.h"
#include "http_core.h"
#include "http_config.h"
#include "http_log.h"
#include "http_protocol.h"
#include "ap_config.h"
#include "apr_optional.h"

#include "modsecurity.h"

/**
 * This function is just a placeholder in this template.
 */
static int hook_pre_config(apr_pool_t *mp, apr_pool_t *mplog, apr_pool_t *mptmp) {
    /* Empty for now, but will be used later. */
    return OK;
}

/**
 * Register to be invoked before configuration begins.
 */
static void register_hooks(apr_pool_t *p) {
    ap_hook_pre_config(hook_pre_config, NULL, NULL, APR_HOOK_LAST);
}

/**
 * This structure is used by Apache to determine that a dynamic
 * library it is loading is a genuine module.
 */
```

```
module AP_MODULE_DECLARE_DATA security_template_module = {
    STANDARD20_MODULE_STUFF,
    NULL,
    NULL,
    NULL,
    NULL,
    NULL,
    register_hooks
};
```

There are three points of interest in the module:

1. The security_template_module structure is used by Apache to verify that the dynamic library is indeed a module. The name is important and should be unique. You'll use the same name when you instruct Apache to load the module later on.

2. The security_template_module initialization structure points to the register_hook callback, which is going to be the module's main initialization entry point.

3. The register_hook callback registers another callback, hook_pre_config, which is invoked every time Apache is reconfigured. This callback doesn't do anything in the template module, but we'll add to it later.

You'll be compiling the template module using the apxs Apache tool. If it isn't in your path, it will be in the bin/ subfolder of your Apache installation. Assuming you placed the source code in the file called mod_security_template.c, invoke the following to compile the template module:

```
$ apxs -cia \
    -I/path/to/modsecurity/source_code \
    -I/usr/include/libxml2 \
    mod_security_template.c
```

> **Note**
>
> On Linux, processes are known to crash when the dynamic libraries they're using change. It's a best practice to shut down Apache before adding or removing any of its modules.

The apxs command line in the example uses five switches, which perform the following functions:

1. Compile the module (switch -c).

2. Copy the compiled module to the directory in which all other Apache modules are stored (switch -i).

3. Activate the module by adding the correct LoadModule directive to the configuration (switch -a).

---

4. Point to the location of the ModSecurity include files (switch `-I/path/to/modsecurity/source_code`).

5. Point to the location of the libxml2 include files (switch `-I/usr/include/libxml2`).

The activation step will work if you have at least one existing `LoadModule` directive in your configuration. The last line will say something similar to the following:

```
[activating module 'security_template' in /usr/local/apache/conf/httpd.conf]
```

If you have a more elaborate configuration layout and the `apxs` tool can't find at least one existing `LoadModule` directive in your `httpd.conf`, you'll have to activate the module manually by adding the following line to the configuration:

```
LoadModule security_template_module modules/mod_security_template.so
```

The first parameter must match the module name used in the source code. You should always place a ModSecurity extension module after the `LoadModule` line that activates ModSecurity itself. If you don't, ModSecurity might not be able to recognize the newly added function.

If Apache starts with the new `LoadModule` line in the configuration, you've successfully completed this step.

Adding a Transformation Function

Starting from the template module, implementing a new transformation function requires two steps. First, you need to implement a single function, which will be called by ModSecurity every time a transformation is needed. All transformation functions (in C) use the following signature:

```
static int reverse(apr_pool_t *mptmp, unsigned char *input,
    long int input_len, char **rval, long int *rval_len)
{
    /* Transformation code here. */

    /* Return 1 if you change the input, 0 if you don't/ */
    return 1;
}
```

To examine the implementation of the built-in transformation functions, refer to the `re_tfns.c` file in the ModSecurity source code.

In general, you should use the same name for the C function as you intend to use for the transformation function in ModSecurity. The five parameters in the signature are as follows:

1. `apr_pool_t *mptmp`: APR memory pool you can use to allocate memory from

Chapter 14: Extending the Rule Language

2. `unsigned char *input`: Pointer to the input string you need to transform

3. `long int input_len`: Length of the input string

4. `char **rval`: Pointer in which to return the output string

5. `long int rval_len`: Length of the output string

> **Note**
>
> Remember that ModSecurity doesn't use NUL-terminated strings. Always use the input_len parameter, which contains the input length.

If your transformation always results in an output string that's equal to or shorter than the input string, you should make your changes in place, overwriting the input string. By doing so, you save on memory allocation, thus speeding up your transformation function. In this case, the `rval` pointer should point to the input string on return.

If the output can be longer, use the `mptmp` memory pool to allocate from, then point `rval` to the newly allocated memory chunk. The memory you allocate will be deallocated automatically when ModSecurity clears the temporary memory pool. Any other memory allocation method would create a memory leak, because deallocation is always manual and you won't have an opportunity to invoke it.

The following is the complete source code of the transformation function example included with ModSecurity:

```
/**
 * This function will be invoked by
 * ModSecurity to transform input.
 */
static int reverse(apr_pool_t *mptmp, unsigned char *input,
    long int input_len, char **rval, long int *rval_len)
{
    /* Transformation functions can choose to do their
     * thing in-place, overwriting the existing content. This
     * is normally possible only if the transformed content
     * is of equal length or shorter.
     *
     * If you need to expand the content use the temporary
     * memory pool mptmp to allocate the space.
     */

    /* Reverse the string in place, but only if it's long enough. */
    if (input_len > 1) {
        long int i = 0;
        long int j = input_len - 1;
        while(i < j) {
            char c = input[i];
```

```
                input[i] = input[j];
                input[j] = c;
                i++;
                j--;
            }
        }

        /* Tell ModSecurity about the content
         * we have generated. In this case we
         * merely point back to the input buffer.
         */
        *rval = (char *)input;
        *rval_len = input_len;

        /* Must return 1 if the content was
         * changed, or 0 otherwise.
         */
        return 1;
    }
```

The return value from a transformation function should always be 1 if the content you're returning is different than the content you received on input, and 0 otherwise. Even if you placed the output in a newly allocated memory chunk, if it's the same, the return code should be 0. Returning the correct response code will allow ModSecurity to work slightly faster when there are no changes, but you shouldn't worry too much about it. If keeping track of whether you made a change is difficult or expensive, just return 1.

Now that you have the function, you need to register it with ModSecurity. To do so, use the Apache mechanism called *optional functions*, which is a two-step process:

1. Ask Apache to find the registration function, which will have been exported by ModSecurity beforehand.

2. Register the new transformation function.

The following example is an implementation of this process:

```
/**
 * Register transformation function with ModSecurity.
 */
static int hook_pre_config(apr_pool_t *mp, apr_pool_t *mplog, apr_pool_t *mptmp) {
    void (*fn)(const char *name, void *fn);

    /* Look for the registration function
     * exported by ModSecurity.
     */
    fn = APR_RETRIEVE_OPTIONAL_FN(modsec_register_tfn);
    if (fn) {
        /* Use it to register our new
```

```
      * transformation function under the
      * name "reverse".
      */
     fn("reverse", (void *)reverse);
  } else {
     ap_log_error(APLOG_MARK, APLOG_ERR | APLOG_NOERRNO, 0, NULL,
        "mod_tfn_reverse: Unable to find modsec_register_tfn.");
  }

  return OK;
}
```

Once you restart Apache, the new transformation function will be equal to those that come with ModSecurity. You should always test your new functionality; for example, add the following rule to the configuration:

```
SecRule ARGS "@rx test" \
    id:2000,phase:2,deny,t:none,t:reverse,log
```

Then, if you send a request with parameter p for which the value is set to tset (the opposite of test), you should get a 403 response in return. The following debug log excerpt shows the new reverse transformation function working as expected:

```
[4] Recipe: Invoking rule 939638; [file "/usr/local/modsecurity/rules.conf] ↵
[line "139"] [id "2000"].
[5] Rule 939638: SecRule "ARGS" "@rx test" "phase:2,id:1007,deny,t:reverse,log"
[9] T (0) reverse: "test"
[4] Transformation completed in 12 usec.
[4] Executing operator "rx" with param "test" against ARGS:p.
[9] Target value: "test"
[4] Operator completed in 9 usec.
[4] Rule returned 1.
[9] Match, intercepted -> returning.
[1] Access denied with code 403 (phase 2). Pattern match "test" at ARGS:p. [file ↵
"/usr/local/modsecurity/rules.conf"] [line "139"] [id "2000"]
```

Adding an Operator

Creating new operators is slightly more difficult, because two functions are needed: there's an additional (and optional) initialization step, which allows your code to do some work at configure-time and reuse it at runtime. The split of the work sometimes allows for significant performance improvements. In ModSecurity, the source code for the built-in operators is in the re_operators.c file.

The new operator example adds a new string-matching function based on the Boyer-Moore-Horspool algorithm.[2] I won't show the code for the algorithm itself here, instead assuming that the following two functions are already implemented:

```
static void initBoyerMooreHorspool(const char *pattern, int patlength,
    int *bm_badcharacter_array);

static int BoyerMooreHorspool(const char *pattern, int patlength,
    const char *text, int textlen, int *bm_badcharacter_array);
```

If you're curious, of course, you can always look at the implementation at the end of the mod_op_strstr.c file (included with ModSecurity). The string-matching algorithm does require initialization, so we'll be using both steps. The initialization code is as follows:

```
/**
 * Operator parameter initialization entry point.
 */
static int op_strstr_init(msre_rule *rule, char **error_msg) {
    /* Operator initialization function will be called once per
     * statement where operator is used. It is meant to be used
     * to check the parameters to see whether they are present
     * and if they are in the correct format.
     */

    /* In this example we just look for a simple nonempty parameter. */
    if ((rule->op_param == NULL)||(strlen(rule->op_param) == 0)) {
        *error_msg = apr_psprintf(rule->ruleset->mp,
          "Missing parameter for operator 'strstr'.");
        return 0; /* ERROR */
    }

    /* If you need to transform the data in the parameter into something
     * else you should do that here. Simply create a new structure to hold
     * the transformed data and place the pointer to it into rule->op_param_data.
     * You will have access to this pointer later on.
     */
    rule->op_param_data = apr_pcalloc(rule->ruleset->mp,
  ALPHABET_SIZE * sizeof(int));
    initBoyerMooreHorspool(rule->op_param, strlen(rule->op_param),
  (int *)rule->op_param_data);

    /* OK */
    return 1;
}
```

---

[2] Boyer-Moore-Horspool algorithm [fsty.uk/m48] (Wikipedia, retrieved 5 January 2017)

Unlike with the transformation function example, here we get to work with ModSecurity structures directly. The first parameter of the operator initialization is a pointer to the msre_rule structure (full definition in re.h). There are two fields in this structure that you'll want to use:

- op_param: A NUL-terminated string that may contain a parameter for your operator
- op_param_data: A generic pointer for your operators' use

The idea is to check the parameter available in op_param and do something with it, then perform the initialization work and store a pointer to the results in op_param_data. When your operator is invoked at runtime, it will have access to the same msre_rule structure and thus to op_param_data. Should you need an example, the code for the @rx and @pm operators demonstrates how parameter preparation is done. Also note the following important points:

- If you need to allocate memory, use the memory pool in rule->ruleset->mp, as in the example.
- If your initialization fails, generate an error string, store it in error_msg (the second function parameter), and return a zero.

The operator execution code is equally simple:

```
/**
 * Operator execution entry point.
 */
static int op_strstr_exec(modsec_rec *msr, msre_rule *rule,
    msre_var *var, char **error_msg)
{
    /* Here we need to inspect the contents of the supplied variable. */

    /* In a general case it is possible for the value
     * to be NULL. What you need to do in this case
     * depends on your operator. In this example we return
     * a "no match" response.
     */
    if (var->value == NULL) return 0; /* No match. */

    /* Another thing to note is that variables are not C strings,
     * meaning the NULL byte is not used to determine the end
     * of the string. Variable length var->value_len should be
     * used for this purpose.
     */

    if (BoyerMooreHorspool(rule->op_param, strlen(rule->op_param),
        var->value, var->value_len, (int *)rule->op_param_data) >= 0)
    {
        *error_msg = apr_psprintf(msr->mp, "Pattern match \"%s\" at %s.",
            rule->op_param, var->name);
```

```
        return 1; /* Match. */
    }

    return 0; /* No match. */
}
```

This time, you'll receive four parameters:

1. `modsec_rec *msr`: The structure in which all transaction data is stored

2. `msre_rule *rule`: The same rule structure you received in the initialization phase

3. `msre_var *var`: The variable structure, which holds the data you need to inspect

4. `char **error_msg`: An error message pointer, which you can point at an error message

The data you need to inspect is stored in a `msre_var` instance, which has the following layout:

```
struct msre_var {
    const char          *name;
    const char          *value;
    unsigned int         value_len;
    const char          *param;
    const void          *param_data;
    msre_var_metadata *metadata;
    msc_regex_t         *param_regex;
    unsigned int         is_negated;
    unsigned int         is_counting;
};
```

Although it looks complex, you only need to be concerned with two fields:

- `const char *value`: Pointer to the variable the operator needs to inspect

- `unsigned int value_len`: Length of the variable

After you inspect the variable, return 0 if there's no match and 1 if there is.

The operator registration step is conceptually identical to that used for transformation functions, except that you use the `modsec_register_operator` optional function:

```
static int hook_pre_config(apr_pool_t *mp, apr_pool_t *mplog,
    apr_pool_t *mptmp)
{
    void (*fn)(const char *name, void *fn_init, void *fn_exec);

    /* Look for the registration function
     * exported by ModSecurity.
     */
    fn = APR_RETRIEVE_OPTIONAL_FN(modsec_register_operator);
    if (fn) {
```

```
    /* Use it to register our new
     * transformation function under the
     * name "reverse".
     */
    fn("strstr", (void *)op_strstr_init, (void *)op_strstr_exec);
} else {
    ap_log_error(APLOG_MARK, APLOG_ERR | APLOG_NOERRNO, 0, NULL,
        "mod_op_strstr: Unable to find modsec_register_operator.");
}

return OK;
}
```

When you compile and enable this module, it gives you access to the new @strstr operator. You can use it in your rules as follows:

```
SecRule ARGS "@strstr attack" \
    id:2000,phase:2,deny,log
```

Adding a Variable

To generate new variables, you typically need to implement one function call. The example that comes with ModSecurity is split across three functions, but that's done for code reuse. Here's the simplified code:

```
static int var_remote_addr_port_generate(modsec_rec *msr, msre_var *var,
    msre_rule *rule, apr_table_t *vartab, apr_pool_t *mptmp)
{
    msre_var *rvar = NULL;

    const char *value = apr_psprintf(mptmp, "%s:%d",
        msr->remote_addr, msr->remote_port);
    if (value == NULL) return 0;

    /* Generate new variable. */
    rvar = apr_pmemdup(mptmp, var, sizeof(msre_var));
    rvar->value = value;
    rvar->value_len = strlen(rvar->value);

    /* Add variable to the collection. */
    apr_table_addn(vartab, rvar->name, (void *)rvar);

    return 1;
}
```

The following parameters are provided:

1. `modsec_rec *msr`: Structure in which all transaction data is stored

2. `msre_var *var`: Variable template

3. `apr_table_t *vartab`: Collection of the variables being prepared for inspection

4. `apr_pool_t *mptmp`: Memory pool from which you can allocate memory

Creating new variables is a four-step process:

1. Create the variable data. How you do that depends on the nature of the data, but it can be as easy as using a single `apr_sprintf()` call (as in the example).

2. Create a new `msre_var` structure, duplicating from the one already provided in `var`, and populate the `value` and `value_len` fields.

3. Using `apr_table_addn()`, add the newly created `msre_var` structure to the `vartab` collection.

4. Return 1 to indicate that you've added one variable to the collection. If you create more than one variable (by repeating steps 1 through 3), keep track of how many new variables there are and return the correct value at the end of the function.

Variable registration is slightly more involved, but only because you need to help ModSecurity do most of the runtime work for you:

```
static int hook_pre_config(apr_pool_t *mp, apr_pool_t *mplog,
    apr_pool_t *mptmp)
{
    void (*register_fn)(const char *name, unsigned int type,
                        unsigned int argc_min, unsigned int argc_max,
                        void *fn_validate, void *fn_generate,
                        unsigned int is_cacheable, unsigned int availability);

    /* Look for the registration function
     * exported by ModSecurity.
     */
    register_fn = APR_RETRIEVE_OPTIONAL_FN(modsec_register_variable);
    if (register_fn) {
        /* Use it to register our new
         * variable under the
         * name "REMOTE_ADDR_PORT".
         */
        register_fn(
            "REMOTE_ADDR_PORT",
            VAR_SIMPLE,
            0, 0,
            NULL,
            var_remote_addr_port_generate,
            VAR_DONT_CACHE,
            PHASE_REQUEST_HEADERS
```

```
            );
        } else {
            ap_log_error(APLOG_MARK, APLOG_ERR | APLOG_NOERRNO, 0, NULL,
                "mod_var_remote_addr_port: Unable to find modsec_register_variable.");
        }

        return OK;
    }
```

To register a variable, you need to use eight parameters, but apart from that, the registration process doesn't hold any surprises:

1. `const char *name`: Variable name.

2. `unsigned int type`: Variable type; use `VAR_SIMPLE` to indicate that you will return only one value, or `VAR_LIST` to indicate the possibility of returning multiple values.

3. `unsigned int argc_min`: Variable parameter definition; use 0 if you don't need to use a parameter, or 1 if you do.

4. `unsigned int argc_max`: Variable parameter definition; use 0 if you don't allow a parameter, or 1 if you do.

5. `void *fn_validate`: Optional pointer to the parameter validation function.

6. `void *fn_generate`: Pointer to the generation function.

7. `unsigned int is_cacheable`: Is the variable cacheable? If generating the variable is expensive and the value isn't likely to change during the duration of a transaction, set it to `VAR_CACHE`. Otherwise, set it to `VAR_DONT_CACHE`.

8. `unsigned int availability`: Phase in which the variable becomes available: `PHASE_REQUEST_HEADERS`, `PHASE_REQUEST_BODY`, `PHASE_RESPONSE_HEADERS`, `PHASE_RESPONSE_BODY`, or `PHASE_LOGGING`. ModSecurity should use this value to ensure that the variable isn't referenced in the rules before it's available. (I say *should* because ModSecurity doesn't do so at the moment.)

As you know, in ModSecurity variables can have parameters. For example, you use `ARGS:p` to request the parameter named `p`, and `ARGS:/^p/` to request all the parameters that start with p. If you allow parameters for your variables, the single parameter will be placed in `var->param`. How you interpret the parameter depends on the nature of the variable. For inspiration, you can look up the `var_args_generate()` function in `re_variables.c`, which implements the `ARGS` collection.

Finally, if you think you can speed up variable retrieval by using configure-time initialization, supply a separate validation function when you register your variable—for example:

```
static char *var_generic_list_validate(msre_ruleset *ruleset, msre_var *var) {
    /* Is it OK if there's no parameter provided? Return NULL if
     * it is. If you require a parameter and you correctly registered
```

```
 * the variable, your validation function will never be invoked.
 */
if (var->param == NULL) return NULL;

/* Validate the value in var->param. */
// ...

/* Perform your initialization work. */
// ...

/* Store initialization data for subsequent retrieval. */
var->param_data = my_opaque_pointer;

/* No error. */
return NULL;
}
```

If you need more examples, all the ModSecurity variables are implemented in the re_variables.c file.

Adding a Request Body Processor

Every request body processor needs to implement three entry points: initialization, data processing, and finalization. The initialization and finalization functions will be invoked only once per request body, but the data-processing function may be invoked many times, each time with a chunk of request body data. The example in this section implements a simple request body processor that counts only the number of bytes seen.

First, register your request body processor in the hook_pre_config() function:

```
static int hook_pre_config(apr_pool_t *mp, apr_pool_t *mplog,
    apr_pool_t *mptmp)
{
    void (*fn)(const char *name,
              void *fn_init, void *fn_process, void *fn_complete);

    /* Look for the registration function exported by ModSecurity. */
    fn = APR_RETRIEVE_OPTIONAL_FN(modsec_register_reqbody_processor);
    if (fn) {
        /* Use it to register our new request body parser functions under
         * the name "EXAMPLE".
         */
        fn("EXAMPLE",
            (void *)example_init,
            (void *)example_process,
            (void *)example_complete);
    }
```

```
    else {
        ap_log_error(APLOG_MARK, APLOG_ERR | APLOG_NOERRNO, 0, NULL,
            "mod_reqbody_example: Unable to register");
    }

    return OK;
}
```

Before we can move to the initialization, we need to define a structure to store the example context. Let's keep this simple in our example by defining a structure that holds only the length of the body:

```
/**
 * Define the example context structure
 */
typedef struct example_ctx {
    unsigned long length;
} example_ctx;
```

Initialization is usually straightforward; use it to create a request body processor context, which you'll need to keep the state during parsing:

```
/**
 * This function will be invoked to initialize the processor.  This is
 * probably only needed for streaming parsers that must create a context.
 */
static int example_init(modsec_rec *msr, char **error_msg) {
    if (error_msg == NULL) return -1;
    *error_msg = NULL;

    ap_log_error(APLOG_MARK, APLOG_INFO | APLOG_NOERRNO, 0, NULL,
        "mod_reqbody_example: init()");

    msr->reqbody_processor_ctx = apr_pcalloc(msr->mp, sizeof(example_ctx));
    if (msr->reqbody_processor_ctx == NULL) {
        /* Set error message and return -1 if unsuccessful */
        *error_msg = apr_pstrdup(msr->mp,
            "failed to create example reqbody processor context");
        return -1;
    }

    /* Return 1 on success */
    return 1;
}
```

Finalization is usually equally simple, although some parsers will need to do more work here. Remember that you shouldn't deallocate your context. Because all allocation is performed from a memory pool, ModSecurity will release the allocated memory all at once at the end of transaction.

In our example, at the end of parsing, we'll simply print the number of bytes seen in the request body to the log:

```
/**
 * This function is called to signal the parser that the request body is
 * complete. Here you should do any final parsing.  For nonstreaming parsers
 * you can parse the data in msr->msc_reqbody_buffer of length
 * msr->msc_reqbody_length.  See modsecurity_request_body_end_urlencoded() in
 * msc_reqbody.c for an example of this.
 */
static int example_complete(modsec_rec *msr, char **error_msg) {
    example_ctx *ctx = (example_ctx *)msr->reqbody_processor_ctx;

    if (error_msg == NULL) return -1;
    *error_msg = NULL;

    ap_log_error(APLOG_MARK, APLOG_INFO | APLOG_NOERRNO, 0, NULL,
        "mod_reqbody_example: complete()");

    ap_log_error(APLOG_MARK, APLOG_INFO | APLOG_NOERRNO, 0, NULL,
        "mod_reqbody_example: request body length=%lu", ctx->length);

    /* Return 1 on success */
    return 1;
}
```

The processing function is usually where all the work happens. You'll be provided data in small pieces as it's received from the client. On every invocation, you'll retrieve your context, perform some processing, and return, signaling success or failure.

There's one additional duty that you need to perform: keeping track of the actual data bytes seen in a request body. There's no universal definition of data bytes, so you're free to define it as you see fit. For example, the multipart/form-data parser will exclude markup and file content when counting data bytes. The data size you calculate here is what's checked for limits specified by the SecRequestBodyNoFilesLimit directive:

```
/**
 * This function will be invoked whenever ModSecurity has data to
 * be processed.  You probably at least need to increment the no_files
 * length, but otherwise this is only useful for a streaming parser.
 */
static int example_process(modsec_rec *msr, const char *buf,
    unsigned int size, char **error_msg)
{
    example_ctx *ctx = (example_ctx *)msr->reqbody_processor_ctx;
```

```
    if (error_msg == NULL) return -1;
    *error_msg = NULL;

    ap_log_error(APLOG_MARK, APLOG_INFO | APLOG_NOERRNO, 0, NULL,
        "mod_reqbody_example: process()");

    /* Need to increment the no_files length if this is not an uploaded file.
     * Failing to do this will disrupt some other limit checks.
     */
    msr->msc_reqbody_no_files_length += size;

    /* Check for an existing context and do something interesting
     * with the chunk of data we have been given.
     */
    if (ctx != NULL) {
        ctx->length += size;
    }

    /* Return 1 on success */
    return 1;
}
```

Summary

In this final chapter of the book (not counting the reference manual that follows in the second part), I led you through the process of adding new elements to the ModSecurity rule language. The extension mechanism of ModSecurity really is a case of standing on the shoulders of giants: you get to use a polished and well-documented extension mechanism implemented for Apache, while the developers (of ModSecurity) get to support extensions with only a dozen lines of code.

With this chapter, you've reached the end of the book, and you now know pretty much everything you need to about ModSecurity. This may be where your real work begins, because although you now know the tool, keeping up with web application security—which you need to understand in order to use ModSecurity in the right way—is often a full-time job.

But it's a fun one!

II Reference Manual

This part of the book contains an unofficial ModSecurity Reference Manual, which started its life in February 2010 as a fork of the official documentation (with permission of Breach Security, Inc.). Although the intention was to contribute all improvements back to ModSecurity, with version 2.6 the project moved the documentation from DocBook into a wiki, which effectively made synchronization impossible.

15 Directives

This chapter documents the configuration directives currently available in ModSecurity. There are three types of directives: base configuration items, directives that make up the rule language, and a group that is best summarized under advanced and optional features. The type is indicated with every directive.

With the ModSecurity directives being part of the web server's configuration, they need to conform to that configuration format—namely, that of Apache. This makes some of the ModSecurity directives hard to read. This is especially the case with the SecRule command, the workhorse of the ModSecurity rule language.

With every directive described in this chapter, you'll see the syntax, the default value, a usage example, the scope, and the version in which the directive appeared. Where no default value is defined (either due to being part of the rule language, for which this wouldn't make any sense, or due to being an advanced feature activated via setting a value), this is indicated.

The scope within the Apache configuration is usually Any. This means that a directive can be used on the main server level, within a virtual host, and also within a container context. However, some directives are limited to a certain scope, whereas others are inherited downwards and can be overwritten. When there's an exception to this rule, it's explained in the text.

Finally, there's an indication of when a certain directive or feature appeared in ModSecurity. Some directives have been removed from ModSecurity or have been renamed; these directives are listed with their name and an indication of when they were removed.

SecAction

Description: Unconditionally processes the action list it receives as the first and only parameter. The syntax of the parameter is identical to that of the third parameter of SecRule.

Syntax: SecAction "action1,action2,action3,..."

Default: none

Example: `SecAction "id:2000,phase:2,pass,log,msg:'Example'"`

Directive type: Rule language

Scope: Any

Version: 2.0.0

This directive is commonly used to set variables and initialize persistent collections using the `initcol` action—for example:

```
SecAction "id:1000,phase:1,nolog,initcol:RESOURCE=%{REQUEST_FILENAME}"
```

> **Note**
>
> Starting with ModSecurity 2.7.0, it's mandatory to assign a unique rule ID to every SecAction and SecRule directive that appears in your configuration.

SecArgumentSeparator

Description: Specifies which character to use as the separator for `application/x-www-form-urlencoded` content.

Syntax: `SecArgumentSeparator CHARACTER`

Default: `&`

Example: `SecArgumentSeparator ;`

Directive type: Configuration

Scope: Any; main before 2.7.0

Version: 2.0.0

This directive is needed if a backend web application is using a nonstandard argument separator. Applications are sometimes (very rarely) written to use a semicolon separator. You shouldn't change the default setting unless you establish that the application you're working with requires a different separator. If this directive is not set properly for each web application, then ModSecurity will not be able to parse the arguments appropriately and the effectiveness of the rule matching will be significantly decreased.

SecAuditEngine

Description: Configures the audit logging engine.

Syntax: `SecAuditEngine On|Off|RelevantOnly`

Default: `Off`

Example: `SecAuditEngine RelevantOnly`

Directive type: Configuration

Scope: Any

Version: 2.0.0

The `SecAuditEngine` directive is used to configure the audit engine, which logs complete transactions. The audit engine is described in detail in the section called "Audit Log" in Chapter 4. ModSecurity is currently able to log most but not all transactions. Transactions involving errors (e.g., 400 and 404 transactions) use a different execution path, which Mod-Security doesn't support.

> **Note**
>
> If you need to change the audit log engine configuration on a per-transaction basis (e.g., in response to some transaction data), use the `ctl` action.

The following example demonstrates how `SecAuditEngine` is used:

```
SecAuditEngine RelevantOnly
SecAuditLog /var/log/apache/modsec-audit.log
SecAuditLogParts ABCFHZ
SecAuditLogType Serial
SecAuditLogRelevantStatus ^(?:5|4\d[^4])
```

The possible values for the audit log engine are as follows:

- `On`: Log all transactions.
- `Off`: Do not log any transactions.
- `RelevantOnly`: Only log the transactions that have triggered a warning or an error or that have a status code considered to be relevant (as determined by the `SecAuditLogRelevantStatus` directive).

SecAuditLog

Description: Defines the path to the main audit log file (serial logging format) or the concurrent logging index file (concurrent logging format). When used in combination with `mlogc` (only possible with concurrent logging), this directive defines the `mlogc` location and command line.

Syntax: `SecAuditLog LOG_PATH`

Default: None

Example: `SecAuditLog /var/log/apache/modsec-audit.log`

Directive type: Configuration

Scope: Any

Version: 2.0.0

This file will be used to store audit log entries if the serial audit logging format is used. If the concurrent audit logging format is used, this file will be used as an index and will contain a record of all audit log files created. If you're planning to use concurrent audit logging to send your audit log data off to a remote server, you'll need to deploy the ModSecurity Log Collector (mlogc), like this:

```
SecAuditLog "|/usr/bin/mlogc /etc/modsecurity/mlogc.conf"
```

> **Note**
>
> This audit log file is opened on startup, when the server typically still runs as root. You shouldn't allow non-root users to have write privileges for this file or for the directory it's stored in.

SecAuditLog2

Description: Defines the location and command-line parameters of a secondary remote logging facility. See SecAuditLog for more details.

Syntax: SecAuditLog2 "|MLOGC_PATH MLOGC_CONFIG_PATH"

Default: None

Example: SecAuditLog2 "|/usr/bin/mlogc /etc/modsecurity/mlogc2.conf"

Directive type: Configuration

Scope: Any

Version: 2.1.2

The purpose of SecAuditLog2 is to make logging to two remote servers possible, which is typically achieved by running two instances of the mlogc tool, each with a different configuration (in addition, one of the instances will need to be instructed not to delete the files it submits). This directive can be used only if SecAuditLog was previously configured and only if the concurrent logging format is used.

SecAuditLogDirMode

Description: Configures the mode (permissions) of any directories created for the concurrent audit logs, using an octal mode value as a parameter (as used in chmod).

Syntax: SecAuditLogDirMode OCTAL_MODE

Default: 0750

Example: SecAuditLogDirMode 0700

Directive type: Configuration

Scope: Any

Version: 2.5.10

The default mode for new audit log directories (0750) only grants read/write access to the owner (typically the account under which Apache is running—e.g., apache) and read access to its group. If access from other accounts is needed (e.g., for use with mpm-itk), then you may use this directive to grant additional read and/or write privileges. You should use this directive with caution to avoid exposing potentially sensitive data to unauthorized users. This feature isn't available on operating systems that do not support octal file modes.

> **Note**
>
> The process umask may still limit the mode if it's being more restrictive than the mode set using this directive.

SecAuditLogFileMode

Description: Configures the mode (permissions) of any files created for concurrent audit logs using an octal mode (as used in chmod).

Syntax: SecAuditLogFileMode OCTAL_MODE

Default: 0640

Example: SecAuditLogFileMode 0600

Directive type: Configuration

Scope: Any

Version: 2.5.10

This feature isn't available on operating systems that do not support octal file modes. The default mode only grants read/write access to the account writing the file. If access from another account is needed (using mpm-itk is a good example), then this directive may be required. However, use this directive with caution to avoid exposing potentially sensitive data to unauthorized users.

> **Note**
>
> The process umask may still limit the mode if it's being more restrictive than the mode set using this directive.

See SecAuditLogDirMode for controlling the mode of created audit log directories.

SecAuditLogFormat

Description: Define the format of the audit log file or files.

Syntax: SecAuditLogFormat JSON|Native

Default: Native

Example: SecAuditLogFormat JSON

Directive type: Configuration

Scope: Any

Version: 2.9.1

The alternative JSON audit log format is available only if support for it has been compiled into the ModSecurity module. This depends on the availability of the YAJL library during the compilation.

SecAuditLogParts

Description: Defines which parts of each transaction are going to be recorded in the audit log. Each part is assigned a single letter; when a letter appears in the list, the corresponding part will be recorded. The list of all parts is included in the following information.

Syntax: SecAuditLogParts PART_LETTERS

Default: ABCFHZ

Example: SecAuditLogParts ABEFHIJZ

Directive type: Configuration

Scope: Any

Version: 2.0.0

> **Note**
>
> The format of the audit log format is documented in detail in the section called "Audit Log" in Chapter 20.

Available audit log parts:

- A: Audit log header (mandatory).
- B: Request headers.
- C: Request body (present only if the request body exists and ModSecurity is configured to intercept it).

- D: Reserved for original response headers; not implemented yet.

- E: Original response body (present only if ModSecurity is configured to intercept response bodies, and if the audit log engine is configured to record it). Intermediary response body is the same as the actual response body unless ModSecurity intercepts the intermediary response body, in which case the actual response body will contain the error message (either the Apache default error message, or the `ErrorDocument` page).

- F: Final response headers (excluding the `Date` and `Server` headers, which are always added by Apache in the late stage of content delivery).

- G: Reserved for the actual response body; not implemented yet.

- H: Audit log trailer.

- I: This part is a replacement for part C. It will log the same data as C in all cases, except when `multipart/form-data` encoding is used, in which case it will log a fake `application/x-www-form-urlencoded` body that contains information about parameters but not about the files. This is handy if you don't want to have (often large) files stored in your audit logs.

- J: Contains information on the uploaded files (requests using `multipart/form-data` encoding). Available as of 2.6.0.

- K: This part contains a full list of every rule that matched (one per line) in the order they were matched. The rules are fully qualified and will thus show inherited actions and default operators. Available as of 2.5.0.

- Z: Final boundary; signifies the end of the entry (mandatory).

> **Note**
>
> When listing the parts you want to see in the log, you should keep them in alphabetical order. Doing otherwise may result in unexpected behavior.

SecAuditLogRelevantStatus

Description: Configures which response status code is to be considered relevant for the purpose of audit logging.

Syntax: `SecAuditLogRelevantStatus REGEX`

Default: None

Example: `SecAuditLogRelevantStatus ^(?:5|4(?!04))`

Directive type: Configuration

Scope: Any

Version: 2.0.0

The main purpose of this directive is to allow you to configure audit logging for only transactions that have a status code that matches the supplied regular expression. For example, you might want to log all application errors (status code 500). Although you could achieve the same effect with a rule in phase 5, SecAuditLogRelevantStatus is sometimes better, because it continues to work even when SecRuleEngine is disabled.

> **Note**
>
> Make sure you set this directive if you want to log requests depending on the status code. Leaving it empty will have ModSecurity ignore the response status code as far as the audit log is concerned, because there is no default value for this directive.

SecAuditLogStorageDir

Description: Configures the directory in which concurrent audit log entries are to be stored.

Syntax: SecAuditLogStorageDir DIR_PATH

Default: None

Example: SecAuditLogStorageDir /var/log/modsecurity/audit

Directive type: Configuration

Scope: Any

Version: 2.0.0

This directive is only needed when concurrent audit logging is used. The directory must already exist and must be writable by the web server user. Audit log entries are created at runtime, after Apache switches to a non-root account.

> **Note**
>
> As with all logging mechanisms, ensure that you specify a filesystem location that has adequate disk space and is not on the main system partition.

SecAuditLogType

Description: Configures the type of audit logging mechanism to be used.

Syntax: SecAuditLogType Serial|Concurrent

Default: None

Example: SecAuditLogType Serial

Directive type: Configuration

Scope: Any

Version: 2.0.0

The possible values are as follows:

Serial

Audit log entries will be stored in a single file, as specified by SecAuditLog. This is convenient for casual use, but it can slow down the server, because only one audit log entry can be written to the file at any one time.

Concurrent

One file per transaction is used for audit logging. This approach is more scalable when heavy logging is required (multiple transactions can be recorded in parallel). It's also the only choice if you need to use remote logging.

SecCacheTransformations

Description: Controls the caching of transformations, which may speed up the processing of complex rulesets. This feature is disabled by default starting with 2.5.6, when it was deprecated and downgraded back to experimental.

Syntax: SecCacheTransformations On|Off [OPTIONS]

Default: Off

Example: SecCacheTransformations On "minlen:64,maxlen:0"

Directive type: Configuration (deprecated)

Scope: Any

Version: 2.5.0; deprecated in 2.5.6

The first directive parameter can be one of the following:

- On: Cache transformations (per transaction, per phase) allowing identical transformations to be performed only once.

- Off: Do not cache any transformations, leaving all transformations to be performed every time they're needed.

The following options are allowed (multiple options must be comma-separated):

- incremental:on|off: Enabling this option will cache every transformation instead of just the final transformation. The default is off.

- maxitems:N: Do not allow more than N transformations to be cached. Cache will be disabled once this number is reached. A zero value is interpreted as unlimited. This option may be useful to limit caching for a form with a large number of variables. The default value is 512.

- `minlen:N`: Do not cache the transformation if the variable's length is less than `N` bytes. The default setting is 32.

- `maxlen:N`: Do not cache the transformation if the variable's length is more than `N` bytes. A zero value is interpreted as unlimited. The default setting is 1024.

SecChrootDir

Description: Configures the directory path that will be used to jail the web server process.

Syntax: SecChrootDir DIR_PATH

Default: None

Example: SecChrootDir /chroot

Directive type: Other (advanced feature)

Scope: Main

Version: 2.0.0 (not supported on Windows)

The internal chroot functionality provided by ModSecurity works great for simple setups. One example of a simple setup is Apache serving only static files or running applications using only built-in modules. You might encounter the following problems with more complex setups:

1. DNS lookups do not work (because this feature requires a shared library loaded on demand, after chroot takes place).

2. You cannot send email from PHP, because it wants to use `sendmail` that resides outside the jail.

3. In some cases, when you separate Apache from its configuration, restarts and graceful reloads no longer work.

The best way to use `SecChrootDir` is as follows:

1. Create `/chroot` to be your main jail directory.

2. Create `/chroot/usr/local/apache` inside the jail.

3. Create a symlink from `/usr/local/apache` to `/chroot/usr/local/apache`.

4. Now install Apache into `/chroot/usr/local/apache`.

You should be aware that the internal chroot feature might not be 100 percent reliable. Due to the large number of default and third-party modules available for the Apache web server, it isn't possible to verify that the internal chroot works reliably with all of them. A module working from within Apache can do things that make it easy to break out of the jail. In particular, if you're using any of the modules that fork in the module initialization phase (e.g., `mod_fastcgi`, `mod_fcgid`, `mod_cgid`), you're advised to examine each Apache process and observe its current working directory, process root, and list of open files. Consider what your options are and make your own decision.

SecCollectionTimeout

Description: Configures the default timeout value for all new collections.

Syntax: SecCollectionTimeout TIMEOUT_IN_SECONDS

Default: 3600

Example: SecCollectionTimeout 900

Directive type: Configuration

Scope: Any

Version: 2.6.3

Use SecCollectionTimeout to set the default timeout value for all your collections at once. You can specify any value up to 2,592,000 (30 days).

SecComponentSignature

Description: Appends a component signature to the ModSecurity signature.

Syntax: SecComponentSignature "COMPONENT_NAME/X.Y.Z (COMMENT)"

Default: None

Example: SecComponentSignature "Local Rules/1.2.3"

Directive type: Rule language

Scope: Main

Version: 2.5.0

This directive should be used to make the presence of significant rulesets known. The entire signature will be recorded in the transaction audit log and appended to the Producer line in the H part of the log file.

SecConnEngine

Description: Enables the connection tracking engine, which counts active requests in read and write states. Enabling the engine is a precondition to limit active requests so that you can protect yourself from certain DoS attacks. This is done via the SecConnReadStateLimit and SecConnWriteStateLimit directives.

Syntax: SecConnEngine On|Off|DetectionOnly

Default: SecConnEngine Off

Example: SecConnEngine DetectionOnly

Directive type: Other (advanced feature)

Scope: Any

Version: 2.8.0

If SecConnEngine is set to off, the SecConnReadStateLimit and SecConnWriteStateLimit directives are ignored. When set to DetectionOnly, the engine runs in monitoring-only mode, in which there is no blocking. To enable blocking, set SecConnEngine to On.

SecConnReadStateLimit

Description: Establishes a per–IP address limit on how many connections are allowed to be in the request reading state within the Apache request lifecycle (SERVER_BUSY_READ state).

Syntax: SecConnReadStateLimit LIMIT [IP_MATCH_OPERATOR]

Default: None

Example: SecConnReadStateLimit 64 "!@ipMatch 192.168.0.0/16"

Directive type: Other (advanced feature)

Scope: Main

Version: 2.8.0 (Apache only)

You need to enable SecConnEngine as a precondition to use this directive. There is an optional IP match operator (one of @ipMatch, @ipMatchF, or @ipMatchFromFile), which can be used to construct whitelists and blacklists. You need to write multiple SecConnReadStateLimit directives if you want to apply multiple IP matching conditions. If you do this, however, only the limit defined in the final SecConnReadStateLimit applies. The other limits are ignored. Thus, it isn't possible to assign different limits to different IP addresses or ranges.

Controlling the number of connections in the reading state from the same IP address can be effective against clients that deliberately submit HTTP headers very slowly in order to keep your server busy with a single request. However, ModSecurity can only bring limited coverage in this case; Apache's mod_reqtimeout provides better defense via more granular controls.

> **Note**
>
> Apache switches a request from SERVER_BUSY_READ to SERVER_BUSY_WRITE surprisingly early in the lifecycle: the moment the request headers have been read by the server. This means that reading the request body can't be limited via SecConnReadStateLimit; you need to use SecConnWriteStateLimit instead.

SecConnWriteStateLimit

Description: Establishes a per-IP address limit on how many connections are allowed to be in the writing state within the Apache request lifecycle (SERVER_BUSY_WRITE state).

Syntax: SecConnWriteStateLimit LIMIT [IP_MATCH_OPERATOR]

Default: None

Example: SecConnWriteStateLimit 10 "!@ipMatch 192.168.0.0/16"

Directive type: Other (advanced feature)

Scope: Main

Version: 2.8.0 (Apache only)

This directive replaces the former SecWriteStateLimit. You need to enable SecConnEngine as a precondition to use this directive. There is an optional IP match operator (one of @ipMatch, @ipMatchF, or @ipMatchFromFile), which can be used to construct whitelists and blacklists. You need to write multiple SecConnWriteStateLimit directives if you want to apply multiple IP matching conditions. If you do this, however, only the limit defined in the final SecConnWriteStateLimit applies. The other limits are ignored. Thus, it isn't possible to assign different limits to different IP addresses or ranges.

Controlling the number of connections in the writing state from the same IP address can be effective against clients that deliberately send their request bodies very slowly or read the responses slowly. They do this as a means to keep a server busy with a single request for as long as possible (DoS). For the reading of the request body, the Apache module mod_reqtimeout provides better defense via more granular control. This does not apply to the generation of the response and the transfer, for which SecConnWriteStateLimit can provide some protection.

> ### Note
> Apache switches a request to SERVER_BUSY_WRITE as soon as the request headers have been read by the server. Therefore, even if the request body is still being read, the request is already in the writing state. The reading of request bodies, the generation of the response, and its transfer are thus summed up together.

SecContentInjection

Description: Enables content injection using the append and prepend actions.

Syntax: SecContentInjection On|Off

Default: Off

Example: SecContentInjection On

Directive type: Other (advanced feature)

Scope: Any

Version: 2.5.0

This directive provides an easy way to control content injection, no matter what the rules want to do. It isn't necessary to have response body buffering enabled in order to use content injection.

SecCookieFormat

Description: Selects the cookie format that will be used in the current configuration context.

Syntax: SecCookieFormat 0|1

Default: 0

Example: SecCookieFormat 1

Directive type: Configuration

Scope: Any

Version: 2.0.0

The possible values are as follows:

- 0: Use version 0 (Netscape) cookies. This is what most applications use.
- 1: Use version 1 cookies, as defined in RFC 2109.[1]

SecCookieV0Separator

Description: This directive allows you to define an alternative separator for multiple cookies on the request header Cookie of the version 0 cookie format.

Syntax: SecCookieV0Separator SEPARATOR

Default: ;

Example: SecCookieV0Separator ,

Directive type: Configuration

Scope: Main, virtual host

Version: 2.7.0

---

[1] RFC 2109: HTTP State Management Mechanism [fsty.uk/m49] (IETF, February 1997)

SecDataDir

Description: Path at which persistent data (e.g., IP address data, session data, and so on) is to be stored.

Syntax: SecDataDir DIR_PATH

Default: None

Example: SecDataDir /var/log/modsecurity/data

Directive type: Configuration

Scope: Main

Version: 2.0.0

This directive must be provided before initcol, setsid, and setuid can be used. The directory to which the directive points must be writable by the web server user.

SecDebugLog

Description: Path to the ModSecurity debug log file.

Syntax: SecDebugLog LOG_PATH

Default: None

Example: SecDebugLog /var/log/apache/modsec-debug.log

Directive type: Configuration

Scope: Any

Version: 2.0.0

SecDebugLogLevel

Description: Configures the verbosity of the debug log data.

Syntax: SecDebugLogLevel 0|1|2|3|4|5|6|7|8|9

Default: 0

Example: SecDebugLogLevel 5

Directive type: Configuration

Scope: Any

Version: 2.0.0

Messages at levels 1–3 are always copied to the Apache error log. Therefore, you can use level 0 as the default logging level if you're very concerned with performance. Higher logging levels are not recommended in production, because heavy logging affects performance adversely.

The possible values for the debug log level are as follows:

- 0: No logging
- 1: Errors (intercepted requests) only
- 2: Warnings
- 3: Notices
- 4: Details of how transactions are handled and performance data
- 5: The exact syntax of the rule
- 6-8: Not used (same as 5)
- 9: Very detailed debugging information, including macro expansion and the setting of variables

SecDefaultAction

Description: Defines the default list of actions, which will be inherited by the rules in the same configuration context.

Syntax: SecDefaultAction "action1,action2,action3"

Default: "phase:2,log,auditlog,pass"

Example: SecDefaultAction "phase:2,log,deny,tag:'experimental ruleset'"

Directive type: Rule language

Scope: Any

Version: 2.0.0

Every rule following a previous SecDefaultAction directive in the same configuration context will inherit its settings unless more specific actions are used. Every SecDefaultAction directive must specify a disruptive action and a processing phase and cannot contain meta-data actions. As of 2.7.0, the use of transformation functions in SecDefaultAction is deprecated and results in a warning message at startup.

> **Warning**
>
> SecDefaultAction is not inherited across configuration contexts. For a complete description of why this may be a problem, see the section called "SecDefaultAction Inheritance Anomaly" in Chapter 7.

SecDisableBackendCompression

Description: Disables backend compression while leaving frontend compression enabled. This directive is necessary in reverse proxy mode when the backend servers support response compression but you want to inspect response bodies. Unless you disable backend compression, ModSecurity will see only compressed content, which is not very useful. This directive is not necessary in embedded mode because ModSecurity performs inspection before response compression takes place.

Syntax: SecDisableBackendCompression On|Off

Default: Off

Example: SecDisableBackendCompression On

Directive type: Other (advanced feature)

Scope: Any

Version: 2.6.0

Backend servers use compression only when clients request it. Thus, to prevent backend response compression, ModSecurity removes the Accept-Encoding request header from the request just before it's proxied. That way, the backend server will always send a noncompressed response body.

SecGeoLookupDb

Description: Defines the path to the database that will be used for geolocation lookups.

Syntax: SecGeoLookupDb DB_PATH

Default: None

Example: SecGeoLookupDb /usr/share/GeoIP/GeoLiteCity.dat

Directive type: Other (advanced feature)

Scope: Any

Version: 2.5.0

ModSecurity relies on the free GeoLite City and GeoLite Country geolocation databases, which can be obtained from MaxMind.[2]

SecGsbLookupDb

Description: Defines the path to the database that will be used for Google's safe browsing lookups. This lookup only works with a former version of the Google project. It is thus currently broken and can't be used.

Syntax: SecGsbLookupDb DB_PATH

Default: None

Example: SecGsbLookupDb /var/log/modsecurity/gsb/goog-hash-malware.dat

Directive type: Other (advanced feature, broken)

Scope: Any

Version: 2.6.0; deprecated in 2.7.0

> **Note**
>
> This directive is now deprecated. ModSecurity's interface with Google's Safe Browsing database relied on an old and now unsupported version of the API. Until the code is upgraded to use a newer version of the API, the Safe Browsing functionality can't be used.

Configures a Safe Browsing database for use with the @gsbLookup operator. Databases can be obtained from Google's Safe Browsing project.[3] You'll be required to register for an API key, after which you'll be presented with one or more URLs that you can use to make local copies of the database(s). Upon startup, ModSecurity loads the databases into memory. After you refresh the databases on the filesystem, you'll also need to reconfigure Apache in order for the changes to be propagated to ModSecurity.

SecGuardianLog

Description: Configures an external program that will receive the information about every transaction via piped logging.

Syntax: SecGuardianLog "|HTTPD_GUARDIAN_PATH"

Default: None

---

[2] MaxMind web site [fsty.uk/m50] (MaxMind, retrieved 5 January 2017)

[3] Google Safe Browsing project [fsty.uk/m51] (Google Transparency Report, retrieved 5 January 2017)

Example: `SecGuardianLog "|/usr/bin/httpd-guardian"`

Directive type: Other (advanced feature)

Scope: Main

Version: 2.0.0

Guardian logging is designed to send information about every request to an external program. Because Apache is typically deployed in a multiprocess fashion, which makes information sharing between processes difficult, the idea is to deploy a single external process to observe all requests in a stateful manner, providing additional protection.

Currently, the only tool known to work with guardian logging is `httpd-guardian`, which is part of the *Apache httpd tools* project.[4] The `httpd-guardian` tool is designed to defend against denial of service attacks. It uses the `blacklist` tool (from the same project) to interact with an iptables-based (on a Linux system) or pf-based (on a BSD system) firewall, dynamically blacklisting the offending IP addresses. Assuming `httpd-guardian` is already configured (look into the source code for the detailed instructions), you only need to set `SecGuardianLog` in your Apache configuration to deploy it.

`SecGuardianLog` sends an access log line resembling an enriched combined format to the program defined in the path. The script is spawned at the startup of the server. When `httpd-guardian` is used, it parses each log line it receives, calculates the number of requests in a given interval, and takes action if necessary. Because of the way Apache interacts with programs that use piped logging, all `httpd-guardian` output will be recorded to the error log.

SecHashEngine

Description: Enables the ModSecurity hash engine, which can be used to cryptographically sign all links that appear in an application's HTML pages or HTTP redirection responses. The hash engine later verifies protected links and refuses to accept those for which signatures are invalid. This is an advanced security feature that rejects all links that have been tampered with.

Syntax: `SecHashEngine On|Off`

Default: `Off`

Example: `SecHashEngine On`

Directive type: Other (advanced feature)

Scope: Any

Version: 2.7.1

---

[4] Apache httpd tools [fsty.uk/m52] (SourceForge, retrieved 5 January 2017)

The hash engine can work on links and form actions in HTML responses, and links in HTTP redirect responses. The engine will only activate on responses that use the text/html content type.

The setting is inherited from the main server scope to the virtual host scope and from there to the various containers. It is thus possible to overwrite the configuration for a limited scope so that the hash engine is used only in one part of the application.

A full example with a detailed walkthrough has been presented as a *ModSecurity Advanced Topic of the Week*.[5]

SecHashKey

Description: Defines the secret key used by the hash engine to generate security HMAC tokens.

Syntax: SecHashKey rand|KEY KeyOnly|SessionID|RemoteIP

Default: rand KeyOnly

Example: SecHashKey 414f6f36-2558-11e6-bc9b-a3019dbf2a81 KeyOnly

Directive type: Other (advanced feature)

Scope: Any

Version: 2.7.1

SecHashKey defines the secret key used to generate HMAC tokens. If the keyword rand is used, then a random key is created at web server startup. A reload of the server configuration will also reinitialize this secret. Alternatively, use a custom key that you enter instead of rand.

The three options (KeyOnly, SessionID, and RemoteIP) serve to customize the HMAC token. With KeyOnly, all clients will receive the same token (which doesn't provide the same level of protection). SessionID and RemoteIP will assign individual tokens for each client or session. SessionID depends on the initialization of the session collection in phase 1 via setsid.

SecHashMethodPm

Description: Uses fast text matching to define which elements should receive the hash engine's security token.

Syntax: SecHashMethodPm ELEMENT_TYPE "string1 [string2 string3 ...]"

Default: None

---

[5] ModSecurity Advanced Topic of the Week: HMAC Token Protection [fsty.uk/m53] (SpiderLabs Blog, 24 January 2014)

Example: `SecHashMethodPm HashFormAction ".asp .html .php"`

Directive type: Other (advanced feature)

Scope: Any

Version: 2.7.1

The `SecHashMethodPm` directive uses a fast text matching algorithm (the same one used for the `@pm` operator) to find elements that need to be processed by the hash engine. The first parameter specifies the element type; the remaining parameters specify the strings to use for the matching. It's possible to issue this directive multiple times for multiple element types or multiple times for the same element type with different string expressions.

> **Note**
>
> Be careful when using this directive with multiple inheriting configuration scopes. If a parent scope selects an element for processing, it's not possible to undo its decision in the child scope.

ModSecurity supports the following element types:

- `HashHref`: Inject token into `href` attributes of all tags
- `HashFormAction`: Inject token into `action` attributes (typically used by `form` tags)
- `HashIframeSrc`: Inject token into `src` attributes of `iframe` tags
- `HashFrameSrc`: Inject token into `src` attributes of `frame` tags
- `HashLocation`: Inject token into URI destinations in response location headers

> **Note**
>
> Token injection is activated only when there is at least one usage of the `SecHashMethodPm` or `SecHashMethodRx` directive in the ModSecurity configuration.

SecHashMethodRx

Description: Uses regular expressions to define which elements should receive the hash engine's security token.

Syntax: `SecHashMethodRx ELEMENT_TYPE REGEX`

Default: None

Example: `SecHashMethodRx HashHref "\.(aspx?|html|php)"`

Directive type: Other (advanced feature)

Scope: Any

Version: 2.7.1

The SecHashMethodRx directive uses regular expressions to find elements that need to be processed by the hash engine. The first parameter specifies the element type; the second parameter specifies the regular expression to use for matching. It's possible to issue this directive multiple times for multiple element types or multiple times for the same element type with different regular expressions. See SecHashMethodPm for a detailed list of the element types.

> **Note**
>
> Be careful when using this directive with multiple inheriting configuration scopes. If a parent scope selects an element for processing, it's not possible to undo its decision in the child scope.

The following example adds a security token to all local links, passing over fully qualified references to ensure that external entities don't receive our token:

```
SecHashMethodRx HashHref "^(?!https?:\/\/)"
```

> **Warning**
>
> There are several ways to define a link. This makes it hard to construct a regular expression that will catch all links all of the time. The previous example will fail on external links defined without the protocol (e.g., //test.example.com/index.html), a form of a link that's rarely used but supported by all major browsers. Extensive testing of the hash engine configuration with your content is necessary to reveal problems as this.

> **Note**
>
> Token injection is activated only when there is at least one usage of the SecHashMethodPm or SecHashMethodRx directive in the ModSecurity configuration.

SecHashParam

Description: Specifies the name of the URL parameter used to transport HMAC tokens when the hash engine is active.

Syntax: SecHashParam PARAMETER_NAME

Default: crypt

Example: SecHashParam hmac

Directive type: Other (advanced feature)

Scope: Any

Version: 2.7.1

The HMAC token is appended to the links within the HTML body of the response. The following fragment gives an example of what the output looks like after it has been changed by ModSecurity:

```
<form action="/search?query=test&crypt=fb34fccbc5343a6b4276ce2ab1c8b00cec7ec5f">
```

SecHttpBlKey

Description: This directive configures the API key for the Project Honey Pot HTTP black list.

Syntax: SecHttpBlKey KEY

Default: None

Example: SecHttpBlKey 09f2b0e9-10f1-4e85

Directive type: Other (advanced feature)

Scope: Main, virtual host

Version: 2.7.0

An API key is required before the Project Honey Pot HTTP black list can be used; contact the project to receive a registered to key to use this functionality.[6] This directive only configures the API key; the @rbl operator is used to access the API.

SecInterceptOnError

Description: When enabled, this directive makes ModSecurity stop processing a phase when a rule error occurs.

Syntax: SecInterceptOnError On|Off

Default: Off

Example: SecInterceptOnError On

Directive type: Configuration

Scope: Any

Version: 2.6.0

Rule errors are rare and are usually the result of a faulty rule (e.g., the @ipMatch operator used against something that's not an IP address, or—more frequent, in this case—PCRE limit errors when using the OWASP ModSecurity Core Rule Set). [7]

---

[6] Honeypot Project [fsty.uk/m32] (Project Honey Pot, retrieved 5 January 2017)

[7] OWASP ModSecurity Core Rule Set [fsty.uk/m7] (OWASP, retrieved 5 January 2017)

> **Note**
>
> It is counterintuitive that SecInterceptOnError doesn't stop processing altogether and drop a request immediately (or intercept it, so to speak). In that light, this directive is of limited value in practice.

SecMarker

Description: Adds a fixed, alphanumeric rule marker that can be used as a target in a skipAfter action.

Syntax: SecMarker MARKER

Default: None

Example: SecMarker WHITELISTING_END

Directive type: Rule language

Scope: Any

Version: 2.5.0

The SecMarker directive can be used to construct conditional *if-then* and *if-then-else* blocks. For a complete example, see the section called "If-Then-Else " in Chapter 6.

SecPcreMatchLimit

Description: Sets the match limit in the PCRE library.

Syntax: SecPcreMatchLimit LIMIT_IN_BYTES

Default: 1500

Example: SecPcreMatchLimit 100000

Directive type: Configuration

Scope: Main

Version: 2.5.12

PCRE uses two arbitrary limits to prevent using too much memory or processing power when a regular expression is being processed. The PCRE limit configured with this directive corresponds to the match_limit field. More information is available on the pcreapi man page.

SecPcreMatchLimitRecursion

Description: Sets the match limit recursion in the PCRE library.

Syntax: SecPcreMatchLimitRecursion LIMIT_IN_BYTES

Default: 1500

Example: SecPcreMatchLimitRecursion 100000

Directive type: Configuration

Scope: Main

Version: 2.5.12

PCRE uses two arbitrary limits to prevent using too much memory or processing power when a regular expression is being processed. The PCRE limit configured with this directive corresponds to the match_limit_recursion field. More information is available on the pcreapi man page.

Note

The default value for SecPcreMatchLimit is very low, which means that your rule-sets will always need to set a different (sane) value. Head to the section called "Regular Expression Denial of Service" in Chapter 9 for more information on this topic.

SecReadStateLimit

This directive has been replaced by SecConnReadStateLimit starting with ModSecurity 2.8.0.

SecRemoteRules

Description: This directive allows you to load ModSecurity rules from a remote server during the startup of the server. This can be useful if you want to keep your rules in a central location.

Syntax: SecRemoteRules REMOTE_KEY REMOTE_URL

Default: None

Example: SecRemoteRules ProdWAF1 https://example.com/rules.txt

Directive type: Other (advanced feature)

Scope: Any

Version: 2.9.0

This directive can be used anywhere, but *only once per server*. To ensure transport security, only HTTPS URLs are allowed. ModSecurity will use two requests to fetch the rules, using the modsecurity user agent identification. Every request will provide certain metadata specified in three special request headers:

- ModSec-unique-id: Contains an anonymous server identifier that remains stable across requests.

- ModSec-status: Contains server information such as software and library version numbers; see SecStatusEngine for details.

- ModSec-key: Contains the key specified within the SecRemoteRules directive.

> **Warning**
>
> When using this directive, consider which SecRemoteRulesFailAction setting will best match your setup. Be aware that the default setting for SecRemoteRulesFailAction is Abort. If your server fails to load the remote rules during startup, then an error log entry with the severity *notice* (!) will be issued during the startup.

The error and audit log entries of the remote rules triggered on the local server will carry remote server as the filename for any rule hits, and the line number will always be -1.

SecRemoteRulesFailAction

Description: Use this directive to define the behavior when remote rules can't be loaded at startup or during a restart and reload of the server.

Syntax: SecRemoteRulesFailAction Abort|Warn

Default: Abort

Example: SecRemoteRulesFailAction Warn

Directive type: Other (advanced feature)

Scope: Any

Version: 2.9.0

> **Warning**
>
> When issuing a reload or graceful reload of the server, ModSecurity will also attempt to reload any remote rules it has in the configuration. If SecRemoteRules is

> set to Abort and the rules can't be fetched, then the reload of the server is aborted and a message indicating the problem is displayed on STDERR of the command issuing the reload. However, there will be no information indicating the problem in the error log of the server.
>
> When set to Warn and the remote call fails, you lose the rules loaded from the remote server previously.

Remote rule loading is an interesting feature, but using it correctly is hard. In fact, it's so hard that you'll want to think twice before you use SecRemoteRules in a production setting.

If you use the default SecRemoteRulesFailAction setting of Abort, you create a point of failure in your system. If the remote server is under your control, you need to make sure the server is accessible and remains accessible for every restart of a server. This sounds easy, but it might prove a liability in an emergency. If the remote server isn't under your control, then you introduce a dependency on a different organization, which could be a problem—unless you really trust that organization and the accessibility of its server.

On the other hand, if you set SecRemoteRulesFailAction to Warn, then problems accessing the remote server will mean that your server loses the previously loaded remote rules and might miss attacks because of it. To make matters worse, in this case your error log won't contain an indication that you're not running with your full rules.

In an extreme scenario, a DoS attack on the server containing your remote rules or on your connection to it might also be used as a way of bypassing your defense.

> **Note**
>
> If you want to set this directive to Warn, then SecRemoteRulesFailAction has to be issued before the SecRemoteRules directive.

SecRequestBodyAccess

Description: Configures whether request bodies will be buffered and processed by ModSecurity.

Syntax: SecRequestBodyAccess On|Off

Default: Off

Example: SecRequestBodyAccess On

Directive type: Configuration

Scope: Any

Version: 2.0.0

This directive is required if you want to inspect the data transported in request bodies (e.g., POST parameters, file uploads). Request buffering is also required in order to make reliable blocking possible.

The possible values are as follows:

- On: Buffer and process request bodies
- Off: Don't buffer request bodies

SecRequestBodyInMemoryLimit

Description: Configures the maximum request body size that ModSecurity will store in memory.

Syntax: SecRequestBodyInMemoryLimit LIMIT_IN_BYTES

Default: 131072 (128 KB)

Example: SecRequestBodyInMemoryLimit 262144

Directive type: Configuration

Scope: Any

Version: 2.0.0

When a multipart/form-data request is being processed, the request body will be redirected into a temporary file on disk once the in-memory limit is reached.

SecRequestBodyLimit

Description: Configures the maximum request body size ModSecurity will accept for buffering.

Syntax: SecRequestBodyLimit LIMIT_IN_BYTES

Default: 134217728 (128 MB)

Example: SecRequestBodyLimit 262144

Directive type: Configuration

Scope: Any

Version: 2.0.0

Anything over the limit will be rejected with HTTP status code 413 (Request Entity Too Large) by default. There is a hard limit of 1 GB.

SecRequestBodyLimitAction

Description: Controls what happens once a request body limit configured with SecRequestBodyLimit and SecRequestBodyNoFilesLimit is encountered.

Syntax: SecRequestBodyLimitAction Reject|ProcessPartial

Default (blocking mode): SecRequestBodyLimitAction Reject

Default (detection-only mode): SecRequestBodyLimitAction ProcessPartial

Example: SecRequestBodyLimitAction ProcessPartial

Directive type: Configuration

Scope: Any

Version: 2.6.0

By default, ModSecurity will reject a request body that's longer than specified. Some sites may not want to allow ModSecurity to reject requests, and they can use this directive to instruct ModSecurity to proceed even when it has only a partial request body. The INBOUND_DATA_ERROR flag will be raised when ModSecurity has only a partial request body.

SecRequestBodyNoFilesLimit

Description: Configures the maximum request body size ModSecurity will accept for buffering, excluding the size of any files being transported in the request.

Syntax: SecRequestBodyNoFilesLimit LIMIT_IN_BYTES

Default: 1048576 (1 MB)

Example: SecRequestBodyLimit 65536

Directive type: Configuration

Scope: Any

Version: 2.5.0

This directive is useful to reduce susceptibility to DoS attacks when someone is sending request bodies of very large sizes. Web applications that require file uploads must configure SecRequestBodyLimit to a high value, but because large files are streamed to disk, file uploads won't increase memory consumption. However, it's still possible for someone to take advantage of a large request body limit and send nonupload requests with large body sizes. This directive eliminates that loophole.

In general, the default value isn't small enough. For most applications, you should be able to reduce it down to 128 KB or lower. Anything over the limit will be rejected with status code 413 (Request Entity Too Large) by default. There is a hard limit of 1 GB.

SecResponseBodyAccess

Description: Configures whether response bodies are to be buffered and processed.

Syntax: SecResponseBodyAccess On|Off

Default: Off

Example: SecResponseBodyAccess On

Directive type: Configuration

Scope: Any

Version: 2.0.0

This directive is required if you plan to inspect HTML responses and implement response blocking.

Possible values are as follows:

- On: Buffer response bodies (but only if the response MIME type matches the list configured with SecResponseBodyMimeType) and process them
- Off: Don't buffer response bodies

SecResponseBodyLimit

Description: Configures the maximum response body size that will be accepted for buffering.

Syntax: SecResponseBodyLimit LIMIT_IN_BYTES

Default: 524228 (512 KB)

Example: SecResponseBodyLimit 2096912

Directive type: Configuration

Scope: Any

Version: 2.0.0

Anything over this limit will be rejected with status code 500 (Internal Server Error) by default. This setting will not affect responses with MIME types that aren't selected for buffering. There is a hard limit of 1 GB.

SecResponseBodyLimitAction

Description: Controls what happens once a response body limit, configured with SecResponseBodyLimit, is encountered.

Syntax: SecResponseBodyLimitAction Reject|ProcessPartial

Default (blocking mode): Reject

Default (detection-only mode): ProcessPartial

Example: SecResponseBodyLimitAction Reject

Directive type: Configuration

Scope: Any

Version: 2.5.0

By default, ModSecurity will reject a response body that's longer than specified. Some web sites, however, will produce very long responses, making it difficult to come up with a reasonable limit. Such sites would have to raise the limit significantly to function properly, defying the purpose of having the limit in the first place (to control memory consumption). With the ability to choose what happens once a limit is reached, site administrators can choose to inspect only the first part of the response, the part that can fit into the desired limit, and let the rest through. Some could argue that allowing parts of responses to go uninspected is a weakness. This is true in theory, but applies only to cases in which the attacker controls the output (e.g., can make it arbitrarily long). In such cases, however, it isn't possible to prevent leakage anyway. The attacker could compress, obfuscate, or even encrypt data before it's sent back and therefore bypass any monitoring device.

SecResponseBodyMimeType

Description: Configures which MIME types are to be considered for response body buffering.

Syntax: SecResponseBodyMimeType MIMETYPE [MIMETYPE [...]]

Default: text/plain text/html

Example: SecResponseBodyMimeType text/plain text/html text/xml

Directive type: Configuration

Scope: Any

Version: 2.0.0

Multiple SecResponseBodyMimeType directives can be used to add MIME types. Use SecResponseBodyMimeTypesClear to clear previously configured MIME types and start over.

SecResponseBodyMimeTypesClear

Description: Clears the list of MIME types considered for response body buffering, allowing you to start populating the list from scratch.

Syntax: SecResponseBodyMimeTypesClear

Default: None

Example: SecResponseBodyMimeTypesClear

Directive type: Other (advanced feature)

Scope: Any

Version: 2.0.0

SecRule

Description: Creates a rule that will analyze the selected variables using the selected operator. Most ModSecurity rules will be defined using this directive.

Syntax: SecRule VARIABLES OPERATOR [ACTIONS]

Default: None

Example: SecRule ARGS "@rx attack" "phase:2,id:2000,log,deny"

Directive type: Rule language

Scope: Any

Version: 2.0.0

Every rule must provide one or more variables, along with the operator that should be used to inspect them. If no actions are provided, the default list will be used. (There is always a default list, even if one was not explicitly set with SecDefaultAction.) If there are actions specified in a rule, they'll be merged with the default list to form the final actions that will be used. (The actions in the rule will overwrite those in the default list.) Refer to SecDefaultAction for more information.

> **Note**
>
> Starting with version 2.7.0, it's mandatory to assign a unique rule ID for every SecRule in the list of actions.

SecRuleEngine

Description: Controls the operating mode of the ModSecurity rule engine.

Syntax: SecRuleEngine On|Off|DetectionOnly

Default: Off

Example: SecRuleEngine On

Directive type: Configuration

Scope: Any

Version: 2.0.0

The possible values are as follows:

- On: Process rules, using blocking when appropriate
- Off: Don't process rules
- DetectionOnly: Process rules but never intercept transactions, even when rules are configured to block

> **Note**
>
> The ModSecurity Apache module is active even when the rule engine is disabled. Parsing the configuration, reading the requests, and optionally logging transactions using the audit engine will all carry on as usual. To fully disable ModSecurity, comment-out its LoadModule directive.

SecRuleInheritance

Description: Configures whether the current context will inherit rules from the parent context.

Syntax: SecRuleInheritance On|Off

Default: On

Example: SecRuleInheritance Off

Directive type: Configuration

Scope: Any

Version: 2.0.0

Sometimes when you create a more specific configuration context (e.g., using the <Location> container), you may want to use a different set of rules than those used in the parent context. By setting SecRuleInheritance to Off, you prevent the parent rules from being inherited, which allows you to start from scratch.

The possible values are as follows:

- On: Inherit rules from the parent context
- Off: Don't inherit rules from the parent context

> **Note**
>
> In Apache, the <Directory>, <Files>, <Location>, <Proxy>, and <VirtualHost> directives are all used to create configuration contexts, or sections in which different settings apply. For more information, please refer to the Apache documentation.[8]

> **Note**
>
> This directive doesn't affect how configuration options are inherited.

SecRulePerfTime

Description: Configures the processing time threshold after which a rule will be considered slow.

Syntax: SecRulePerfTime MICROSECONDS

Default: None

Example: SecRulePerfTime 1000

Directive type: Other (advanced feature)

Scope: Any

Version: 2.7.0

Starting with version 2.7.0, ModSecurity contains a simple profiling facility that keeps track of rule performance in order to identify slow rules. The rules that go over the threshold configured using SecRulePerfTime will be recorded in the audit log, in the Rules-Performance-Info part H header. They will also be kept in the PERF_RULES collection—which is handy, because you can keep track of them in real time (with additional rules, of course).

SecRuleRemoveById

Description: Removes the matching rules from the current configuration context.

Syntax: SecRuleRemoveById ID [ID_RANGE [...]]

Default: None

Example: SecRuleRemoveByID 1000 1004 "2101-2200"

Directive type: Rule language

Scope: Any

Order: After rule declaration

---

[8] Configuration Sections [fsty.uk/m54] (Apache HTTP Server 2.4 Documentation, retrieved 5 January 2017)

Version: 2.0.0

This directive supports multiple parameters, each of which can be a rule ID or a range. Parameters that contain spaces must be delimited using double quotes.

> **Note**
>
> The SecRuleRemoveById directive affects only rules that exist in the configuration when the directive is processed. Any rules with the matching IDs that follow this directive won't be affected by it.

SecRuleRemoveByMsg

Description: Removes the matching rules from the current configuration context.

Syntax: SecRuleRemoveByMsg REGEX

Default: None

Example: SecRuleRemoveByMsg "experimental"

Directive type: Rule language

Scope: Any

Order: After rule declaration

Version: 2.0.0

Normally, you would use SecRuleRemoveById to remove rules by referencing their IDs, but this directive allows you to find rules for removal based on the text specified in their msg actions.

SecRuleRemoveByTag

Description: Removes the matching rules from the current configuration context.

Syntax: SecRuleRemoveByTag REGEX

Default: None

Example: SecRuleRemoveByTag "OWASP_CRS/WEB_ATTACK/XSS"

Directive type: Rule language

Order: After rule declaration

Scope: Any

Version: 2.6.0

This directive is very useful if you want to quickly remove an entire family of rules that have been tagged systematically.

SecRuleScript

Description: This directive creates a special rule that executes a Lua script to decide whether to match.

Syntax: SecRuleScript LUA_SCRIPT_PATH [ACTIONS]

Default: None

Example: SecRuleScript "scripts/inspect.lua" "phase:2,id:2402,deny"

Directive type: Rule language

Scope: Any

Version: 2.5.0

This directive's main difference from SecRule is that there are no targets or operators. The script has access to any variable in the ModSecurity context, and it can use any Lua code to test them. The second optional parameter is the list of actions, the meaning of which is identical to that of SecRule.

All Lua scripts are compiled at configuration time and cached in memory. To reload scripts, you must reload the entire ModSecurity configuration by restarting Apache. You can find out more about Lua by visiting its web site.[9]

The following is an example Lua script:

```
-- Your script must define the main entry
-- point, as below.
function main()
    -- Log something at level 1. Normally you shouldn't be
    -- logging anything, especially not at level 1, but this is
    -- just to show you can. Useful for debugging.
    m.log(1, "Hello world!");

    -- Retrieve one variable.
    local var1 = m.getvar("REMOTE_ADDR");

    -- Retrieve one variable, applying one transformation function.
    -- The second parameter is a string.
    local var2 = m.getvar("ARGS", "lowercase");

    -- Retrieve one variable, applying several transformation functions.
```

---

[9] Lua web site [fsty.uk/m17] (Lua.org, retrieved 5 January 2017)

```
-- The second parameter is now a list. You should note that m.getvar()
-- requires the use of dot to separate collection names from
-- variable names.
local var3 = m.getvar("ARGS.p", { "lowercase", "compressWhitespace" } );

-- If you want this rule to match return a string containing the
-- error message. Otherwise, simply return nil.
-- It is considered good practice to return the name of the variable,
-- where the problem is located. The error message will written to
-- the error log and the audit log as part of the standard error message.

if var3 == "attack" then
        return "Variable ARGS:p looks suspicious!";
else
        return nil;
end

end
```

In this first example, we were only retrieving one variable at a time. In this case, the name of the variable is known to you. In many cases, however, you'll want to examine variables for which you won't know the names in advance, such as script parameters.

The following example shows the use of m.getvars() to retrieve many variables at once:

```
function main()
    -- Retrieve script parameters.
    local d = m.getvars("ARGS", { "lowercase", "htmlEntityDecode" } );

    -- Loop through the parameters.
    for i = 1, #d do
        -- Examine parameter value.
        if (string.find(d[i].value, "<script")) then
            -- Always specify the name of the variable where the
            -- problem is located in the error message.
            return ("Suspected XSS in variable " .. d[i].name .. ".");
        end
    end

    -- Nothing wrong found.
    return nil;
end
```

> **Note**
>
> Lua support in ModSecurity has been used in production by various organizations
> for many years. However, it's still marked *experimental*, because the programming

> interface may change in a future version of ModSecurity—namely, the next major release of ModSecurity.

SecRuleUpdateActionById

Description: Updates the action list of the specified rule.

Syntax: SecRuleUpdateActionById RULEID[:CHAIN_OFFSET] ACTIONLIST

Default: None

Example: SecRuleUpdateActionById 1002 "phase:1,deny"

Directive type: Rule language

Scope: Any

Order: After rule declaration

Version: 2.5.0; offset support added in 2.6.0

This directive will overwrite the action list of the specified rule with the actions provided in the second parameter. It has two limitations: it cannot be used to change the ID or phase of a rule. Only actions that can appear only once are overwritten. Actions that are allowed to appear multiple times in a list will be appended to the end of the list:

```
SecRule ARGS "@rx attack" \
    "phase:2,id:2000,t:lowercase,log,pass,msg:'Message text'"

SecRuleUpdateActionById 2000 \
    "t:none,t:compressWhitespace,deny,status:403,msg:'New message text'"
```

The rule effectively resulting from the previous example will be as follows:

```
SecRule ARGS "@rx attack" \
    "phase:2,id:2000,t:lowercase,t:none,t:compressWhitespace,\
    deny,status:403,msg:'New Message text'"
```

The addition of t:none will neutralize any previous transformation functions specified (t:lowercase, in the example).

In 2.6.0, SecRuleUpdateActionById was updated to support chain offsets, which is needed when you want to change rules that are part of the chain. In such cases, first use a rule ID to locate the entire chain, then use the offset to locate the desired rule within the chain.

The following example illustrates using SecRuleUpdateActionById on a chained rule:

```
SecRule ARGS:foo "@rx attack" \
    "phase:2,id:2001,chain,block,log,msg:'Rule hit'"
    SecRule ARGS:foo "@rx script" "setvar:TX.bar=1"
```

```
SecRuleUpdateActionById 2001:1 "setvar:TX.bar=2"
```

The rule resulting from this example will be as follows:

```
SecRule ARGS:foo "@rx attack" \
    "phase:2,id:2001,chain,block,log,msg:'Rule hit'"
    SecRule ARGS:foo "@rx script" "setvar:TX.bar=2"
```

> **Warning**
>
> In the current implementation, when changing a rule that originally has chain, the replacement action list must specify chain, too.

SecRuleUpdateTargetById

Description: Updates the list of targets for the specified rule.

Syntax: SecRuleUpdateTargetById RULEID TARGET1[,TARGET2,...] [NEW_TARGETS]

Default: None

Example: SecRuleUpdateTargetById 2000,2001 !ARGS:foo

Directive type: Rule language

Scope: Any

Order: After rule declaration

Version: 2.6.0

This is a very useful directive if you run into a rule that inspects parameters that you would rather ignore. Previously, you would have to remove the entire rule and copy and modify it. With this directive, you can simply change the rule at configuration time to do what you want. For example, to prevent a rule from looking at a named parameter, use this directive:

```
# The rule that you want to change, defined in a
# separate file that you'd rather leave unchanged
SecRule ARGS "@rx attack" "id:2000,phase:2,log,deny"

# Configuration-time modification of rule #2000
SecRuleUpdateTargetById 2000 "!ARGS:username"
```

In the previous example, the target list of rule 2000 is changed from ARGS to ARGS|!ARGS:username, effectively protecting the parameter username from inspection.

Using an alternative syntax, you can also directly replace a variable with something else. For example:

```
# Configuration-time modification of rule #100
SecRuleUpdateTargetById 2000 ARGS ARGS_GET
```

In this latter example, the target list of rule 2000 is changed from ARGS to ARGS_GET, effectively changing it to inspect *only* query string parameters.

The SecRuleUpdateTargetById directive operates at configure-time and is thus a bit faster. If you need to change rules at runtime (either appending or replacing), use the equivalent ctl action variant ruleUpdateTargetById.

SecRuleUpdateTargetByMsg

Description: Updates the list of targets for a group of rules identified via their message.

Syntax: SecRuleUpdateTargetByMsg REGEX TARGET1[,TARGET2,...] [NEW_TARGET]

Default: None

Example: SecRuleUpdateTargetByMsg Experimental "!ARGS:foo,!ARGS:bar"

Directive type: Rule language

Scope: Any

Order: After rule declaration

Version: 2.7.0

This directive works like SecRuleUpdateTargetById. However, unlike that directive, it identifies a rule not by its ID but by its message. This allows to address a group of rules, which share their message or part thereof.

The alternative form, with the replacement of a parameter, looks like the following:

```
SecRuleUpdateTargetByMsg Experimental ARGS:bar ARGS:foo
```

In this example, we replace the target parameter foo with the new target parameter bar. Therefore, all the rules with a message containing the text Experimental will no longer inspect parameter foo but parameter bar instead.

SecRuleUpdateTargetByTag

Description: Updates the list of targets for a group of rules identified via their tag.

Syntax: SecRuleUpdateTargetByTag REGEX TARGET1[,TARGET2,...] [NEW_TARGET]

Default: None

Example: SecRuleUpdateTargetByTag "attack-sqli" "!ARGS:foo,!ARGS:bar"

Directive type: Rule language

Scope: Any

Order: After rule declaration

Version: 2.7.0

With SecRuleUpdateTargetByTag, you can manipulate the target list of a group of rules identified by one of their tags or by a substring occurring within one of their tags. It is identical to SecRuleUpdateTargetByMsg in all other aspects.

SecSensorId

Description: Configures the sensor ID.

Syntax: SecSensorId SENSORID

Default: None

Example: SecSensorId ProdWAF1

Directive type: Configuration

Scope: Main

Version: 2.7.0

Prior to the addition of SecSensorId, ModSecurity audit logs didn't contain any information that might help you identify the source. The mlogc utility has a parameter named SensorUsername, but that's used only for authentication during audit log transit. Starting with 2.7.0, if you're running a site that might be served by two or more servers, assigning unique IDs to ModSecurity instances will help you differentiate among them. The ID you configure using this directive will appear in the Sensor-Id header in part H of the audit log in double quotes.

> **Tip**
>
> If you're using mlogc for remote audit logging, make sure to use the same value for the SecSensorId directive in ModSecurity configuration and for the SecUsername parameter in mlogc.conf.

SecServerSignature

Description: Instructs ModSecurity to replace the data Apache sends out in the Server response header.

Syntax: SecServerSignature NEW_SERVER_SIGNATURE

Default: None

Example: SecServerSignature "Acme Web Server 19.99"

Directive type: Other (advanced feature)

Scope: Main

Version: 2.0.0

In order for this directive to work, you must set the Apache `ServerTokens` directive to `Full`. ModSecurity will overwrite the server signature data held in this memory space with the data set in this directive. If `ServerTokens` is not set to `Full`, then the memory space is most likely not large enough to hold the new data we're looking to insert.

SecStatusEngine

Description: This call sends information about your web server to the ModSecurity team.

Syntax: SecStatusEngine On|Off

Default: Off

Example: SecStatusEngine On

Directive type: Other (advanced feature)

Scope: Any

Version: 2.8.0

The `SecStatusEngine` directive instructs the server to send a DNS request to the ModSecurity name server via UDP on standard port 53. The hostname of the DNS request is a base32-encoded collection of information about your server and the various libraries in use. The data is then cut and encoded to get multiple snippets of 32 bytes, which will make up a virtual server name and various subdomains of the *status.modsecurity.org* domain, with a time-stamp forming another subdomain right after the information about your server.

The exact data is being written into the error log of the server under the `notice` severity. Here are the fields in order:

- ModSecurity version (e.g., 2.9.1)
- Web server (e.g., Apache)
- Compiled APR version (e.g., 1.5.2)
- Loaded APR version (e.g., 1.5.2)
- Compiled PCRE version (e.g., 8.31)
- Loaded PCRE version (e.g., 8.3.12 2012-07-06)
- Lua version (e.g., Lua 5.2)
- LibXML version (e.g., 2.9.1)

- Unique server ID (e.g., 9a3e20d7e4ad5c0f31327e4206f7a3741d4b444c)

The ID of the server is a SHA1 hash of a combination of the MAC-address(es) of the server and its hostname. This data is all encoded in base32. Then, the timestamp in seconds since the Unix time epoch is added, followed finally by the domain *status.modsecurity.org*. All combined, the DNS call will ask for a hostname like that in the following example:

```
GIXDSLRRFRAXAYLDNBSSYMJOGUXDELZR.FY2S4MRMHAXDGMJPHAXDGMJAGIYDCMRN.↵
GA3S2MBWFRGHKYJAGUXDELBSFY4S4MJM.HFQTGZJSGBSDOZJUMFSDKYZQMYZTCMZS.↵
G5STIMRQGZTDOYJTG42DCZBUMI2DINDD.1462431337.status.modsecurity.org
```

The ModSecurity project will then catch this request and use it to determine the use of ModSecurity.

SecStreamInBodyInspection

Description: Instructs ModSecurity to create a copy of the request body and place it in the variable STREAM_INPUT_BODY.

Syntax: SecStreamInBodyInspection On|Off

Default: Off

Example: SecStreamInBodyInspection On

Directive type: Other (advanced feature)

Scope: Any

Version: 2.6.0

When enabled, this directive causes ModSecurity to make the request body available in STREAM_INPUT_BODY in the form of a single memory buffer. Despite the "stream" part in the name of the directive and the corresponding variable, there is no streaming involved.

This directive might be useful if you need access to the raw request body, but it comes with a cost of increased memory usage. In particular, when parsing multipart/form-data, the size of the buffer used by this directive may be as big as the setting in SecRequestBodyLimit instead of the smaller limit set by SecRequestBodyNoFilesLimit.

You'll also need this directive if you want to use the @rsub operator for request body manipulation.

> **Note**
>
> There's also the REQUEST_BODY variable, but unlike STREAM_INPUT_BODY, it won't contain HTTP request bodies in the multipart/form-data format used for file uploads.

SecStreamOutBodyInspection

Description: Instructs ModSecurity to create a copy of the response body and place it in the variable STREAM_OUTPUT_BODY.

Syntax: SecStreamOutBodyInspection On|Off

Default: Off

Example: SecStreamOutBodyInspection On

Directive type: Other (advanced feature)

Scope: Any

Version: 2.6.0

When enabled, this directive causes ModSecurity to make the response body available in STREAM_OUTPUT_BODY as a single memory buffer. Despite the "stream" part in the name of the directive and the corresponding variable, there is no streaming involved.

You might need SecStreamOutBodyInspection if you want to use the @rsub operator against response bodies. Be warned, however, that doing so will likely double the amount of memory used for response buffering.

SecTmpDir

Description: Configures the directory in which temporary files will be created.

Syntax: SecTmpDir DIR_PATH

Default: /tmp

Example: SecTmpDir /var/log/modsecurity/tmp

Directive type: Configuration

Scope: Any

Version: 2.0.0

The location specified needs to be writable by the Apache user process. This is the directory location in which ModSecurity will swap request data to disk if it runs out of memory (i.e., there's more data than was specified in the SecRequestBodyInMemoryLimit directive) during inspection.

SecTmpSaveUploadedFiles

Description: Configures whether the files transported in multipart/form-data requests will be temporarily stored on disk for inspection.

Syntax: SecTmpSaveUploadedFiles On|Off

Default: Off

Example: SecTmpSaveUploadedFiles On

Directive type: Configuration

Scope: Any

Version: 2.9.0

The SecTmpSaveUploadedFiles directive allows you to inspect files embedded in a request; use the FILES_TMPNAMES variable and the @inspectFile operator. The temporary files will be removed after the transaction is complete, regardless of the result of the inspection. If you want to keep the files, use the SecUploadKeepFiles directive.

SecUnicodeCodePage

Description: Configures the code page that will be used for best-effort Unicode character mapping with the t:urlDecodeUni transformation action.

Syntax: SecUnicodeCodePage CODEPAGE

Default: None

Example: SecUnicodeCodePage 28591

Directive type: Configuration (deprecated)

Scope: Main

Version: 2.6.1; deprecated (configure code page via the SecUnicodeMapFile directive)

This directive requires the map file to be configured with SecUnicodeMapFile. To find out what code pages are available, refer to the unicode.mapping file included with ModSecurity.

SecUnicodeMapFile

Description: Configures the location of the file that contains best-effort mappings used for Unicode character conversion with the t:urlDecodeUni transformation action.

Syntax: SecUnicodeMapFile MAPFILE_PATH [CODEPAGE]

Default: None

Example: SecUnicodeMapFile /etc/modsecurity/unicode.mapping 28591

Directive type: Configuration

Scope: Main

Version: 2.6.1 (code page option accepted since 2.7.5)

A default map file, unicode.mapping, is included with ModSecurity.

SecUploadDir

Description: Configures the directory in which intercepted files will be stored.

Syntax: SecUploadDir UPLOAD_DIR_PATH

Default: None

Example: SecUploadDir /var/log/modsecurity/uploads

Directive type: Configuration

Scope: Any

Version: 2.0.0

This directive is used with SecUploadKeepFiles. The directory defined with this command must be on the same filesystem as the temporary directory defined with SecTmpDir. If that isn't the case, moving the temporary file to the upload store will fail and the file will remain in the temporary directory.

SecUploadFileLimit

Description: Configures the maximum number of file uploads processed in a multipart POST.

Syntax: SecUploadFileLimit LIMIT

Default: 100

Example: SecUploadFileLimit 2

Directive type: Configuration

Scope: Any

Version: 2.5.12

You're encouraged to reduce the default value. Any file over the limit will not be extracted, and the MULTIPART_FILE_LIMIT_EXCEEDED and MULTIPART_STRICT_ERROR flags will be set. To prevent bypassing any file checks, you must check for one of these flags.

> **Note**
>
> If the limit is exceeded, the part name and filename will still be recorded in FILES_NAME and FILES; the file size will be recorded in FILES_SIZES, but there will be no record in FILES_TMPNAMES, because a temporary file wasn't created. Likewise, the file won't be stored in the upload file archive.

SecUploadFileMode

Description: Configures the mode (permissions) of any uploaded files using octal mode (as used in chmod).

Syntax: SecUploadFileMode OCTAL_MODE

Default: 0600

Example: SecUploadFileMode 0640

Directive type: Configuration

Scope: Any

Version: 2.1.6

This feature is not available on operating systems that don't support octal file modes. This directive is used when access from another account is needed (e.g., when using clamd). However, use this directive with caution to avoid exposing potentially sensitive data to unauthorized users.

> **Note**
>
> The process umask may still limit the mode if it's being more restrictive than the mode set using this directive.

SecUploadKeepFiles

Description: Configures whether the uploaded files will be kept after the transaction is processed.

Syntax: SecUploadKeepFiles On|Off|RelevantOnly

Default: Off

Example: SecUploadKeepFiles RelevantOnly

Directive type: Configuration

Scope: Any

Version: 2.0.0

This directive requires the storage directory to be defined (using SecUploadDir).

Possible values are as follows:

- On: Keep all uploaded files
- Off: Don't keep uploaded files
- RelevantOnly: Keep only those files that belong to requests deemed relevant

SecWebAppId

Description: Creates an application namespace, allowing for separate persistent session and user storage.

Syntax: SecWebAppId NAME

Default: None

Example: SecWebAppId Service1

Directive type: Configuration

Scope: Any

Version: 2.0.0

Application namespaces are used to avoid collisions between session IDs and user IDs when multiple applications are deployed on the same server. If SecWebAppId isn't used, a collision between session IDs might occur. The following configuration snippet avoids this in an exemplary way:

```
<VirtualHost *:80>
    ServerName app1.example.com
    SecWebAppId "App1"
    ...
</VirtualHost>

<VirtualHost *:80>
    ServerName app2.example.com
    SecWebAppId "App2"
    ...
</VirtualHost>
```

SecWebAppId is being used in conjunction with the Apache <VirtualHost> directives here. Application namespace information is recorded in the audit log using the WebApp-Info header of the H part. See the section called "WebApp-Info" in Chapter 20 for a detailed description of this log header.

> **Note**
>
> The use of this directive will also set a variable named WEBAPPID, which can then be used in subsequent rules. This can be useful to write rules in the server context that only apply to certain virtual hosts, which you mark with this directive.

SecWriteStateLimit

This directive has been replaced by SecConnWriteStateLimit starting with ModSecurity 2.8.0.

SecXmlExternalEntity

Description: This directive configures the loading of external entities during XML parsing in ModSecurity.

Syntax: SecXmlExternalEntity On|Off

Default: Off

Example: SecXmlExternalEntity On

Directive type: Configuration

Scope: Any

Version: 2.7.3

In XML, entities are used as variables or aliases for some other content, usually special characters or larger quantities of text. Entities can be defined in XML itself, either by specifying their value or by referring to a URL that contains the value. Externally defined entities have the capacity to create vulnerability in applications, leading to *XML External Entity* (XXE) attacks. For example, the attacker could define an external entity that refers to a local file and obtain its contents:

```
<!ENTITY xxe SYSTEM "file:///etc/passwd">
```

Other attacks are also possible; DoS attacks are common. Since ModSecurity version 2.7.3, external entity processing isn't allowed by default, thus preventing potential security holes if ModSecurity is used to parse inbound XML (which is always under the control of the attacker). You shouldn't enable XXE processing unless you're certain that you're able to mitigate all the possible attack vectors.

16 Variables

This chapter documents variables and collections. Variables are simple, named data containers that are created by ModSecurity as it processes an HTTP transaction. Collections are sets of variables; they're usually used to group a number of variables that share the same meaning or as an easy way to handle many variables at once. For example, when you use a collection in a rule, ModSecurity will process the rule once for each variable the collection contains.

An important part of using variables is understanding when they become available. Certain variables and collections that depend on the availability of the request body are not going to be available in phase 1, when ModSecurity has only read the request headers. Any data submitted as part of the request body will thus only be available in the phase 2 (the request phase). The same problem affects variables that depend on the availability of data in phase 3 and phase 4 (response).

ModSecurity won't warn you if you use the wrong phase for your rule; if you make a mistake, you'll simply end up with an empty collection or with a collection that contains only some of the desired data. It's generally a good practice to place request rules in phase 2 and response rules in 4; doing so will ensure that your rules always have access to all of the available data.

This chapter lists all variables and collections currently available in ModSecurity. For the variables, there's an example value with every item. The collections come with full examples when it's useful.

ARGS

ARGS is a collection that contains all request parameters, regardless of where they appear in the request (e.g., in the query string or in the request body). All parameters are decoded and appear as they would appear to a web application.

```
SecRule ARGS "@rx attack" \
    "id:2000,phase:2,deny,t:lowercase,msg:'Attack'"
```

ARGS_COMBINED_SIZE

Contains the combined size of all request parameters. Files are excluded from the calculation. This variable can be useful, for example, to create a rule to ensure that the total size of the argument data is below a certain threshold.

Example value: 2500

ARGS_GET

ARGS_GET is similar to ARGS, but it contains only decoded query string parameters.

ARGS_GET_NAMES

ARGS_GET_NAMES is similar to ARGS_NAMES, but it contains only the URL-decoded names of query string parameters.

ARGS_NAMES

This collection contains all request parameter names. You can search for specific parameter names you want to inspect. In a positive policy scenario, you can also whitelist (using an inverted rule with the exclamation point) only authorized argument names.

This example rule allows only two argument names, p and a:

```
SecRule ARGS_NAMES "!@rx ^(p|a)$" "id:2000,phase:2,deny"
```

ARGS_POST

ARGS_POST is similar to ARGS, but it contains only request body parameters.

ARGS_POST_NAMES

ARGS_POST_NAMES is similar to ARGS_NAMES, but it contains only the names of request body parameters.

AUTH_TYPE

This variable holds the authentication method used to validate a user, if any of the methods built into HTTP are used. In a reverse-proxy deployment, this information won't be available if the authentication is handled in the backend web server.

Example value: Basic

DURATION

This variable contains the time elapsed since the beginning of the transaction, in microseconds. Before 2.7.0, the time was specified in milliseconds.

Example value: 46078

ENV

This collection provides access to environment variables. It requires a single parameter to specify the name of the desired variable.

```
# Set environment variable
SecRule REQUEST_FILENAME "@rx printenv" \
    "id:2000,phase:2,pass,setenv:tag=suspicious"

# Inspect environment variable
SecRule ENV:tag "@rx suspicious" "id:2001,phase:2,deny"
```

Use setenv to set environment variables.

FILES

Contains a collection of original filenames in a file upload request (names as provided by the client; usually the name that was on the remote user's filesystem, sometimes including the full path). Available only on inspected multipart/form-data requests.

```
SecRule FILES "@rx \.conf$" "id:2000,phase:2,deny"
```

FILES_COMBINED_SIZE

Contains the total size of the files transported in the request body. Available only on inspected multipart/form-data requests.

Example value: 54834

FILES_NAMES

Contains a collection of form fields that were used for file upload. Available only on inspected multipart/form-data requests.

```
SecRule FILES_NAMES "@rx ^upfile$" "id:2000,phase:2,deny"
```

FILES_SIZES

Contains a list of individual file sizes. Useful for implementing a size limitation on individual uploaded files. Available only on inspected multipart/form-data requests.

```
SecRule FILES_SIZES "@gt 100" "id:2000,phase:2,deny"
```

FILES_TMP_CONTENT

The FILES_TMP_CONTENT collection holds the contents of the individual files in a multipart/form-data request. The key is the argument name of the file being submitted. This directive depends on SecTmpSaveUploadedFiles or SecUploadKeepFiles being enabled.

FILES_TMPNAMES

Contains a list of temporary filenames on the disk. Useful when used together with @inspectFile. Available only on inspected multipart/form-data requests and depends on SecTmpSaveUploadedFiles or SecUploadKeepFiles being enabled.

```
SecRule FILES_TMPNAMES "@inspectFile /path/to/inspect_script.pl" \
    "id:2000,phase:2,deny"
```

FULL_REQUEST

FULL_REQUEST contains the entire request as received from the client, including the request line, all the request headers, and the body if SecRequestBodyAccess is enabled. The request body is only available from phase 2 (request). The size limits on the request are being enforced here as well. This variable is available from 2.8.0.

Example value: GET /index.html HTTP/1.1\r\nHost: example.com\r\n...

FULL_REQUEST_LENGTH

This is the byte count of the request, including the request headers and the body if SecRequestBodyAccess is enabled. The length of the request body is only available from phase 2 (request). The size limits on the request are enforced here as well. This variable is available from 2.8.0.

Example value: 890

> **Note**
>
> Unusually, the length of the request line (the first line in the request that contains the request method, URI, and protocol information) isn't part of the calculation.

GEO

The GEO collection contains the data obtained by the most recent execution of the @geoLookup operator.

Fields within the collection:

- COUNTRY_CODE: ISO 3166 two-character country code—for example, US, GB, and so on.
- COUNTRY_CODE3: ISO 3166 three-character country code—for example, GBR.
- COUNTRY_NAME: The full country name.
- COUNTRY_CONTINENT: The two-character continent on which the country is located.
- REGION: The two-character region. For the United States, this is the state; for Canada, it's the province; and so on.
- CITY: The city name, if supported by the database.
- POSTAL_CODE: The postal code, if supported by the database.
- LATITUDE: The latitude, if supported by the database.
- LONGITUDE: The longitude, if supported by the database.
- DMA_CODE: The metropolitan area code (US only).
- AREA_CODE: The phone system area code (US only).

The following example demonstrates the initialization of the GEO collection and its usage:

```
SecGeoLookupDb /path/to/GeoLiteCity.dat
...
SecRule REMOTE_ADDR "@geoLookup" \
    "id:1000,phase:1,chain,drop,msg:'Non-GB IP address'"
SecRule GEO:COUNTRY_CODE "!@streq GB"
```

GLOBAL

The GLOBAL collection provides a simple mechanism to store information that will persist across transactions and which can be shared by all transactions running on the same server.

As with all other persistent collections, GLOBAL becomes available only after it's initialized using the initcol action.

The following example shows how to count server errors across all server processes and threads:

```
# Initialize global collection
SecAction "id:1000,phase:1,pass,nolog,initcol:global=global"

# Count server errors
SecRule RESPONSE_STATUS "@beginsWith 5" \
    "id:9000,phase:5,pass,log,\
    setvar:GLOBAL.num_errors=+1\
    msg:'This is server error number %{GLOBAL.num_errors}'"
```

HIGHEST_SEVERITY

This variable holds the highest severity of any rules that have matched so far. Severities are optional numeric values that rules can specify via the severity action. By convention, the lower the value, the higher the severity. A value of 255 indicates that no severity has been set. The HIGHEST_SEVERITY variable can be used with numerical comparison operators such as @lt, @gt, and so on.

Example value: 2

INBOUND_DATA_ERROR

This variable is a flag that will be raised when ModSecurity isn't able to buffer the entire request body and SecRequestBodyLimitAction is set to ProcessPartial.

Example value: 1

> **Note**
>
> ModSecurity is distributed with a brief list of recommended rules. In this set, there's a rule with the ID 200002, which stops processing the request if it's too big and you're running in blocking mode. Therefore, the INBOUND_DATA_ERROR variable will only ever be visible if you have set SecRuleEngine to DetectionOnly.

IP

The IP collection is used to store information about an IP address. As all other persistent collections, IP becomes available only after it's initialized using the initcol action.

The following example shows how to initialize the IP collection and how to count requests:

```
# Initialize IP storage
SecAction "id:1000,phase:1,pass,nolog,initcol:ip=%{REMOTE_ADDR}"

# Count transactions
SecAction "id:1001,phase:1,pass,log,\
    msg:'Request number %{IP.num_requests} from ip address %{IP.key}'\
    setvar:IP.num_requests=+1,\
    expirevar:IP.num_requests=300"
```

MATCHED_VAR

This variable holds the value of the most recently matched variable. It's similar to the TX:0, but it's automatically supported by all operators and there's no need to specify the capture action. Because each ModSecurity rule can match against more than one variable, MATCHED_VAR is best used in the action list when referring to a match of the current SecRule. If you want to continue to examine the matched fields in subsequent rules, you should use MATCHED_VARS, which contains all matched variable values.

Example value: further scrutiny

```
SecRule ARGS "@rx foo" \
    "id:2000,log,deny,logdata:%{MATCHED_VAR}"
```

MATCHED_VAR_NAME

This variable holds the full name of the most recently matched variable.

Example value: ARGS:param

```
SecRule ARGS "@rx pattern" \
    "id:2000,phase:2,pass,nolog,setvar:TX.mymatch=%{MATCHED_VAR_NAME}"
...
SecRule TX:MYMATCH "@eq ARGS:param" \
    "id:2001,phase:2,deny"
```

MATCHED_VARS

This collection holds the values of all variables that matched in the most recent rule. You can use MATCHED_VARS to simulate a loop operation, performing multiple progressive checks against a group of variables—for example, as with these two chained rules:

```
SecRule ARGS "@rx foo" \
    "id:2000,phase:2,chain,deny,msg:'Two patterns matched'"
    SecRule MATCHED_VARS "@rx bar"
```

In the previous example, ModSecurity will first loop through the variables in ARGS, checking them against pattern_1 and storing those that match into the MATCHED_VARS collection. In the second rule, ModSecurity will loop through the MATCHED_VARS collection and check them against pattern_2.

MATCHED_VARS_NAMES

This collection holds the names of all variables that matched in the most recent rule.

MODSEC_BUILD

This variable holds the ModSecurity build number. This variable is intended to be used to check the build number prior to using a feature that is available only in a certain build.

Example value: 020901900

The ModSecurity build number consists of nine digits:

1. Major version (two digits, e.g., 02)
2. Minor version (two digits, e.g., 09)
3. Maintenance version (two digits, e.g., 01)
4. Build type (one digit, e.g., 9)
5. Release type (two digits, e.g., 00)

MULTIPART_BOUNDARY_QUOTED

This flag is set on a multipart request that contains a quoted boundary. This flag triggers the MULTIPART_STRICT_ERROR flag automatically.

Example value: 0

MULTIPART_BOUNDARY_WHITESPACE

This flag is set if a multipart request with whitespace in the boundary string is encountered. This flag triggers the MULTIPART_STRICT_ERROR flag automatically.

Example value: 1

MULTIPART_CRLF_LF_LINES

This flag will be set to 1 whenever a multipart request uses mixed line terminators. The multipart/form-data RFC requires that the CRLF sequence be used to terminate lines. Because some client implementations use only LF to terminate lines, you might want to allow them to proceed under certain circumstances (if you want to do this, you'll need to stop using MULTIPART_STRICT_ERROR and check each multipart flag variable individually, avoiding MULTIPART_LF_LINE). However, mixing CRLF and LF line terminators is dangerous, as it can allow for evasion. Therefore, in such cases, you'll have to add a check for MULTIPART_CRLF_LF_LINES.

This variable is considered a special case, and the MULTIPART_CRLF_LF_LINES flag doesn't trigger MULTIPART_STRICT_ERROR automatically.

Example value: 0

MULTIPART_DATA_AFTER

This flag is triggered if there's data after the final boundary in a multipart request. This flag triggers the MULTIPART_STRICT_ERROR flag automatically.

Example value: 0

MULTIPART_DATA_BEFORE

This flag is set if data has been encountered in a multipart request before the first boundary. This flag triggers the MULTIPART_STRICT_ERROR flag automatically.

Example value: 0

MULTIPART_FILE_LIMIT_EXCEEDED

Whenever a multipart request submits more files than the limit defined in SecUploadFileLimit, this flag is set. It triggers the MULTIPART_STRICT_ERROR flag automatically.

Example value: 0

MULTIPART_FILENAME

This variable is filled with the contents of the filename field in a multipart request—usually the name of the file on the client's filesystem, sometimes including the full path. If more than one file is being uploaded, then MULTIPART_FILENAME will only contain the value of the last filename in the request. If you want all filenames, then the FILES collection is a better choice. MULTIPART_FILENAME has been available since 2.7.3.

Example value: report.odt

MULTIPART_HEADER_FOLDING

This flag is set after header folding has been encountered in a multipart request. Header folding is defined in RFC 2557 and rarely occurs in practice. This flag triggers the MULTIPART_STRICT_ERROR flag automatically.

Example value: 0

MULTIPART_INVALID_HEADER_FOLDING

This flag is set if an invalid header folding has been discovered in a multipart request. Header folding is defined in RFC 2557. This flag triggers the MULTIPART_STRICT_ERROR flag automatically.

Example value: 0

MULTIPART_INVALID_PART

This flag will be set on a multipart request that contains a part that is either malformed or missing a name. It was added in 2.7.0 in response to an advisory from SEC Consult that documents a bypass in which ModSecurity interprets an evasion attempt differently from the tested backend application.[1] This flag triggers the MULTIPART_STRICT_ERROR flag automatically.

Example value: 0

MULTIPART_INVALID_QUOTING

Technically, the single quote character is considered invalid when quoting in a multipart request, but some backends will allow it. Whenever invalid quoting is encountered, processing continues, but this flag is set. This flag triggers the MULTIPART_STRICT_ERROR flag automatically.

Example value: 0

MULTIPART_LF_LINE

Multipart requests are meant to use CRLF line terminators. If only LF is used, this flag is set. It triggers the MULTIPART_STRICT_ERROR flag automatically.

---

[1] SEC Consult SA-20121017-0 :: ModSecurity multipart/invalid part ruleset bypass [fsty.uk/m55] (Seclists.org, 17 October 2012)

Example value: 0

MULTIPART_MISSING_SEMICOLON

If the `Content-Type` header in a multipart request lacks the necessary semicolon after the `multipart/form-data` string, then this flag is set. It triggers the `MULTIPART_STRICT_ERROR` flag automatically.

Example value: 0

MULTIPART_NAME

This variable is filled with the contents of the name field in a multipart request—usually the name of the field of the upload form. If more than one file is being uploaded, then `MULTIPART_NAME` will only contain the value of the last field name in the request. If you want all field names, then the `FILES_NAMES` collection is the better variable to use. `MULTIPART_NAME` has been available since 2.7.3.

Example value: `uploadFile`

MULTIPART_STRICT_ERROR

The `multipart/form-data` format is complex and ambiguous, but most implementations don't follow the specification in every detail. ModSecurity uses a dual approach when handling this format: parsing is permissive, but violations are flagged and exposed in the rule language. A violation may not be a sign of malice, but it should be taken into consideration in most cases.

Example value: 1

The `MULTIPART_STRICT_ERROR` variable is used as an indicator of the problems detected during the parsing of `multipart/form-data`. It will be set if any of the following are set:

- `MULTIPART_BOUNDARY_QUOTED`
- `MULTIPART_BOUNDARY_WHITESPACE`
- `MULTIPART_DATA_AFTER`
- `MULTIPART_DATA_BEFORE`
- `MULTIPART_FILE_LIMIT_EXCEEDED`
- `MULTIPART_HEADER_FOLDING`
- `MULTIPART_INVALID_HEADER_FOLDING`

- `MULTIPART_INVALID_PART`

- `MULTIPART_INVALID_QUOTING`

- `MULTIPART_LF_LINE`

- `MULTIPART_MISSING_SEMICOLON`

- `REQBODY_PROCESSOR_ERROR`

Except for REQUEST_BODY_PROCESSOR_ERROR, which is set when a major error occurs, each of the listed variables covers one unusual (although sometimes legal) aspect of the request body in multipart/form-data format. Your policies should *always* contain a rule to check MULTIPART_STRICT_ERROR (which is easier, because there's only one value to check) or one or more individual variables (if you know exactly what you're looking for). Depending on the rate of false positives and your default policy, you should decide whether to block or just warn when the rule is triggered.

The best way to use this variable is as in the following example, which is also part of the set of recommended rules distributed together with ModSecurity:

```
SecRule MULTIPART_STRICT_ERROR "!@eq 0" \
  "id:'200003',phase:2,t:none,log,deny,status:400, \
  msg:'Multipart request body failed strict validation: \
  PE %{REQBODY_PROCESSOR_ERROR}, \
  BQ %{MULTIPART_BOUNDARY_QUOTED}, \
  BW %{MULTIPART_BOUNDARY_WHITESPACE}, \
  DB %{MULTIPART_DATA_BEFORE}, \
  DA %{MULTIPART_DATA_AFTER}, \
  HF %{MULTIPART_HEADER_FOLDING}, \
  LF %{MULTIPART_LF_LINE}, \
  SM %{MULTIPART_MISSING_SEMICOLON}, \
  IQ %{MULTIPART_INVALID_QUOTING}, \
  IP %{MULTIPART_INVALID_PART}, \
  IH %{MULTIPART_INVALID_HEADER_FOLDING}, \
  FL %{MULTIPART_FILE_LIMIT_EXCEEDED}'"
```

MULTIPART_UNMATCHED_BOUNDARY

This flag is set to 1 when, during the parsing phase of a multipart/request-body, ModSecurity encounters what seems like a boundary but isn't. Such an event may occur when evasion of ModSecurity is attempted.

Example value: 0

Unlike other multipart flags, this one doesn't trigger MULTIPART_STRICT_ERROR automatically. It's also not part of the recommended rule 200003 but is handled separately in the recommended rule 200004:

```
SecRule MULTIPART_UNMATCHED_BOUNDARY "!@eq 0" \
    "id:'200004',phase:2,t:none,log,deny,\
    msg:'Multipart parser detected a possible unmatched boundary.'"
```

In practice, this rule flag is set often due to snippets of text resembling an unmatched boundary. Therefore, it's likely you'll have to switch this rule from deny to detection only (pass).

OUTBOUND_DATA_ERROR

This variable is a flag that will be raised when ModSecurity isn't able to buffer the entire response body.

Example value: 0

PATH_INFO

This variable contains the extra request URI information, also known as *path info*. It's available only in embedded deployments and not in phase 1.

Example value: /article/475664

Consider the URI /index.php/123?foo: The PATH_INFO value is /123.

PERF_ALL

This special variable contains a string that's a combination of all other performance variables, arranged in the same order in which they appear in the Stopwatch2 audit log header. It's intended for use in custom Apache logs, as described in the section called "Performance Logging" in Chapter 10.

Example value: combined=57334, p1=19327, p2=28699, p3=2837, p4=6471, p5=0, sr=7721, sw=0, l=0, gc=0

> **Note**
>
> If used within a ModSecurity rule, some of the values will be zero, because the processing phases in question won't have finished yet.

PERF_COMBINED

Contains the time, in microseconds, spent in ModSecurity during the current transaction. The value in this variable is derived by adding all the performance variables except

PERF_SREAD (the time spent reading from persistent storage is already included in the phase measurements).

Example value: 57334

PERF_GC

Contains the time, in microseconds, spent performing garbage collection.

Example value: 15

PERF_LOGGING

Contains the time, in microseconds, spent in audit logging. This value is known only after the handling of a transaction is finalized, which means that it can only be logged using mod_log_config and the %{VARNAME}M syntax. When used within an ordinary rule, it will carry the value 0.

Example value: 12

PERF_PHASE1

Contains the time, in microseconds, spent processing phase 1.

Example value: 19327

PERF_PHASE2

Contains the time, in microseconds, spent processing phase 2 (request).

Example value: 28699

PERF_PHASE3

Contains the time, in microseconds, spent processing phase 3.

Example value: 2837

PERF_PHASE4

Contains the time, in microseconds, spent processing phase 4 (response).

Example value: 6471

PERF_PHASE5

Contains the time, in microseconds, spent processing phase 5 (logging).

Example value: 120

PERF_RULES

This collection keeps a list of slow rules that ran during the current transaction. To use this collection, you first need to define a slowness threshold using the SecRulePerfTime directive. After that, every rule with a total running time above the threshold will be recorded.

One possible way to use PERF_RULES is as part of a self-diagnostic system that runs in phase 5. The usual approach is to use two different thresholds: one to record a slow rule in PERF_RULES and another to decide whether to issue a warning—for example:

```
# Consider anything over 100 microseconds to be slow
SecRulePerfTime 100

# Determine if we had any slow rules and report rules taking at least 250 ↵
microseconds

SecRule &PERF_RULES "@eq 0" \
    "id:95000,phase:5,pass,log,msg:'All rules performed below time limit.'"
SecRule PERF_RULES "@ge 250" \
    "id:95001,phase:5,pass,log,msg:'Rule %{MATCHED_VAR_NAME}: %{MATCHED_VAR} ↵
usec.'"
```

If you care only about a particular rule, it's possible to reference its performance counter by its ID, as in the following example:

```
SecRule FILES_TMPNAMES "@inspectFile /usr/local/bin/runav.pl" \
    "id:10001,phase:2,deny,log,msg:'Virus scan detected an error.'"

SecRule PERF_RULES:10001 "@ge 0" \
    "id:95002,phase:5,pass,log,msg:'File inspection took %{MATCHED_VAR} usec.'"
```

> **Note**
>
> If a rule is executed multiple times in order to handle several input variables, Mod-Security compares the accumulated running time to SecRulePerfTime.

PERF_SREAD

Contains the time, in microseconds, spent reading from persistent storage.

Example value: 12

PERF_SWRITE

Contains the time, in microseconds, spent writing to persistent storage.

Example value: 4

QUERY_STRING

Contains the query string part of a request URI. The value in QUERY_STRING is always provided raw, without URL decoding taking place.

Example value: foo=bar

REMOTE_ADDR

This variable holds the IP address of the remote client.

Example value: 192.168.1.101

In some setups, one IP address is not sufficient to fully describe the source of a transaction. At the transport level, there is always only one TCP IP address, but a user agent may be communicating with the final destination via one or more proxies. Most proxies will preserve the original user agent IP address in a request header—for example, Via or X-Forwarded-For. This information can be used, but only if received from a trusted proxy, because a client can fake these values.

With Apache 2.4, there is a module called mod_remoteip that helps with the correct interpretation of these headers. It allows you to declare trusted proxies that may appear in the aforementioned headers. Let's assume your server runs behind a trusted proxy with IP address 192.168.1.55. You can configure the module as follows and have Apache assign the client IP address to REMOTE_ADDR, which will also lead to the correct client IP being used in ModSecurity's log messages:

```
RemoteIPHeader        X-Forwarded-For
RemoteIPInternalProxy 192.168.1.55
```

There is a distinction between internal and external proxy hosts built into mod_remoteip. Here, we used an internal proxy host. Refer to the module documentation for more information on how to use it correctly.[2]

REMOTE_HOST

If the Apache directive HostnameLookups is set to On, then this variable will hold the remote hostname resolved through DNS. If the directive is set to Off, this variable will hold the remote IP address (same as REMOTE_ADDR). Possible uses for this variable include denying known bad client hosts or network blocks or, conversely, allowing authorized hosts in.

Example value: www.feistyduck.com

REMOTE_PORT

This variable holds information on the source port that the client used when initiating the connection to the web server.

Example value: 35268

REMOTE_USER

This variable holds the username of the authenticated user. If there are no password access controls in place (basic or digest authentication or a custom authentication scheme filling this internal Apache variable), then this variable will be empty. Apache authentication happens between ModSecurity phase 1 and 2 (request).

Example value: john_smith

In a reverse-proxy deployment, this information won't be available if the authentication is handled in the backend web server.

REQBODY_ERROR

Contains the status of the request body processor used for request body parsing. The values can be 0 (no error) or 1 (error). This variable will be set by request body processors (typically the multipart/request-data parser or the XML parser) when they fail to do their work.

Example value: 0

---

[2] Module mod_remoteip [fsty.uk/m56] (Apache HTTP Server 2.4 documentation, retrieved 5 January 2017)

> **Note**
>
> Your policies *must* have a rule to check for request body processor errors at the very beginning of phase 2. Failure to do so will leave the door open for impedance mismatch attacks. It's possible, for example, that a payload that can't be parsed by ModSecurity can be parsed successfully by a more tolerant parser operating in the application. If your policy dictates blocking, then you should reject the request if an error is detected. When operating in detection-only mode, your rule should alert with high severity when request body processing fails.
>
> The recommended rules that are part of the ModSecurity distribution contain a rule with id 200002 to achieve this.

REQBODY_ERROR_MSG

If there's been an error during request body parsing, this variable will contain an error message. For the XML body processor, this message is fairly general in nature, but with the JSON processor, it can be quite detailed.

Example value: 1

REQBODY_PROCESSOR

Contains the name of the currently used request body processor. The possible values are URLENCODED, MULTIPART, JSON, XML, or empty. This variable is typically used in conjunction with a format check or a similar construct.

Example value: MULTIPART

A typical use for this variable is within a chained rule that calls an operator specific to a certain request body processor:

```
SecRule REQBODY_PROCESSOR "@streq XML" \
    "id:2000,phase:2,chain,log,msg:'XML DTD validation error'"
  SecRule XML "@validateDTD /path/to/xml.dtd"
```

REQUEST_BASENAME

This variable holds just the filename part of REQUEST_FILENAME.

Example value: index.html

> **Note**
>
> Please note that anti-evasion transformations are not applied to this variable by default. REQUEST_BASENAME will recognize both / and \ as path separators. Be aware

that the value of this variable depends on what was provided in the request and that it doesn't have to correspond to the resource (on disk) that will be used by the web server.

REQUEST_BODY

Holds the raw request body. By default, this variable is available only if the URLENCODED request body processor was used, which will occur when the application/x-www-form-urlencoded content type is detected.

Example value: yourEmail=john.smith@example.com&supportMessage=I+was+lo...

If you want to force the presence of REQUEST_BODY, you can do so as follows:

```
SecAction "id:1000,phase:1,pass,nolog,ctl:forceRequestBodyVariable=On"
```

REQUEST_BODY_LENGTH

Contains the number of bytes read from a request body.

Example value: 720

REQUEST_COOKIES

This variable is a collection of all request cookies (values only).

REQUEST_COOKIES_NAMES

This variable is a collection of the names of all request cookies. For example, the following rule will trigger if the JSESSIONID cookie is not present:

```
SecRule &REQUEST_COOKIES_NAMES:JSESSIONID "@eq 0" \
    "id:1000,phase:1,deny"
```

REQUEST_FILENAME

This variable holds the relative request URL, without the query string part but including the path info, if any.

Example value: /subfolder/index.html

> **Warning**
>
> In phase 1, this variable contains the relative request URL as submitted by the client and as described in the example. However, between phase 1 and 2 there is an

implicit path normalization happening and evasions such as ".." are applied to the variable. Therefore, if you want to test for these evasions, you need your rule to run in phase 1, or you need to use the REQUEST_URI_RAW variable instead.

REQUEST_HEADERS

This variable can be used either as a collection of all of the request headers or to inspect selected headers (by using the REQUEST_HEADERS:Header-Name syntax).

```
SecRule REQUEST_HEADERS:Host "@rx ^[\d\.]+$" \
    "id:1000,phase:1,deny,log,status:400,msg:'Host header is a numeric IP address'"
```

REQUEST_HEADERS_NAMES

This variable is a collection of the names of all of the request headers.

```
SecRule REQUEST_HEADERS_NAMES "@rx ^x-forwarded-for" \
    "id:1000,phase:1,log,deny,status:403,t:lowercase,msg:'Proxy server used'"
```

REQUEST_LINE

This variable holds the complete request line sent to the server (including the request method and HTTP version information).

Example value: GET /index.html HTTP/1.1

```
# Allow only POST, GET and HEAD request methods,
# and only valid protocol versions
SecRule REQUEST_LINE "!@rx ^(?:(?:POS|GE)T|HEAD) /[^ ]* HTTP/(:?(1\.[01]))$" \
    "id:1000,phase:1,log,block,t:none"
```

REQUEST_METHOD

This variable holds the request method used in the transaction.

Example value: POST

REQUEST_PROTOCOL

This variable holds the request protocol version information.

Example value: HTTP/1.1

REQUEST_URI

This variable holds the full request URL, including the query string data and the optional path info. However, it will never contain a domain name, even if one was provided on the request line.

Example value: /app/index.php?p=X

> ### Warning
>
> In phase 1, this variable contains the request URL as submitted by the client and as described previously. However, between phase 1 and 2 there is an implicit path normalization happening and evasions such as ".." are mapped to the path in the variable. Therefore, if you want to test for these evasions, you need your rule to run in phase 1, or you need to use the REQUEST_URI_RAW variable instead.

REQUEST_URI_RAW

This variable holds the full request URL, including the query string data and the path info, if any. In addition, it will contain the domain name if it was provided on the request line (e.g., https://www.example.com/index.php?p=X). Unlike REQUEST_URI, no normalizations will be applied to this variable and it will remain unaltered throughout the full request lifecycle.

Example value: /app/index.php?p=X

RESOURCE

This variable is a persistent collection used to store information about a certain resource on the server. As with all other persistent collections, RESOURCE becomes available only after it's initialized using the initcol action.

Resources usually are meant to be scripts or filenames, but a wider definition is applicable—as shown in the following example, which counts login attempts to an individual account:

```
# Initialize resource collection with username as key
SecRule &ARGS:username "!@eq 0" \
    "id:2000,phase:2,pass,nolog,\
    initcol:RESOURCE=%{ARGS.username},\
    setvar:RESOURCE.num_login_attempts=+1,\
    expirevar:RESOURCE.num_login_attempts=60"

# Check number of login attempts to account
SecRule RESOURCE:num_login_attempts "@ge 5" \
    "id:2001,phase:2,deny,log,\
    msg:'5 or more login attempts within 60 seconds.'"
```

RESPONSE_BODY

This variable holds the data for the response body, but only when response body buffering is enabled.

Example value: `<!DOCTYPE html>\n<html lang=...`

RESPONSE_CONTENT_LENGTH

Response body length in bytes. This variable can be available starting with phase 3, but it doesn't have to be (as the length of the response body isn't always announced in the response headers). If the size isn't known, this variable will contain a zero. If `RESPONSE_CONTENT_LENGTH` contains a zero in phase 5, that means the actual size of the response body was 0.

Example value: `14578`

The value of this variable can change between phases if the body is modified. For example, `mod_deflate` can compress the response body between phases 4 and 5.

RESPONSE_CONTENT_TYPE

Response content type. Available only starting with phase 3. The value available in this variable is taken directly from the internal structures of Apache, which means that it may contain information that isn't yet available in response headers. In embedded deployments, you should always refer to this variable, rather than to `RESPONSE_HEADERS:Content-Type`.

Example value: `text/html`

RESPONSE_HEADERS

This variable refers to the response headers collection, like `REQUEST_HEADERS` refers to request headers.

This variable may not have access to some headers when running in embedded mode. Headers such as `Server`, `Date`, `Connection`, and `Content-Type` could be added just prior to sending data to the client. This data should be available in phase 5 or when deployed in proxy mode.

RESPONSE_HEADERS_NAMES

This variable is a collection of response header names. The same limitations as those discussed in RESPONSE_HEADERS apply.

RESPONSE_PROTOCOL

This variable holds the HTTP response protocol information.

Example value: HTTP/1.1

RESPONSE_STATUS

This variable holds the HTTP response status code.

Example value: 200

> **Warning**
>
> In embedded mode, it isn't always possible to work with this variable. In cases in which the value of the variable would be interesting (i.e., errors), it's possible for Apache to choose to break out of the request cycle early and bypass ModSecurity (and other Apache modules). All ModSecurity rules, including those referring to RESPONSE_STATUS, would thus be bypassed.

RULE

This is a special collection that provides access to the accuracy, id, logdata, maturity, msg, rev, severity, and ver fields of the rule that triggered the action. It can be used to refer to only the same rule in which it resides. Use it in a construct like the following:

```
SecRule ARGS "@rx attack" \
    "id:1000,phase:2,deny,log,accuracy:3,\
    setenv:accuracy_%{RULE.id}=%{RULE.accuracy}"
```

For a request containing attack, this rule would set the environment variable accuracy_1000 and assign it a value of 3.

> **Note**
>
> For logdata and msg, the variables contain the format description of the field as defined in the rule—that is, without any macros resolved.

It's also noteworthy that as of this writing, this collection is not available inside a message field.

SCRIPT_BASENAME

This variable holds just the filename part of SCRIPT_FILENAME. Not available in phase 1.

Example value: index.html

> ## Warning
>
> If used in proxy mode, this variable can't be trusted, because mapping the request to the filename will only happen on the backend. An attacker can therefore add PATH_INFO to the request and ModSecurity will use it as SCRIPT_BASENAME.

SCRIPT_FILENAME

This variable holds the absolute filesystem path to the file or script that will be used to serve the request. The variable isn't available in phase 1. In proxy mode, the variable contains the full proxy URL, with the prefix proxy.

Example value (embedded): /usr/lib/cgi-bin/login.action

Example value (proxy): proxy:https://localhost:8443/index.html

SCRIPT_GID

This variable holds the numerical identifier of the group owner of the file or script requested. In phase 1 and in proxy mode, this variable will be set to 0.

Example value: 1000

SCRIPT_GROUPNAME

This variable holds the name of the group owner of the file or script. In phase 1 and in proxy mode, this variable will be set to root.

Example value: staff

SCRIPT_MODE

This variable holds the script's permissions mode data. In phase 1 and in proxy mode, this variable will be set to 0000.

Example value: 0644

SCRIPT_UID

This variable holds the numerical identifier of the owner of the script. In phase 1 and in proxy mode, this variable will be set to 0.

Example value: 1000

SCRIPT_USERNAME

This variable holds the username of the owner of the script. In phase 1 and in proxy mode, this variable will be set to root.

Example value: myuser

SDBM_DELETE_ERROR

On rare occasions, the server fails to delete entries in the persistent storage data files on disk. When this happens, this flag will be set to 1.

Example value: 0

SERVER_ADDR

This variable contains the IP address of the server or listener serving the request.

Example value: 192.168.1.100

SERVER_NAME

This variable contains the transaction's hostname, or IP address if there is no hostname. Usually, this is the server name as defined in the Apache configuration. However, if the Apache configuration setting UseCanonicalName is disabled (which is the default), then this is the Host request header, which means that in principle it shouldn't be trusted.

Example value: example.com

SERVER_PORT

This variable contains the local port of the server or listener serving the request.

Example value: 443

SESSION

This variable is a persistent collection that contains session information. It becomes available only after `setsid` is executed to initialize the collection for the request or to retrieve the collection if it's been initialized during another transaction.

The following example shows how to initialize SESSION using `setsid`, how to use `setvar` to increase an arbitrary variable (SESSION.score), how to set a second variable (SESSION.blocked), and, finally, how to deny the connection based on this variable:

```
# Initialize session storage
SecRule REQUEST_COOKIES:PHPSESSID "!@rx ^$" \
    "id:1000,phase:2,pass,log,msg:'Initializing session (%{SESSIONID})', \
    setsid:%{REQUEST_COOKIES.PHPSESSID}"

# Increment session score on attack
SecRule ARGS "@rx attack" \
    "id:2000,phase:2,t:none,t:lowercase,pass,log, \
    msg:'Attack; raising score (%{SESSION.score})',setvar:SESSION.score=+10"

# Detect too many attacks in a session
SecRule SESSION:score "@gt 50" \
    "id:8998,phase:2,pass,log, \
    msg:'Score (%{MATCHED_VAR}) higher than threshold',setvar:SESSION.blocked=1"

# Enforce session block
SecRule SESSION:blocked "@eq 1" \
    "id:8999,phase:2,deny,log,msg:'Blocking request'"

SecRule SESSIONID "!@rx ^$" \
    "id:9999,phase:5,pass,log, \
    msg:'Session %{MATCHED_VAR}: final score: %{SESSION.score}, blocked variable: ↵
%{SESSION.blocked}'"
```

The SESSION.score variable will be raised on every perceived attack (i.e., rule 2000). Once the threshold is reached, blocking will start for every request of the session until the session expires.

SESSIONID

This variable contains the ID value of the SESSION collection set with `setsid`. See SESSION for a complete example.

Example value: `j8v4if2fpvbfr1cjp49e3del55`

STREAM_INPUT_BODY

This variable contains the raw request body as a single memory buffer. It isn't created by default and needs to be configured using the `SecStreamInBodyInspection` directive. This variable is designed for use in combination with the `@rsub` operator.

Example value: `yourEmail=john.smith@example.com&supportMessage=I+was+lo...`

STREAM_OUTPUT_BODY

This variable contains the raw response body as a single memory buffer. It isn't created by default and needs to be configured using the `SecStreamOutBodyInspection` directive. This variable is designed for use in combination with the `@rsub` operator.

Example value: `<html><body><h1>It works!</h1></body></html>`

TIME

This variable holds a formatted string representing the time, in a format that lists the individual integers from year to second without any separator.

Example value: `20160523063440`

TIME_DAY

This variable holds the current day of the month (1–31).

Example value: `23`

TIME_EPOCH

This variable holds the time, in seconds, since the start of the Unix time epoch (January 1, 1970).

Example value: `1463978119`

TIME_HOUR

This variable holds the current hour value (00–23).

Example value: 06

TIME_MIN

This variable holds the current minute value (00–59).

Example value: 34

TIME_MON

This variable holds the current month value (01–12).

Example value: 05

TIME_SEC

This variable holds the current second value (0–59).

Example value: 40

TIME_WDAY

This variable holds the current weekday value (0–6). Sunday is represented by 0; Saturday is thus 6.

Example value: 0

TIME_YEAR

This variable holds the current four-digit year value.

Example value: 2017

TX

This is the transient transaction collection, which is used to store pieces of data during the lifetime of a single transaction or request.

Some variable names in the TX collection are reserved and can't be used:

- TX:0: The matching value when using the @rx, @pm, or @pmf operator with the capture action

---

- `TX:1-TX:9`: The captured subexpression value when using the `@rx` operator with capturing parentheses and the `capture` action
- `TX:MSC_.*`: ModSecurity processing flags
  - `MSC_PCRE_LIMITS_EXCEEDED`: Set to nonzero if PCRE match limits are exceeded. See `SecPcreMatchLimit` and `SecPcreMatchLimitRecursion` for more information.

UNIQUE_ID

Exposes the unique ID assigned to the current transaction by the `mod_unique_id` Apache module.

Example value: `VOKKOn8AAQEAAEj3TMUAAAAA`

URLENCODED_ERROR

This flag is raised when an invalid URL encoding is encountered during the parsing of a query string (on every request) or during the parsing of an `application/x-www-form-urlencoded` request body (only on requests that use the `URLENCODED` request body processor). An invalid URL encoding error will be triggered, for example, if the percent sign initiating a URL-encoded format character is followed only by a single character and not the usual two.

Example value: 1

USER

This is a persistent collection containing user information. It becomes available only after `setuid` is executed to initialize the collection for the request or to retrieve the collection if it's been initialized during another transaction.

USERAGENT_IP

When used with Apache 2.4 and higher, this variable contains the IP address of the user agent, which may be communicating with the server via one or more proxy servers. To enable this functionality in the Apache web server, use the `mod_remoteip` module to extract the user agent IP address from headers that contain this information (e.g., `X-Forwarded-For`). Available starting with 2.7.0—and only when used in combination with Apache 2.4 or better.

Example value: `192.168.32.15`

USERID

This variable contains the ID value of the USER collection set with setuid.

Example value: guest

In the following example, the USER collection is initialized with the REMOTE_USER set by one of Apache's authentication modules. In the subsequent rule, the value is checked and guest access blocked.

```
# Initialize user tracking
SecAction "id:2000,phase:2,nolog,pass,setuid:%{REMOTE_USER}"

# Is the current user the administrator?
SecRule USERID "@rx guest" \
    "id:2001,phase:2,log,deny,msg:'Blocking guest access'"
```

WEBAPPID

This variable contains the current application name, which is set using the SecWebAppId directive.

Example value: App2

WEBSERVER_ERROR_LOG

This collection contains zero or more error messages produced by the web server. This variable is best accessed from phase 5 (logging). ModSecurity messages written to the server's error log will also be added to this collection.

XML

This is a special collection used to interact with the XML parser. It's used standalone as a variable for the validateDTD and validateSchema operator and serves as a target for these validation calls. However, it also can be used to designate specific locations within the XML document via a valid XPath expression, which will then be evaluated against a previously parsed XML DOM tree. The following example illustrates some advanced XPath uses:

```
SecRule REQUEST_HEADERS:Content-Type "@rx ^text/xml$" \
    "phase:1,id:1000,t:lowercase,pass,log, \
        msg:'Enable XML processor',ctl:requestBodyProcessor=XML"

SecRule REQBODY_PROCESSOR            "!@rx ^XML$"       "phase:2,id:2000,log,pass, \
        msg:'XML processor is not enabled. Skipping XML checks.',skipAfter:END↵
```

```
_XML_CHECKS"

SecRule XML       "@validateDTD /path/to/note.dtd" "id:2001,phase:2,deny,log, \
        msg:'XML DTD check failed"

SecRule XML:/note/to              "@rx extern"       "id:2002,phase:2,deny,log"
SecRule XML:/note/from            "@rx attacker"     "id:2003,phase:2,deny,log"
SecRule XML:/note/transfer        "!@rx ^direct$"    "id:2004,phase:2,deny,log"
SecRule XML:/note/item[last()]    "@rx attack"       "id:2005,phase:2,deny,log"
SecRule XML:/note/item[last()-1]  "@rx attack"       "id:2006,phase:2,deny,log"
SecRule XML:/note/item/@type      "@rx core"         "id:2007,phase:2,deny,log"
SecRule XML://to                  "@rx extern"       "id:2008,phase:2,deny,log"

SecMarker END_XML_CHECKS
```

17 Transformation Functions

Transformation functions are used to alter input data before it's used in matching (i.e., operator execution). The input data is never modified; whenever you request a transformation function to be used, ModSecurity will create a copy of the data, transform it, and then run the operator against the result.

In the following example, the request parameter values are converted to lowercase before matching:

```
SecRule ARGS "@rx xp_cmdshell" \
    "id:2000,phase:2,deny,t:lowercase"
```

Multiple transformation actions can be used in the same rule, forming a *transformation pipeline*. The transformations will be performed in the order in which they appear in the rule.

In most cases, the order in which transformations are performed is important. In the following example, a series of transformation functions is performed to counter evasion. Performing the transformations in any other order would allow a skillful attacker to evade detection:

```
SecRule ARGS "@rx (asfunction|javascript|vbscript|data|mocha|livescript):" \
    "id:2000,phase:2,deny, \
    t:htmlEntityDecode,t:lowercase,t:removeNulls,t:removeWhitespace"
```

The matching of the input data happens after the final transformation, but it's also possible to execute the matching after every transformation step separately. Use the multiMatch action to configure the transformation pipeline in such a way.

> **Warning**
>
> Currently, it's possible to use SecDefaultAction to specify a default list of transformation functions, which will be applied to all rules that follow the SecDefaultAction directive. However, this practice is deprecated since 2.7.0 and results in a warning message at startup. Although being able to configure default

> transformation functions seemed like a good idea originally, this feature made rules more difficult to understand, because their functionality would depend not only on what was in the rule, but also on all the context in which they were executing.

The remainder of this chapter documents the transformation functions currently available in ModSecurity. Every transformation is accompanied by an example that illustrates the transformation process. When the transformation works on binary input or when the output is binary, no example is given.

base64Decode

Decodes a base64-encoded string, as defined in RFC 2045.[1]

Before: L2Jpbi9jYXQgL2V0Yy9wYXNzd2Q=

After: /bin/cat /etc/passwd

base64DecodeExt

Decodes a base64-encoded string. Unlike base64Decode, this version uses a forgiving implementation, which ignores invalid characters.

Before: @=L#2Jpbi9@@jYXQ$gL2{VOY}y9wYXNzd2#Q§(=)#$@

After: /bin/cat /etc/passwd

base64Encode

Encodes an input string using base64-encoding, as defined in RFC 2045.

Before: Dear John,\nWhen we talked about ...

After: RGVhciBKb2huLFxuV2hlbiB3ZSBOYWxrZWQgYWJvdXQgLi4u

cmdLine

Performs several transformations that simulate how input would be treated in an attack aimed at command execution:

1. Deletes backslash characters
2. Deletes double quote characters

---

[1] RFC 2045: MIME Part One: Format of Internet Message Bodies [fsty.uk/m57] (IETF, November 1996)

3. Deletes single quote characters

4. Deletes caret characters

5. Deletes whitespace before a forward slash character

6. Deletes whitespace before an open parenthesis character

7. Replaces each comma with a space

8. Replaces each semicolon with a space

9. Compresses multiple whitespace characters (any of 0x20, \t, \r, and \n) into a single space

10. Converts all characters to lowercase

Before: `"cat /^e^t^c/passwd;cat /etc/shadow"`

After: `cat/etc/passwd cat/etc/shadow`

compressWhitespace

Converts any of the whitespace characters (0x20, \f, \t, \n, \r, \v, 0xa0) to spaces (0x20), compressing multiple consecutive space characters into one.

Before: `cat      /etc/passwd`

After: `cat /etc/passwd`

cssDecode

Decodes characters encoded using the CSS 2.x escape rules.[2] CSS escaping works with a backslash followed by up to six hexadecimal characters identifying a Unicode character. ModSecurity will only ever interpret the final two characters and ignore the other ones. This transformation is useful to uncover CSS-encoded ASCII characters that wouldn't normally be encoded. If a backslash is used in front of a nonhexadecimal digit (e.g., for evasion purposes), the backslash is ignored. Finally, CSS escaping allows for a space character to terminate an encoding string of five or fewer digits. This whitespace termination character is thus ignored by ModSecurity.

Before: `cat\000020\/e\tc\2f \pa\ss\wd\020\26`

After: `cat /etc/passwd &`

---

[2] CSS 2.x escape rules [fsty.uk/m58] (W3C, retrieved 5 January 2017)

escapeSeqDecode

Decodes ANSI C escape sequences: \a, \b, \f, \n, \r, \t, \v, \\, \?, \', \", \xHH (hexadecimal), and \000 (octal). Invalid encodings are left in the output.

Before: cats\x08\040\/dogs\010\x08\010\x08et\x07c\/pain\010\x08ss\001w\ad

After: cat /etc/passwd

hexDecode

Decodes a string by replacing each pair of hexadecimal characters with their corresponding ASCII characters. The resulting string may contain binary characters.

Before: 636174202f6574632f706173737764

After: cat /etc/passwd

hexEncode

Encodes a string (possibly containing binary characters) by replacing each input byte with two hexadecimal characters.

Before: cat /etc/passwd

After: 636174202f6574632f706173737764

htmlEntityDecode

Decodes characters encoded as HTML entities.[3] The following variants are supported:

- &#xHH and &#xHH; (where H is any hexadecimal number)
- &#DDD and &#DDD; (where D is any decimal number)
- &quot and "
-   and
- &lt and <
- &gt and >

This function converts every detected HTML entity into just one byte, possibly resulting in a loss of information if the entity refers to a character that requires two or more bytes. It's thus useful to uncover bytes that would otherwise not need to be encoded, but this function can't do anything meaningful with characters from the range above 0xff.

---

[3] HTML entities [fsty.uk/m59] (W3C, retrieved 5 January 2017)

Before: cats&#008dogs&#008&#x08&#008&#x08&#x020&#047etc&#x2fpas&#115w&#x64

After: cat /etc/passwd

jsDecode

Decodes JavaScript escape sequences, as defined in the ECMAScript standard. [4] The following variants are supported:

- \uHHHH (where H is any hexadecimal number)
- \xHH (where H is any hexadecimal number)
- \OOO (where O is any octal number)

If a \uHHHH code is in the range of FF01–FF5E (the full-width ASCII codes), then the higher byte is used to detect and adjust the lower byte. Otherwise, only the lower byte will be used and the higher byte zeroed (leading to possible loss of information).

Single-character escape sequences are left untouched (\b, \f, \n, \r, \t, \v, \0, and \\).

Before: \143\u0061\x74+\u002fet\u0002c\u002f\x70ass\u0077d

After: cat /etc/passwd

length

Looks up the length of the input string in bytes, placing it (as a string) in output. For example, if it gets ABCDE on input, this transformation function will return 5 on output.

Before: Dear John,\nWhen we talked about ...

After: 36

lowercase

Converts all characters to lowercase using the current C locale.

Before: CAT /ETC/PASSWD

After: cat /etc/passwd

md5

Calculates an MD5 hash from the data in input. The computed hash is in a raw binary form and needs to be further encoded for printing or logging. Hash functions are commonly used

---

[4] ECMAScript [fsty.uk/m60] (ECMA International, retrieved 5 January 2017)

in combination with hexEncode (e.g., t:md5,t:hexEncode). Given that MD5 is now considered insecure, you should use this transformation function only with compatibility with existing systems.

none

Not an actual transformation function, but an instruction to ModSecurity to remove all transformation functions associated with the current rule.

normalisePath

Removes multiple slashes, directory self-references, and directory back references (except when at the beginning of the input) from the input string.

Before: /../././../etc/./php.ini

After: /etc/php.ini

normalisePathWin

Same as normalisePath, but first converts backslash characters to forward slashes.

Before: \..\windows\php.ini

After: /windows/php.ini

normalizePath

Alias for normalisePath.

normalizePathWin

Alias for normalisePathWin.

parityEven7bit

Calculates even parity of seven-bit data, replacing the eighth bit of each target byte with the calculated parity bit.

---

parityOdd7bit

Calculates odd parity of seven-bit data, replacing the eighth bit of each target byte with the calculated parity bit.

parityZero7bit

Calculates zero parity of seven-bit data, replacing the eighth bit of each target byte with a zero-parity bit, which allows inspection of even/odd parity seven-bit data as ASCII7 data.

removeComments

This transformation function will remove comments that start with /* and end with */, but replace # and -- occurrences with spaces elsewhere.

Before: cat /*dog not included*//etc/passwd#short for password

After: cat /etc/passwd

removeCommentsChar

Removes characters and character combinations typically used to create comments: /*, */, --, and #.

Before: cat /* *//e#t--c/#pass#w#d

After: cat /etc/passwd

removeNulls

Removes all NUL bytes from input.

removeWhitespace

Removes all whitespace characters from input.

Before: c a t / e t c /pass w d

After: cat/etc/passwd

replaceComments

Replaces each occurrence of a C-style comment (/* ... */) with a single space (multiple consecutive occurrences of which will not be compressed). Unterminated comments will also be replaced with a space (ASCII 0x20). However, a standalone termination of a comment (*/) will not be acted upon.

Before: `cat/*dog not included*//etc/passwd`

After: `cat /etc/passwd`

replaceNulls

Replaces NUL bytes in input with space characters (ASCII 0x20).

sha1

Calculates a SHA1 hash from the input string. The computed hash is in a raw binary form and needs to be further encoded for printing or logging. Hash functions are commonly used in combination with hexEncode (e.g., `t:sha1,t:hexEncode`).

sqlHexDecode

Decodes SQL-style hexadecimal encodings.

Before: `0x53454C45435420*0x2046524F4D 0x55534552;`

After: `SELECT * FROM USER;`

trim

Removes whitespace from both the left and right ends of the input string. To make the example usage easier to follow, we used underscores to represent whitespace characters.

Before: ____cat____

After: cat

trimLeft

Removes whitespace from the left end of the input string. To make the example usage easier to follow, we used underscores to represent whitespace characters.

Before: ____cat____

After: cat____

trimRight

Removes whitespace from the right end of the input string. To make the example usage easier to follow, we used underscores to represent whitespace characters.

Before: ___cat___

After: ___cat

urlDecode

Decodes a *percent-encoded* (or *URL-encoded*) input string, as defined in RFC 3986.[5] Invalid encodings (i.e., those that use nonhexadecimal characters or those that are at the end of string and have one or two bytes missing) are not converted, but no error is raised. To detect invalid encodings, use the @validateUrlEncoding operator on the input data first. The transformation function shouldn't be used against variables that have already been URL-decoded (such as request parameters) unless it's your intention to perform URL decoding twice!

Before: /index.html%2F%2E%2E%2F%2E%2E%2F%65%74%63%2F%70%68%70%2E%69%6E%69

After: /index.html/../../etc/php.ini

urlDecodeUni

Like urlDecode, but with support for the Microsoft-specific %uHHHH encoding. If the code is in the range of FF01-FF5E (the full-width ASCII codes), then the higher byte is used to detect and adjust the lower byte. If SecUnicodeMapFile and SecUnicodeCodePage were used, the two-byte Unicode code point will be converted into a single byte using best-effort mapping. If these directives were not used, only the lower byte will be used and the higher byte will be ignored.

Before: /index%u005C%u002E%2E%5C%77%69%6E%64%6F%77%73%5C%70%68%70%2E%69%6E%69

After: /index\..\windows\php.ini

urlEncode

Encodes an input string using percent (URL) encoding.

Before: cat /etc/passwd

After: cat+%2fetc%2fpasswd

---

[5] RFC 3986: URI: Generic Syntax [fsty.uk/m61] (IETF, January 2005)

utf8toUnicode

Converts all UTF-8 characters (code point 128 and higher) to Unicode using the %uHHHH syntax. Available as of 2.7.0.

Before: ćat¯'/etç/passwd'

After: %u0107at%u00af%u2019/et%u00e7/passwd%u2019

18 Operators

In ModSecurity, operators are used to evaluate parameter values and make decisions about rule matching. If an operator matches, the entire rule matches and the associated action list is processed. In this chapter, we document the operators currently available in ModSecurity.

Most operators compare the variables specified in the SecRule directive with the supplied operator parameter. In the following example, the value of the REQUEST_METHOD variable is compared to the POST string:

```
SecRule REQUEST_METHOD "!@streq POST" \
    "phase:1,id:2000,deny,log,msg:'Wrong method'"
```

Some operators work without a parameter. A few special operators perform more advanced checks, and some interface to external libraries and even remote servers. In the special case of geoLookup, the operator is used to initialize a collection.

beginsWith

Returns true if the parameter string is found at the beginning of the input. Macro expansion is performed on the parameter string before comparison.

```
# Deny access to admin interface of service
SecRule REQUEST_URI "@beginsWith /admin" \
    "id:1000,phase:1,deny"
```

contains

Returns true if the parameter string is found anywhere in the rule's input. Macro expansion is performed on the parameter string before comparison.

```
# Detect ".php" anywhere in the request line
SecRule REQUEST_URI "@contains .php" \
    "id:1000,phase:1,deny"
```

containsWord

Returns true if the parameter string is found in the input variable. Unlike `contains`, this operator matches only if the parameter appears in the input as a whole word, not just a part of it. Macro expansion is performed on the parameter string before comparison. This operator was added in 2.7.1.

```
# Detect PHP function name "eval" in input ("medieval" won't match)
SecRule ARGS "@containsWord eval" \
    "id:2000,phase:2,deny"
```

detectSQLi

Checks input for SQL injection attacks. This operator relies on libinjection,[1] a special-purpose library designed to detect injection attacks. This library is embedded in ModSecurity itself.

```
# Detect sql injection using libinjection
SecRule ARGS "@detectSQLi" \
    "id:2000,phase:2,deny"
```

The `detectSQLi` operator was added in 2.8.0 but has seen significant updates since its introduction thanks to improvements in libinjection.

detectXSS

Checks input for cross-site scripting attacks. This operator relies on libinjection,[1] a special-purpose library designed to detect injection attacks. This library is embedded in ModSecurity itself.

```
# Detect XSS using libinjection
SecRule ARGS "@detectXSS" \
    "id:2000,phase:2,deny"
```

The `detectSQLi` operator was added in 2.8.0 but has seen significant updates since its introduction thanks to improvements in libinjection.

endsWith

Returns true if the parameter string is found at the end of the input. Macro expansion is performed on the parameter string before comparison.

---

[1] libinjection [fsty.uk/m62] (GitHub, retrieved 5 January 2017)

```
# Detect a request line that does not end with "HTTP/1.1"
SecRule REQUEST_LINE "!@endsWith HTTP/1.1" \
    "id:1000,phase:1,deny"
```

eq

Performs numerical comparison and returns true if the input value is *equal* to the provided parameter. Macro expansion is performed on the parameter string before comparison.

```
# Detect a connection problem with backend server
SecRule RESPONSE_STATUS "@eq 503" \
    "id:9000,phase:5,log,pass,exec:'alarm-backend-down.sh'"
```

fuzzyHash

The @fuzzyHash operator checks if a file resembles some other known file. A *fuzzy hash* (also called *context triggered piecewise hash* or *CTPH*) helps to identify malicious files even when they've been altered in order to defeat more common strict hash checking, such as MD5 or SHA1.

In order to use this operator, the ssdeep library needs to be available when ModSecurity is compiled. You also need a database of fuzzy hashes. The ssdeep library comes with a tool that can be used to build your own database. A more detailed description of @fuzzyHash can be found at the SpiderLabs Blog.[2] This operator was added to ModSecurity in 2.9.0.

The @fuzzyHash operator requires two parameters. The first parameter should be the path to the fuzzy hash database, and the second parameter is the percentage threshold of relative closeness, which serves as a limit to assume that two files are identical. If the call to the ssdeep library returns a percentage value above this limit, then the operator @fuzzyHash matches.

```
# Check file uploads against malware database
SecUploadKeepFiles On
SecRule FILES_TMP_CONTENT "@fuzzyHash fuzzy-hashes.txt 90" \
    "id:2000,phase:2,deny,msg:'Malware found in file attachment'"
```

ge

Performs numerical comparison and returns true if the input value is *greater than or equal to* the provided parameter. Macro expansion is performed on the parameter string before comparison.

---

[2] Detecting Malware with Fuzzy Hashing [fsty.uk/m63] (SpiderLabs Blog, retrieved 5 January 2017)

---

eq   353

```
# Detect 15 or more request headers
SecRule &REQUEST_HEADERS_NAMES "@ge 15" \
    "id:1000,phase:1,deny"
```

geoLookup

Performs a geolocation lookup using the IP address in input against the geolocation database previously configured using SecGeoLookupDb. The operator itself doesn't have a parameter. If the lookup is successful, then the obtained information is captured in the GEO collection.

The geoLookup operator matches on success and is thus best used in combination with nolog,pass. If you want to block on a failed lookup (which may be over the top, depending on how accurate the geolocation database is), the following example demonstrates how best to do it:

```
# Configure geolocation database
SecGeoLookupDb /path/to/GeoLiteCountry.dat
...
# Look up IP address
SecRule REMOTE_ADDR "@geoLookup" \
    "id:1000,phase:1,nolog,pass"

# Block IP address for which geolocation failed
SecRule &GEO "@eq 0" \
    "id:1001,phase:1,deny,msg:'Failed to lookup IP'"
```

See the GEO variable for more information on the various fields available.

> **Note**
>
> The @geoLookup operator is executed on every request, and the result is not cached. Despite this, the performance of this operation is quite good, because modern operating systems cache file contents in memory. The overall operator cost is similar to that of the regular expression operator.

gsbLookup

This operator was used to perform a lookup against one of the databases from Google's Safe Browsing project.[3] This operator is now deprecated, because it works only with an obsolete version of the Safe Browsing API that is no longer available.

---

[3] Google Safe Browsing project [fsty.uk/m64] (Google, retrieved 5 January 2017)

gt

Performs a numerical comparison between a variable and parameter and returns true if the input value is greater than the operator parameter.

```
# Count occurrences of "username" parameter; block request if more
# than one instance is encountered (parameter pollution attack).
SecRule &ARGS:username "@gt 1" \
    "id:2000,phase:2,deny"
```

inspectFile

Executes an external program for every variable in the target list. The contents of the variable are provided to the script as the first parameter on the command line. The program must be specified as the first parameter to the operator. If the supplied program filename is not absolute, it's treated as relative to the directory in which the configuration file resides. If the filename is determined to be a Lua script (based on its .lua extension), the script will be processed by the internal Lua engine. Internally processed scripts often run faster (there's no process creation overhead) and have full access to the transaction context of ModSecurity.

The @inspectFile operator was initially designed for file inspection (hence the name), but it can also be used in any situation that requires decision-making using external logic.

The following example uses an external program:

```
# Execute external program to validate uploaded files
SecRule FILES_TMPNAMES "@inspectFile /path/to/inspect_file.pl" \
    "id:2000,phase:2,deny"
```

The next example uses a Lua script (placed in the same directory as the configuration file):

```
SecRule FILES_TMPNAMES "@inspectFile inspect.lua" \
    "id:2000,phase:2,deny"
```

The contents of inspect.lua are as follows:

```
function main(filename)
    -- Do something to the file to verify it. In this example, we
    -- read up to 10 characters from the beginning of the file.
    local f = io.open(filename, "rb");
    local d = f:read(10);
    f:close();

    -- Return null if there is no reason to believe there is anything
    -- wrong with the file (no match). Returning any text will be taken
    -- to mean a match should be triggered.
```

```
        return null;
    end
```

ipMatch

Performs a match against one or more IPv4 or IPv6 IP addresses or network segments.

```
# Check remote client against one IPv4 address
SecRule REMOTE_ADDR "@ipMatch 192.168.2.254" \
    "id:1000,phase:1,deny"

# Check remote client against two IPv4 network segments
SecRule REMOTE_ADDR "@ipMatch 192.168.2.0/24,192.168.3.0/24" \
    "id:1001,phase:1,deny"

# Check remote client against the loopback IPv6 address
SecRule REMOTE_ADDR "@ipMatch ::1/128" \
    "id:1002,phase:1,deny"

# Check remote client against one IPv6 network segment
SecRule REMOTE_ADDR "@ipMatch 2001:DB8::/48" \
    "id:1003,phase:1,deny"
```

> ### Warning
>
> The use of CIDR notation in @ipMatch was affected by a bug in ModSecurity 2.8.0.
> Although the bug was fixed long ago, the old and flawed version still remains in
> various Linux distributions.

ipMatchF

Alias for @ipMatchFromFile. Available starting with 2.7.0.

ipMatchFromFile

Same as @ipMatch, but uses a file that contains one IP address or network segment per line.
Available starting with 2.7.0.

```
# Check client against the IP blacklist
SecRule REMOTE_ADDR "@ipMatchFromFile ip-blacklist.txt" \
    "id:1000,phase:1,deny"
```

> **Note**
>
> This operator loads the contents of the parameter files at startup and doesn't refresh
> them until the web server is restarted or reloaded.

le

Performs numerical comparison and returns true if the input value is *less than or equal to*
the operator parameter. Macro expansion is performed on the parameter string before comparison.

```
# Detect 5 or fewer headers in a request (likely a robot)
SecRule &REQUEST_HEADERS_NAMES "@le 5" \
    "id:2000,phase:2,deny,msg:'Suspiciously few request headers'"
```

lt

Performs numerical comparison and returns true if the input value is *less than* the operator
parameter. Macro expansion is performed on the parameter string before comparison.

```
# Detects a successful request
SecRule RESPONSE_STATUS "@lt 400" \
    "id:9000,phase:5,pass,msg:'Request successful'"
```

noMatch

A special-purpose operator that never matches. Use @noMatch without an operator parameter.

```
SecRule REMOTE_ADDR "@noMatch" \
    "id:2000,phase:2,pass,msg:'This will never match'"
```

pm

Performs a case-insensitive match of the provided phrases against the input value. The operator uses a set-based matching algorithm (Aho-Corasick), which means that it will match
any number of keywords in parallel. When matching a large number of keywords is needed,
this operator performs much better than a regular expression.

```
# Detect suspicious client by looking at the user agent identification
SecRule REQUEST_HEADERS:User-Agent "@pm WebZIP WebCopier Webster WebStripper \
    SiteSnagger ProWebWalker CheeseBot" \
    "id:2000,phase:2,log,deny"
```

The @pm operator supports Snort-style binary data embedded in patterns, for which you can switch from text to binary using the pipe character. In the following example, we look for AAA in request parameters:

```
SecRule ARGS "@pm A|41|A" \
    "id:2000,phase:2,log,deny"
```

The pipe character is used to switch from text to binary mode and back. When in binary mode, bytes are represented by their hexadecimal values.

pmf

The @pmf operator is an alias for @pmFromFile.

pmFromFile

Performs a case-insensitive match of the provided phrases against the input value. The operator uses a set-based matching algorithm (Aho-Corasick), which means that it will match any number of keywords in parallel. When matching a large number of keywords is needed, this operator performs much better than a regular expression.

This operator is the same as @pm, except that it takes a list of files as arguments. It will match any one of the phrases listed in the file(s) anywhere in the target value.

```
# Detect suspicious user agents using the keywords in
# the files /path/to/blacklist1 and blacklist2 (the latter
# must be placed in the same folder as the configuration file)
SecRule REQUEST_HEADERS:User-Agent "@pm /path/to/blacklist1 blacklist2" \
    "id:2000,phase:2,deny"
```

Note the following points:

1. Files must contain exactly one phrase per line. End-of-line markers (both LF and CRLF) will be stripped from each phrase and any whitespace trimmed from both the beginning and the end. Empty lines and comment lines (those beginning with the # character) will be ignored.

2. To allow easier inclusion of phrase files with rulesets, relative paths may be used. In this case, the path of the file containing the rule is prepended to the phrase file path.

3. The @pm operator phrases don't support metacharacters.

4. Because this operator doesn't check for boundaries when matching, false positives are possible in some cases. For example, if you want to use @pm for PHP function names,

the phrase eval will potentially match more than one word (e.g., it will also match evaluation or medieval).

rbl

Looks up the input value in the desired *real-time block list* (RBL), given as the operator parameter.

```
# Look up IP address on real-time block list via DNS request
SecRule REMOTE_ADDR "@rbl multi.surbl.org" \
    "id:2000,phase:2,deny"
```

RBLs rely on the DNS protocol to expose reputation information for hostnames and IP addresses. Internally, the check is performed by constructing a special hostname, which is then looked up via the system DNS. For example, to check the reputation of 127.0.0.2 in the multi.surbl.org RBL, the @rbl operator looks up hostname 2.0.0.127.multi.surbl.org. If the DNS call returns a positive result (hostname found), the target hostname or IP address is blacklisted and the @rbl operator matches. If the response is negative (hostname not found), the target is not blacklisted and the operator will not match.

> **Warning**
>
> Each invocation of this parameter will potentially cause a network operation, which might take a significant time to complete. For best performance, consider deploying a local caching DNS server.

The @rbl operator is known to work with the following RBL providers:

- Spamhaus[4]
- SURBL[5]
- URIBL[6]
- Project Honey Pot[7]

The first three providers offer multiple lists with various blacklist criteria. They are best looked up and compared on the providers' web sites. Note that these RBL services come with usage restrictions for heavy or commercial use. Project Honey Pot needs an API key that has to be defined with the SecHttpBlKey directive.

---

[4] The Spamhaus Project [fsty.uk/m29] (Spamhaus, retrieved 5 January 2017)

[5] SURBL URI reputation data [fsty.uk/m30] (SURBL, retrieved 5 January 2017)

[6] URIBL—real-time URI blacklist [fsty.uk/m31] (URIBL, retrieved 5 January 2017)

[7] Project Honey Pot [fsty.uk/m32] (Unspam Technologies, Inc., retrieved 5 January 2017)

---

rsub

Use @rsub to change request and response bodies. This operator relies on the regular expression substitution feature to update the STREAM_INPUT_BODY and SEC_OUTPUT_BODY variables.

```
SecRule STREAM_INPUT_BODY "@rsub s/regex/replacement/i" \
    "id:2000,phase:2,nolog,pass"
```

Note the following points:

- STREAM_INPUT_BODY must be enabled with SecStreamInBodyInspection.

- STREAM_OUTPUT_BODY must be enabled with SecStreamOutBodyInspection.

- SecContentInjection must be enabled if you want to use @rsub.

- The optional i flag after the last slash will make the pattern case-insensitive.

- The @rsub operator works only on STREAM_INPUT_BODY and SEC_OUTPUT_BODY. It will fail if used on other input values.

- Performing a substitution in STREAM_INPUT_BODY won't affect variables such as ARGS, ARGS_NAMES, and the like. These are set at the beginning of phase 2 (request) and kept as a copy that isn't resynced after the @rsub operation. It's possible to use the updated STREAM_INPUT_BODY in subsequent rules, however.

rx

Performs a regular expression match of the pattern provided as a parameter. This is the default operator; the rules that don't explicitly specify an operator default to @rx.

```
# Detect Nikto scanner
SecRule REQUEST_HEADERS:User-Agent "@rx nikto" \
    "id:1000,phase:1,deny,t:lowercase"

# Detect Nikto scanner with a case-insensitive pattern
SecRule REQUEST_HEADERS:User-Agent "@rx (?i)nikto" \
    "id:1001,phase:1,deny,t:none"

# Detect Nikto scanner with a case-insensitive pattern
SecRule REQUEST_HEADERS:User-Agent "(?i)nikto" \
    "id:1002,phase:1,deny"
```

Regular expressions are handled by the PCRE library.[8] ModSecurity compiles its regular expressions with the following settings:

---

[8] Perl Compatible Regular Expressions [fsty.uk/m18] (PCRE, retrieved 5 January 2017)

1. The entire input is treated as a single line, even when there are newline characters present.

2. All matches are case-sensitive. To perform case-insensitive matching, you can either use the `lowercase` transformation function or force case-insensitive matching by prefixing the regular expression pattern with the `(?i)` modifier (a PCRE feature; you'll find many similar features in the PCRE documentation).

3. The `PCRE_DOTALL` and `PCRE_DOLLAR_ENDONLY` flags are set during regular expression compilation, meaning that a single dot will match any character, including the newlines, and a `$` end anchor will not match a trailing newline character.

Regular expressions are a very powerful tool. You're strongly advised to read the PCRE documentation to become acquainted with its features.

streq

Performs a string comparison and returns true if the parameter string is identical to the input string. Macro expansion is performed on the parameter string before comparison.

```
# Detect request parameters "foo" that do not
# contain "bar", exactly.
SecRule ARGS:foo "!@streq bar" \
    "id:2000,phase:2,deny"
```

strmatch

This is an alternative to `@contains` that uses the Boyer-Moore-Horspool algorithm and comes without variable expansion. This algorithm is a single-pattern matching technique with better performance on large parameter values.

```
SecUploadKeepFiles On

# Detect "http" anywhere in the uploaded files
SecRule FILES_TMP_CONTENT "@strmatch http" \
    "id:2000,phase:2,deny"
```

unconditionalMatch

This is a special-purpose operator that always matches. Use `@unconditionalMatch` without an operator parameter.

```
SecRule REMOTE_ADDR "@unconditionalMatch" \
    "id:2000,phase:2,pass,nolog,t:sha1,t:hexEncode,\
    setvar:TX.ip_hash=%{MATCHED_VAR}"
```

The @unconditionalMatch operator doesn't look very useful at first sight, but if you examine the example carefully, you'll realize it provides the fastest way to fill the TX.ip_hash variable without any matching overhead.

validateByteRange

Validates that the byte values used in input fall into the range specified by the operator parameter. This operator matches on an input value that contains bytes that aren't in the specified range.

```
# Enforce very strict byte range for request parameters (only
# works for applications that do not use languages other
# than English).
SecRule ARGS "@validateByteRange 10, 13, 32-126" \
    "id:2000,phase:2,deny"
```

The validateByteRange operator is most useful for detecting the presence of NUL bytes, which don't have a legitimate use but are often used as an evasion technique.

```
# Do not allow NUL bytes
SecRule ARGS "@validateByteRange 1-255" \
    "id:2000,phase:2,deny"
```

validateDTD

Validates the XML DOM tree against the supplied DTD. The DOM tree must have been built previously using the XML request body processor. This operator matches when the validation fails.

```
# Parse the request bodies that contain XML
SecRule REQUEST_HEADERS:Content-Type "@rx ^text/xml$" \
    "id:1000,phase:1,nolog,pass,t:lowercase,\
    ctl:requestBodyProcessor=XML"

# Validate XML payload against the DTD
SecRule XML "@validateDTD /path/to/xml.dtd" \
    "id:2000,phase:2,deny,msg:'Failed DTD validation'"
```

validateHash

Validates the HMAC security tokens that have been configured by the hash engine. This operator retrieves the token value from the correct request parameter (based on the current ModSecurity configuration) and validates its contents.

```
# Check for correct HMAC token in URI
SecRule REQUEST_URI "@validateHash \.(aspx?|php)" \
    "id:2000,phase:2,deny"
```

validateSchema

Validates the XML DOM tree against the supplied XML Schema. The DOM tree must have been built previously using the XML request body processor. This operator matches when the validation fails.

```
# Parse the request bodies that contain XML
SecRule REQUEST_HEADERS:Content-Type "@rx ^text/xml$" \
    "id:1000,phase:1,nolog,pass,t:lowercase,\
    ctl:requestBodyProcessor=XML"
```

```
# Validate XML payload against the schema
SecRule XML "@validateSchema /path/to/xml.xsd" \
    "id:2000,phase:2,deny,msg:'Failed DTD validation'"
```

validateUrlEncoding

Validates the URL-encoded characters in the provided input string.

```
# Validate URL-encoded characters in the request URI
SecRule REQUEST_URI_RAW "@validateUrlEncoding" \
    "id:1000,phase:1,deny"
```

ModSecurity will automatically decode the URL-encoded characters in request parameters, which means that there's little sense in applying the @validateUrlEncoding operator to them —that is, unless you know that some of the request parameters were URL-encoded more than once. Use this operator against raw input or against input that you know is URL-encoded. For example, some applications will URL-encode cookies, although that's not in the standard. Because it isn't in the standard, ModSecurity will neither validate nor decode such encodings.

validateUtf8Encoding

Check whether the input is a valid UTF-8 string.

```
# Make sure all request parameters contain only valid UTF-8
SecRule ARGS "@validateUtf8Encoding" \
    "id:2000,phase:2,deny"
```

The @validateUtf8Encoding operator detects the following problems:

Not enough bytes

UTF-8 supports two-, three-, four-, five-, and six-byte encodings. ModSecurity will locate cases in which one or more bytes is/are missing from a character.

Invalid characters

The two most significant bits in most characters should be fixed to 0x80. Some attack techniques use different values as an evasion technique.

Overlong characters

ASCII characters are mapped directly into UTF-8, which means that an ASCII character is one UTF-8 character at the same time. However, in UTF-8 many ASCII characters can also be encoded with two, three, four, five, and six bytes. This is no longer legal in newer versions of Unicode, but many older implementations still support it. The use of overlong UTF-8 characters is common for evasion.

Note the following points:

- Most but not all applications use UTF-8. If you're dealing with an application that does, validating that all request parameters are valid UTF-8 strings is a great way to prevent a number of evasion techniques that use the assorted UTF-8 weaknesses. False positives are likely if you use this operator in an application that doesn't use UTF-8.

- Many web servers will also allow UTF-8 in request URIs. If yours does, you can verify the request URI using @validateUtf8Encoding.

verifyCC

Detects credit card numbers in input. This operator will first use the supplied regular expression to perform an initial match, following up with the Luhn algorithm calculation to minimize false positives.

```
# Detect credit card numbers in parameters and
# prevent them from being logged to audit log
SecRule ARGS "@verifyCC \d{13,16}" \
    "id:2000,phase:2,log,pass,msg:'Possible credit card number',sanitiseMatched"
```

verifyCPF

Detects Brazilian social security numbers. This operator will use the supplied regular expression to perform an initial match and follow up with a further match against the CPF calculation algorithm.

```
# Detect Brazilian social security numbers and
# prevent them from being logged to audit log
```

```
SecRule ARGS "@verifyCPF /^([0-9]{3}\.){2}[0-9]{3}-[0-9]{2}$/" \
    "id:2000,phase:2,log,pass,msg:'Possible CPF number',sanitiseMatched"
```

verifySSN

Detects US social security numbers. This operator will use the supplied regular expression to perform an initial match and follow up with a further match against the SSN calculation algorithm.

```
# Detect US social security numbers in parameters and
# prevent them from being logged to audit log
SecRule ARGS "@verifySSN \d{3}-?\d{2}-?\d{4}" \
    "id:2000,phase:2,log,pass,msg:'Possible social security number',\
    sanitiseMatched"
```

within

Returns true if the rule's input is found anywhere within the parameter. Macro expansion is performed on the parameter string before comparison.

```
# Detect request methods other than GET, POST and HEAD
SecRule REQUEST_METHOD "!@within GET,POST,HEAD" \
    "id:2000,phase:2"
```

19 Actions

This chapter documents the actions currently available in ModSecurity. Actions are executed when an individual rule matches. They are heterogeneous in nature and fall into multiple categories, but generally a distinction is drawn between two basic groups: disruptive actions versus nondisruptive actions.

Disruptive actions are used to block a transaction in some way. However, if you want to tell ModSecurity that a rule isn't to interfere with a request, there is the pass action, which falls into this group as well. In general, a rule can only have one disruptive action.

Nondisruptive actions are instructions to the rule engine. Use them to control logging, set variables, tweak ModSecurity behavior for the current transaction, alter the flow of the rules, and set metadata. You can queue multiple nondisruptive actions in an individual rule, and some of them can even be used multiple times within the same rule.

accuracy

This utility field stores rule accuracy on a scale from 1 (very inaccurate) to 9 (very accurate). What these values mean is for the rule authors to determine and document.

```
# My experimental rule for XSS detection
SecRule ARGS "@rx [<>]" \
    "id:2000,phase:2,log,block,accuracy:1,maturity:1"
```

Available starting with 2.7.0.

allow

The allow action is a disruptive action that stops rule processing.

```
# Allow unrestricted access from 192.168.1.100
SecRule REMOTE_ADDR "@ipMatch 192.168.1.100" \
    "id:1000,phase:1,nolog,allow"
```

The following constraints apply:

1. If used on its own, as in the previous example, `allow` will affect the entire transaction, stopping processing of the current phase but also skipping over all other phases apart from the logging phase. (The logging phase is special; it always executes.)

2. If used as `allow:phase`, the engine stops processing the current phase. Other phases will continue as normal.

3. If used as `allow:request`, the engine stops processing the current phase; the next phase to be processed will be the `RESPONSE_HEADERS` phase.

For example:

```
# Do not process current phase
SecRule REMOTE_ADDR "@ipMatch 192.168.1.100" \
    "id:1000,phase:1,nolog,allow:phase"

# Do not process request but process response
SecRule REMOTE_ADDR "@ipMatch 192.168.1.100" \
    "id:1001,phase:1,nolog,allow:request"
# Do not process transaction (request and response)
SecRule REMOTE_ADDR "@ipMatch 192.168.1.100" \
    "id:1002,phase:1,nolog,allow"
```

If you want to allow a response through, put a rule into the `RESPONSE_HEADERS` phase and simply use `allow` on its own:

```
# Allow response through
SecRule REMOTE_ADDR "@ipMatch 192.168.1.100" \
    "id:6000,phase:3,nolog,allow"
```

append

Appends text given as parameter to the end of the response body. Content injection must be enabled (using the `SecContentInjection` directive). No content type checks are made, which means that before using any of the content injection actions, you must check whether the content type of the response is adequate for injection.

The following rule injects content into the response body after checking its content type:

```
SecRule RESPONSE_CONTENT_TYPE "@rx ^text/html" \
    "id:8000,phase:3,nolog,pass,append:'<hr>Footer'"
```

> **Warning**
>
> Although macro expansion is allowed in the additional content, you are strongly cautioned against inserting user-defined data fields into the output. Doing so

would create a *cross-site scripting* (XSS) vulnerability, which is an unfortunate thing for a security tool to do.

auditlog

Marks the current transaction to be logged in the audit log.

```
# Always log transactions from 192.168.1.100
SecRule REMOTE_ADDR "@ipMatch 192.168.1.100" \
    "id:1000,phase:1,nolog,auditlog"
```

block

Performs the default disruptive action defined with the most recent SecDefaultAction directive. This action is a placeholder intended for use by rule writers to request a blocking action without specifying how the blocking is to be done. The idea is to allow rule users to chose how blocking is done or to override it altogether if they so desire.

```
# Specify how blocking is to be done
SecDefaultAction "phase:2,deny,status:403,log,auditlog"

# Detect attacks where we want to block
SecRule ARGS "@rx attack1" "id:2000,phase:2,block"

# Detect attacks where we want only to warn
SecRule ARGS "@rx attack2" "id:2001,phase:2,pass"
```

It's possible to use the SecRuleUpdateActionById directive to override how a rule handles blocking. This is useful in three cases:

- A rule has blocking hard-coded, and you want it to use the policy you determine

- A rule was written to block, but you want it to only warn

- A rule was written to only warn, but you want it to block

The following example demonstrates the first case, in which the hard-coded block is removed in favor of the user-controllable block:

```
# Specify how blocking is to be done
SecDefaultAction "phase:2,pass,log,auditlog"

# Detect attacks and block
SecRule ARGS "@rx attack1" "id:2000,phase:2,deny"
```

```
# Change how rule ID 2000 blocks
SecRuleUpdateActionById 2000 block
```

capture

When used together with the regular expression operator (@rx), the capture action will create copies of the regular expression captures and place them in the transaction variable collection.

```
# Get the first byte of the debug parameter and save it in TX.debug
SecRule ARGS_GET:debug "@rx ^(.)" \
    "id:1000,phase:1,nolog,pass,capture,setvar:TX.debug=%{TX.1}"
```

Up to 10 captures will be copied on a successful pattern match, each with a single-digit name from 0 to 9. The TX.0 variable always contains the entire area that the regular expression matched. All the other variables will contain the captured values in the order in which the capturing parentheses appear in the regular expression.

> **Note**
>
> The capture action allows you to extract a piece out of a variable. The variables and collections MATCHED_VAR, MATCHED_VAR_NAME, MATCHED_VARS, and MATCHED_VARS_NAMES always contain the last matched input string and don't depend on the capture action.

chain

Chains the current rule with the rule that immediately follows it, creating a *rule chain*. Chained rules allow for more complex processing logic.

```
# Refuse to accept POST requests that do not contain Content-Length header.
# (Do note that this rule should be preceded by a rule
# that verifies only valid request methods are used.)
SecRule REQUEST_METHOD "@rx ^POST$" "id:1000,phase:1,log,block,chain"
    SecRule &REQUEST_HEADERS:Content-Length "@eq 0"
```

> **Note**
>
> Rule chains allow you to simulate logical AND. The disruptive actions specified in the first portion of the chained rule will be triggered only if all of the variable checks in the chained rules return positive hits. If any one aspect of a chained rule comes back negative, then the entire rule chain will fail to match. Also note that disruptive actions, execution phases, metadata actions (id, rev, msg), skip, and skipAfter actions can be specified only by the chain starter rule.

The following directives can be used in rule chains:

- `SecAction`

- `SecRule`

- `SecRuleScript`

Special rules control the usage of actions in chained rules:

- Any actions that affect the rule flow (i.e., disruptive actions, `skip`, and `skipAfter`) can be used only in the chain starter. They'll be executed only if the entire chain matches.

- Nondisruptive actions can be used anywhere in the chain. They'll be executed immediately after an individual rule matches.

- The metadata actions (e.g., `id`, `rev`, `msg`) can be used only in the chain starter.

ctl

Changes ModSecurity configuration on a transient, per-transaction basis. Any changes made using this action will affect only the transaction in which the action is executed. The default configuration, as well as the other transactions running in parallel, will be unaffected. If used to manipulate a rule, the `ctl` action has to run first, before the target rule runs.

The `ctl` action is accompanied by a parameter that is used to indicate which aspect of the configuration should be changed. With the exception of the `requestBodyProcessor` and `forceRequestBodyVariable` parameters, each parameter corresponds to one configuration directive. The various parameters are each described in separate entries that follow.

ctl:auditEngine

Controls the audit logging engine and corresponds with the `SecAuditEngine` directive.

```
# Disable audit logging when accessed from a trusted local address
SecRule REMOTE_ADDR "@ipMatch 192.168.1.100" \
    "id:1000,phase:1,pass,nolog,ctl:auditEngine=Off"
```


ctl:auditLogParts

Defines which parts of a transaction are recorded in the audit log; corresponds with theSecAuditLogParts directive. This `ctl` parameter supports incremental changes of the audit log when the + and - symbols are used. Use them to add or subtract individual parts from audit log entries in response to specific information in HTTP transactions.

```
# Enable logging of request body when post parameter "searchstring" is encountered
SecRule &ARGS_POST_NAMES:searchstring "@ge 1" \
    "id:2000,phase:2,pass,nolog,ctl:auditLogParts=+C"
```

ctl:debugLogLevel

Adjusts the verbosity level of the debug log data and corresponds with the SecDebugLogLevel directive.

```
# Enable full debug log
SecRule &ARGS:debug "@ge 1" \
    "id:1000,phase:1,pass,nolog,ctl:debugLogLevel=9"
```

ctl:forceRequestBodyVariable

Allows you to force the REQUEST_BODY variable to be set when there is no request body processor configured. This allows for inspection of request bodies of unknown types. This action has to be performed in phase 1 (request headers) so that the REQUEST_BODY variable can be prepared for phase 2 (request).

```
# Enable REQUEST_BODY variable for special content type text/calendar
SecRule REQUEST_HEADERS:Content-Type "@beginsWith text/calendar" \
    "id:1000,phase:1,pass,nolog,t:lowercase,ctl:forceRequestBodyVariable=On"
```

ctl:hashEnforcement

Controls the checking of security tokens using the hash engine. There is no corresponding directive for this ctl action.

```
# Add exception to HMAC security token enforcement
SecRule REQUEST_URI "@beginsWith /rest/api/emptyBasket" \
    "id:1000,phase:1,pass,nolog,ctl:hashEnforcement=Off"
```

ctl:hashEngine

Enables or disables the hash engine for the current transaction. The action corresponds with the SecHashEngine directive. However, unlike SecHashEngine, this action does not enable checking of the security tokens automatically (see ctl:hashEnforcement).

```
# Enable the hash engine for the comment section
SecRule REQUEST_URI "@beginsWith /comment" \
    "id:1000,phase:1,pass,nolog,t:normalizePath,t:lowercase,ctl:hashEngine=On"
```

ctl:requestBodyAccess

Controls request body buffering and processing. The ctl:requestBodyAccess action corresponds with the SecRequestBodyAccess directive.

```
# Disable processing of big form submissions for performance reasons
SecRule REQUEST_URI "@beginsWith /reports/submit.do" \
    "id:1000,phase:1,pass,nolog,ctl:requestBodyAccess=Off"
```

ctl:requestBodyLimit

Overrides the default request body size for the current transaction. This action corresponds with the SecRequestBodyLimit directive.

```
# Strict size limit on login requests
SecRule REQUEST_URI "@beginsWith /login" \
    "id:1000,phase:1,pass,nolog,t:normalizePath,t:lowercase,\
    ctl:requestBodyLimit=100"
```

ctl:requestBodyProcessor

Allows runtime configuration of the request body processor. By default, ModSecurity will automatically use the URLENCODED and MULTIPART processors to process application/x-www-form-urlencoded and multipart/form-data bodies, respectively. Two additional processors, JSON and XML, are also supported, but they're not used automatically. To activate a specific processor, place a rule containing ctl:requestBodyProcessor in the REQUEST_HEADERS processing phase.

```
# Parse requests with Content-Type "text/xml" as XML
SecRule REQUEST_CONTENT_TYPE "@beginsWith text/xml" \
    "id:1001,phase:1,pass,nolog,ctl:requestBodyProcessor=XML"
```

Request body processors will not interrupt a transaction if an error occurs. Instead, they'll set the REQBODY_PROCESSOR_ERROR and REQBODY_PROCESSOR_ERROR_MSG variables, which can be inspected in the REQUEST_BODY phase and an appropriate action taken.

ctl:responseBodyAccess

Controls the response body buffering and processing. The ctl:responseBodyAccess action corresponds with the SecResponseBodyAccess directive.

```
# Don't inspect static content
SecRule REQUEST_URI "@beginsWith /static" \
    "id:1000,phase:1,pass,nolog,ctl:responseBodyAccess=Off"
```

ctl:responseBodyLimit

Overrides the default given response body size limit for the current transaction. This action corresponds with the SecResponseBodyLimit directive.

```
# Cover for large css files
SecRule REQUEST_URI "@beginsWith /css" \
    "id:1000,phase:1,pass,nolog,ctl:responseBodyLimit=2048000"
```

ctl:ruleEngine

Disables the rule engine for the current transaction. This action corresponds with the SecRuleEngine directive.

```
# Disable ModSecurity from this trusted IP address
SecRule REMOTE_ADDR "@ipMatch 192.168.1.100" \
    "id:1000,phase:1,pass,nolog,ctl:ruleEngine=Off"
```

ctl:ruleRemoveById

Removes one or more rules from the configuration for the duration of the current transaction only. Use this action multiple times if you want to remove multiple individual rules. This action corresponds with the SecRuleRemoveById directive.

```
# Disable the Anti-XSS rules from
# the OWASP ModSecurity Core Rules for path
SecRule REQUEST_URI "@beginsWith /app2" \
    "id:1000,phase:1,pass,nolog,ctl:ruleRemoveById=941000-941999"
```

ctl:ruleRemoveByMsg

Removes rules with matching messages from the configuration for the duration of the current transaction only. This action corresponds with the SecRuleRemoveByMsg directive.

```
# Disable the experimental rules for path
SecRule REQUEST_URI "@beginsWith /app2" \
    "id:1000,phase:1,pass,nolog,ctl:ruleRemoveByMsg=experimental"
```

ctl:ruleRemoveByTag

Deactivates matching rules for the current transaction. This action corresponds with the SecRuleRemoveByTag directive.

```
# Disable the SQL injection rules for this path
SecRule REQUEST_URI "@beginsWith /graphs" \
    "id:1000,phase:1,pass,nolog,ctl:ruleRemoveByTag=attack-sqli"
```

ctl:ruleRemoveTargetById

Use to exclude the processing of a given target (request parameter, header or cookie, etc.) by a rule. The syntax has the form ctl:ruleRemoveTargetById=<id>;<target>. The rule ID can be a range; if the target is a collection, you can specify an individual element within the collection after a colon. This action corresponds loosely with the SecRuleUpdateTargetById directive.

```
# Disable rule 942110 for parameter address on given path
SecRule REQUEST_URI "@beginsWith /subscription" \
    "id:1000,phase:1,pass,nolog,ctl:ruleRemoveTargetById=942110;ARGS:address"
```

ctl:ruleRemoveTargetByMsg

Use to exclude the processing of a given target (request parameter, header or cookie, etc.) by a rule, identified by the rule's msg action. The syntax has the form ctl:ruleRemoveTargetByMsg=<msg regex>;<target>. If the target is a collection, you can specify an individual element within the collection after a colon. This action corresponds loosely with SecRuleUpdateTargetByMsg.

```
# Disable group of rules for parameter address on given path
SecRule REQUEST_URI "@beginsWith /subscription" \
    "id:1000,phase:1,pass,nolog,\
    ctl:ruleRemoveTargetByMsg=Restricted SQL Character.*Detection;ARGS:address"
```

ctl:ruleRemoveTargetByTag

Use to exclude the processing of a given target (request parameter, header or cookie, etc.) from being processed by a rule, identified by the rule's tag. The syntax has the form ctl:ruleRemoveTargetByTag=<tag regex>;<target>. If the target is a collection, you can specify an individual element within the collection after a colon. This action corresponds loosely with SecRuleUpdateTargetByTag.

```
# Disable the sql injection rules for parameter dimension on given path
SecRule REQUEST_URI "@beginsWith /graphs" \
```

```
    "id:1000,phase:1,pass,nolog,\
ctl:ruleRemoveTargetByTag=SQL_INJECTION;ARGS:dimension"
```

deny

Stops rule processing and intercepts the transaction. This is a disruptive action.

```
SecRule REQUEST_HEADERS:User-Agent "@contains nikto" \
    "id:1000,phase:1,log,deny,msg:'Nikto scanner identified'"
```

By default, deny blocks requests using HTTP status code 403 (Forbidden). You can set a different status code with the help of the status action.

deprecatevar

Decrements a numerical value over time. This action can be used only with variables that are recorded in persistent storage.

The following example decrements the counter by 60 every 300 seconds:

```
SecAction "id:9000,phase:5,nolog,pass,deprecatevar:SESSION.score=60/300"
```

Counter values are always positive, meaning that the value never goes below zero. Unlike expirevar, the deprecate action must be executed on every request. The value of the specified variable is reduced when the rule containing deprecatevar is processed.

drop

This disruptive action initiates an immediate closing of the TCP connection by sending a FIN packet.

```
SecRule ARGS "@rx attack" \
    "id:2000,phase:2,drop,msg:'TCP connection dropped'"
```

This action is useful for responding to brute force and denial of service attacks, when you want to minimize both the network bandwidth and the data returned to the client. In addition, the Apache worker (process or thread, depending on the deployment mode) bound to the connection is released immediately. The drop action causes the following error message to appear in the Apache log: AH00470: network write failure in core output filter.

> **Warning**
>
> This action isn't available on Windows-based builds. If used on this platform, the 500 HTTP status code will be returned instead.

---

exec

Executes the external program specified in the parameter. If the parameter supplied to exec is a Lua script (determined by the `.lua` extension), the script will be processed using the internal Lua engine, giving you direct access to the request context from the script.

```
# Run external program on rule match
SecRule REQUEST_URI "@beginsWith /cgi-bin/script.pl" \
    "id:2000,phase:2,pass,t:lowercase,t:normalizePath,block,\
    exec:/usr/local/apache/bin/test.sh"

# Run Lua script on rule match
SecRule ARGS:p "@rx attack" \
    "id:2000,phase:2,block,exec:/usr/local/apache/conf/exec.lua"
```

The exec action is executed independently from any disruptive actions specified. External scripts will always be called with no parameters. Some transaction information will be placed in environment variables. All the usual CGI environment variables will be there. The script you execute must write something (anything) to stdout; if it doesn't, ModSecurity will assume that the script failed and will record the failure. Internal Lua scripts have the option to return values via environment variables. For external scripts, there is no return value. However, the first line of stdout is written to the ModSecurity debug log at log level 4.

expirevar

Configures a collection variable to expire after the given time period (in seconds).

```
# Set up session tracking based on the content of the JSESSIONID cookie
SecRule REQUEST_COOKIES:JSESSIONID "!@rx ^$" \
    "id:1000,phase:1,nolog,pass,chain"
    SecAction setsid:%{REQUEST_COOKIES:JSESSIONID}

# Treat sessions that attempt access to the CGI folder as suspicious,
# but only for up to one hour (3600 seconds)
SecRule REQUEST_URI "@beginsWith /cgi-bin/script.pl" \
    "id:2000,phase:1,log,pass,t:lowercase,t:normalizePath,\
    setvar:session.suspicious=1,expirevar:session.suspicious=3600"
```

You should use the expirevar actions at the same time that you use setvar actions in order to keep the intended expiration time. If they're used on their own (perhaps in a SecAction directive), the expire time will be reset.

id

Assigns a unique ID to the rule or chain in which it appears.

```
SecRule &REQUEST_HEADERS:Host "@eq 0" \
    "phase:1,id:1000,block,severity:2,msg:'Request missing a host header'"
```

These are the reserved ID ranges:

- 1–99,999: Reserved for local (internal) use. Use as you see fit, but do not use this range for rules that are distributed to others.

- 100,000–199,999: Reserved for Oracle.

- 200,000–209,999: Reserved for the ModSecurity project.

- 210,000–299,999: Reserved for Comodo.

- 300,000–399,999: Reserved for Atomicorp (previously gotroot).

- 400,000–429,999: Unused (available for reservation).

- 430,000–439,999: Reserved for Flameeyes.

- 440,000–599,999: Unused (available for reservation).

- 600,000–699,999: Reserved for Akamai.

- 700,000–799,999: Reserved for Ivan Ristić.

- 800,000–899,999: Unused (available for reservation).

- 900,000–999,999: Reserved for the OWASP ModSecurity Core Rule Set Project.

- 1,000,000–1,009,999: Reserved for the Red Hat Security Team.

- 1,010,000–1,999,999: Unused (available for reservation).

- 2,000,000–2,999,999: Reserved for Trustwave.

- 3,000,000–3,999,999: Reserved for Akamai.

- 4,000,000–8,999,999: Unused (available for reservation).

- 9,000,000–9,999,999: Reserved for the OWASP ModSecurity Core Rule Set Project.

- 10,000,000 and above: Unused (available for reservation).

ModSecurity doesn't enforce these ranges, and the reservations are only informal. However, if you plan to distribute rules, it makes sense to take assigned rule ranges into consideration, or your users will run into conflicts if they combine multiple rulesets.

initcol

Initializes a named persistent collection, either by loading data from storage or by creating a new collection in memory.

The following example initiates IP address tracking, which is best done in phase 1:

```
SecAction "id:1000,phase:1,nolog,pass,initcol:ip=%{REMOTE_ADDR}"
```

Collections are loaded into memory on demand, when the `initcol` action is executed. A collection will be persisted only if a change was made to it in the course of transaction processing.

> **Note**
>
> Use initcol to initialize the IP, GLOBAL, and RESOURCE collections. The SESSION and USER collections are initialized via setsid and setuid, respectively.

log

Indicates that a successful match of the rule needs to be logged.

```
SecAction "id:1000,phase:1,initcol:ip=%{REMOTE_ADDR},log,pass"
```

This action will log a rule match to the web server's error log. Whenever the `log` action is used, an implicit `auditlog` will also be added to the rule. If, for whatever reason, you want to log only to the error log, use `log,noauditlog` in the same rule.

logdata

Logs a data fragment as part of the alert message to the audit and error logs.

```
SecRule ARGS:p "@rx <script>" \
    "id:2000,phase:2,log,pass,logdata:%{MATCHED_VAR}"
```

The `logdata` information appears in the error and audit log files in the `data` field. The information is properly escaped so that even binary data can be logged.

maturity

This is a utility field that stores rule maturity on a scale from 1 (very immature) to 9 (very mature). What these values really mean is for rule authors to determine and document.

```
# My experimental rule for XSS detection
SecRule ARGS "@rx [<>]" \
    "id:2000,phase:2,log,block,accuracy:1,maturity:1"
```

Available starting with 2.7.0.

msg

Assigns a custom message to the rule or chain in which it appears. The message will be logged along with every alert to the audit and error logs. Macro expansion is supported.

```
SecRule &REQUEST_HEADERS:Host "@eq 0" \
    "id:1000,phase:1,block,severity:2,msg:'Request missing a host header'"
```


multiMatch

If enabled, ModSecurity will perform multiple operator invocations for every target: before the first anti-evasion transformation is performed and after every transformation.

```
SecRule ARGS "@rx attack" \
    "id:2000,phase:2,log,deny,t:removeNulls,t:base64Decode,t:lowercase,multiMatch"
```

Normally, variables are inspected only once per rule, and only after all transformation functions have been completed.

noauditlog

Prevents a rule match from triggering a transaction write to the audit log.

```
SecRule REQUEST_HEADERS:User-Agent "@rx Test" \
    "id:1000,phase:1,allow,noauditlog"
```


nolog

Prevents a rule match from appearing in the error log. This action is typically used with utility and configuration rules, which have no need to log anything.

```
SecRule REQUEST_HEADERS:User-Agent "@rx Test" \
    "id:1000,phase:1,allow,nolog"
```

This action implies noauditlog, but you can override this by using nolog,auditlog together.

---

pass

Continues processing the current phase with the next rule in spite of a successful match.

```
SecRule REQUEST_HEADERS:User-Agent "@rx Test" \
    "id:1000,phase:1,log,pass"
```

When using pass with a SecRule with multiple targets, all variables are inspected and all nondisruptive actions triggered on every match. In the following example, the TX.score variable is incremented once for every request parameter matching goal:

```
# Set TX.test to zero
SecAction "id:2000,phase:2,nolog,pass,setvar:TX.score=0"

# Increment TX.score for every request parameter containing "goal"
SecRule ARGS "@rx goal" \
    "id:2001,phase:2,log,pass,setvar:TX.score=+1"
```

pause

Pauses transaction processing for the specified number of milliseconds.

```
# Slow down the response
SecRule REQUEST_HEADERS:User-Agent "@rx Test" \
    "id:1000,phase:1,log,pause:5000"
```

The pause action is a disruptive action with an implicit allow behavior, which means that you can't pause and block at the same time. Once pause is executed, the current phase will be terminated and all subsequent phases skipped. As with allow, the logging phase (5) is not affected.

Also starting with 2.7.0, the pause parameter supports macro expansion.

> ### Warning
>
> This feature can be of limited benefit for slowing down brute force authentication attacks, but use it with care. If you're under a denial of service attack, the pause feature may make matters worse, because it will cause an entire Apache worker (process or thread, depending on the deployment mode) to sit idle until the pause is completed.

phase

Places the rule or chain into one of five available processing phases (1–5). Starting with ModSecurity 2.7.0, some phases also have text aliases:

---

pass

- 1: Request headers

- 2: Request body (alias `request`)

- 3: Response headers

- 4: Response body (alias `response`)

- 5: Logging (alias `logging`)

With the aliases, phases are now easier to specify. In addition, only the more relevant and useful phases have aliases, which should hopefully make it easier to choose where to place rules.

The following example initializes persistent tracking of IP address behavior. Because this is essentially a service that needs to be available to all rules, we need to place the initialization as early as possible. For that reason, we use the first phase for the rule:

```
# Initialize IP address tracking in phase 1
SecAction "id:1000,phase:1,nolog,pass,initcol:IP=%{REMOTE_ADDR}"
```

Keep in mind that if you specify an incorrect phase, the variables used in the rule may not yet be available. This could lead to false negatives; your variables and operator may be correctly specified, but they may miss malicious data because the phase is wrong.

prepend

Prepends the text given as a parameter to the response body. Content injection must be enabled (using the SecContentInjection directive). No content type checks are made, which means that before using any of the content injection actions, you must check whether the content type of the response is adequate for injection.

```
SecRule RESPONSE_CONTENT_TYPE "@beginsWith text/html" \
    "id:8000,phase:3,nolog,pass,prepend:'Header<br>'"
```

> **Note**
>
> Although macro expansion is allowed in the injected content, you're strongly cautioned against inserting user-defined data fields into output. Doing so would create a cross-site scripting vulnerability.

proxy

Intercepts the current transaction by forwarding the request to another web server using the proxy backend. The forwarding is carried out transparently to the HTTP client (i.e., there's no external redirection taking place).

```
SecRule REQUEST_HEADERS:User-Agent "@rx Test" \
    "phase:1,log,proxy:http://www.example.com"
```

For this disruptive action to work, mod_proxy also must be installed. This action is useful if you want to proxy matching requests onto a honeypot web server, especially in combination with an IP address or session tracking.

redirect

Intercepts a transaction by issuing an external (client-visible) redirection to the given location as a disruptive action—for example:

```
SecRule REQUEST_HEADERS:User-Agent "@rx Test" \
    "id:1000,phase:1,log,redirect:http://www.example.com/failed.html"
```

By default, HTTP status code 302 will be used for the redirection. If the status action is present on the same rule and its value can be used for a redirection (i.e., it's one of the following: 301, 302, 303, or 307), that value will be used for the redirection status code.

rev

Specifies rule revision. This action is useful to provide an indication that a rule has been updated. It's best used in combination with the id action.

```
SecRule REQUEST_METHOD "!@rx ^(GET|HEAD|POST|PUT)$" \
    "id:1000,rev:2,phase:1,log,deny,severity:2,msg:'Restricted HTTP method'"
```

sanitiseArg

Prevents sensitive request parameter data from being logged to the audit log. Each byte of the named parameter(s) is replaced with an asterisk.

```
# Never log passwords
SecAction "id:2000,nolog,pass,phase:2,sanitiseArg:password,\
    sanitiseArg:newPassword,sanitiseArg:oldPassword"
```

> ### Warning
>
> The sanitise family of actions affect data only as it's logged to the audit log. It will still be logged to the Apache error log, the access log could contain sensitive data from the request URI, and even high-level debug logs may contain sensitive data.

sanitiseMatched

Prevents the matched variable (request argument, request header, or response header) from being logged to the audit log. Each byte of the named parameter(s) is replaced with an asterisk. The warning noted for sanitiseArg applies here as well.

```
# Do not log any parameter that contains "password" in name
SecRule ARGS_NAMES "@rx password" \
    "id:2000,phase:2,nolog,pass,sanitizeMatched"
```

sanitiseMatchedBytes

In combination with an operator based on regular expressions (e.g., @rx, @verifyCPF, @verifyCC, @verifySSN), sanitizeMatchedBytes performs partial sanitization, hiding just the variable part that matched. Specifying capture in the same rule is required for the correct operation.

```
SecRule ARGS "@rx test" \
    "id:2000,phase:2,nolog,pass,sanitizeMatchedBytes,capture
```

With an optional parameter, sanitizeMatchedBytes can leave some of the matched bytes intact. This behavior could be useful if, for example, you wanted to preserve some of the credit card digits in order to be able to identify the credit card.

```
SecRule ARGS "@verifyCC \d{13,16}" \
    "id:2000,phase:2,nolog,pass,sanitizeMatchedBytes:4/4,capture
```

The warning noted for sanitiseArg applies here as well.

sanitiseRequestHeader

Prevents a named request header from being logged to the audit log. Each byte of the named request header is replaced with an asterisk.

```
SecAction "phase:1,nolog,pass,sanitiseRequestHeader:Authorization"
```

sanitiseResponseHeader

Prevents a named response header from being logged to the audit log. Each byte of the named response header is replaced with an asterisk.

```
SecAction "phase:3,nolog,pass,sanitiseResponseHeader:Set-Cookie"
```

sanitizeArg

Alias for sanitiseArg.

sanitizeMatched

Alias for sanitiseMatched.

sanitizeMatchedBytes

Alias for sanitiseMatchedBytes.

sanitizeRequestHeader

Alias for sanitiseRequestHeader.

sanitizeResponseHeader

Alias for sanitiseResponseHeader.

severity

Assigns a severity to the rule in which it's used.

Table 19.1. Severity values

Numerical value	Text value
0	EMERGENCY
1	ALERT
2	CRITICAL
3	ERROR
4	WARNING
5	NOTICE
6	INFO
7	DEBUG

```
SecRule REQUEST_METHOD "@streq PUT" \
    "id:1000,phase:1,deny,severity:CRITICAL,msg:'Restricted HTTP function'"
```

Severity values in ModSecurity follow those of syslog, as shown in Table 19.1.

> **Warning**
>
> Although it's possible to specify severity levels using either the numerical values or the text values, the use of the numerical values is deprecated and may be removed in a subsequent update.

setuid

This special-purpose action initializes the USER collection, using the username provided as a parameter.

```
SecAction "id:1000,phase:1,nolog,pass,setuid:%{REMOTE_USER}"
```

After initialization takes place, the USERID variable will be available for use in subsequent rules. This action understands application namespaces (configured using SecWebAppId) and will use one if it's configured.

setsid

This special-purpose action initializes the SESSION collection, using the session token provided as a parameter.

```
# Initialize session variables using the session cookie value
SecRule REQUEST_COOKIES:PHPSESSID "!@rx ^$" \
    "id:2000,phase:2,nolog,pass,\
    setsid:%{REQUEST_COOKIES.PHPSESSID}"
```

After the initialization takes place, the SESSIONID variable will be available for use in subsequent rules. This action understands application namespaces (configured using SecWebAppId) and will use one if it's configured.

setenv

Creates, removes, or updates environment variables, which can be used to communicate with other Apache modules and with the web application (when running in embedded mode).

To create a new variable and set its value to 1 (usually used for setting flags), use:

```
setenv:name
```

To create a variable and choose its value, use the following:

```
setenv:name=value
```

To remove a variable, use the following:

```
setenv:!name
```

setvar

Creates, removes, or updates custom ModSecurity variables, which reside in the TX collection. Variable names are case-insensitive.

To create a variable and set its value to 1 (usually used for setting flags), use the following:

```
setvar:TX.score
```

To create a variable and initialize it at the same time, use the following:

```
setvar:TX.score=10
```

To remove a variable, prefix the name with an exclamation point, as follows:

```
setvar:!TX.score
```

To increase or decrease variable value, use + and - characters in front of a numerical value, as follows:

```
setvar:TX.score=+5
```

skip

Skips one or more rules (or chains) on a successful match—for example:

```
# Require Accept header, but not when accessed from localhost
SecRule REMOTE_ADDR "@ipMatch 127.0.0.1" \
    "id:1000,phase:1,nolog,skip:1"
# This rule will be skipped over when REMOTE_ADDR is 127.0.0.1
SecRule &REQUEST_HEADERS:Accept "@eq 0" \
    "id:1001,phase:1,deny,msg:'Request missing an Accept header'"
```

The skip action works only with rules that belong to the same processing phase and not necessarily in the order in which the rules appear in the configuration file. If you place a phase 2 rule after a phase 1 rule that uses skip, it won't skip over the phase 2 rule; it will skip over the next phase 1 rule that follows it in the phase. For this reason, it's generally better to use the skipAfter action, which works across phases.

skipAfter

Skips one or more rules (or chains), resuming execution immediately after the rule with the provided ID. Alternatively, use skipAfter in combination with a marker created by

SecMarker. In the following example, a match in the first rule will cause the second rule to be skipped:

```
# Require Accept header, but not from access from the localhost
SecRule REMOTE_ADDR "@ipMatch 127.0.0.1" \
    "id:1000,phase:1,nolog,skipAfter:IGNORE_LOCALHOST"
# This rule will be skipped over when REMOTE_ADDR is 127.0.0.1
SecRule &REQUEST_HEADERS:Accept "@eq 0" \
    "id:1001,phase:1,deny,msg:'Request missing an Accept header'"
SecMarker IGNORE_LOCALHOST
```

status

Specifies the response status code to use with the deny and redirect actions.

```
# Deny with status 403 by default
SecDefaultAction "phase:1,log,deny,status:403"
```

t

This action specifies the desired list of transformation functions that transform the value of each variable appearing in the rule before matching.

```
SecRule ARGS "@rx (asfunction|javascript|vbscript|data|mocha|livescript):" \
    "id:2000,phase:2,t:none,t:htmlEntityDecode,t:lowercase,\
    t:removeNulls,t:removeWhitespace"
```

tag

Assigns a tag (category) to a rule or a chain.

```
SecRule REQUEST_FILENAME "@rx \b(?:n(?:map|et|c)|w(?:guest|sh)|cmd(?:32)?|telnet|rc↵
md|ftp)\.exe\b" \
    "id:1000,phase:1,t:lowercase,deny,msg:'System command access',\
    tag:'WEB_ATTACK/FILE_INJECTION',tag:'OWASP/A2'"
```

The tag information appears along with other rule metadata. The purpose of the tagging mechanism is to allow easy automated categorization of events. Multiple tags are allowed. Although tags are not required to follow a particular format, it's customary to use forward slashes to form hierarchies (as shown in the example).

ver

This is a utility field that stores the version number of the ruleset to which the rule belongs. It's an alternative to the `SecComponentSignature` directive. To uniquely identify individual rules, use the `id` and `rev` actions instead.

```
SecRule ARGS "@rx PATTERN" \
    "id:2000,phase:2,log,block,rev:1,ver:'Acme Rules/0.1'"
```

Available starting with 2.7.0.

xmlns

Configures an XML namespace, which will be used in the execution of XPath expressions.

```
SecRule XML:/soap:Envelope/soap:Body/q1:getInput/id() "@rx 123" \
    "id:2000,phase:2,deny,xmlns:xsd=http://www.w3.org/2001/XMLSchema"
```

20 Data Formats

This chapter describes the formats of the ModSecurity alert messages, transaction logs, and communication protocols, knowledge of which not only is helpful for a better understanding of how ModSecurity works but also allows for an easier integration with third-party tools and products.

Alerts

ModSecurity alerts are either *warnings* (nonfatal problems) or *errors* (fatal problems, which normally lead to the interception of the transaction in which they occur). The alerts are written to the Apache error log and incorporated into the ModSecurity audit logs. Here's an example of one ModSecurity alert:

```
Message: Access denied with code 403 (phase 2).  ↵
Matched phrase "arachni/" at REQUEST_HEADERS:User-Agent.  ↵
[file "/usr/share/modsecurity-crs/rules/REQUEST-13-SCANNER-DETECTION.conf"]  ↵
[line "54"] [id "913100"] [rev "2"] [msg "Request Indicates a Security  ↵
Scanner Scanned the Site"] [data "Matched Data: arachni/ found within  ↵
REQUEST_HEADERS:User-Agent: arachni/v1.4"] [severity "CRITICAL"] [ver  ↵
"OWASP_CRS/3.0.0"] [maturity "9"] [accuracy "9"] [tag "application-multi"]  ↵
[tag "language-multi"] [tag "platform-multi"] [tag "attack-reputation"]  ↵
[tag "reputation-scanner"] [tag "OWASP_CRS/AUTOMATION/SECURITY_SCANNER"]  ↵
[tag "WASCTC/WASC-21"] [tag "OWASP_TOP_10/A7"] [tag "PCI/6.5.10"]
```

Each alert entry begins with the engine message, which describes what ModSecurity did and why—for example:

```
Message: Access denied with code 403 (phase 2).  ↵
Matched phrase "arachni/" at REQUEST_HEADERS:User-Agent.
```

Alert Action Description

The engine message is designed to provide some indication of what happened and why, even when the rules themselves don't explain it. The first part of the message tells whether

ModSecurity acted to prevent a request or response. As you will see later, there are several variations of the message, depending on what exactly happened.

> **Note**
>
> Many messages presented in this section and throughout this chapter are templates that contain placeholders (e.g., *%0*, *%1*, and so on) to indicate where dynamic information should be inserted. At runtime, when this information is available, the rule engine will construct the final messages, removing all placeholders from the templates.

The first part of the engine message uses the following format:

1. If the alert is only a warning and no interception took place, the first sentence will simply say *Warning*.

2. If the transaction was intercepted, the first sentence will begin with *Access denied*. What follows is the list of possible messages related to transaction interception:

   - *Access denied with code %0*: A response with status code %0 was sent.

   - *Access denied with connection close*: The connection was abruptly closed.

   - *Access denied with redirection to %0 using status %1*: A redirection to URI %0 was issued using status %1.

3. Different wording will be used when an `allow` action is executed. There are three variations in this case:

   - *Access allowed*: The rule engine stopped processing rules (transaction was unaffected).

   - *Access to phase allowed*: The rule engine stopped processing rules in the current phase only. Subsequent phases will be processed normally. The transaction wasn't affected by this rule, but it may be affected by any of the rules in the subsequent phase.

   - *Access to request allowed*: The rule engine stopped processing rules in the current phase. Phases prior to request execution in the backend (phases 1 and 2) won't be processed. The response phases (phases 3 and 4) and the logging phase (phase 5) will be processed as usual. The transaction was not affected by this rule.

Alert Justification Description

The second part of the engine message explains *why* the alert was generated. Because it's automatically generated from the rules, the explanation will be very technical in nature, talking about operators and their parameters and giving you insight into what the rule looked like. However, this message can't give you insight into the reasoning behind the rule. A well-written rule will always specify a human-readable message (using the `msg` action) to provide further information.

The format of the second part of the engine message depends on whether it was generated by the operator (which happens on a match) or by the rule processor (which happens when there isn't a match, but negation was used):

- `@beginsWith`: *String match %0 at %1.*

- `@contains`: *String match %0 at %1.*

- `@containsWord`: *String match %0 at %1.*

- `@detectSQLi`: *Detected SQLi using libinjection with fingerprint %1.*

- `@detectXSS`: *Detected XSS using libinjection.*

- `@endsWith`: *String match %0 at %1.*

- `@eq`: *Operator EQ matched %0 at %1.*

- `@fuzzyHash`: *Fuzzy hash of %0 matched with %1 (from: %2) Score: %3.*

- `@ge`: *Operator GE matched %0 at %1.*

- `@geoLookup`: *Geo lookup for %0 succeeded at %1.*

- `@gt`: *Operator GT matched %0 at %1.*

- `@inspectFile`: *File %0 rejected by the approver script %1: %2.*

- `@ipMatch`: *IPmatch: %0 matched at %1.*

- `@ipMatchFromFile`: *IPmatchFromFile: %0 matched at %1.*

- `@le`: *Operator LE matched %0 at %1.*

- `@lt`: *Operator LT matched %0 at %1.*

- `@noMatch`: *No match.*

- `@pm`: *Matched phrase %0 at %1.*

- `@pmFromFile`: *Matched phrase %0 at %1.*

- `@rbl`: *RBL lookup of %0 succeeded at %1.*

- `@rx`: *Pattern match %0 at %1.*

- `@streq`: *String match %0 at %1.*

- `@strmatch`: *Pattern match %0 at %1.*

- `@unconditionalMatch`: *Unconditional match in SecAction.*

- `@validateByteRange`: *Found %0 byte(s) in %1 outside range: %2.*

- `@validateDTD`: *XML: DTD validation failed.*

- @validateSchema: *XML: Schema validation failed.*
- @validateUrlEncoding
  - *Invalid URL Encoding: Non-hexadecimal digits used at %0.*
  - *Invalid URL Encoding: Not enough characters at the end of input at %0.*
- @validateUtf8Encoding
  - *Invalid UTF-8 encoding: not enough bytes in character at %0.*
  - *Invalid UTF-8 encoding: invalid byte value in character at %0.*
  - *Invalid UTF-8 encoding: overlong character detected at %0.*
  - *Invalid UTF-8 encoding: use of restricted character at %0.*
  - *Invalid UTF-8 encoding: decoding error at %0.*
- @verifyCC: *CC# match %0 at %1.*
- @verifyCPF: *CPF# match %0 at %1. [offset %2]*
- @verifySSN: *SSN# match %0 at %1. [offset %2]*
- @within: *String match within %0 at %1.*

Messages not related to operators are as follows:

- When the SecAction directive is processed: *Unconditional match in SecAction.*
- When SecRule doesn't match, but negation is used: *Match of %0 against %1 required.*

> **Note**
>
> The parameters for the @rx and @pm operators (regular expression and text pattern matching, respectively) will be truncated to 252 bytes if they're longer than this limit. In such a case, the parameter in the alert message will be terminated with three dots. Other parameters will be cut at about 1,000 bytes.

Metadata

The metadata fields are always placed at the end of the alert entry. Each metadata field is a text fragment that consists of an open bracket followed by the metadata field name, followed by the value in double quotes and the closing bracket. Here is the text fragment that makes up the id metadata field:

```
[id "960034"]
```

The following metadata fields are currently used (in order of appearance in the alert message):

1. `offset`: The byte offset where a match occurred within the target data; this isn't always available.

2. `file`: Absolute path to the file in which the rule was defined.

3. `line`: The line number of the rule definition within the file. If a rule stretches multiple lines, the number of the last line is displayed. If a rule is a chained rule, the number of the last line of the first rule in the chain is displayed.

4. `id`: Unique rule ID, as specified by the `id` action.

5. `rev`: Rule revision, as specified by the `rev` action.

6. `msg`: Human-readable message, as specified by the `msg` action.

7. `data`: Transaction data fragment, as specified by the `logdata` action.

8. `severity`: Event severity as text, as specified by the `severity` action. The possible values (with their corresponding numerical values in brackets) are EMERGENCY (0), ALERT (1), CRITICAL (2), ERROR (3), WARNING (4), NOTICE (5), INFO (6), and DEBUG (7).

9. `maturity`: Rule maturity, as specified by the `maturity` action.

10. `accuracy`: Rule accuracy, as specified by the `accuracy` action.

11. `tag`: Rule tag, as specified by the `tag` action. Multiple occurrences of this field are possible.

12. `hostname`: The server name, as specified by the Apache `ServerName` directive.

13. `unique_id`: Unique transaction ID, generated automatically.

14. `uri`: Request URI.

Escaping

ModSecurity alerts will always contain text fragments that were taken from the configuration or the transaction. Such text fragments are escaped before they are used in messages in order to sanitize potentially dangerous characters. They're also sometimes enclosed with double quotes. The escaping algorithm is as follows:

1. Characters `0x08` (BACKSPACE), `0x0a` (NEWLINE), `0x10` (CARRIAGE RETURN), `0x09` (HORIZONTAL TAB), and `0x0b` (VERTICAL TAB) will be represented as \b, \n, \r, \t, and \v, respectively.

2. Bytes from the ranges `0x00-0x1f` and `0x7f-0xff` (inclusive) will be represented as \xHH, where HH is the hexadecimal value of the byte.

3. Backslash characters (\) will be represented as \\.

4. Each double-quote character will be represented as \".

Alerts in the Apache Error Log

Every ModSecurity alert conforms to the following format when it appears in the Apache error log:

```
[Fri Jun 24 05:56:52.940618 2016] [-:error] [pid 18627:tid 140172673226496] ↵
[client 192.168.1.101:34311] [client 192.168.1.101] ModSecurity: ALERT_MESSAGE
```

This example shows a ModSecurity alert as it would appear in the Apache error log. As you can see, Apache prepends the alert with some data of its own. In this example, the default Apache error log format is used, but the format can be changed using Apache's ErrorLogFormat directive.

For all practical purposes, the ModSecurity part of the log entry begins with the ModSecurity: prefix. However, if you examine the log entry carefully, you'll see that the client IP address appears twice. The second occurrence of the client IP address is added to the error log by ModSecurity, a leftover element from back when Apache didn't include this information itself. This information is now redundant and may be removed in future versions of ModSecurity.

The actual message (ALERT_MESSAGE in the example) is in the same format as previously described.

> **Note**
>
> Apache further escapes ModSecurity alert messages before writing them to the error log. This means that all backslash characters will be doubled in the error log. In practice, because ModSecurity already represents a single backslash within an untrusted text fragment as two backslashes, the end result in the Apache error log will be *four* backslashes. Thus, if you need to interpret a ModSecurity message from the error log, you should decode the message part after the ModSecurity: prefix first. This step will peel back the first encoding layer.

Alerts in Audit Logs

In addition to being logged to the Apache error log, alerts are recorded to the H section of the ModSecurity audit log. Alerts will appear with each on a separate line and in the order they were generated by ModSecurity. Each line will be in the following format:

```
Message: ALERT_MESSAGE
```

An example of an H section that contains an alert message is given in the next section.

Audit Log

The ModSecurity audit log records information about one transaction in what is essentially a single file. This audit log record comes in two formats: the original native format and the newer JSON format; the latter was added in 2.9.1. This section will describe the native format first and then the JSON format.

The following is an example of the native format:

```
--94bfba28-A--
[29/Jun/2016:05:22:17 +0200] V3M@6X8AAQEAACuQ5dcAAAAO 192.168.1.101 37298 ↵
192.168.1.108 443
--94bfba28-B--
GET / HTTP/1.1
User-Agent: Arachni/v1.4
Accept: text/html,application/xhtml+xml,application/xml;q=0.9,*/*;q=0.8
Accept-Encoding: gzip
Accept-Language: en-GB,*
Host: localhost

--94bfba28-F--
HTTP/1.1 200 OK
Last-Modified: Mon, 06 Jun 2016 03:39:07 GMT
ETag: "2d-53493d08b74e4"
Accept-Ranges: bytes
Content-Length: 45
Content-Type: text/html

--94bfba28-E--
<html><body><h1>It works!</h1></body></html>

--94bfba28-H--
Message: Warning. Matched phrase "arachni/" at REQUEST_HEADERS:User-Agent. ↵
[file "/usr/share/modsecurity-crs/rules/REQUEST-13-SCANNER-DETECTION.conf"] ↵
[line "54"] [id "913100"] [rev "2"] [msg "Request Indicates a Security ↵
Scanner Scanned the Site"] [data "Matched Data: arachni/ found within ↵
REQUEST_HEADERS:User-Agent: arachni/v1.4"] [severity "CRITICAL"] [ver ↵
"OWASP_CRS/3.0.0"] [maturity "9"] [accuracy "9"] [tag "application-multi"] ↵
[tag "language-multi"] [tag "platform-multi"] [tag "attack-reputation"] ↵
[tag "reputation-scanner"] [tag "OWASP_CRS/AUTOMATION/SECURITY_SCANNER"] ↵
[tag "WASCTC/WASC-21"] [tag "OWASP_TOP_10/A7"] [tag "PCI/6.5.10"]
Stopwatch: 1467170537397705 64580 (- - -)
Stopwatch2: 1467170537397705 64580; combined=63402, p1=12879, p2=30615, ↵
p3=3056, p4=6820, p5=9134, sr=569, sw=898, l=0, gc=0
Response-Body-Transformed: Dechunked
Producer: ModSecurity for Apache/2.9.1 (http://www.modsecurity.org/).
Server: Apache
```

```
Engine-Mode: "ENABLED"

--94bfba28-Z--
```

The file consists of multiple sections, each in a different format. Separators are used to define sections:

```
--94bfba28-A--
```

A separator always begins on a newline and conforms to the following format:

1. Two hyphens

2. A unique boundary, which consists of hexadecimal characters

3. A hyphen

4. A section identifier, which is a single uppercase letter

5. Two trailing hyphens

Parts in Native Format

This subsection documents the audit log parts available in ModSecurity:

- A: Audit log header
- B: Request headers
- C: Request body
- D: Original response headers (not implemented)
- E: Original response body
- F: Response headers
- G: Actual response body (not implemented)
- H: Audit log trailer
- I: Reduced multipart request body
- J: Multipart files information
- K: Matched rules information
- Z: Audit log footer

Audit Log Header (A)

ModSecurity audit log entries in the native format always begin with the header part—for example:

```
--7aa36b22-A--
[29/Jun/2016:05:50:43 +0200] V3NFk38AAQEAAFpxaBEAAAAG 192.168.1.101 37368 ↵
192.168.1.108 443
```

The header contains only one line, with the following information on it:

1. Timestamp

2. Unique transaction ID

3. Source IP address (IPv4 or IPv6)

4. Source port

5. Destination IP address (IPv4 or IPv6)

6. Destination port

Request Headers (B)

The request headers part contains the request line and the request headers, but the data recorded need not be identical to the content sent by the client, because Apache doesn't expose raw request line and request headers to its modules. For that reason, ModSecurity sees only processed data provided to it by Apache. Although the end result may be identical to the raw request, differences are possible in some areas:

1. If any of the fields are NUL-terminated, Apache will see only the content prior to the NUL.

2. Headers that span multiple lines (a feature known as *header folding*) will be collapsed into a single line.

3. Multiple headers with the same name will be combined into a single header (as allowed by the HTTP RFC).

Request Body (C)

This part contains the request body of the transaction, after dechunking and decompression (if applicable).

Original Response Headers (D)

This part contains the status line and the request headers that would have been delivered to the client had ModSecurity not intervened. Thus, this part makes sense only for transactions in which ModSecurity altered the data flow. By differentiating between the original and the final response headers, we can record not only what was internally ready for sending but also what was actually sent.

Original Response Body (E)

This part contains the transaction response body (before compression and chunking, when used) that either was sent or would have been sent had ModSecurity not intervened. You can find out whether interception took place by looking at the Action header of part H. If that header is present and the interception took place in phase 3 or 4, then the E part will contain the intended response body. Otherwise, it will contain the actual response body.

> **Note**
>
> Once the G (actual response body) part is implemented, part E will be present only in audit logs that contain a transaction that was intercepted, and there will be no need for further analysis.

Response Headers (F)

This part contains the actual response headers sent to the client. Because ModSecurity doesn't have access to the raw connection data, it constructs part F out of the internal Apache data structures that hold the response headers.

Some headers (the Date and Server response headers) are generated just before they're sent, and ModSecurity isn't able to record those. You should note that if ModSecurity is working as part of a reverse proxy, the backend web server will have generated these two headers; in that case, they'll be recorded.

Response Body (G)

When implemented, this part will contain the actual response body before compression and chunking.

> **Note**
>
> This part is reserved for future use. It's not currently implemented.

Audit Log Trailer (H)

Part H contains additional transaction metadata obtained from the web server or from ModSecurity itself. This part contains a number of trailer headers, which are similar to HTTP headers (without support for header folding). The following list shows the headers in alphabetical order:

1. Action
2. Apache-Error
3. Engine-Mode
4. Message
5. Producer
6. Response-Body-Transformed
7. Rules-Performance-Info
8. Sanitised-Args
9. Sanitised-Request-Headers
10. Sanitised-Response-Headers
11. Server
12. Stopwatch
13. Stopwatch2
14. WebApp-Info

Action

The Action header is present only for the transactions that were intercepted:

```
Action: Intercepted (phase 2)
```

The phase information documents the phase in which the decision to intercept took place.

Apache-Error

The Apache-Error header contains Apache error log messages observed by ModSecurity, excluding those sent by ModSecurity itself—for example:

```
Apache-Error: [file "mod_proxy_http.c"] [line 1264] [level 7] AH01103: read timeout
```

Engine-Mode

Available as of 2.7.0, the Engine-Mode header documents the running mode of the rule engine at the time of the audit log creation. There are three possibilities:

Header not present
    When the rule engine is disabled, the Engine-Mode header will not be present in the audit log.

Header present, with value "DETECTION_ONLY"
> The engine is in detection-only mode.

Header present, with value "ENABLED"
> The engine is fully enabled.

Message

Zero or more Message headers can be present in any trailer, and each such header will represent a single ModSecurity warning or error, displayed in the order they were raised.

The following example was broken across multiple lines to make it fit the page:

```
Message: Access denied with code 403 (phase 2). ↵
Matched phrase "arachni/" at REQUEST_HEADERS:User-Agent. ↵
[file "/usr/share/modsecurity-crs/rules/REQUEST-13-SCANNER-DETECTION.conf"] ↵
[line "54"] [id "913100"] [rev "2"] [msg "Request Indicates a Security ↵
Scanner Scanned the Site"] [data "Matched Data: arachni/ found within ↵
REQUEST_HEADERS:User-Agent: arachni/v1.4"] [severity "CRITICAL"] [ver ↵
"OWASP_CRS/3.0.0"] [maturity "9"] [accuracy "9"] [tag "application-multi"] ↵
[tag "language-multi"] [tag "platform-multi"] [tag "attack-reputation"] ↵
[tag "reputation-scanner"] [tag "OWASP_CRS/AUTOMATION/SECURITY_SCANNER"] ↵
[tag "WASCTC/WASC-21"] [tag "OWASP_TOP_10/A7"] [tag "PCI/6.5.10"]
```

Producer

The Producer header identifies the product that generated the audit log—for example:

```
Producer: ModSecurity for Apache/2.9.1 (http://www.modsecurity.org/).
```

ModSecurity allows rulesets to add their own signatures to the Producer information (via the SecComponentSignature directive). The following is an example of the Producer header with the signature of one component (all one line):

```
Producer: ModSecurity for Apache/2.9.1 (http://www.modsecurity.org/); ↵
MyComponent/1.0.0 (Beta).
```

Response-Body-Transformed

This header will appear in every audit log that contains a response body:

```
Response-Body-Transformed: Dechunked
```

The contents of the header are constant at present, so the header is useful only as a reminder that the recorded response body is not identical to the one sent to the client. The actual content is the same, except that Apache may further compress the body and deliver it in chunks.

Rules-Performance-Info

Available as of 2.7.0, the `Rules-Performance-Info` header will contain the list of slow rules evaluated during the transaction—for example:

```
Rules-Performance-Info: "2000=65", "2001=114".
```

The first number in each pair is the rule ID, and the second number is the rule duration, in microseconds. Use the `SecRulePerfTime` directive to configure the threshold at which a rule will be considered slow.

Sanitised-Args

The `Sanitised-Args` header contains a list of arguments that were sanitized (each byte of their content replaced with an asterisk) before logging—for example:

```
Sanitised-Args: "old_password", "new_password", "new_password_repeat".
```

Sanitised-Request-Headers

The `Sanitised-Request-Headers` header contains a list of request headers that were sanitized before logging—for example:

```
Sanitised-Request-Headers: "Authentication".
```

Sanitised-Response-Headers

The `Sanitised-Response-Headers` header contains a list of response headers that were sanitized before logging—for example:

```
Sanitised-Response-Headers: "My-Custom-Header".
```

Server

The `Server` header identifies the web server—for example:

```
Server: Apache/2.4.20 (Unix) OpenSSL/1.0.1f
```

This information may sometimes be present in any of the parts that contain response headers, but there are two cases in which it isn't:

1. When none of the response headers were recorded

2. When the information in the response headers isn't accurate because server signature masking was used

Stopwatch

The Stopwatch header provides certain diagnostic information that allows you to determine the performance of the web server and of ModSecurity itself. It will typically look like this:

```
Stopwatch: 1467172243542720 29419 (- - -)
```

The first value is the transaction timestamp in microseconds since January 1, 1970. The second is the duration of the transaction, also in microseconds. The three hyphens in parentheses are artifacts from a former version and left in the header for compatibility reasons. This header has been superseded by Stopwatch2.

Stopwatch2

The Stopwatch2 header provides improved performance statistics—for example:

```
Stopwatch2: 1467172243542720 29419; combined=28534, p1=13447, p2=3992, p3=0, ↵
p4=0, p5=10152, sr=518, sw=943, l=0, gc=0
```

The first value is the transaction timestamp in microseconds since January 1, 1970; the second is the transaction duration, also in microseconds.

> **Note**
>
> You should expect that the transaction duration reported by ModSecurity is different from the one reported by Apache itself. This is because ModSecurity concerns itself only with its own operation, whereas Apache takes a larger view and includes other activities.

The performance metrics follow after the semicolon:

- combined: Combined processing time
- p1–p5: Time spent in each of the rule phases
- sr and sw: Time spent reading from and writing to persistent storage, respectively
- l: Time spent on audit logging
- gc: Time spent on garbage collection

All the values are given in microseconds.

WebApp-Info

The WebApp-Info header contains information about the application to which the recorded transaction belongs. This information will appear only if it's known, which will happen if SecWebAppId was set or setsid or setuid executed in the transaction.

The header uses the following format:

```
WebApp-Info: "WEBAPPID" "SESSIONID" "USERID"
```

Each unknown value is replaced with a hyphen.

Reduced Multipart Request Body (I)

Transactions that address file uploads tend to be large, yet the file contents aren't always relevant from a security point of view. The I part was designed to avoid recording raw multipart/form-data request bodies, replacing them with a simulated application/x-www-form-urlencoded body that contains the same key-value parameters.

The reduced multipart request body won't contain any file information. The J part is designed to carry the file information.

Multipart Files Information (J)

The purpose of part J is to record information about the files contained in a multipart/form-data request body. This is handy in cases in which the original request body wasn't recorded or when only a reduced version was recorded (e.g., when part I was used instead of part C).

This part uses the comma-separated values (CSV) format, with each line containing information about one file. The fields are as follows: field number, file size, filename, and file content type. The last line contains the overall size of uploaded files.

The following example represents a multipart/form-data request with two files, one that was present and another that wasn't (for which the size is zero):

```
2,34566,"image.png","image/png"
3,0,"","<Unknown ContentType>"
Total,34566
```

Matched Rules (K)

Matched rules part K contains a record of all ModSecurity rules that matched during transaction processing. All rules that make up a chain are logged, but those rules in the chain that didn't match or didn't run at all are commented-out with a single # character at the beginning of the rule.

Audit Log Footer (Z)

Part Z is a special part that has only a boundary and no content. Its only purpose is to signal the end of an audit log.

Parts in JSON Format

The JSON audit log format was introduced with ModSecurity 2.9.1. Use the SecAuditLogFormat directive to switch from the native format to JSON. The parts of the native audit log format are mapped to a JSON Schema with the following blocks:

- Transaction
- Request
- Uploads (optional)
- Response
- Matched rules
- Audit data

The individual blocks correspond with individual audit log parts in the native format, as described later. The blocks are activated via the SecAuditLogParts directive.

The JSON format audit log lists the blocks in alphabetical order. It comes in a machine-readable form without carriage returns. To read it with human eyes, you'll need to print it.

Transaction (transaction)

The transaction part corresponds with the audit log part A in native format.

```
"transaction": {
  "local_address": "192.168.1.108",
  "local_port": 443,
  "remote_address": "192.168.1.101",
  "remote_port": 37474,
  "time": "29/Jun/2016:06:20:48 +0200",
  "transaction_id": "V3NMoH8AAQEAAFD4AHYAAAAA"
}
```

Request (request)

The request part corresponds with the native audit log part B together with part C.

```
"request": {
  "headers": {
    "Accept": "text/html",
    "Accept-Encoding": "gzip",
    "Accept-Language": "en-GB,*",
    "Host": "localhost",
    "User-Agent": "Arachni/v1.4"
  },
```

```
    "request_line": "GET / HTTP/1.1"
},
```

Uploads (uploads)

The uploads part corresponds with part J in the native audit log format. It's optional and only available if the transaction includes file uploads.

```
"uploads": {
  "info": [
    "file_size",
    8744,
    "file_name",
    "logo.png",
    "content_type",
    "image/png"
  ],
  "total": 8744
},
```

Response (response)

The response part corresponds with the native audit log part F together with part E.

```
"request": {
  "headers": {
    "Accept": "text/html",
    "Accept-Encoding": "gzip",
    "Accept-Language": "en-GB,*",
    "Host": "localhost",
    "User-Agent": "Arachni/v1.4"
  },
  "request_line": "GET / HTTP/1.1"
},
```

Matched Rules (matched_rules)

The matched rules part corresponds with part K in the native audit log format.

```
"matched_rules": [
  {
    "chain": false,
    "rules": [
      {
        "actionset": {
          "accuracy": 9,
```

```
        "id": "913100",
        "is_chained": false,
        "logdata": "Matched Data: arachni/ found within REMOTE_ADDR: 127.0.0.1",
        "maturity": 9,
        "msg": "Request Indicates a Security Scanner Scanned the Site",
        "phase": 2,
        "rev": "2",
        "severity": 2,
        "tags": [
          "application-multi",
          "language-multi",
          "platform-multi",
          "attack-reputation",
          "reputation-scanner",
          "OWASP_CRS/AUTOMATION/SECURITY_SCANNER",
          "WASCTC/WASC-21",
          "OWASP_TOP_10/A7",
          "PCI/6.5.10"
        ],
        "version": "OWASP_CRS/3.0.0"
      },
      "config": {
        "filename": "/usr/share/modsecurity-crs/rules/REQUEST-13-SCANNER-DETECTIO⏎
N.conf",
        "line_num": 54
      },
      "is_matched": true,
      "operator": {
        "negated": false,
        "operator": "pmFromFile",
        "operator_param": "scanners-user-agents.data",
        "target": "REQUEST_HEADERS:User-Agent"
      },
      "unparsed": "SecRule \"REQUEST_HEADERS:User-Agent\" \"@pmFromFile ⏎
scanners-user-agents.data\" \"phase:request,log,msg:'Request Indicates a Security ⏎
Scanner Scanned the Site',severity:CRITICAL,id:913100,rev:2,block,t:none,t:lowercas⏎
e,ver:OWASP_CRS/3.0.0,maturity:9,accuracy:9,capture,logdata:'Matched Data: %{TX.0} ⏎
found within %{MATCHED_VAR_NAME}: %{MATCHED_VAR}',tag:application-multi,tag:languag⏎
e-multi,tag:platform-multi,tag:attack-reputation,tag:reputation-scanner,tag:OWASP⏎
_CRS/AUTOMATION/SECURITY_SCANNER,tag:WASCTC/WASC-21,tag:OWASP_TOP_10/A7,tag:PCI⏎
/6.5.10,setvar:tx.msg=%{rule.msg},setvar:tx.anomaly_score=+%{tx.critical_anomaly⏎
_score},setvar:tx.%{rule.id}-OWASP_CRS/AUTOMATION/SECURITY_SCANNER-%{matched_var⏎
_name}=%{matched_var},setvar:ip.block=1,expirevar:ip.block=%{tx.block⏎
_duration},setvar:ip.block_reason=%{rule.msg}\""
    }
  ]
},
```

Audit data (`audit_data`)

The audit data part corresponds with the native audit log part H, as do the individual items within, which have been explained in the discussion of the native format.

```
"audit_data": {
  "action": {
    "intercepted": true,
    "message": "Matched phrase \"arachni/\" at REQUEST_HEADERS:User-Agent.",
    "phase": 2
  },
  "engine_mode": "ENABLED",
  "error_messages": [
    "[file \"apache2_util.c\"] [line 271] [level 3] [client %s] ModSecurity: %s%s ↵
[uri \"%s\"]%s"
  ],
  "messages": ["Access denied with code 403 (phase 2). Matched phrase \"arachni/\" ↵
at REQUEST_HEADERS:User-Agent. [file \"/usr/share/modsecurity-crs/rules↵
/REQUEST-913-SCANNER-DETECTION.conf\"] [line \"59\"] [id \"913100\"] [rev ↵
\"2\"] [msg \"Found User-Agent associated with security scanner\"] [data \"Matched ↵
Data:  found within REQUEST_HEADERS:User-Agent: arachni/\"] [severity ↵
\"CRITICAL\"] [ver \"OWASP_CRS/3.0.0\"] [maturity \"9\"] [accuracy \"9\"] [tag ↵
\"application-multi\"] [tag \"language-multi\"] [tag \"platform-multi\"] [tag ↵
\"attack-reputation-scanner\"] [tag \"OWASP_CRS/AUTOMATION/SECURITY↵
_SCANNER\"] [tag \"WASCTC/WASC-21\"] [tag \"OWASP_TOP_10/A7\"] [tag \"PCI↵
/6.5.10\"]"],
  "producer": "ModSecurity for Apache/2.9.1 (http://www.modsecurity.org/)",
  "response_body_dechunked": true,
  "server": "Apache",
  "stopwatch": {
    "gc": 0,
    "l": 0,
    "p1": 19828,
    "p2": 5830,
    "p3": 0,
    "p4": 0,
    "p5": 9323,
    "sr": 899,
    "sw": 1341
  }
},
```

> **Note**
>
> The `stopwatch` tag refers to the `Stopwatch2` header in part H of the native audit log format.

Storage Formats

ModSecurity supports two audit log storage formats:

1. Serial audit log format: Multiple audit log files stored in the same file
2. Concurrent audit log format: One file used for every audit log

Serial Audit Log Format

The *serial audit log* format stores multiple audit log entries within the same file (one after another). This is often convenient (because audit log entries are easy to find), but this format is suitable for light logging only, because writing to the file is serialized; only one audit log entry can be written at any one time. On a server that logs too much, a transaction may need to wait for some other transaction to finish writing to the serial audit log file.

Concurrent Audit Log Format

The *concurrent audit log* format uses one file per audit log entry and allows many transactions to be recorded in parallel. A hierarchical directory structure is used to ensure that the number of files created in any one directory remains relatively small—for example:

```
$LOGGING-HOME/20160623/20160623-0535/20160623-053508-V2tY7H8AAQEAAG2JzOEAAAAC
```

The current time is used to work out the directory structure; the filename is constructed using the current time and the transaction ID.

The creation of every audit log in concurrent format is recorded with an entry in the concurrent audit log *index file*. The format of each line resembles the common web server access log format. For example:

```
192.168.1.101 192.168.1.108 - - [23/Jun/2016:05:29:11 +0200] ↵
"GET /index.html HTTP/1.1" 200 45 "-" "-" V1D5h38AAQEAACG9TlkAAAAA ↵
"-" /20160603/20160603-0529/20160603-052911-V1D5h38AAQEAACG9TlkAAAAA ↵
0 1017 md5:e6d5de80b70c2d97c7c1e7d0b8cffd70
```

The tokens on the line are as follows:

1. Server hostname (or IP address, if the hostname is not known)
2. Source IP address
3. Remote user (from HTTP authentication)
4. Local user (from identd)
5. Timestamp
6. Request line

7. Response status

8. Bytes sent (in the response body)

9. Referrer information

10. User-Agent information

11. Unique transaction ID

12. Session ID

13. Audit log filename (relative to the audit logging home, as configured using the SecAuditLogStorageDir directive)

14. Audit log offset

15. Audit log size

16. Audit log hash

The audit log hash begins with the name of the algorithm used, followed by a colon, followed by the hexadecimal representation of the hash itself. This hash can be used to verify that the transaction was correctly recorded and that it hasn't been modified since.

> **Note**
>
> Lines in the index file will be up to 3,980 bytes long, and the information logged will be reduced to fit where necessary. Reduction will occur within the individual fields, but the overall format will remain the same. The character L will appear as the last character on a reduced line. A space will be the last character on a line that wasn't reduced to stay within the limit.

Remote Logging Protocol

Audit logs generated in multisensor deployments are of little use if left on the sensors. More commonly, they'll be transported to a central logging server. ModSecurity supports the following transport protocol:

1. The transport protocol is based on the HTTP protocol.

2. The server uses TLS encryption with HTTP basic authentication.

3. Clients will open a connection to the centralization web server and authenticate (given the end-point URI, the username, and the password).

4. Clients will use a single PUT transaction to submit an entry, placing the file in the body of the request and additional information in the request headers (see the next step for details).

5. The server will process each submission and respond with an appropriate status code:

a. 200 (OK): The submission was processed. The client can delete the corresponding audit log entry if it so desires. The same audit log entry must not be submitted again.

b. 409 (Conflict): The submission is in an invalid format and can't be processed. The client should attempt to fix the problem with the submission and attempt delivery again at a later time. This error generally occurs due to a programming error in the protocol implementation, not because of the content of the audit log entry being transported.

c. 500 (Internal Server Error): The server was unable to correctly process the submission due to some internal problem. The client should reattempt delivery at a later time. A client that starts receiving 500 responses to all its submissions should suspend its operations for a period of time before continuing.

> **Note**
>
> Server implementations are advised to accept all submissions that correctly implement the protocol. Clients are unlikely to be able to overcome problems within audit log entries, so such problems are best resolved on the server side.

Request Headers Information

Each audit log entry submission must contain additional information in the request headers:

1. The X-Content-Hash header must contain the audit log entry hash. Clients should expect the audit log entries to be validated against the hash by the server.

2. The X-ForensicLog-Summary header must contain the entire concurrent format index line.

3. The Content-Length header must be present and must contain the length of the audit log entry.

Index